Kingyo Used Books

3

Seimu Yoshizaki

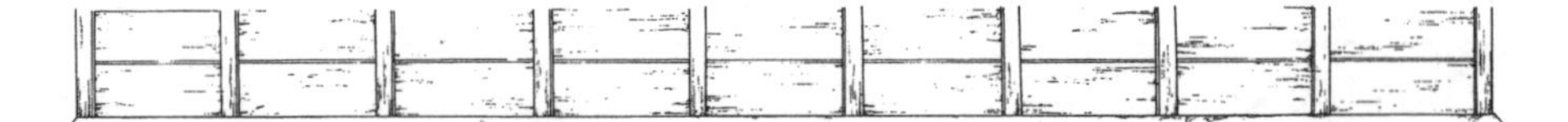
Kingyo
Used
Books

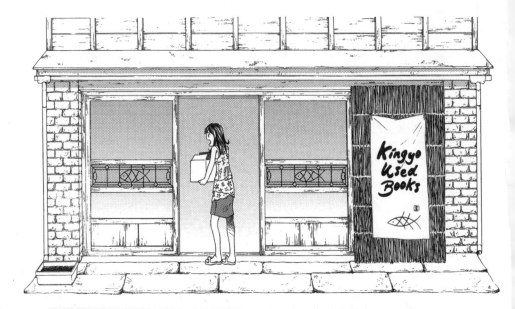

Kingyo Used Books 3

Contents

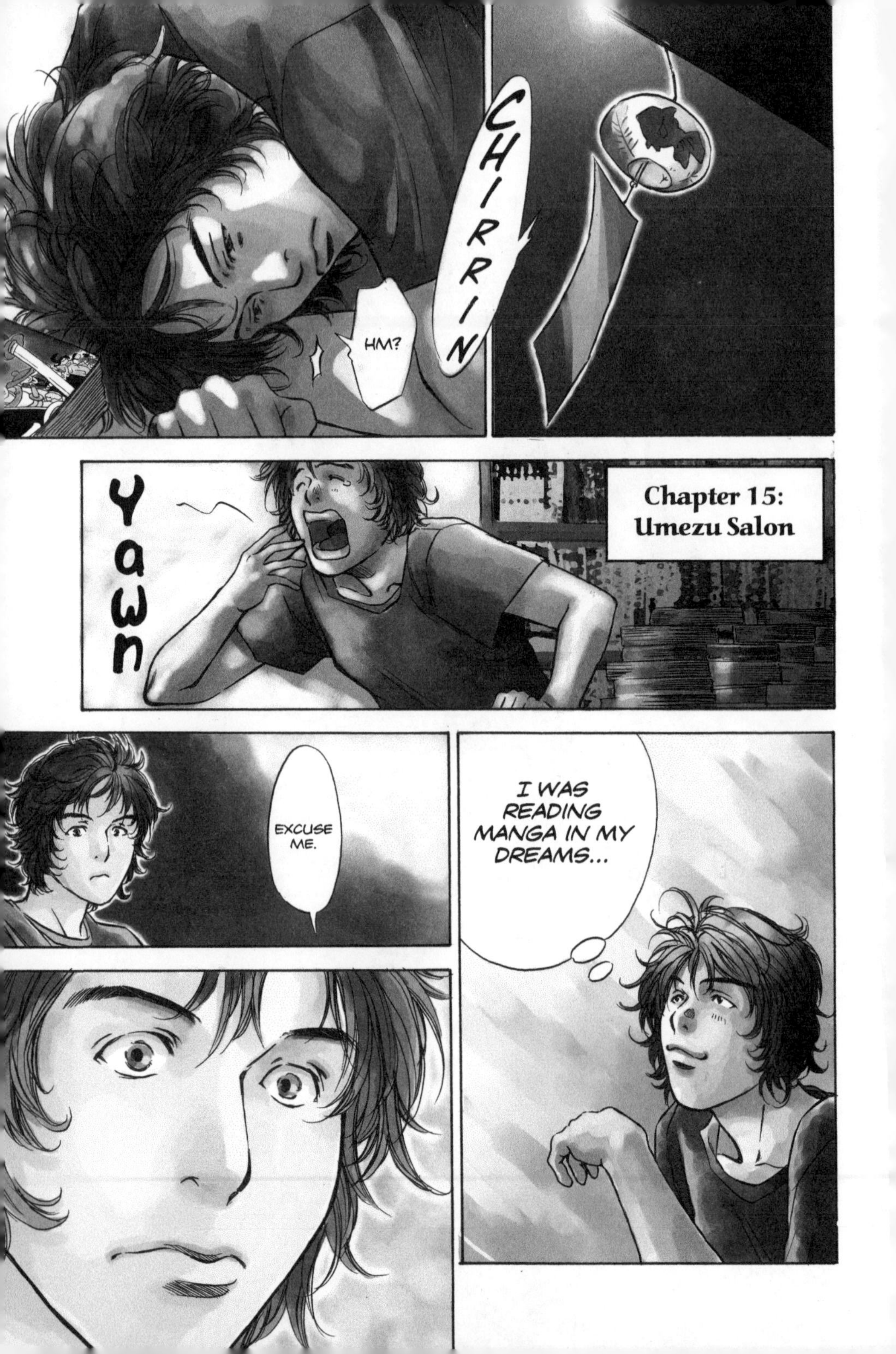
CHIRRIN
HM?
Chapter 15: Umezu Salon
Yawn
I WAS READING MANGA IN MY DREAMS...
EXCUSE ME.

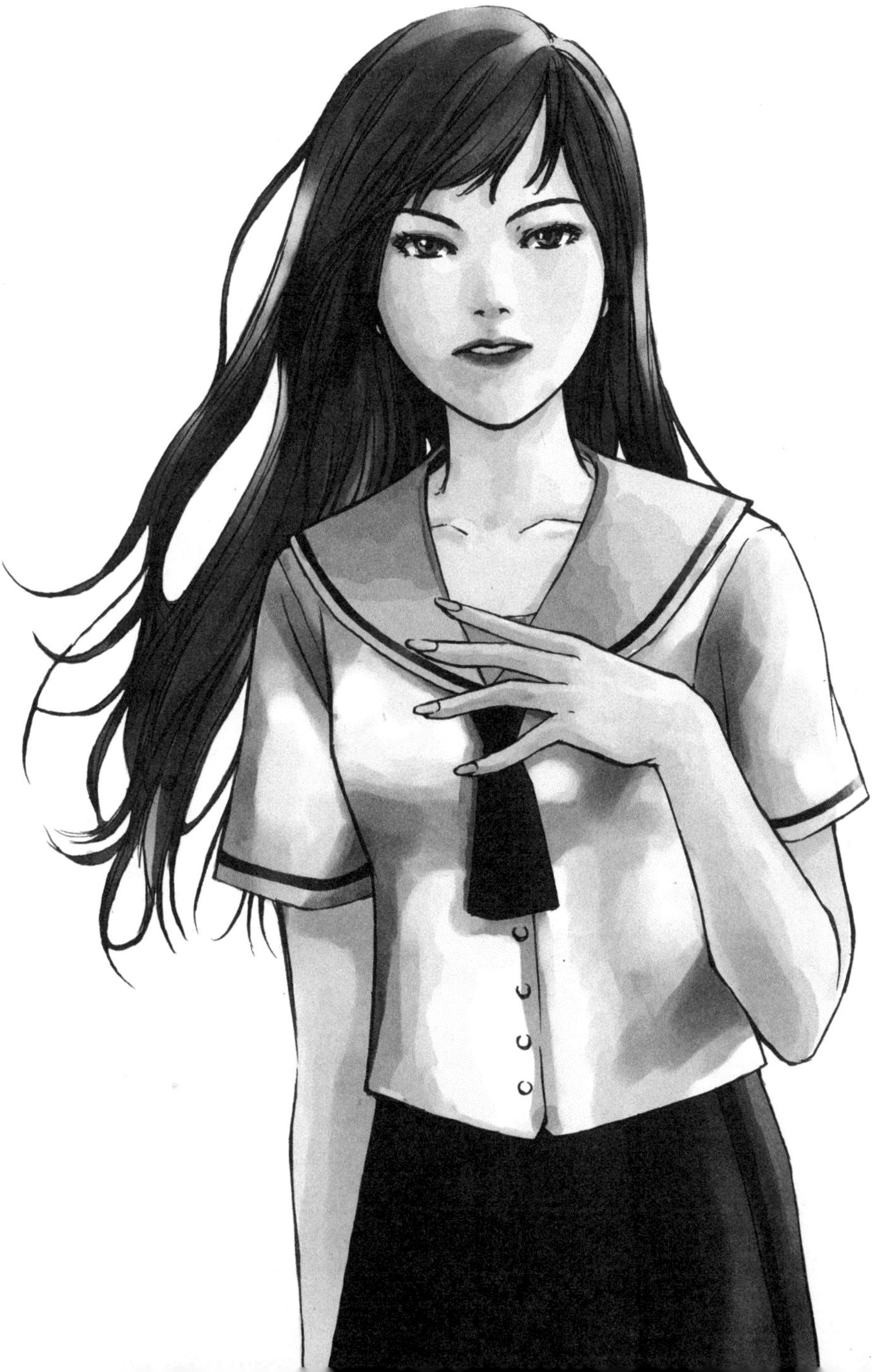

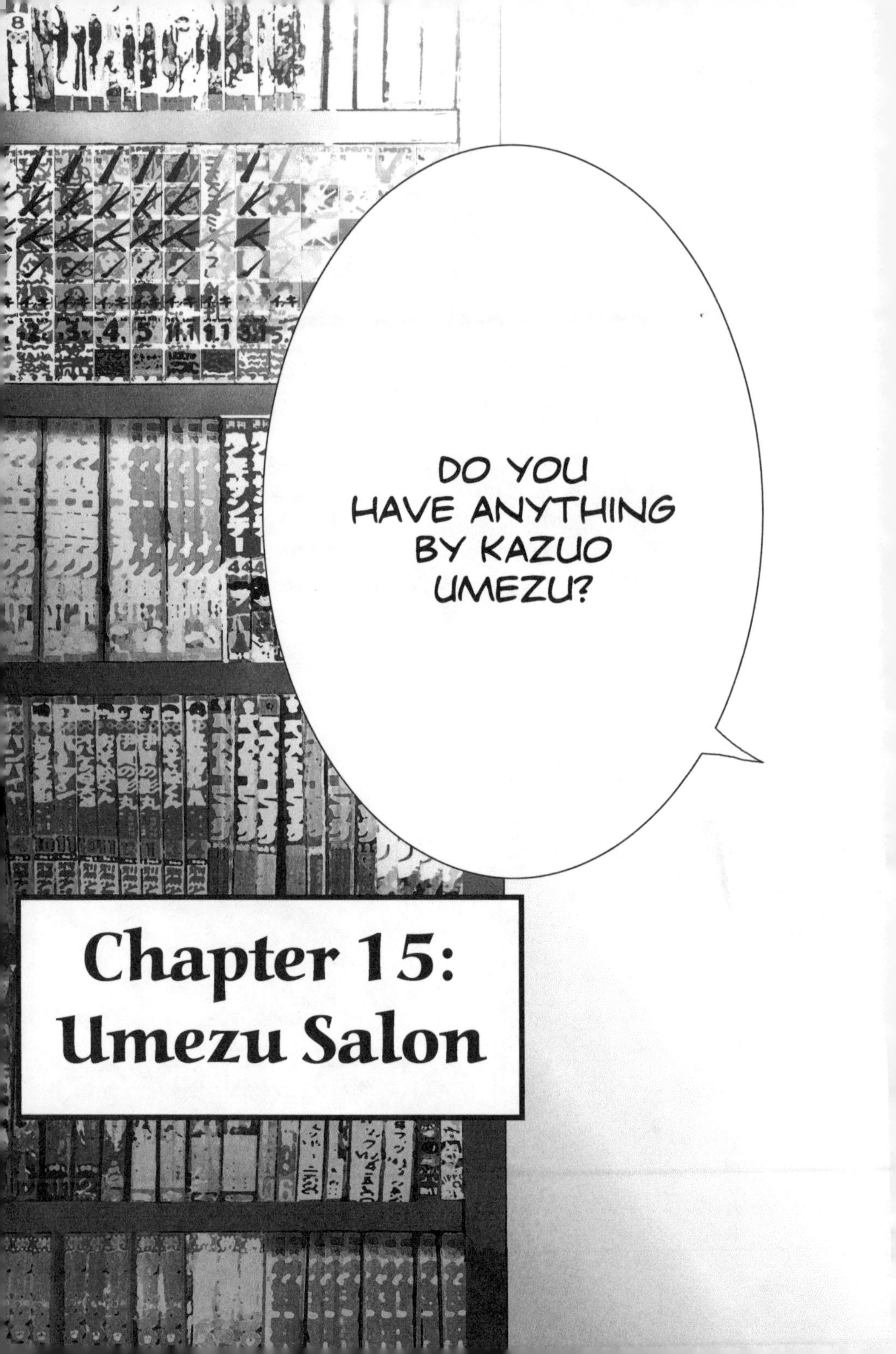
DO YOU HAVE ANYTHING BY KAZUO UMEZU?
Chapter 15: Umezu Salon

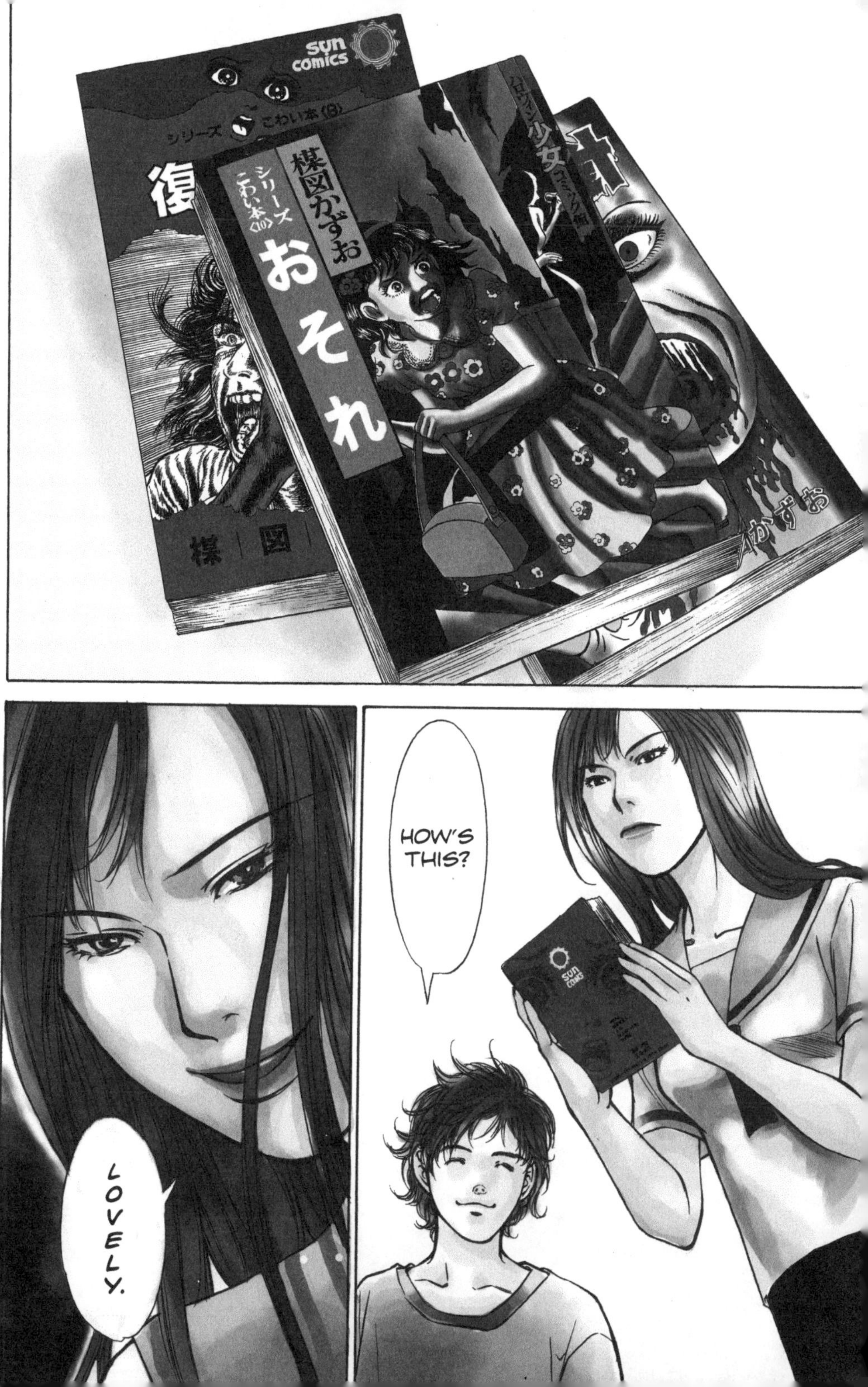
sun comics
シリーズ こわい本(8)
復
楳図かずお
シリーズ こわい本〈10〉
おそれ
楳図
HOW'S THIS?
LOVELY.

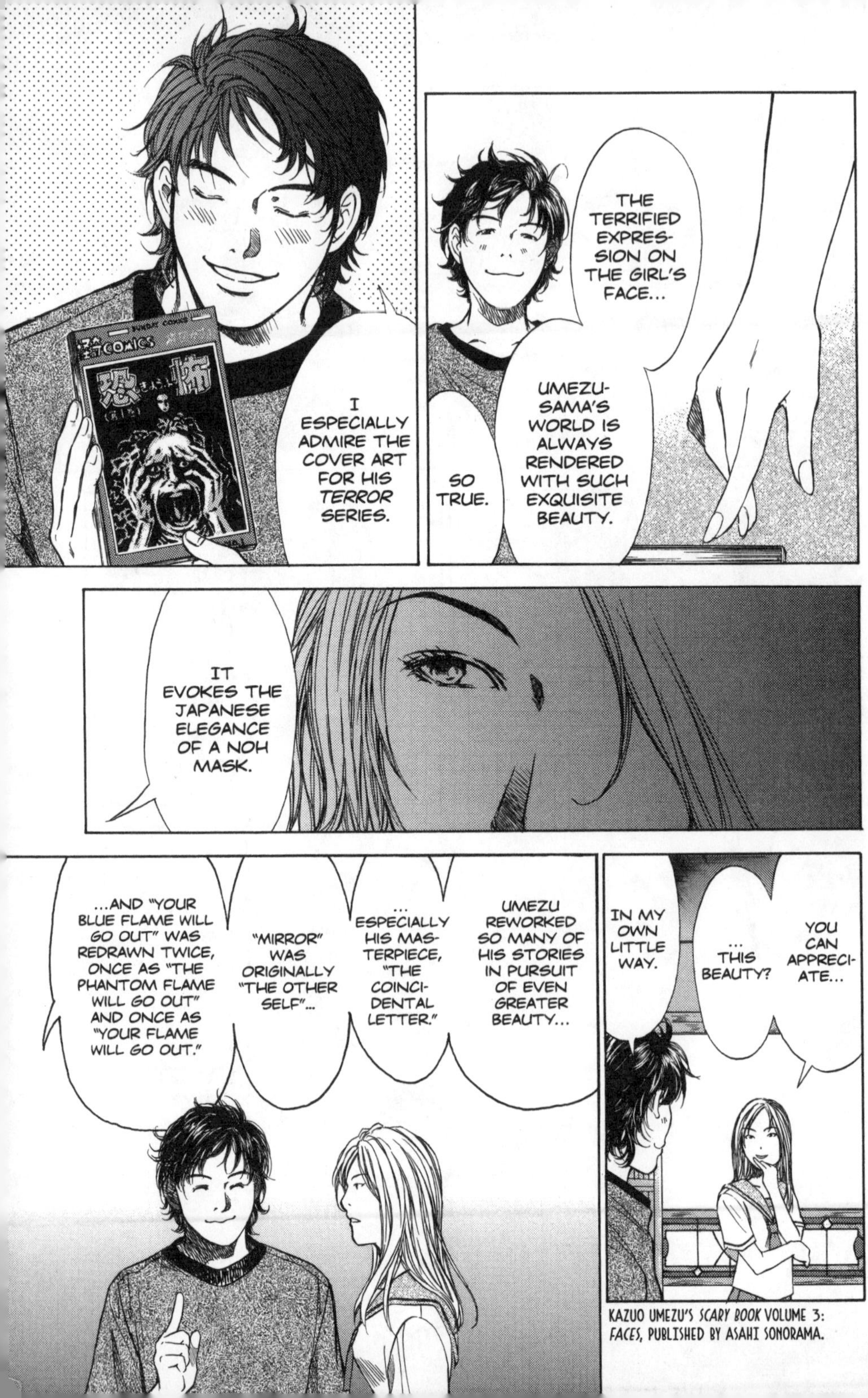
THE TERRIFIED EXPRESSION ON THE GIRL'S FACE...
UMEZU-SAMA'S WORLD IS ALWAYS RENDERED WITH SUCH EXQUISITE BEAUTY.
SO TRUE.
I ESPECIALLY ADMIRE THE COVER ART FOR HIS *TERROR* SERIES.
IT EVOKES THE JAPANESE ELEGANCE OF A NOH MASK.
YOU CAN APPRECIATE...
...THIS BEAUTY?
IN MY OWN LITTLE WAY.
UMEZU REWORKED SO MANY OF HIS STORIES IN PURSUIT OF EVEN GREATER BEAUTY...
...ESPECIALLY HIS MASTERPIECE, "THE COINCIDENTAL LETTER."
"MIRROR" WAS ORIGINALLY "THE OTHER SELF"...
...AND "YOUR BLUE FLAME WILL GO OUT" WAS REDRAWN TWICE, ONCE AS "THE PHANTOM FLAME WILL GO OUT" AND ONCE AS "YOUR FLAME WILL GO OUT."

KAZUO UMEZU'S *SCARY BOOK* VOLUME 3: *FACES*, PUBLISHED BY ASAHI SONORAMA.

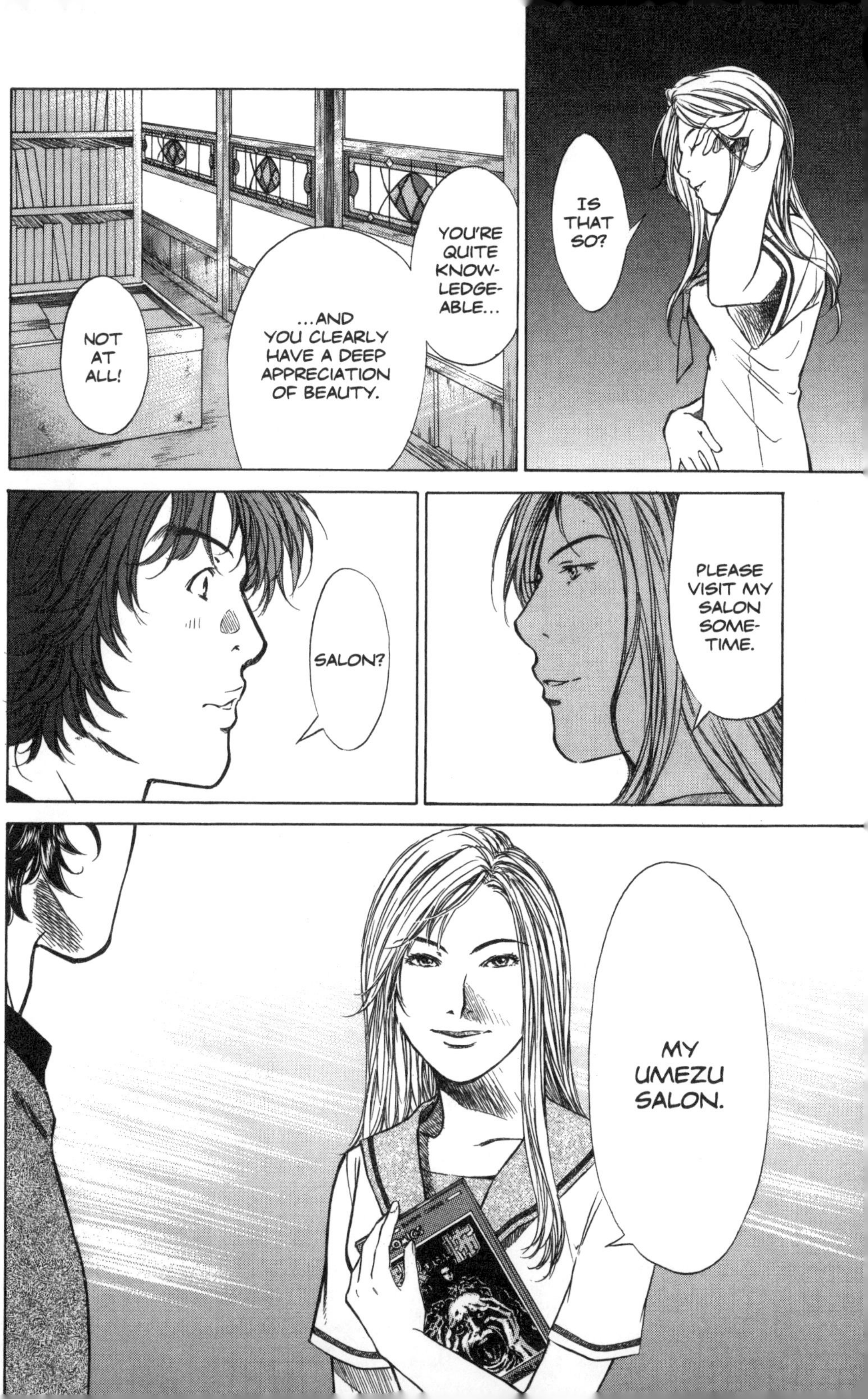
IS THAT SO?
YOU'RE QUITE KNOWLEDGE-ABLE...
...AND YOU CLEARLY HAVE A DEEP APPRECIATION OF BEAUTY.
NOT AT ALL!
PLEASE VISIT MY SALON SOME-TIME.
SALON?
MY UMEZU SALON.

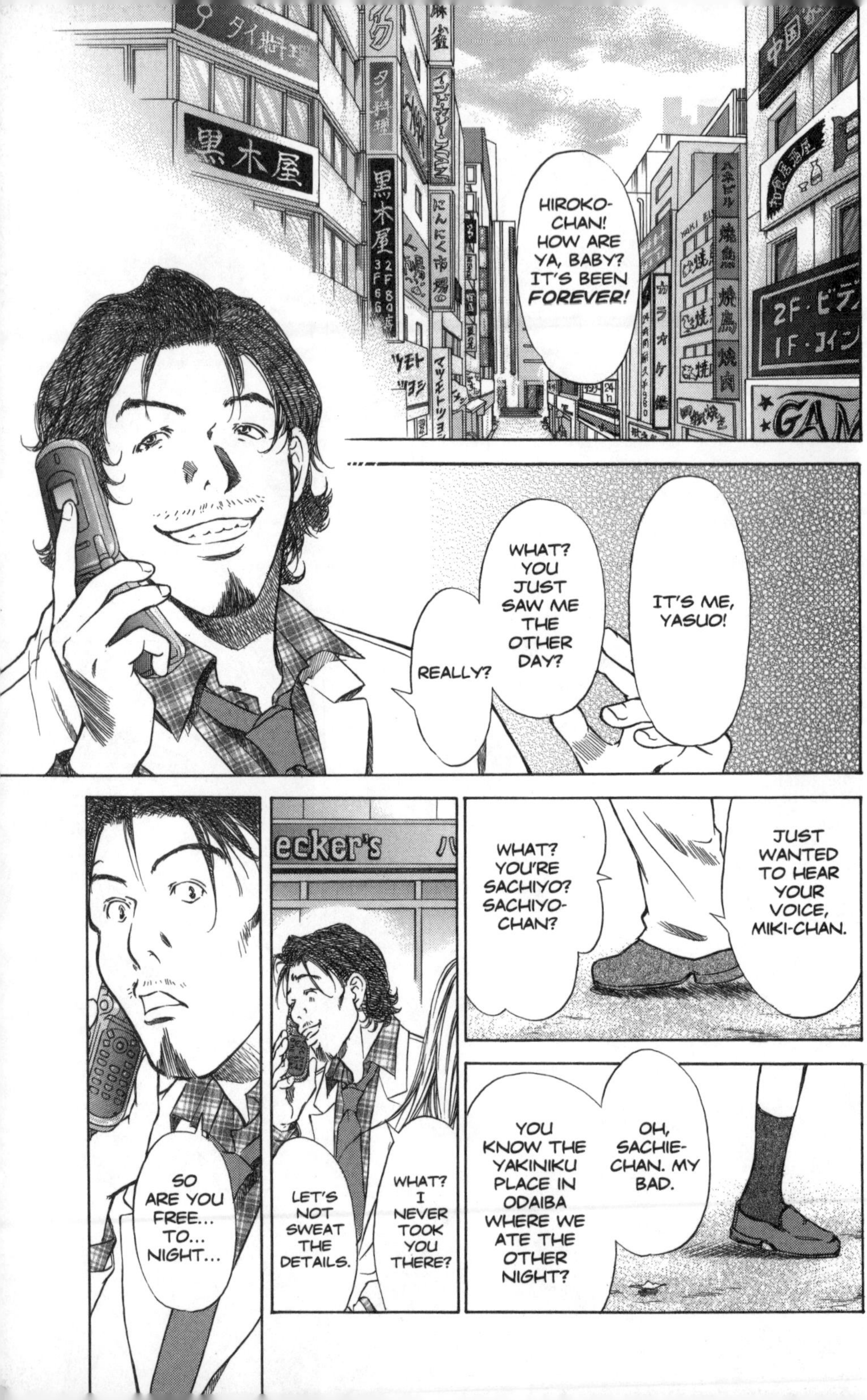
黒木屋
HIROKO-CHAN! HOW ARE YA, BABY? IT'S BEEN *FOREVER!*
IT'S ME, YASUO!
WHAT? YOU JUST SAW ME THE OTHER DAY?
REALLY?
JUST WANTED TO HEAR YOUR VOICE, MIKI-CHAN.
WHAT? YOU'RE SACHIYO? SACHIYO-CHAN?
OH, SACHIE-CHAN. MY BAD.
YOU KNOW THE YAKINIKU PLACE IN ODAIBA WHERE WE ATE THE OTHER NIGHT?
WHAT? I NEVER TOOK YOU THERE?
LET'S NOT SWEAT THE DETAILS.
SO ARE YOU FREE... TO... NIGHT...

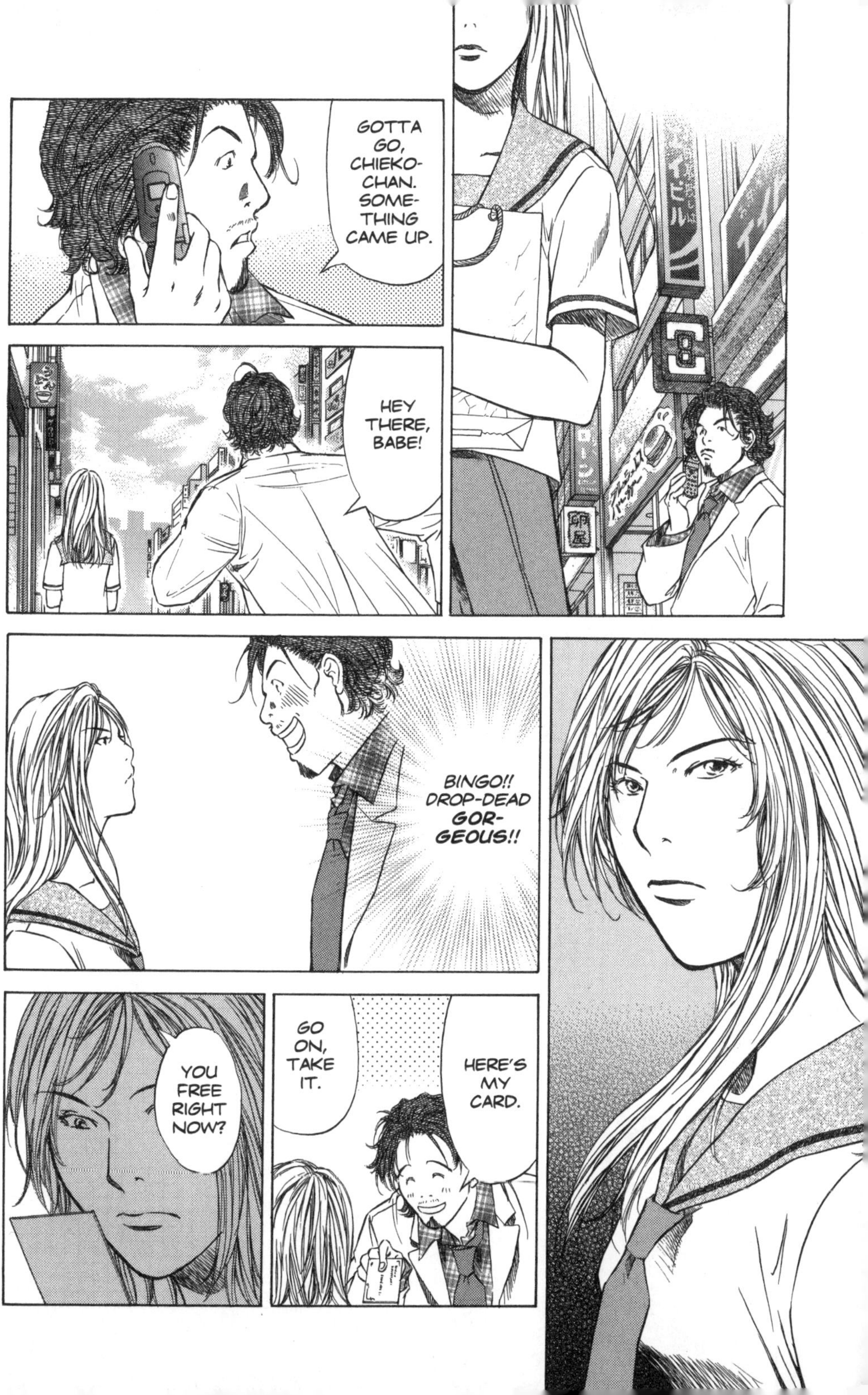
GOTTA GO, CHIEKO-CHAN. SOMETHING CAME UP.
HEY THERE, BABE!
BINGO!! DROP-DEAD GORGEOUS!!
HERE'S MY CARD.
GO ON, TAKE IT.
YOU FREE RIGHT NOW?

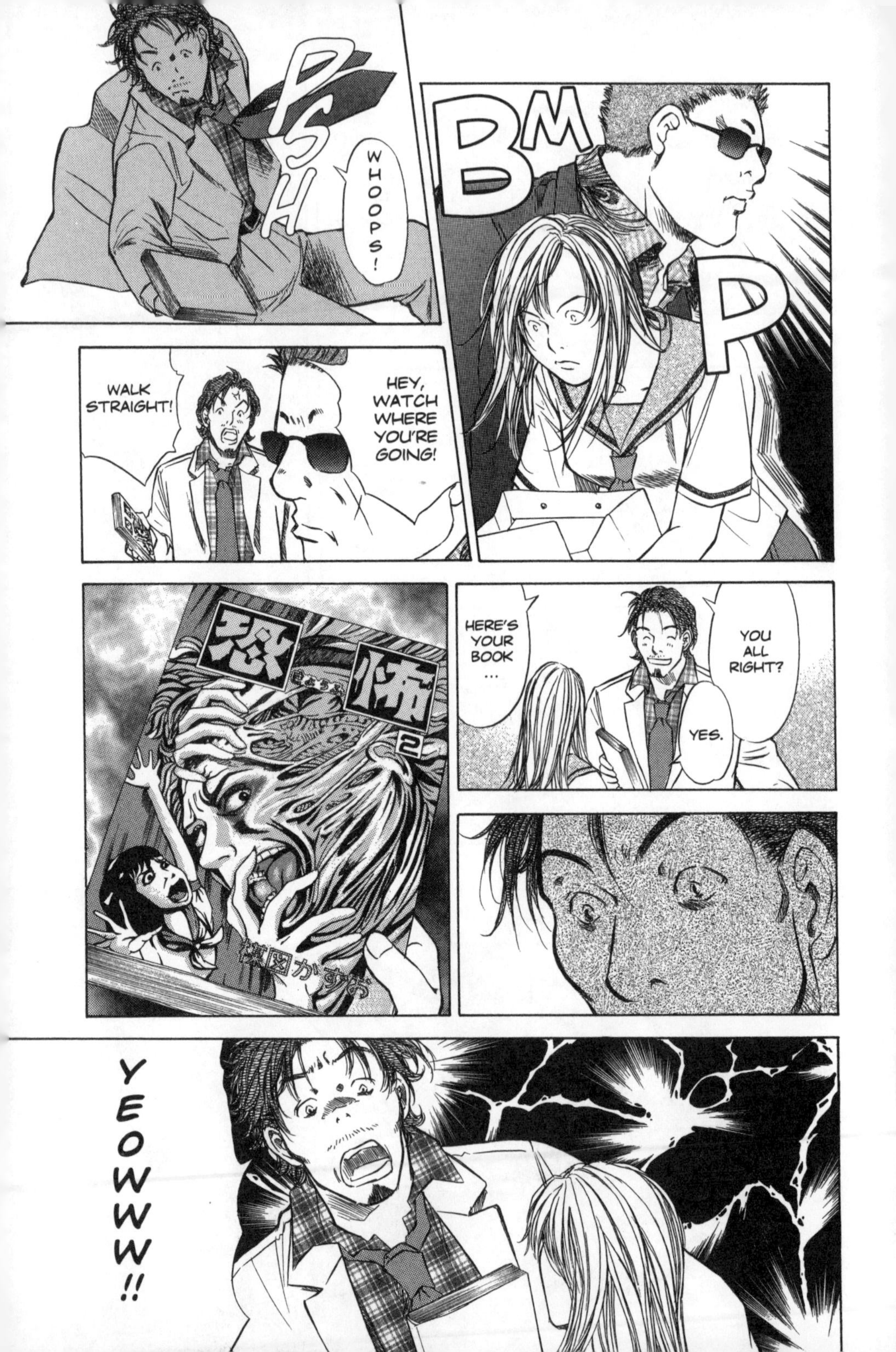
BMP
PSH
WHOOPS!
HEY, WATCH WHERE YOU'RE GOING!
WALK STRAIGHT!
YOU ALL RIGHT?
YES.
HERE'S YOUR BOOK ...
恐怖
2
YEOWWWW!!

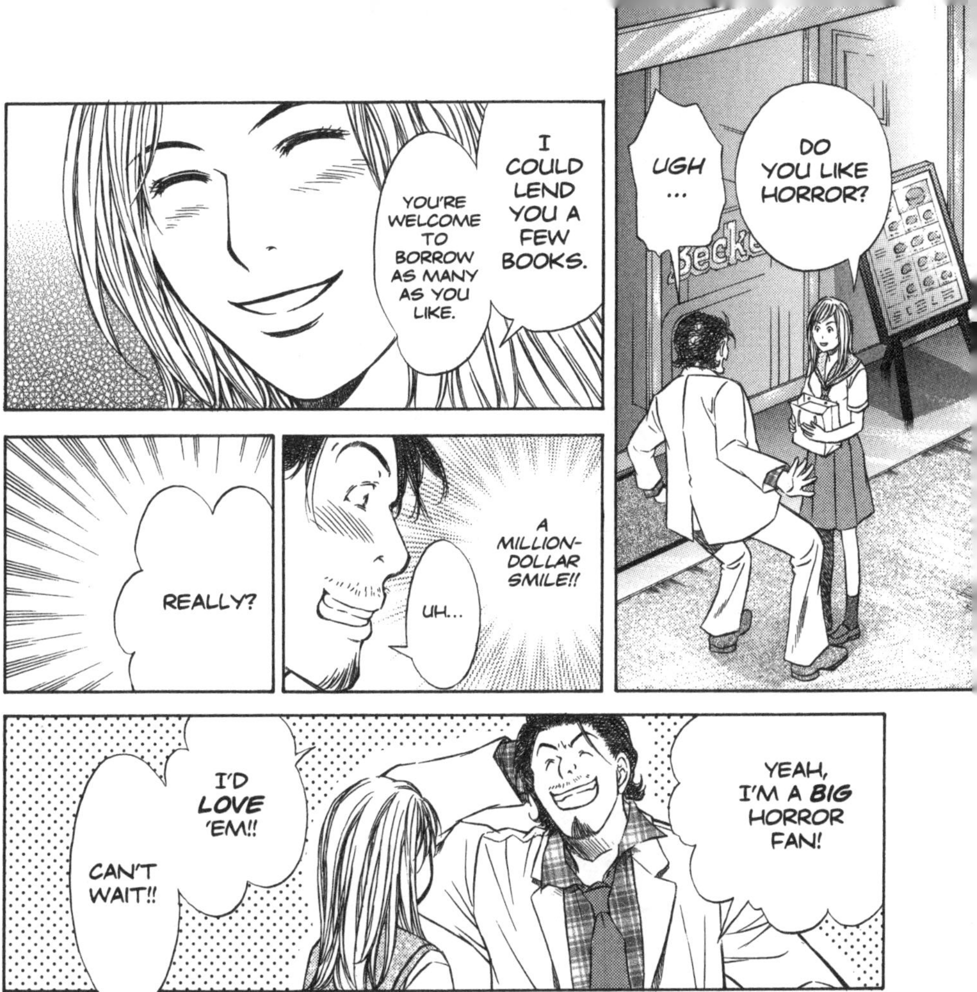
DO YOU LIKE HORROR?
UGH ...
I COULD LEND YOU A FEW BOOKS.
YOU'RE WELCOME TO BORROW AS MANY AS YOU LIKE.
A MILLION-DOLLAR SMILE!!
UH...
REALLY?
YEAH, I'M A ***BIG*** HORROR FAN!
I'D ***LOVE*** 'EM!!
CAN'T WAIT!!

★THE SEAL RESEMBLES A WARD TO CONTAIN EVIL SPIRITS.

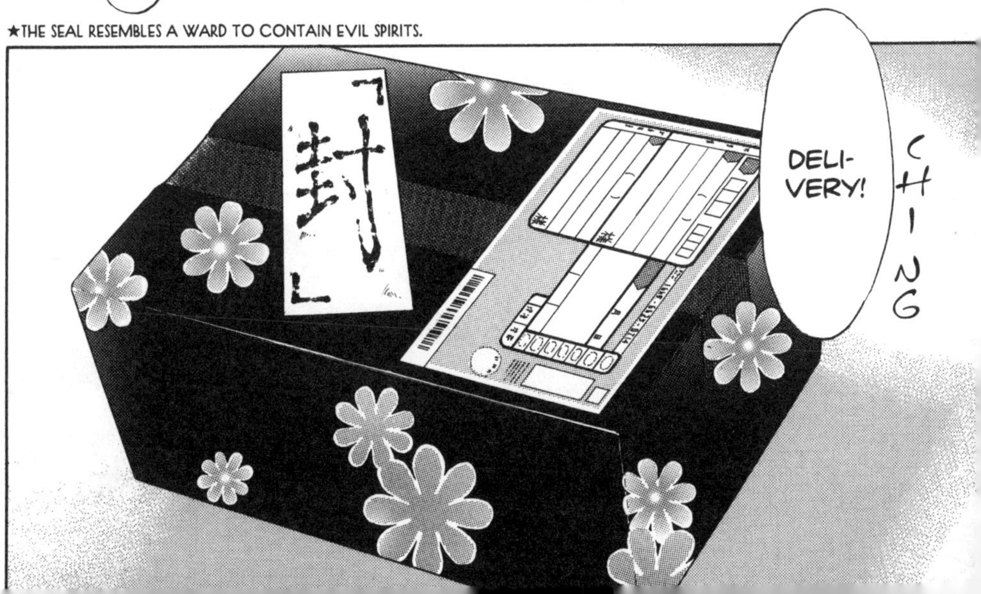
DELI-VERY!
CHING
封

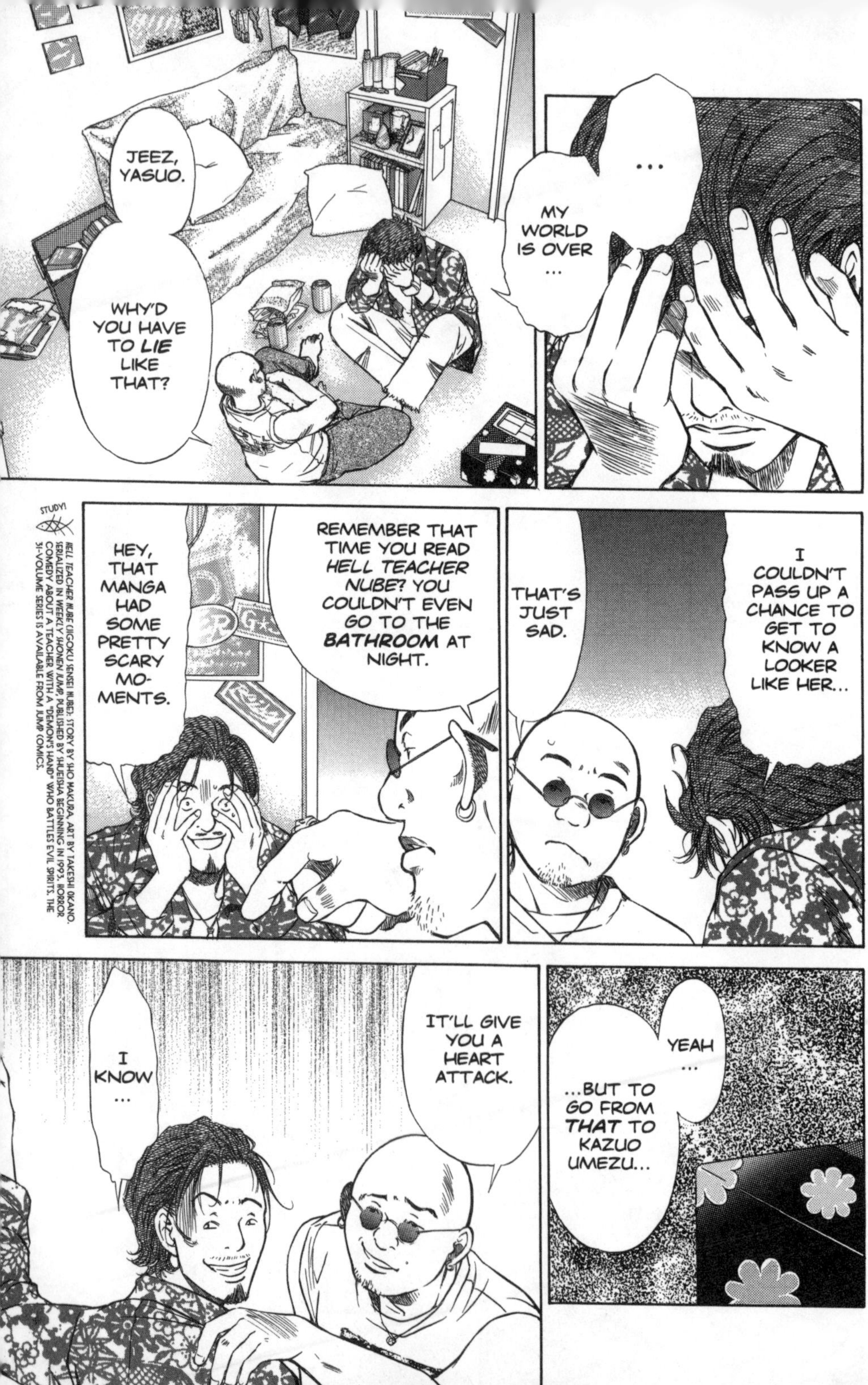
...
MY WORLD IS OVER ...
JEEZ, YASUO.
WHY'D YOU HAVE TO LIE LIKE THAT?
I COULDN'T PASS UP A CHANCE TO GET TO KNOW A LOOKER LIKE HER...
THAT'S JUST SAD.
REMEMBER THAT TIME YOU READ HELL TEACHER NUBE? YOU COULDN'T EVEN GO TO THE BATHROOM AT NIGHT.
HEY, THAT MANGA HAD SOME PRETTY SCARY MO-MENTS.
YEAH ...
...BUT TO GO FROM THAT TO KAZUO UMEZU...
IT'LL GIVE YOU A HEART ATTACK.
I KNOW ...

STUDY!

HELL TEACHER NUBE (JIGOKU SENSEI NUBE): STORY BY SHO MAKURA, ART BY TAKESHI OKANO. SERIALIZED IN WEEKLY SHONEN JUMP PUBLISHED BY SHUEISHA BEGINNING IN 1993. HORROR COMEDY ABOUT A TEACHER WITH A "DEMON'S HAND" WHO BATTLES EVIL SPIRITS. THE 31-VOLUME SERIES IS AVAILABLE FROM JUMP COMICS.

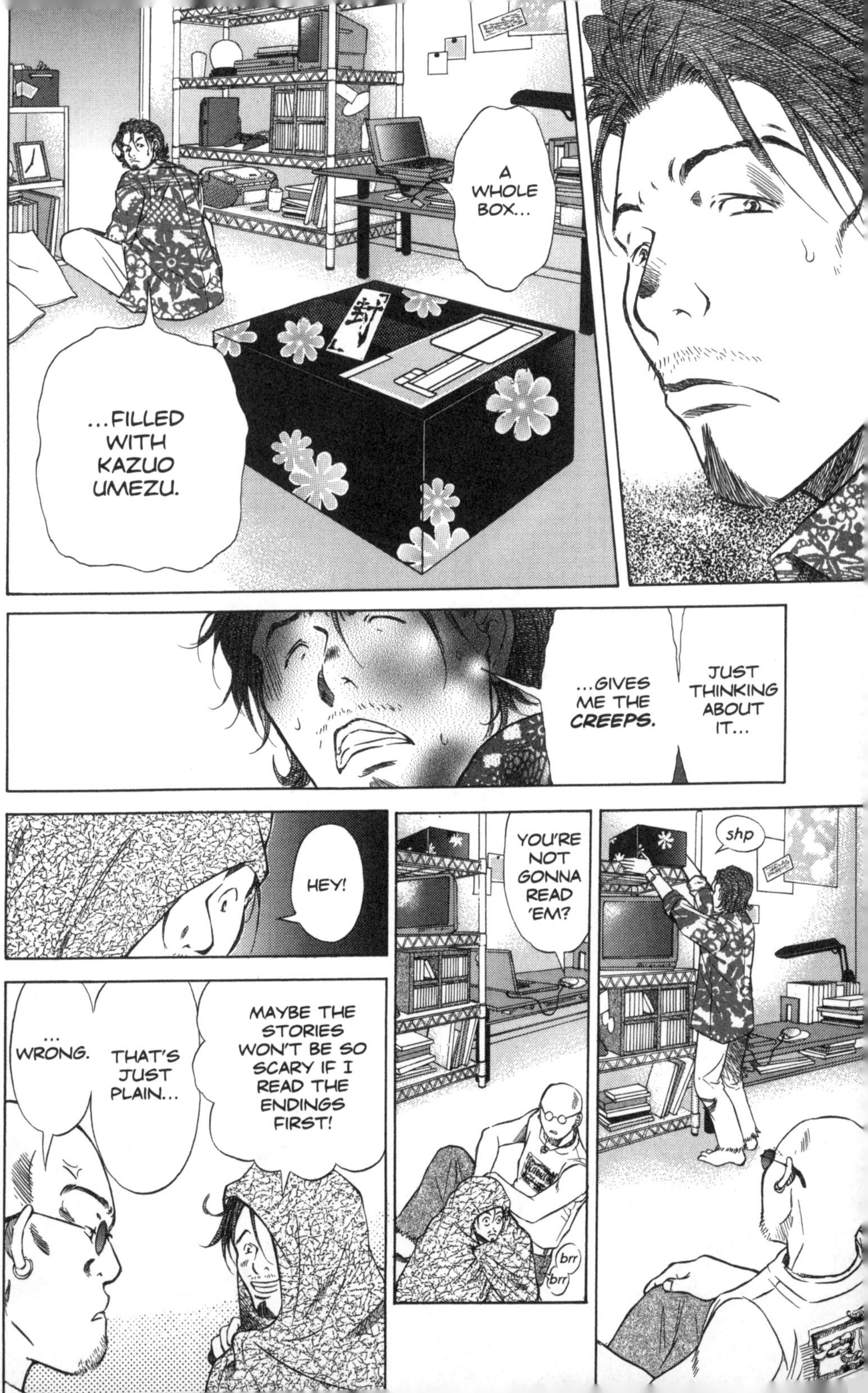
A WHOLE BOX...
...FILLED WITH KAZUO UMEZU.
JUST THINKING ABOUT IT...
...GIVES ME THE CREEPS.
shp
YOU'RE NOT GONNA READ 'EM?
brr
brr
HEY!
MAYBE THE STORIES WON'T BE SO SCARY IF I READ THE ENDINGS FIRST!
THAT'S JUST PLAIN...
...WRONG.

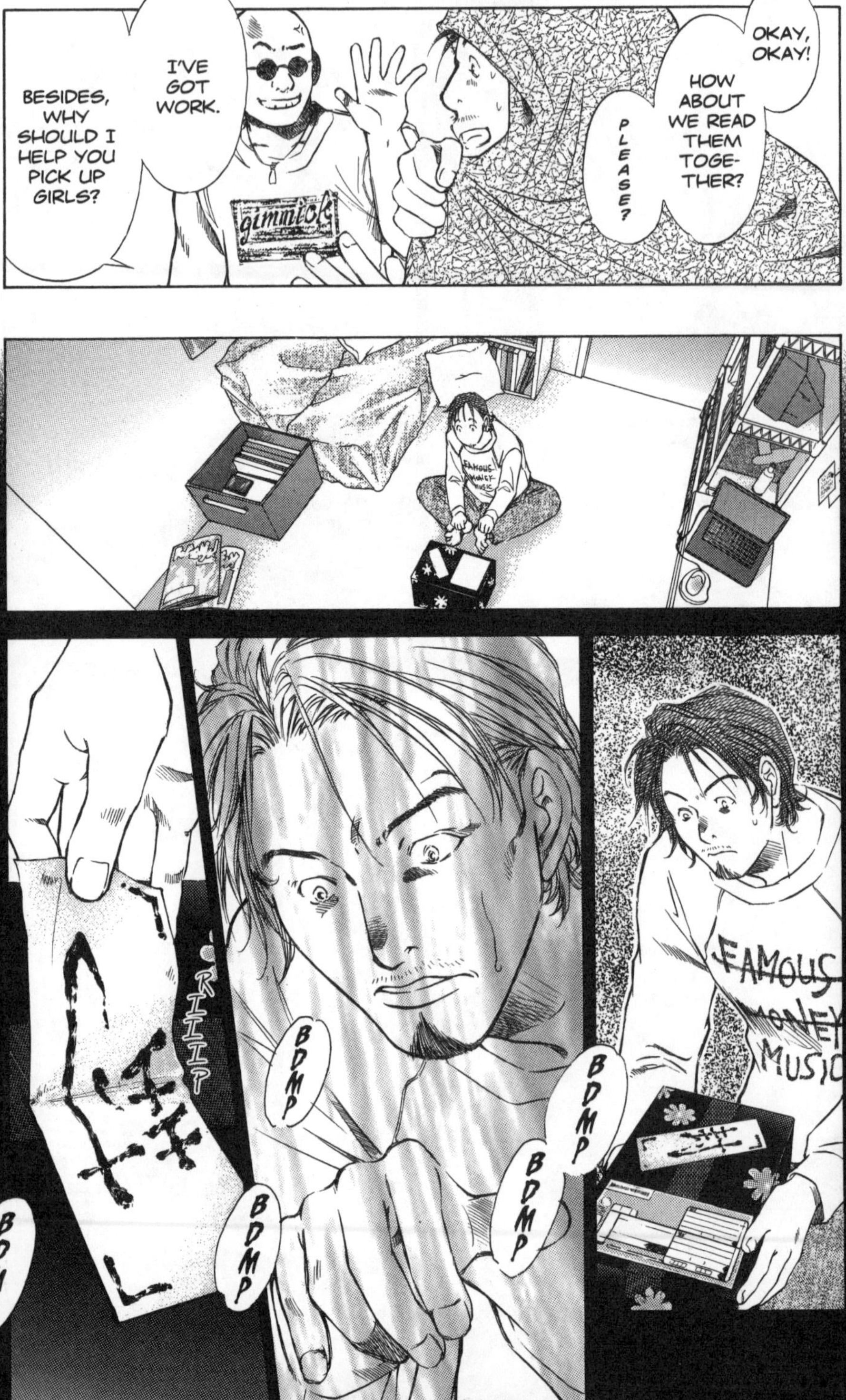
OKAY, OKAY!
HOW ABOUT WE READ THEM TOGE-THER?
PLEASE?
I'VE GOT WORK.
BESIDES, WHY SHOULD I HELP YOU PICK UP GIRLS?
gimmick
FAMOUS MONEY MUSIC
BDMP
BDMP
BDMP
BDMP
RIIIP
BDMP

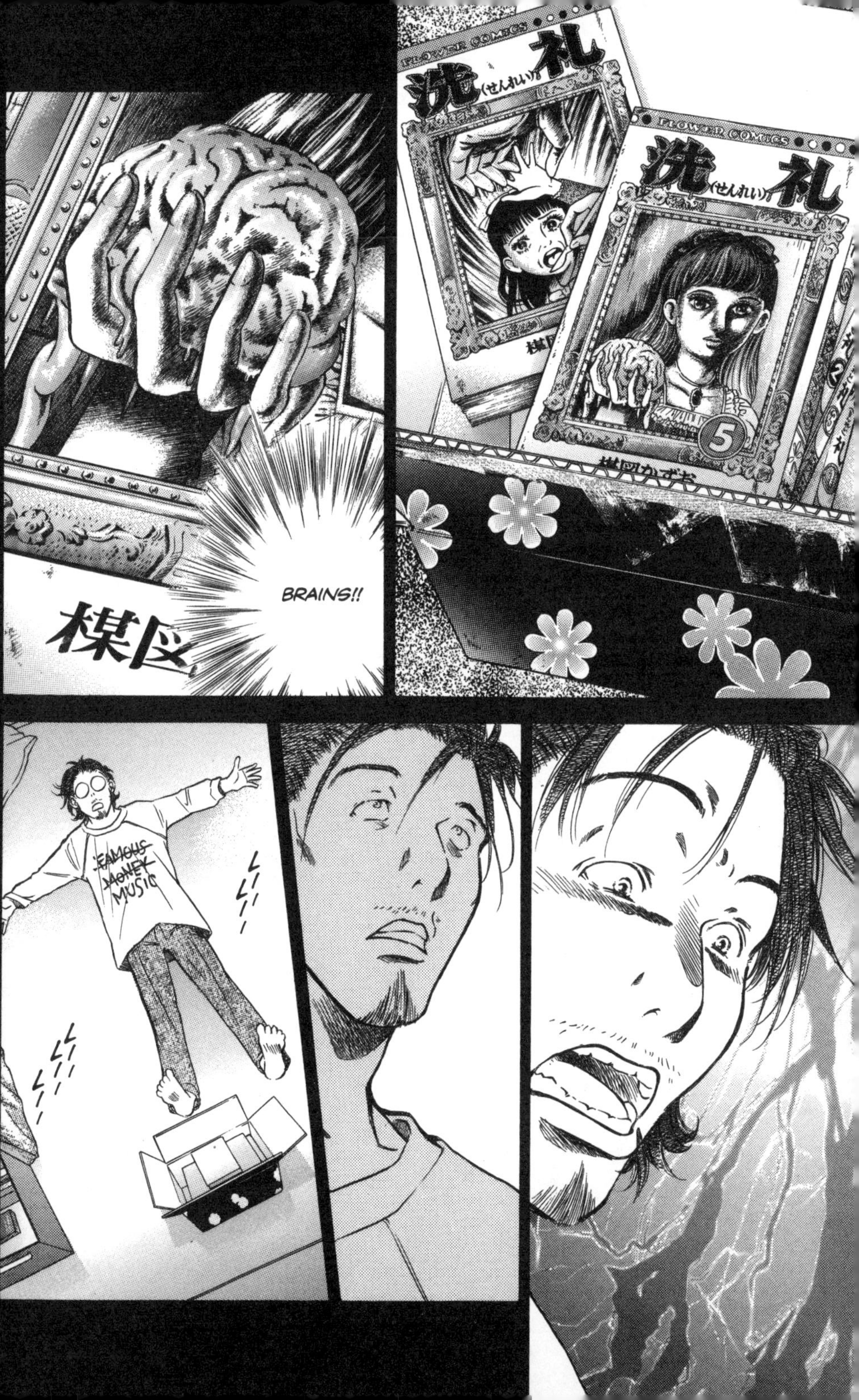
FLOWER COMICS
洗礼(せんれい)
FLOWER COMICS
洗礼(せんれい)
5
楳図
BRAINS!!
FAMOUS
MONEY
MUSIC

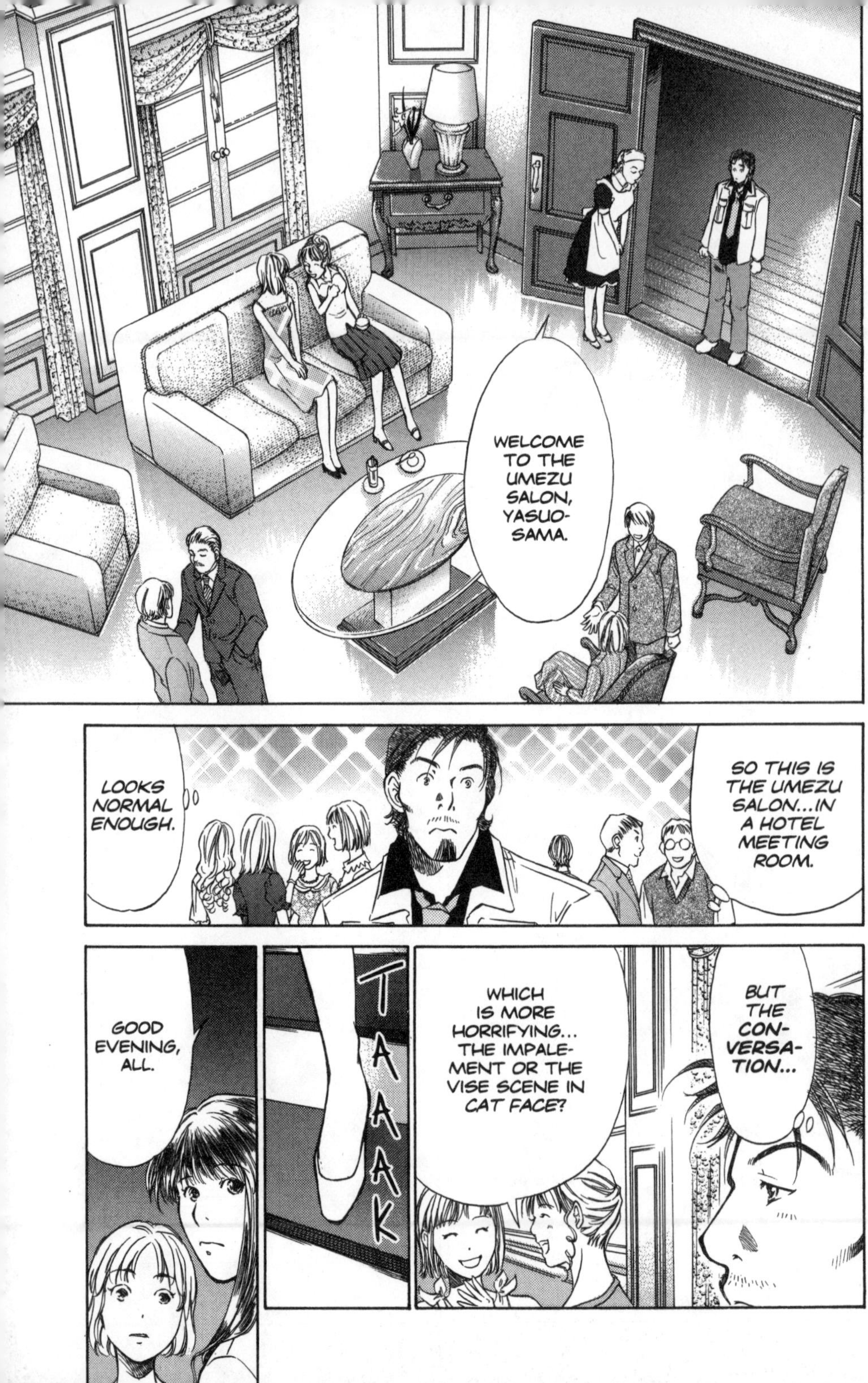
WELCOME TO THE UMEZU SALON, YASUO-SAMA.
SO THIS IS THE UMEZU SALON...IN A HOTEL MEETING ROOM.
LOOKS NORMAL ENOUGH.
BUT THE CON-VERSA-TION...
WHICH IS MORE HORRIFYING... THE IMPALE-MENT OR THE VISE SCENE IN CAT FACE?
TAAAK
GOOD EVENING, ALL.

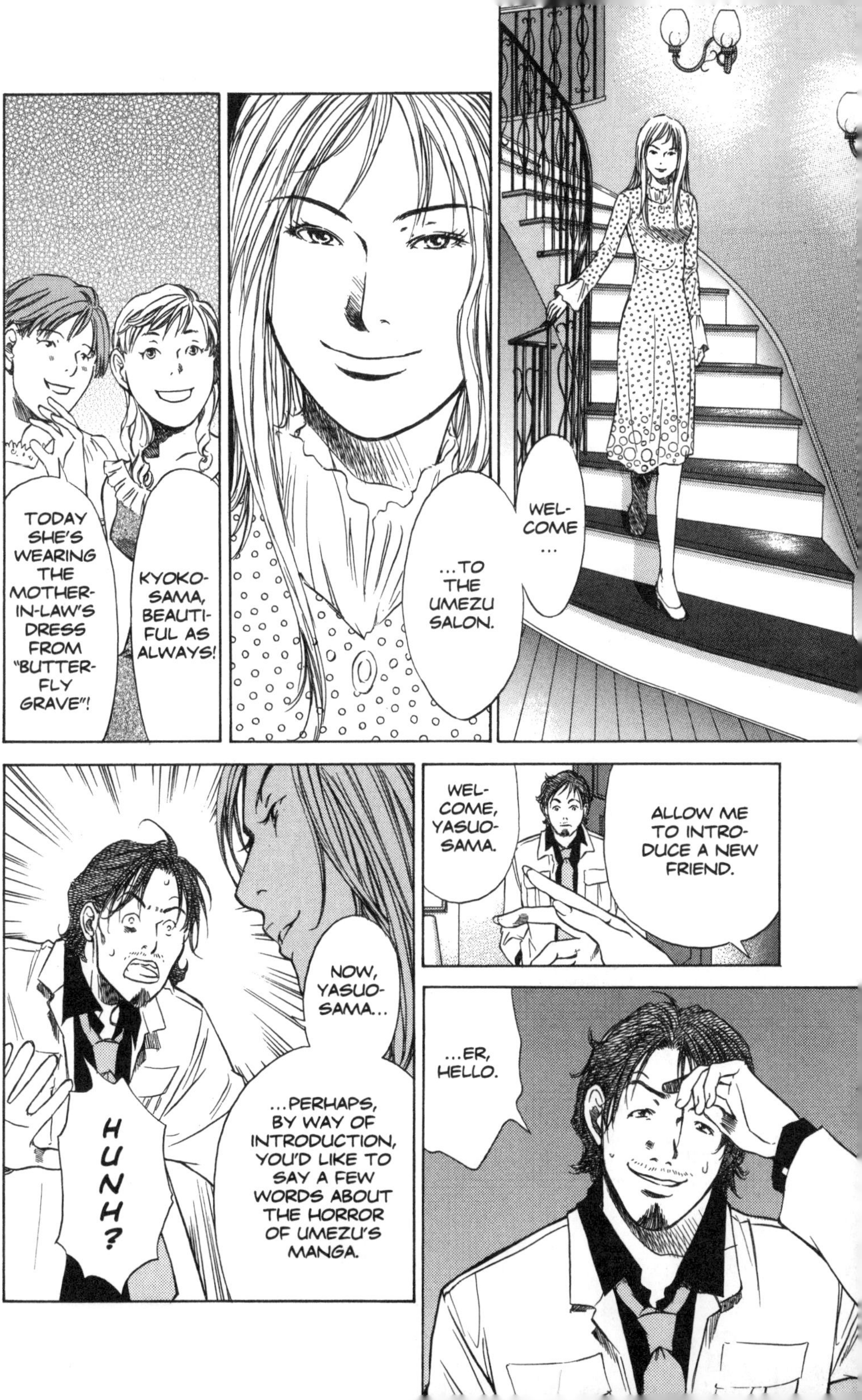
WEL-COME...
...TO THE UMEZU SALON.
KYOKO-SAMA, BEAUTIFUL AS ALWAYS!
TODAY SHE'S WEARING THE MOTHER-IN-LAW'S DRESS FROM "BUTTERFLY GRAVE"!
WEL-COME, YASUO-SAMA.
ALLOW ME TO INTRODUCE A NEW FRIEND.
...ER, HELLO.
NOW, YASUO-SAMA...
...PERHAPS, BY WAY OF INTRODUCTION, YOU'D LIKE TO SAY A FEW WORDS ABOUT THE HORROR OF UMEZU'S MANGA.
HUNH?

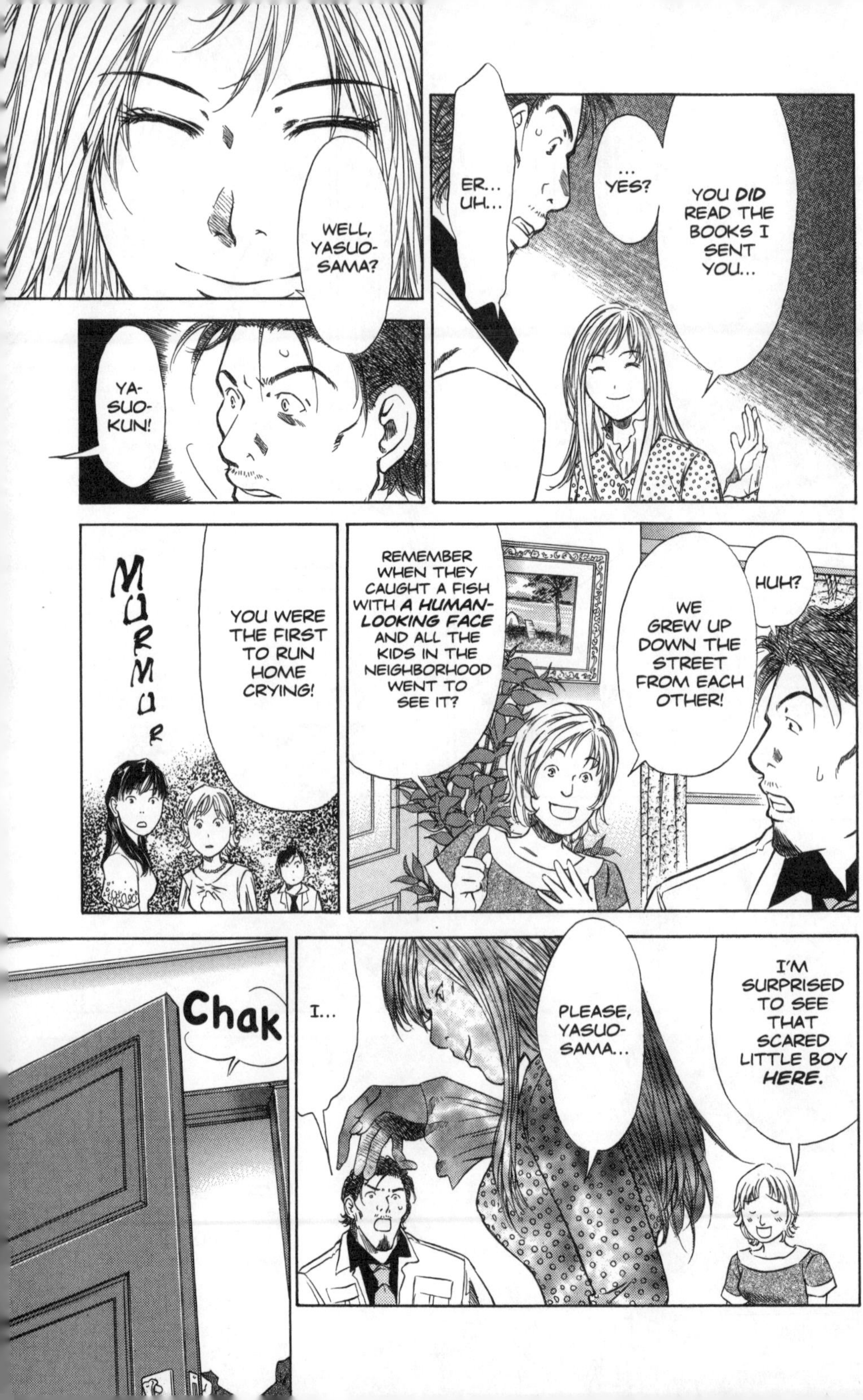
YOU **DID** READ THE BOOKS I SENT YOU...
... YES?
ER... UH...
WELL, YASUO-SAMA?
YA-SUO-KUN!
HUH?
WE GREW UP DOWN THE STREET FROM EACH OTHER!
REMEMBER WHEN THEY CAUGHT A FISH WITH ***A HUMAN-LOOKING FACE*** AND ALL THE KIDS IN THE NEIGHBORHOOD WENT TO SEE IT?
YOU WERE THE FIRST TO RUN HOME CRYING!
MURMUR
I'M SURPRISED TO SEE THAT SCARED LITTLE BOY ***HERE.***
PLEASE, YASUO-SAMA...
I...
Chak

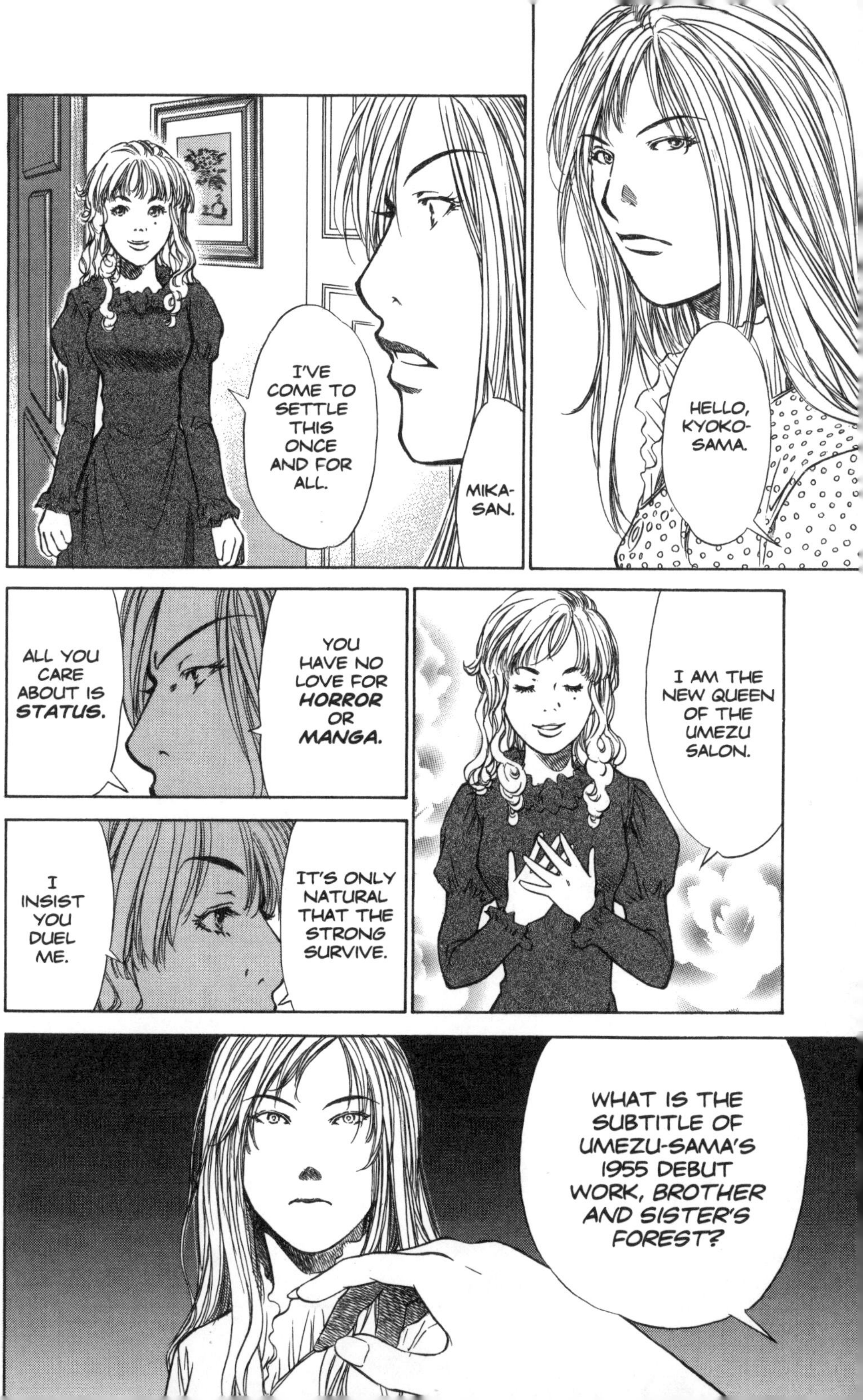
HELLO, KYOKO-SAMA.
MIKA-SAN.
I'VE COME TO SETTLE THIS ONCE AND FOR ALL.
I AM THE NEW QUEEN OF THE UMEZU SALON.
YOU HAVE NO LOVE FOR HORROR OR MANGA.
ALL YOU CARE ABOUT IS STATUS.
IT'S ONLY NATURAL THAT THE STRONG SURVIVE.
I INSIST YOU DUEL ME.
WHAT IS THE SUBTITLE OF UMEZU-SAMA'S 1955 DEBUT WORK, BROTHER AND SISTER'S FOREST?

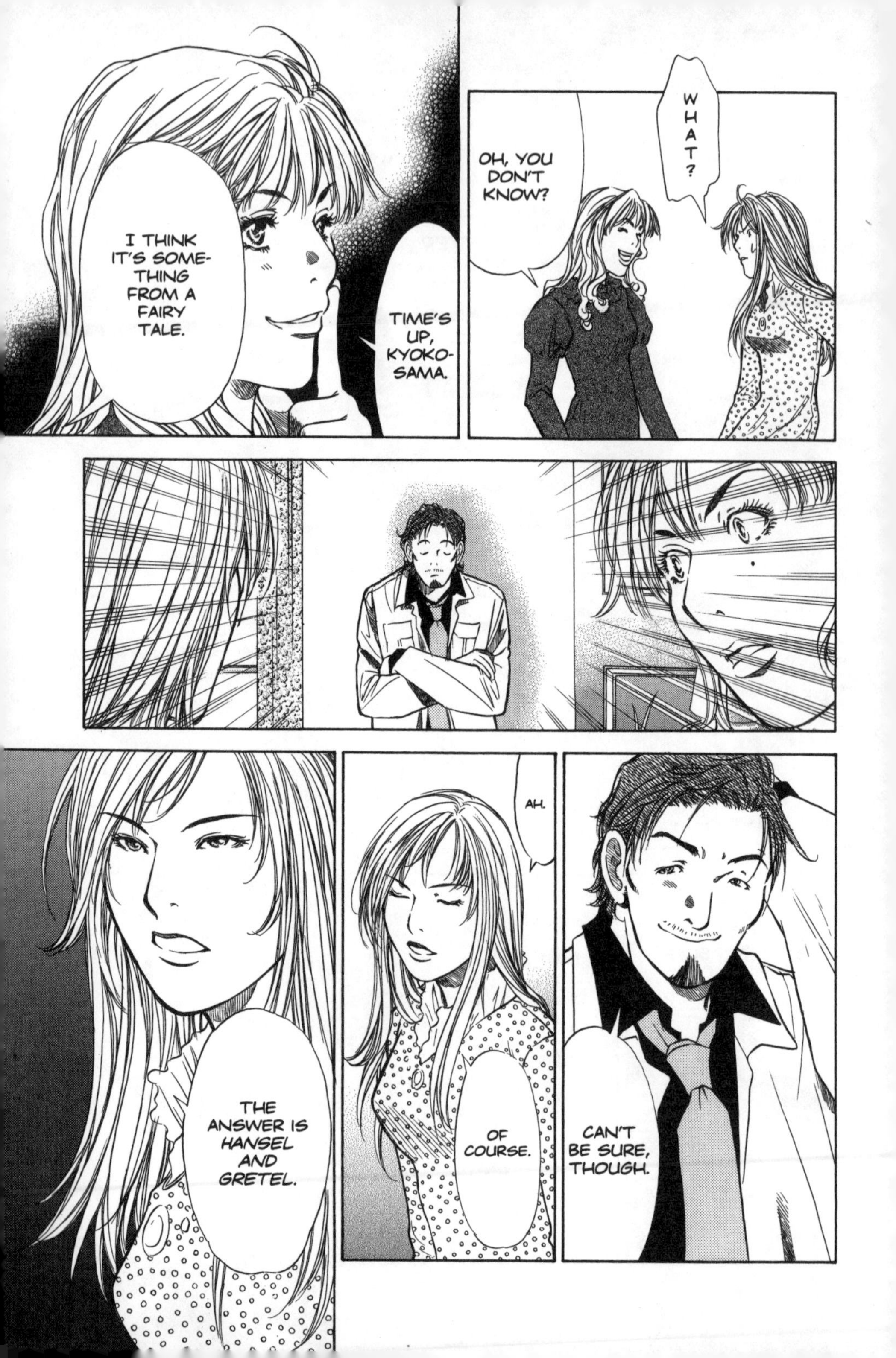
WHAT?
OH, YOU DON'T KNOW?
I THINK IT'S SOME-THING FROM A FAIRY TALE.
TIME'S UP, KYOKO-SAMA.
CAN'T BE SURE, THOUGH.
AH.
OF COURSE.
THE ANSWER IS HANSEL AND GRETEL.

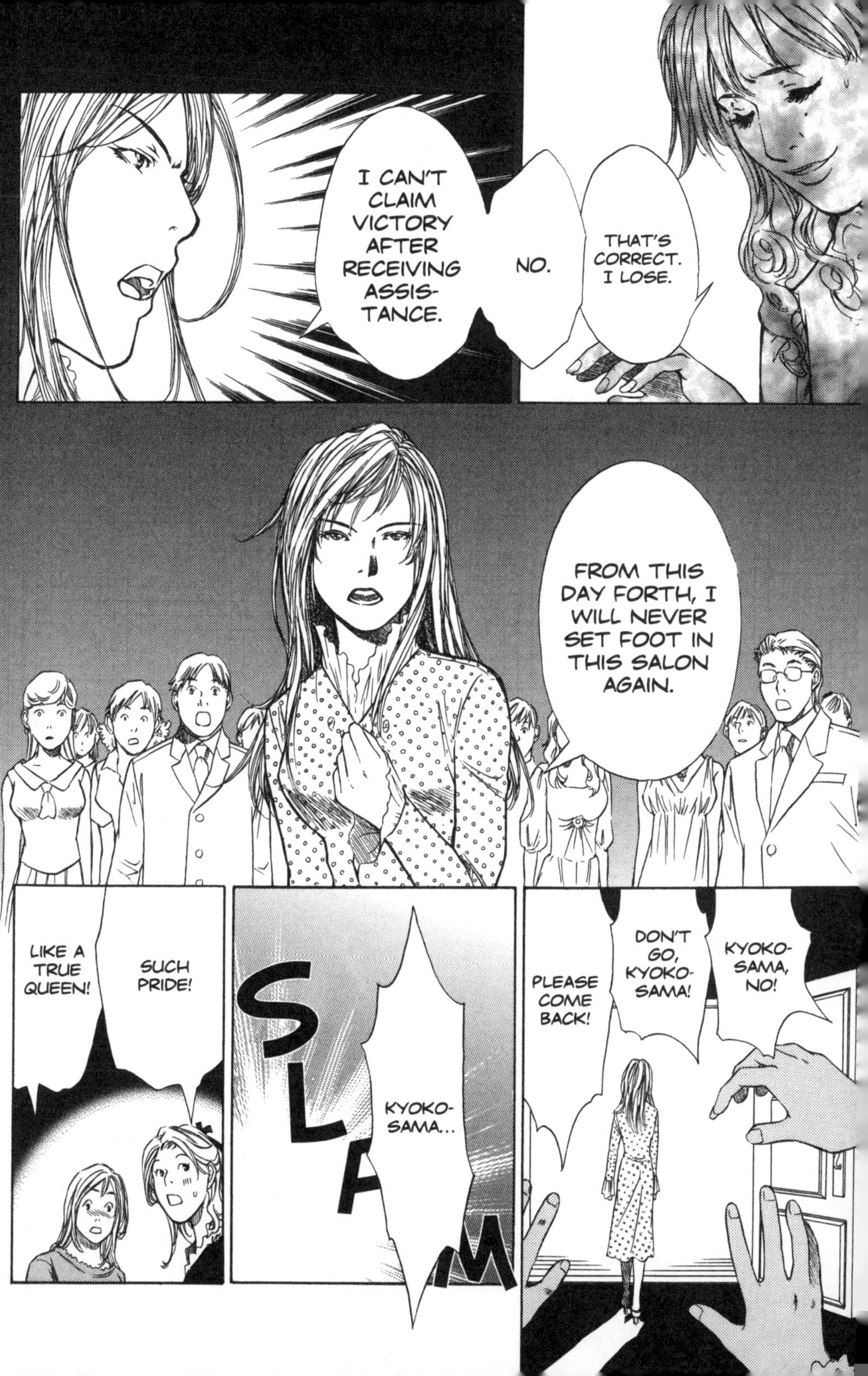
THAT'S CORRECT. I LOSE.
NO.
I CAN'T CLAIM VICTORY AFTER RECEIVING ASSIS-TANCE.
FROM THIS DAY FORTH, I WILL NEVER SET FOOT IN THIS SALON AGAIN.
KYOKO-SAMA, NO!
DON'T GO, KYOKO-SAMA!
PLEASE COME BACK!
SLAM
KYOKO-SAMA...
SUCH PRIDE!
LIKE A TRUE QUEEN!

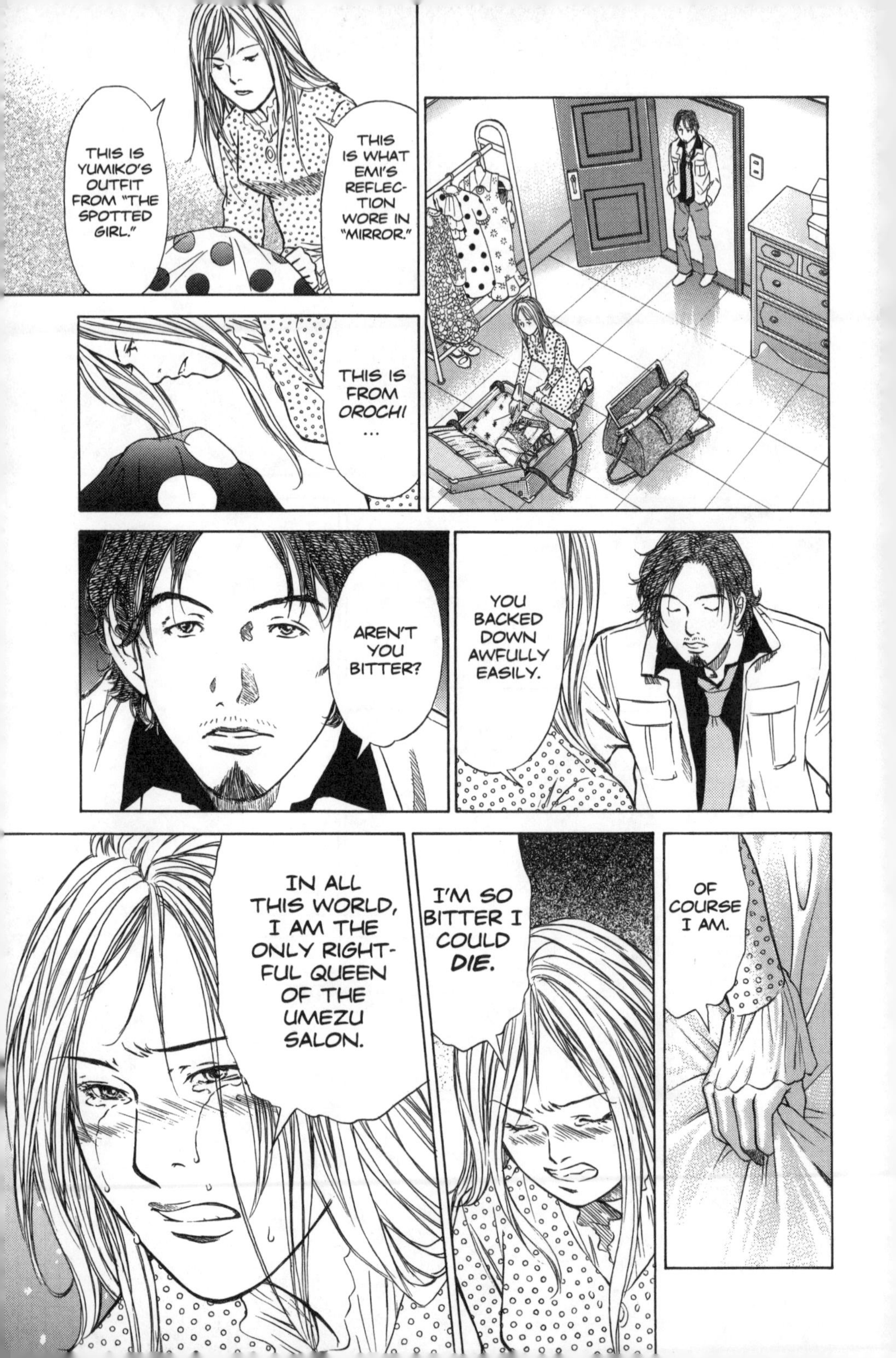
THIS IS WHAT EMI'S REFLECTION WORE IN "MIRROR."
THIS IS YUMIKO'S OUTFIT FROM "THE SPOTTED GIRL."
THIS IS FROM *OROCHI* ...
YOU BACKED DOWN AWFULLY EASILY.
AREN'T YOU BITTER?
OF COURSE I AM.
I'M SO BITTER I COULD ***DIE.***
IN ALL THIS WORLD, I AM THE ONLY RIGHTFUL QUEEN OF THE UMEZU SALON.

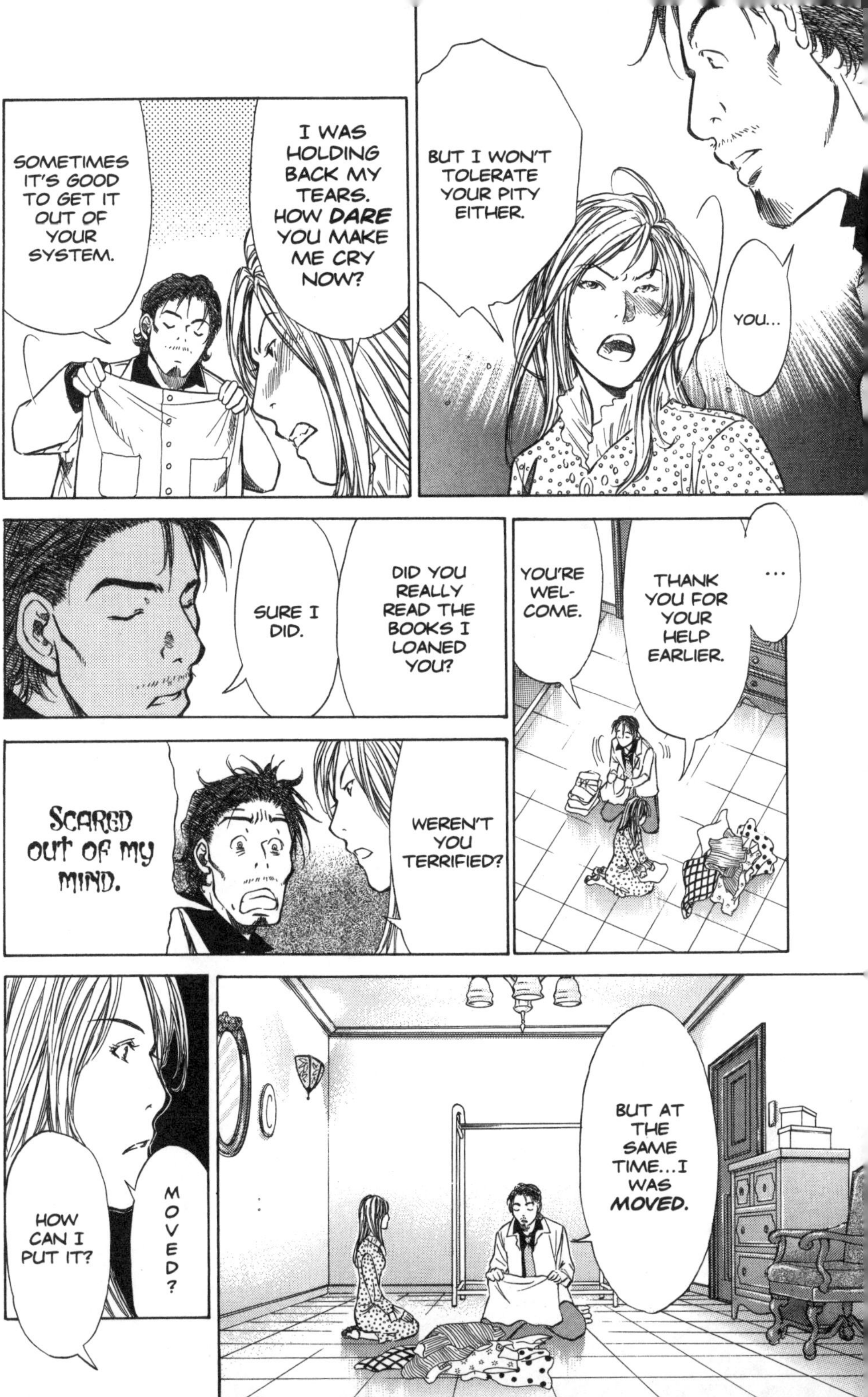
BUT I WON'T TOLERATE YOUR PITY EITHER.
YOU...
I WAS HOLDING BACK MY TEARS. HOW *DARE* YOU MAKE ME CRY NOW?
SOMETIMES IT'S GOOD TO GET IT OUT OF YOUR SYSTEM.
...
THANK YOU FOR YOUR HELP EARLIER.
YOU'RE WEL-COME.
DID YOU REALLY READ THE BOOKS I LOANED YOU?
SURE I DID.
WEREN'T YOU TERRIFIED?
SCARED OUT OF MY MIND.
BUT AT THE SAME TIME...I WAS *MOVED.*
MOVED?
HOW CAN I PUT IT?

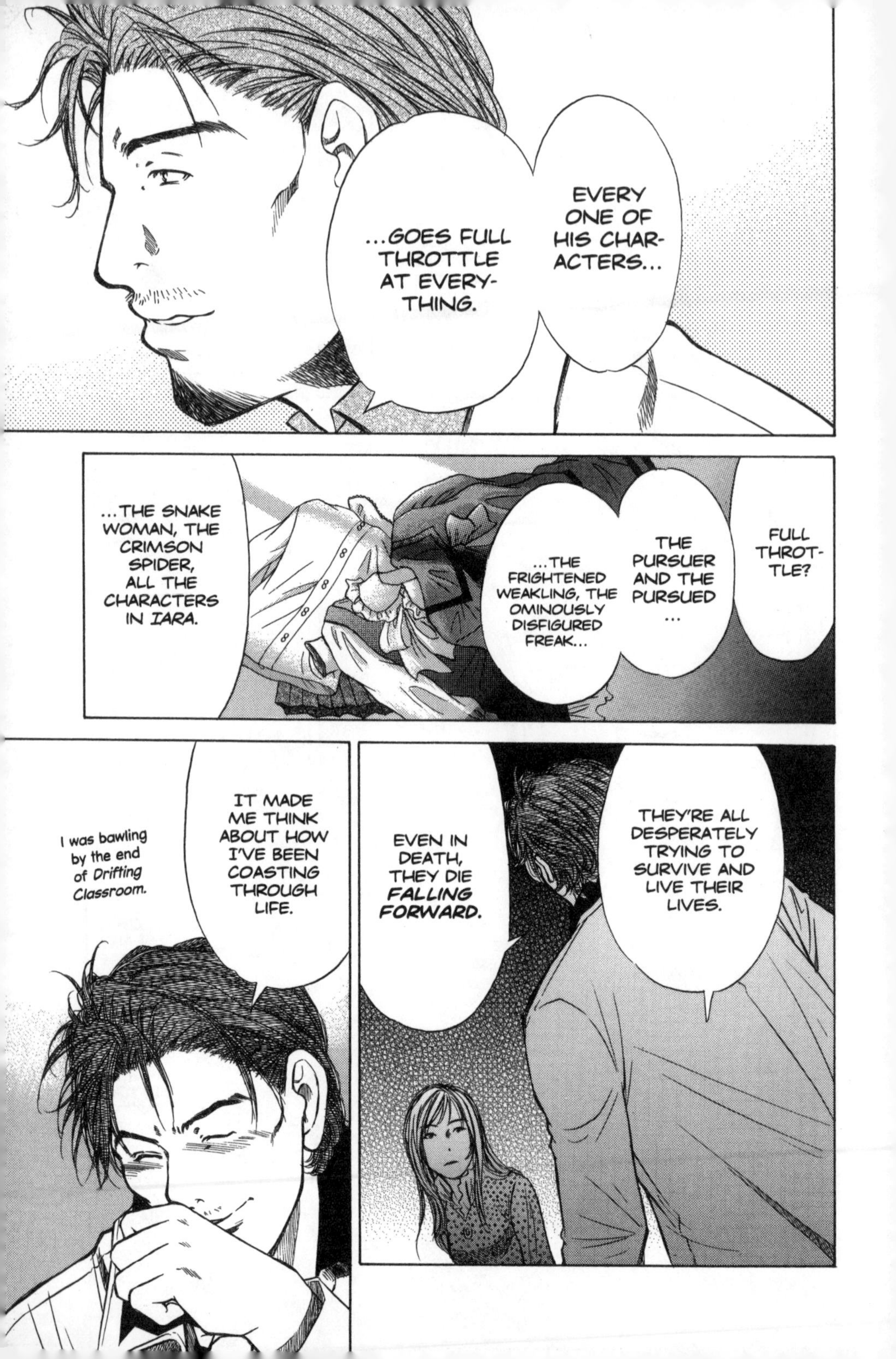
EVERY ONE OF HIS CHARACTERS...
...GOES FULL THROTTLE AT EVERYTHING.
FULL THROTTLE?
THE PURSUER AND THE PURSUED ...
...THE FRIGHTENED WEAKLING, THE OMINOUSLY DISFIGURED FREAK...
...THE SNAKE WOMAN, THE CRIMSON SPIDER, ALL THE CHARACTERS IN *IARA*.
THEY'RE ALL DESPERATELY TRYING TO SURVIVE AND LIVE THEIR LIVES.
EVEN IN DEATH, THEY DIE ***FALLING FORWARD.***
IT MADE ME THINK ABOUT HOW I'VE BEEN COASTING THROUGH LIFE.
I was bawling by the end of *Drifting Classroom.*

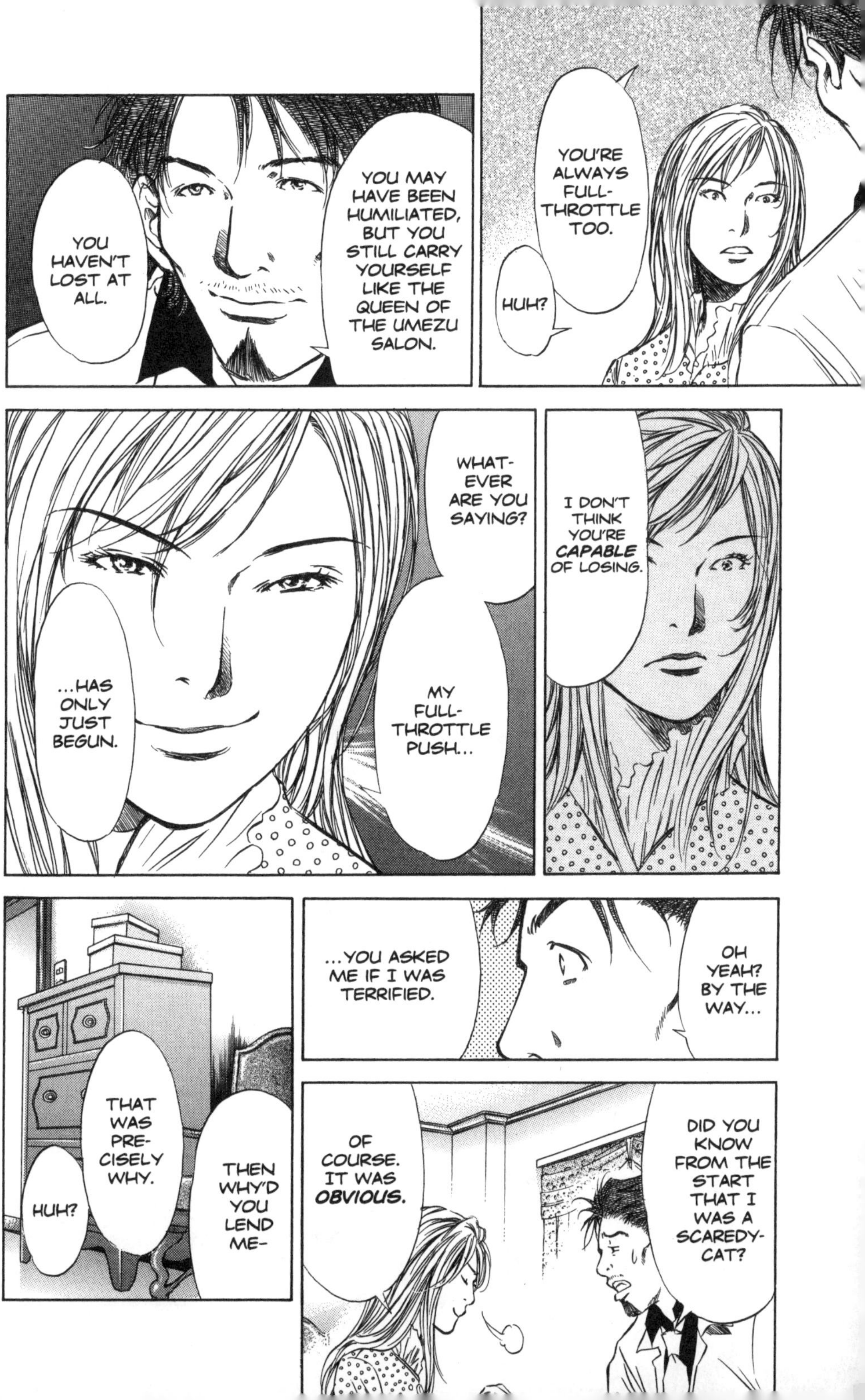
YOU'RE ALWAYS FULL-THROTTLE TOO.
HUH?
YOU MAY HAVE BEEN HUMILIATED, BUT YOU STILL CARRY YOURSELF LIKE THE QUEEN OF THE UMEZU SALON.
YOU HAVEN'T LOST AT ALL.
I DON'T THINK YOU'RE *CAPABLE* OF LOSING.
WHATEVER ARE YOU SAYING?
MY FULL-THROTTLE PUSH...
...HAS ONLY JUST BEGUN.
OH YEAH? BY THE WAY...
...YOU ASKED ME IF I WAS TERRIFIED.
DID YOU KNOW FROM THE START THAT I WAS A SCAREDY-CAT?
OF COURSE. IT WAS ***OBVIOUS.***
THEN WHY'D YOU LEND ME-
THAT WAS PRECISELY WHY.
HUH?

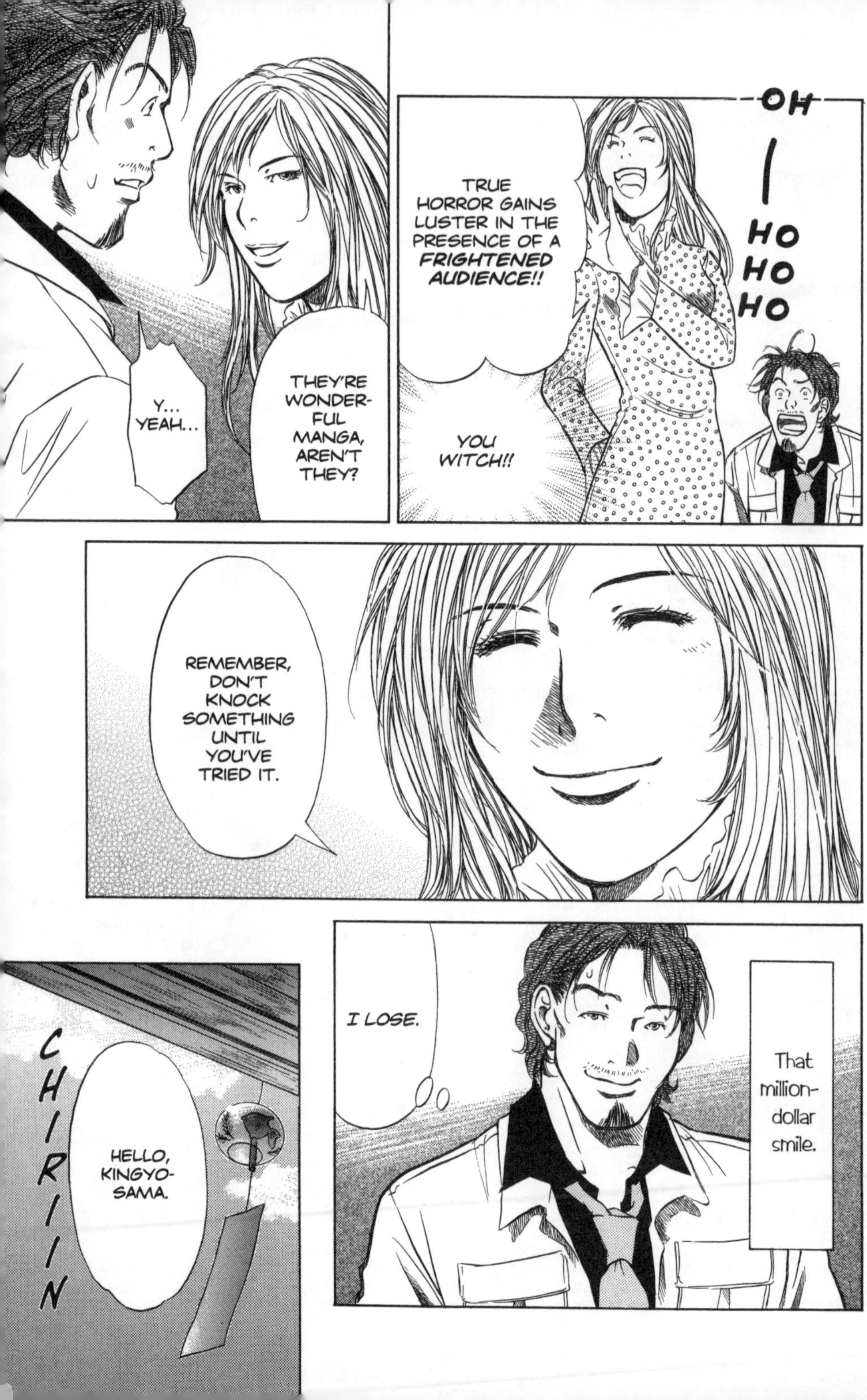
OH—HO HO HO
TRUE HORROR GAINS LUSTER IN THE PRESENCE OF A FRIGHTENED AUDIENCE!!
YOU WITCH!!
THEY'RE WONDERFUL MANGA, AREN'T THEY?
Y... YEAH...
REMEMBER, DON'T KNOCK SOMETHING UNTIL YOU'VE TRIED IT.
That million-dollar smile.
I LOSE.
CHIRIIN
HELLO, KINGYO-SAMA.

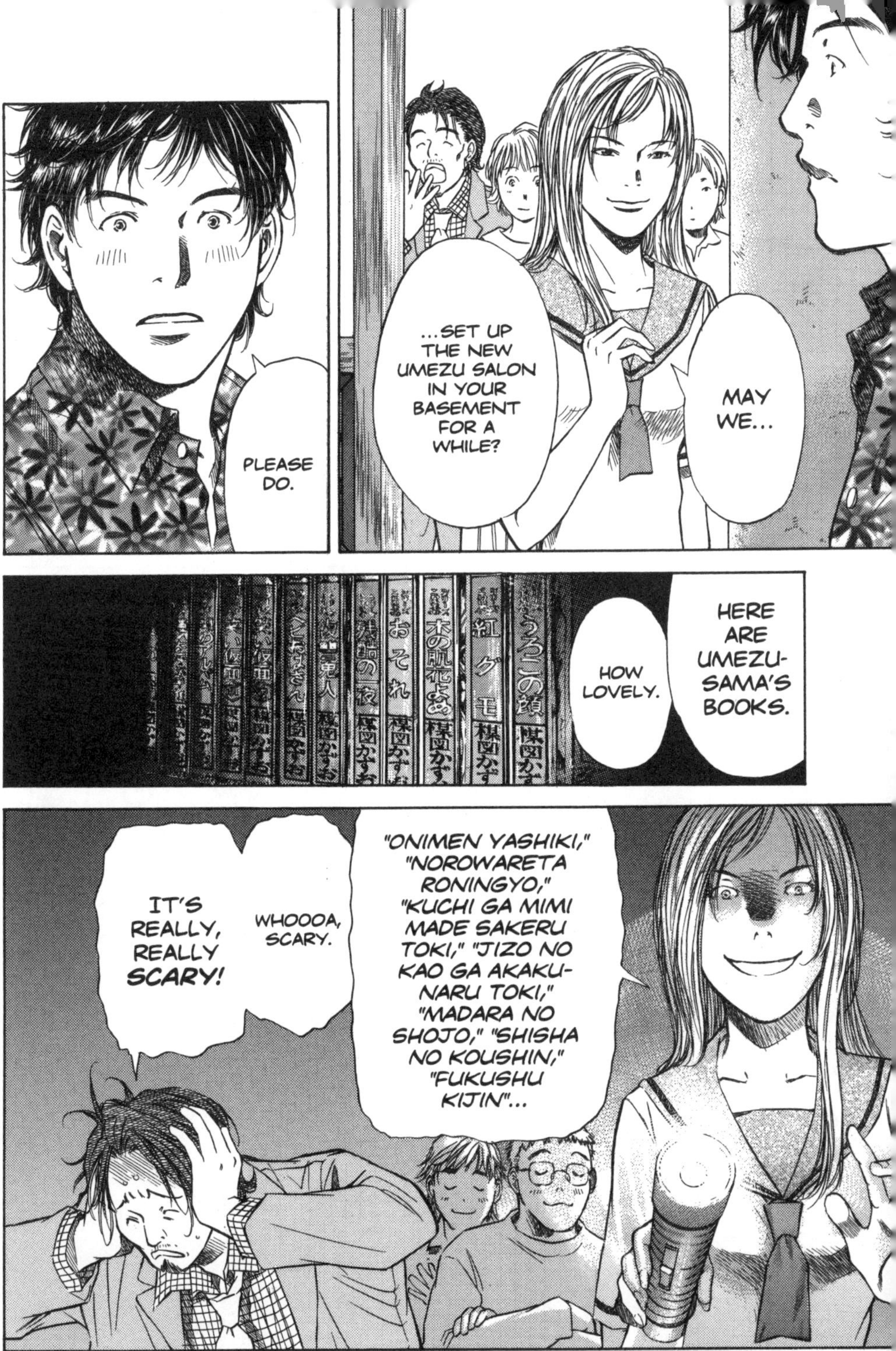
MAY WE...
...SET UP THE NEW UMEZU SALON IN YOUR BASEMENT FOR A WHILE?
PLEASE DO.
HERE ARE UMEZU-SAMA'S BOOKS.
HOW LOVELY.
"ONIMEN YASHIKI," "NOROWARETA RONINGYO," "KUCHI GA MIMI MADE SAKERU TOKI," "JIZO NO KAO GA AKAKU-NARU TOKI," "MADARA NO SHOJO," "SHISHA NO KOUSHIN," "FUKUSHU KIJIN"...
WHOOOA, SCARY.
IT'S REALLY, REALLY SCARY!

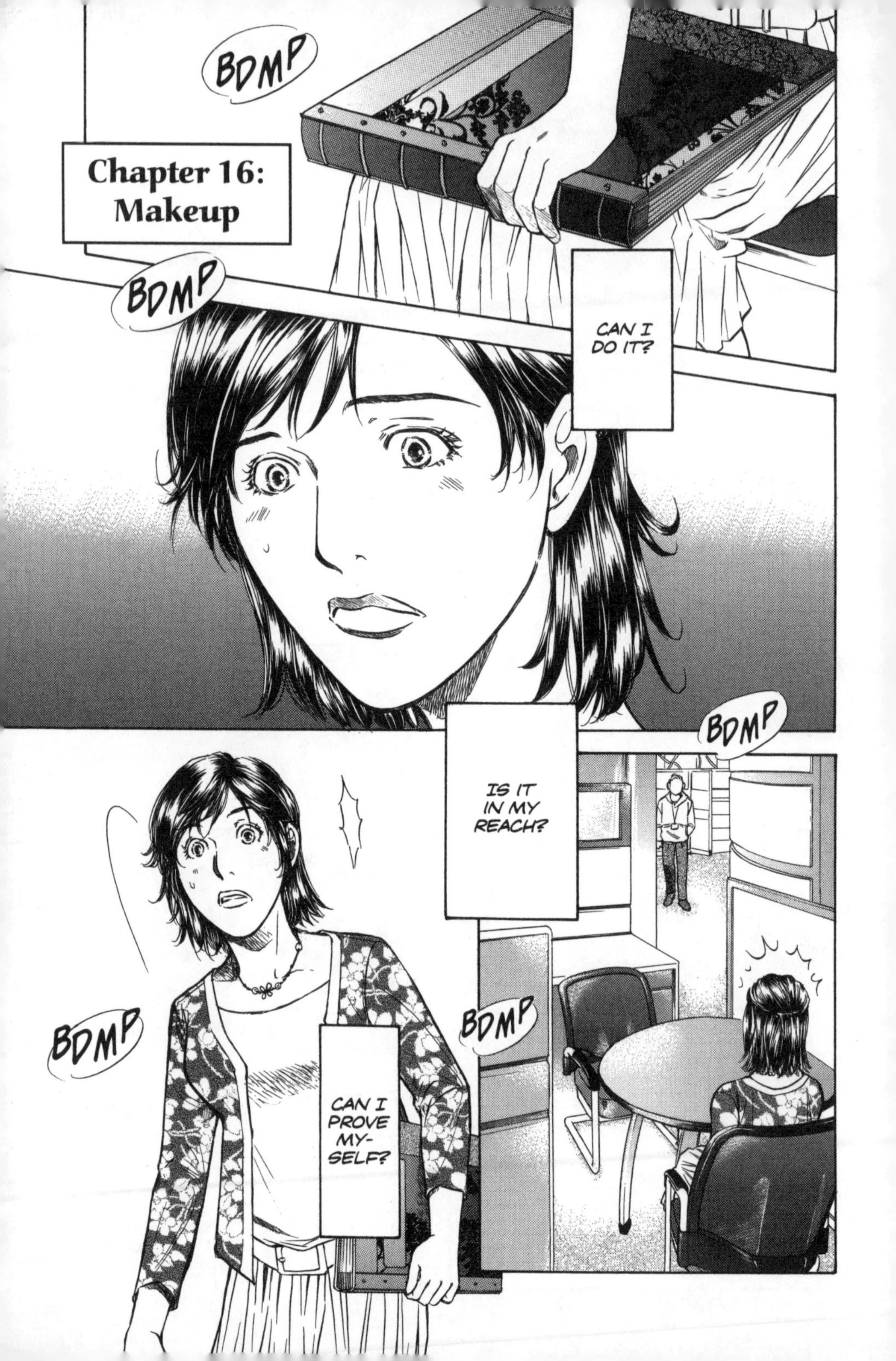
BDMP
Chapter 16: Makeup
BDMP
CAN I DO IT?
BDMP
IS IT IN MY REACH?
BDMP
CAN I PROVE MY-SELF?
BDMP

Chapter 16: Makeup

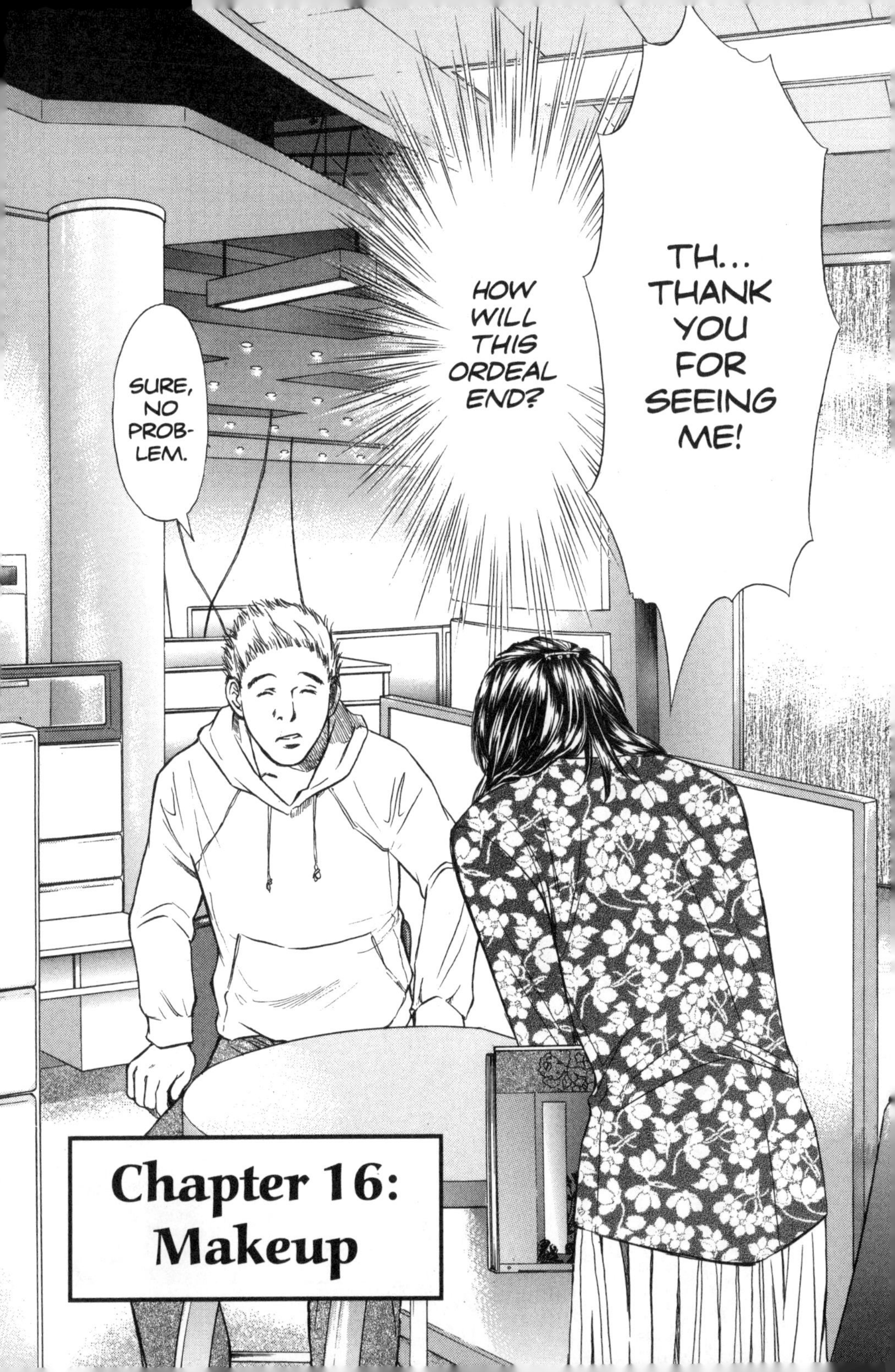
TH... THANK YOU FOR SEEING ME!
HOW WILL THIS ORDEAL END?
SURE, NO PROBLEM.

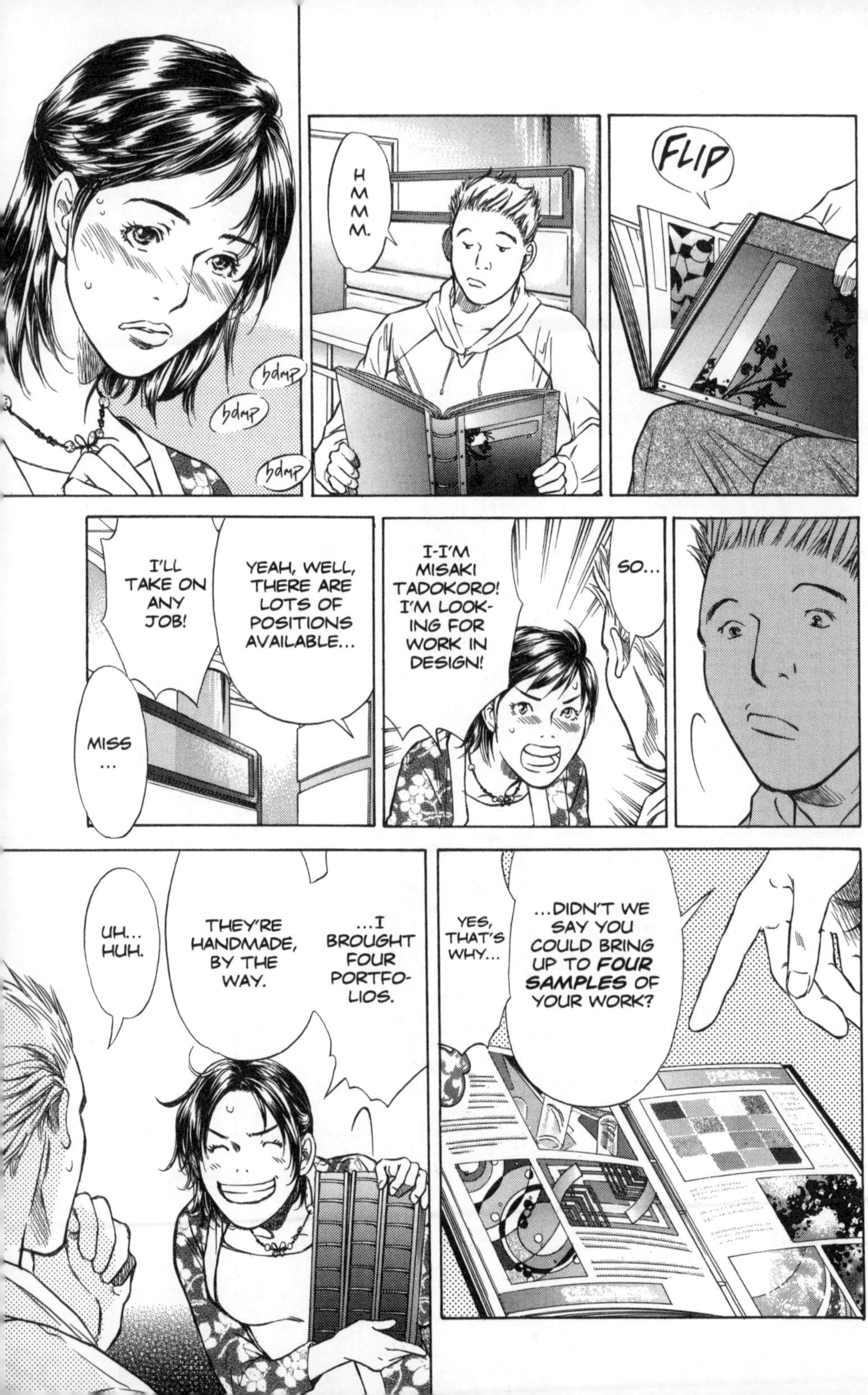
FLIP
HMMM.
bdmp
bdmp
bdmp
SO...
I-I'M MISAKI TADOKORO! I'M LOOKING FOR WORK IN DESIGN!
YEAH, WELL, THERE ARE LOTS OF POSITIONS AVAILABLE...
I'LL TAKE ON ANY JOB!
MISS...
...DIDN'T WE SAY YOU COULD BRING UP TO FOUR SAMPLES OF YOUR WORK?
YES, THAT'S WHY...
...I BROUGHT FOUR PORTFOLIOS.
THEY'RE HANDMADE, BY THE WAY.
UH... HUH.

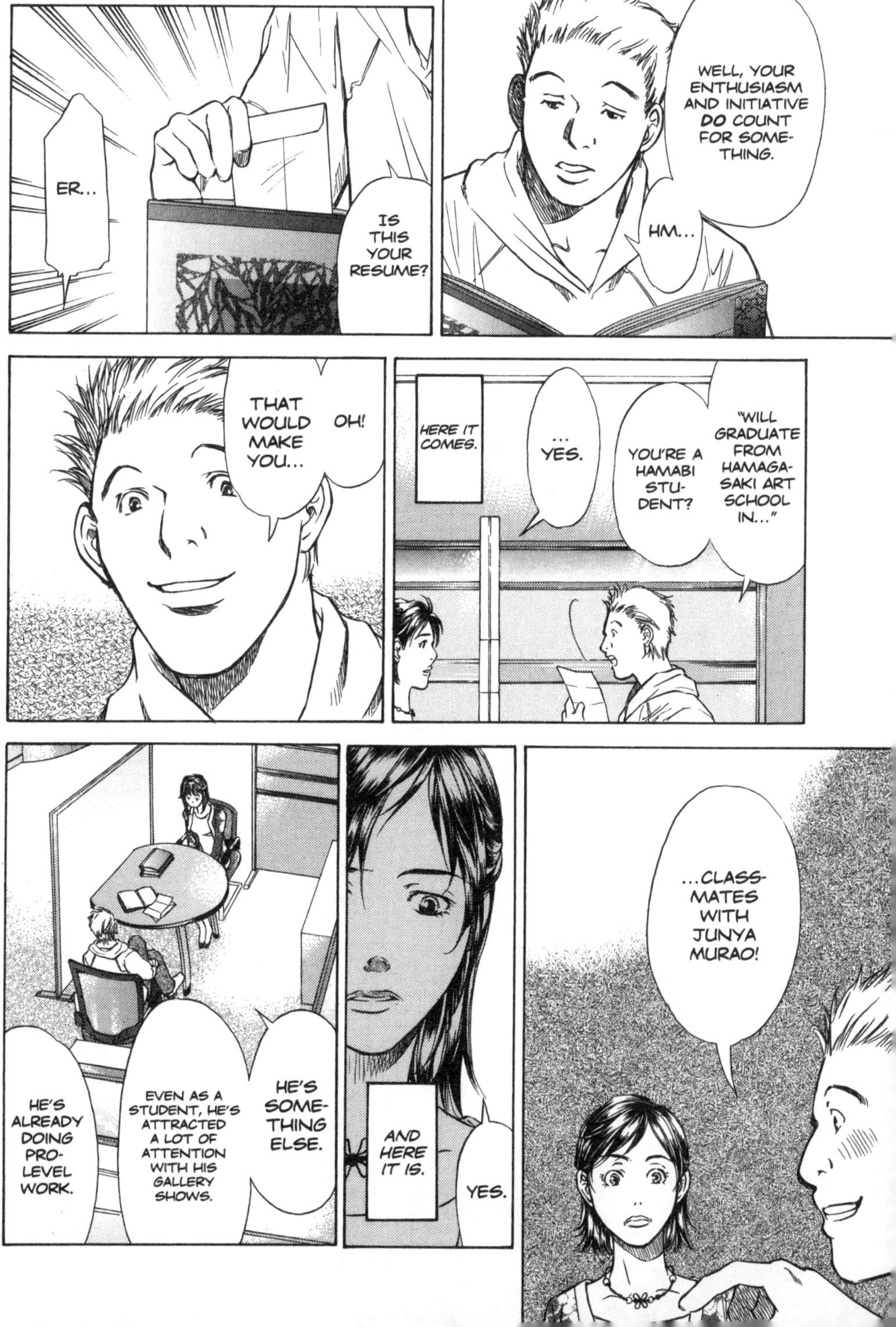
WELL, YOUR ENTHUSIASM AND INITIATIVE **DO** COUNT FOR SOME-THING.
HM...
IS THIS YOUR RESUME?
ER...
"WILL GRADUATE FROM HAMAGA-SAKI ART SCHOOL IN..."
YOU'RE A HAMABI STU-DENT?
... YES.
HERE IT COMES.
OH!
THAT WOULD MAKE YOU...
...CLASS-MATES WITH JUNYA MURAO!
YES.
AND HERE IT IS.
HE'S SOME-THING ELSE.
EVEN AS A STUDENT, HE'S ATTRACTED A LOT OF ATTENTION WITH HIS GALLERY SHOWS.
HE'S ALREADY DOING PRO-LEVEL WORK.

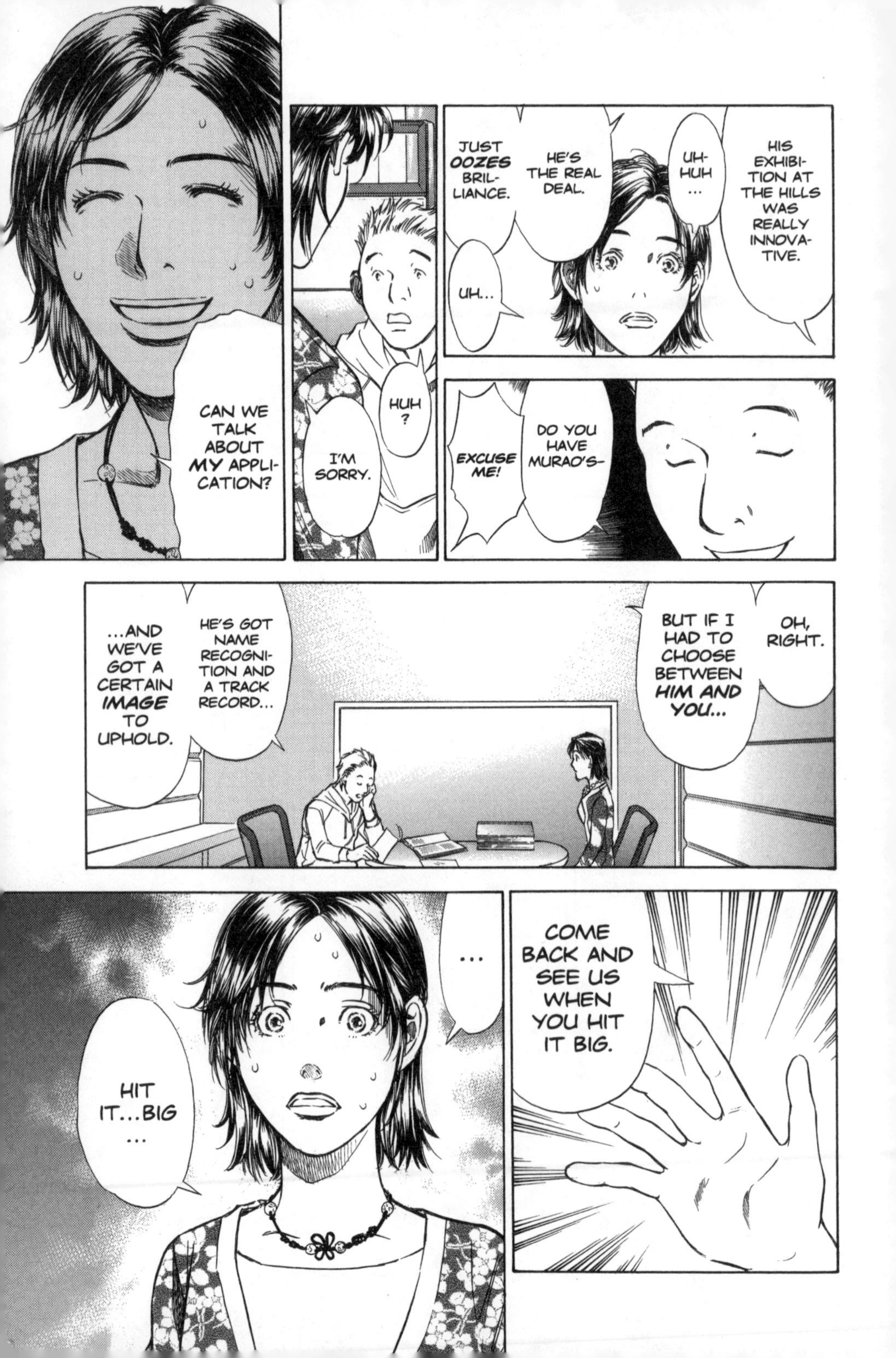
HIS EXHIBITION AT THE HILLS WAS REALLY INNOVATIVE.
UH-HUH...
HE'S THE REAL DEAL.
JUST OOZES BRILLIANCE.
UH...
DO YOU HAVE MURAO'S-
EXCUSE ME!
HUH?
I'M SORRY.
CAN WE TALK ABOUT MY APPLICATION?
OH, RIGHT.
BUT IF I HAD TO CHOOSE BETWEEN HIM AND YOU...
HE'S GOT NAME RECOGNITION AND A TRACK RECORD...
...AND WE'VE GOT A CERTAIN IMAGE TO UPHOLD.
COME BACK AND SEE US WHEN YOU HIT IT BIG.
...
HIT IT...BIG...

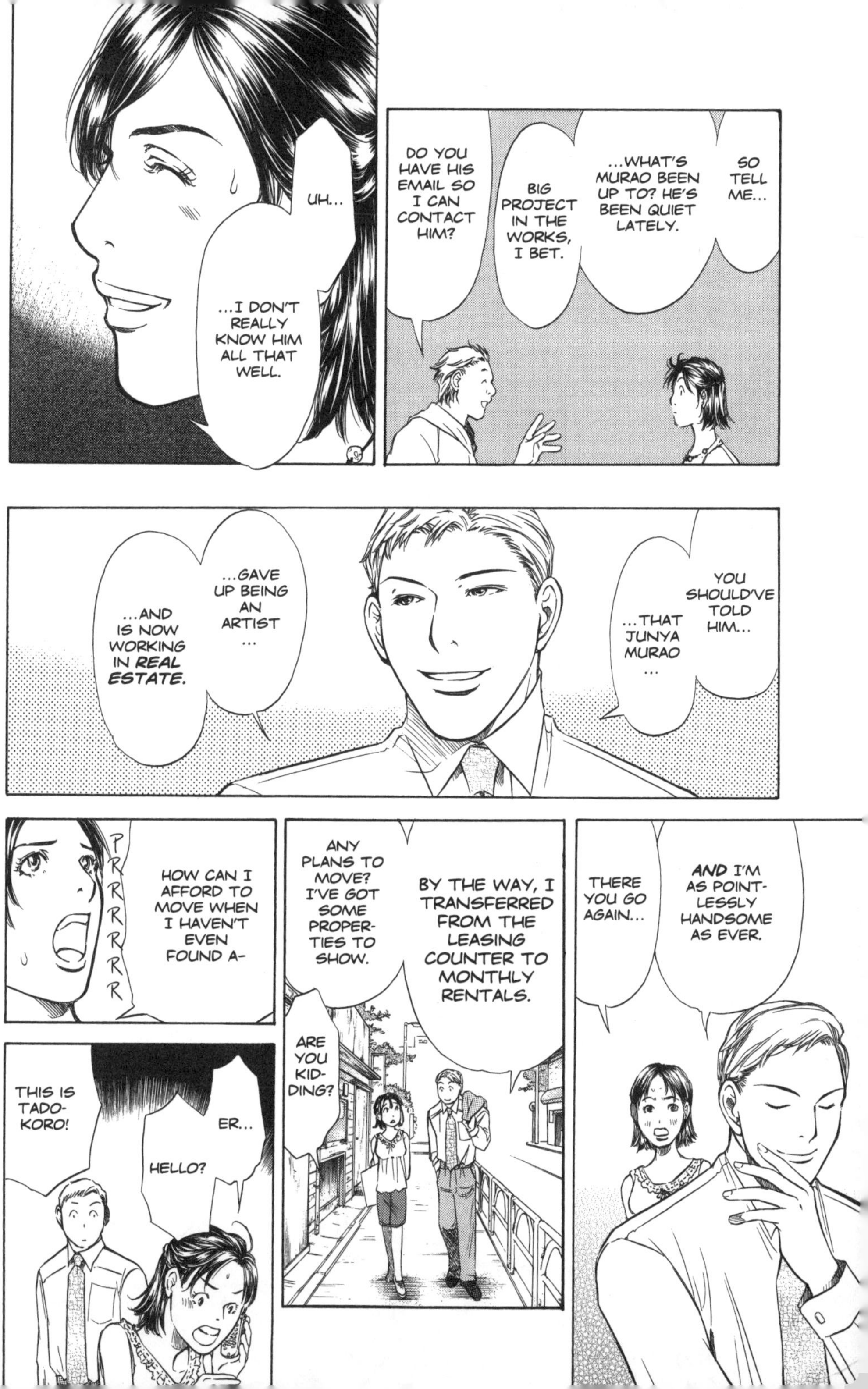
SO TELL ME...
...WHAT'S MURAO BEEN UP TO? HE'S BEEN QUIET LATELY.
BIG PROJECT IN THE WORKS, I BET.
DO YOU HAVE HIS EMAIL SO I CAN CONTACT HIM?
UH...
...I DON'T REALLY KNOW HIM ALL THAT WELL.
YOU SHOULD'VE TOLD HIM...
...THAT JUNYA MURAO ...
...GAVE UP BEING AN ARTIST ...
...AND IS NOW WORKING IN *REAL ESTATE*.
AND I'M AS POINT-LESSLY HANDSOME AS EVER.
THERE YOU GO AGAIN...
BY THE WAY, I TRANSFERRED FROM THE LEASING COUNTER TO MONTHLY RENTALS.
ANY PLANS TO MOVE? I'VE GOT SOME PROPER-TIES TO SHOW.
ARE YOU KID-DING?
PRRRRRRR
HOW CAN I AFFORD TO MOVE WHEN I HAVEN'T EVEN FOUND A-
ER...
HELLO?
THIS IS TADO-KORO!

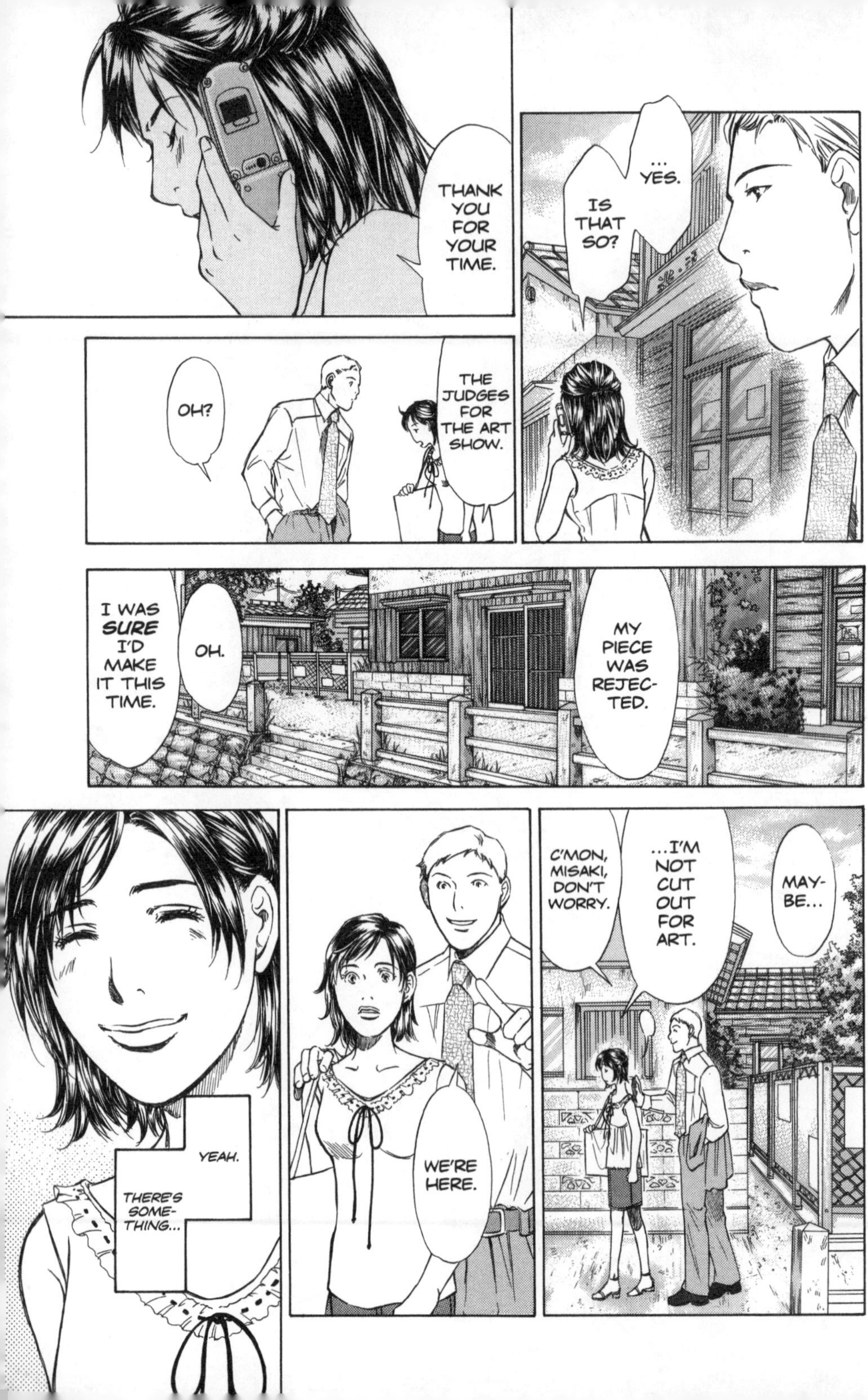
...YES.
IS THAT SO?
THANK YOU FOR YOUR TIME.
THE JUDGES FOR THE ART SHOW.
OH?
MY PIECE WAS REJECTED.
OH.
I WAS **SURE** I'D MAKE IT THIS TIME.
MAY-BE...
...I'M NOT CUT OUT FOR ART.
C'MON, MISAKI, DON'T WORRY.
WE'RE HERE.
YEAH.
THERE'S SOME-THING...

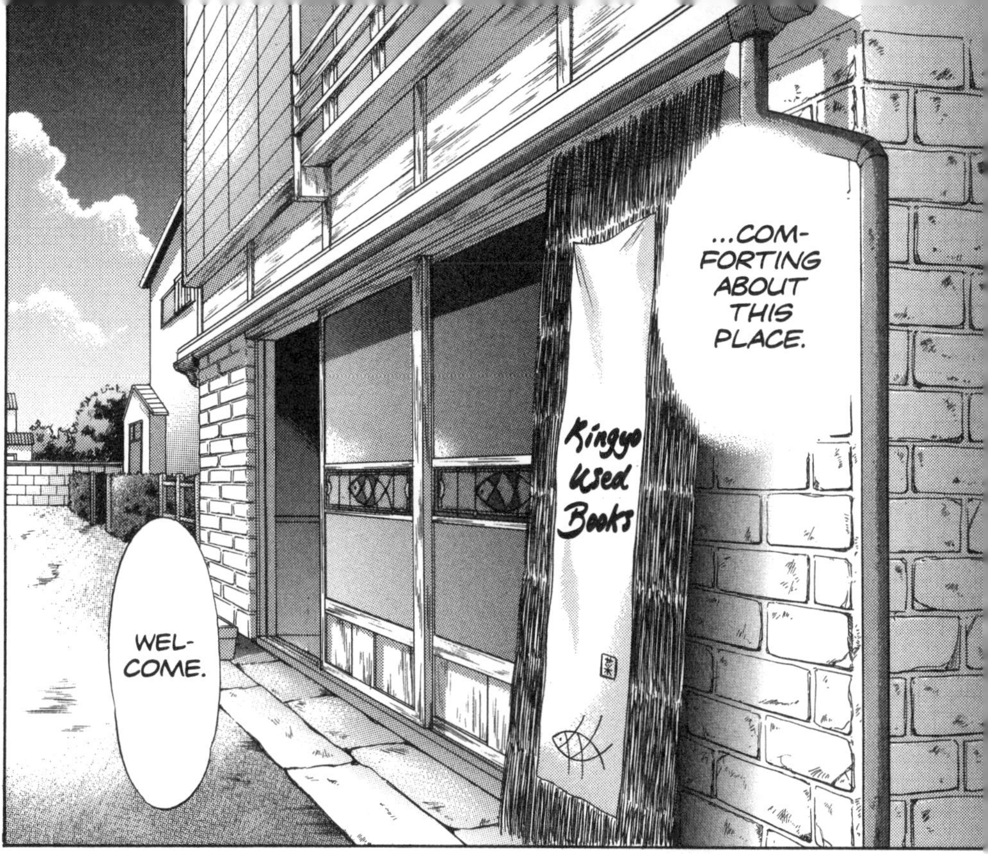
...COM-FORTING ABOUT THIS PLACE.
Kingyo Used Books
WEL-COME.

A WHILE BACK I HAPPENED UPON THIS BOOK-STORE.

SINCE THEN IT'S BECOME A PLACE I VISIT OFTEN.

THEN I FOUND OUT MY FRIEND MURAO-KUN WAS ANOTHER REGULAR...

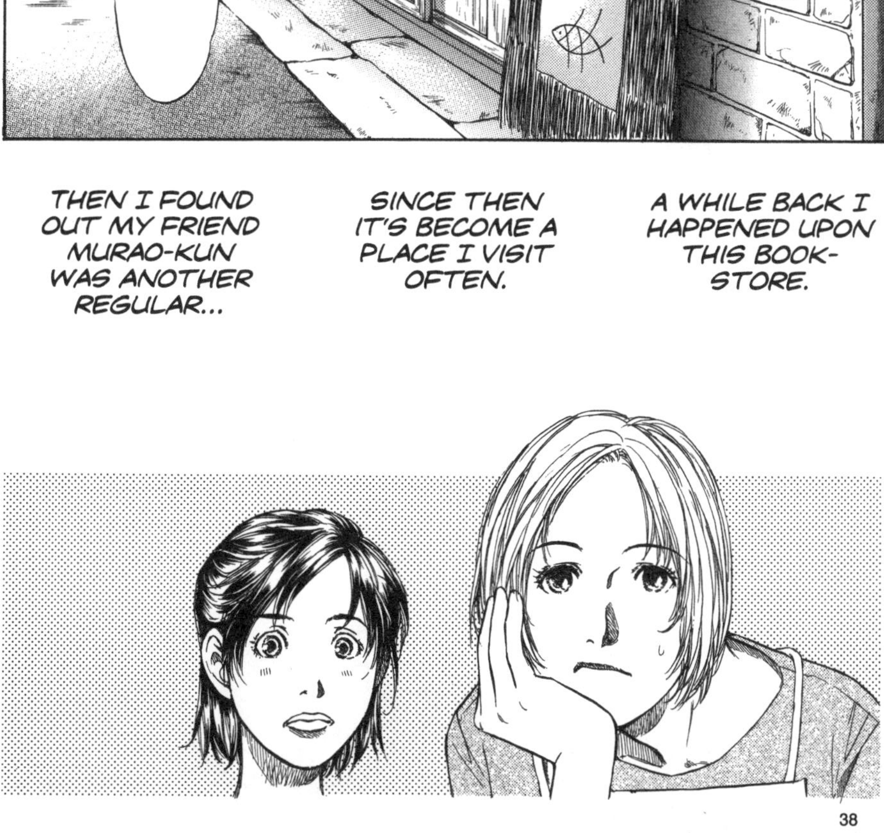

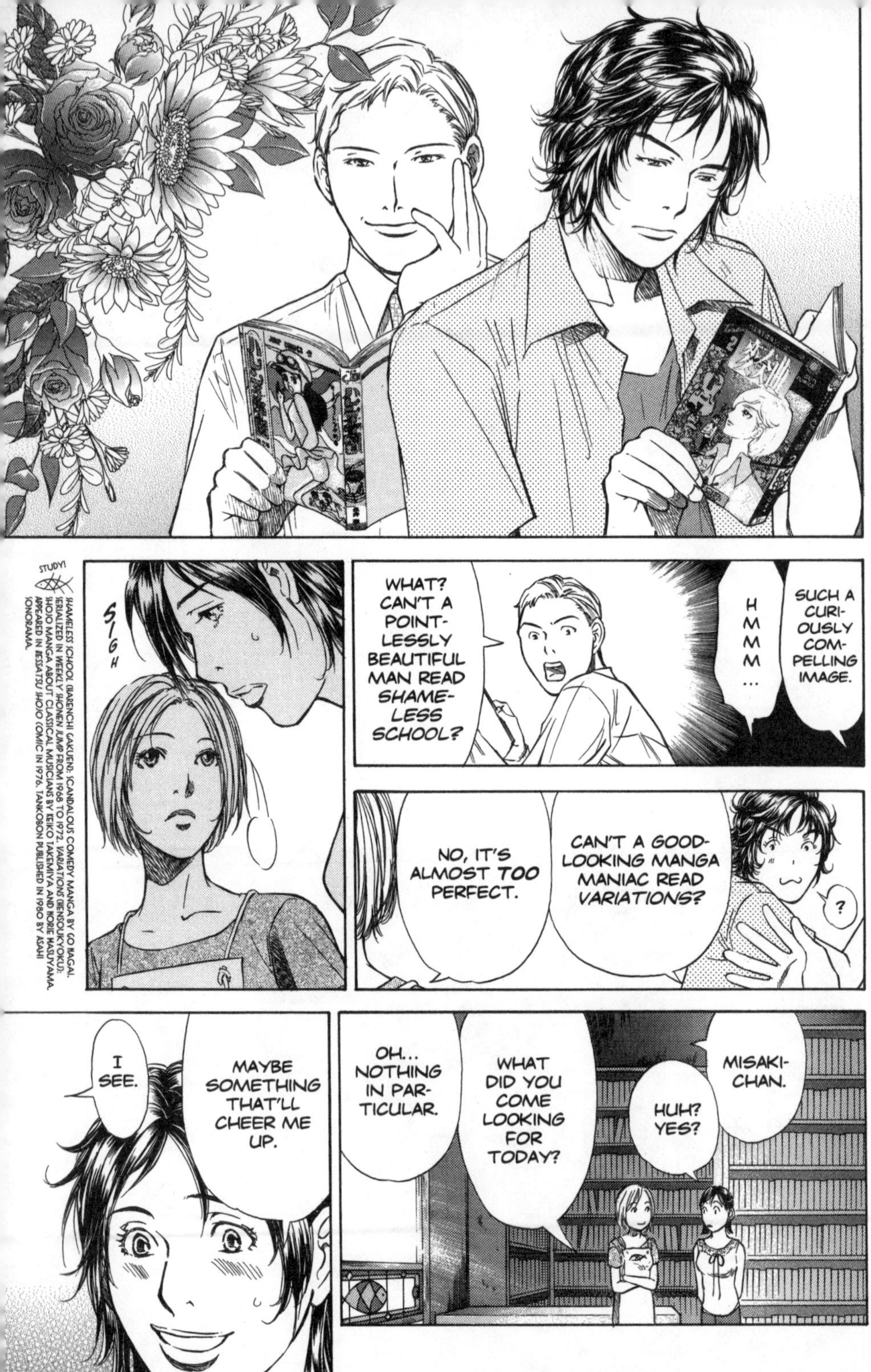
SUCH A CURIOUSLY COMPELLING IMAGE.
HMMM...
WHAT? CAN'T A POINTLESSLY BEAUTIFUL MAN READ SHAMELESS SCHOOL?
CAN'T A GOOD-LOOKING MANGA MANIAC READ *VARIATIONS*?
NO, IT'S ALMOST *TOO* PERFECT.
?
SIGH
STUDY!
SHAMELESS SCHOOL (HARENCHI GAKUEN): SCANDALOUS COMEDY MANGA BY GO NAGAI. SERIALIZED IN WEEKLY SHONEN JUMP FROM 1968 TO 1972. VARIATIONS (HENSOUKYOKU): SHOJO MANGA ABOUT CLASSICAL MUSICIANS BY KEIKO TAKEMIYA AND NORIE MASUYAMA. APPEARED IN BESSATSU SHOJO COMIC IN 1976. TANKOBON PUBLISHED IN 1980 BY ASAHI SONORAMA.
MISAKI-CHAN.
HUH? YES?
WHAT DID YOU COME LOOKING FOR TODAY?
OH... NOTHING IN PARTICULAR.
MAYBE SOMETHING THAT'LL CHEER ME UP.
I SEE.

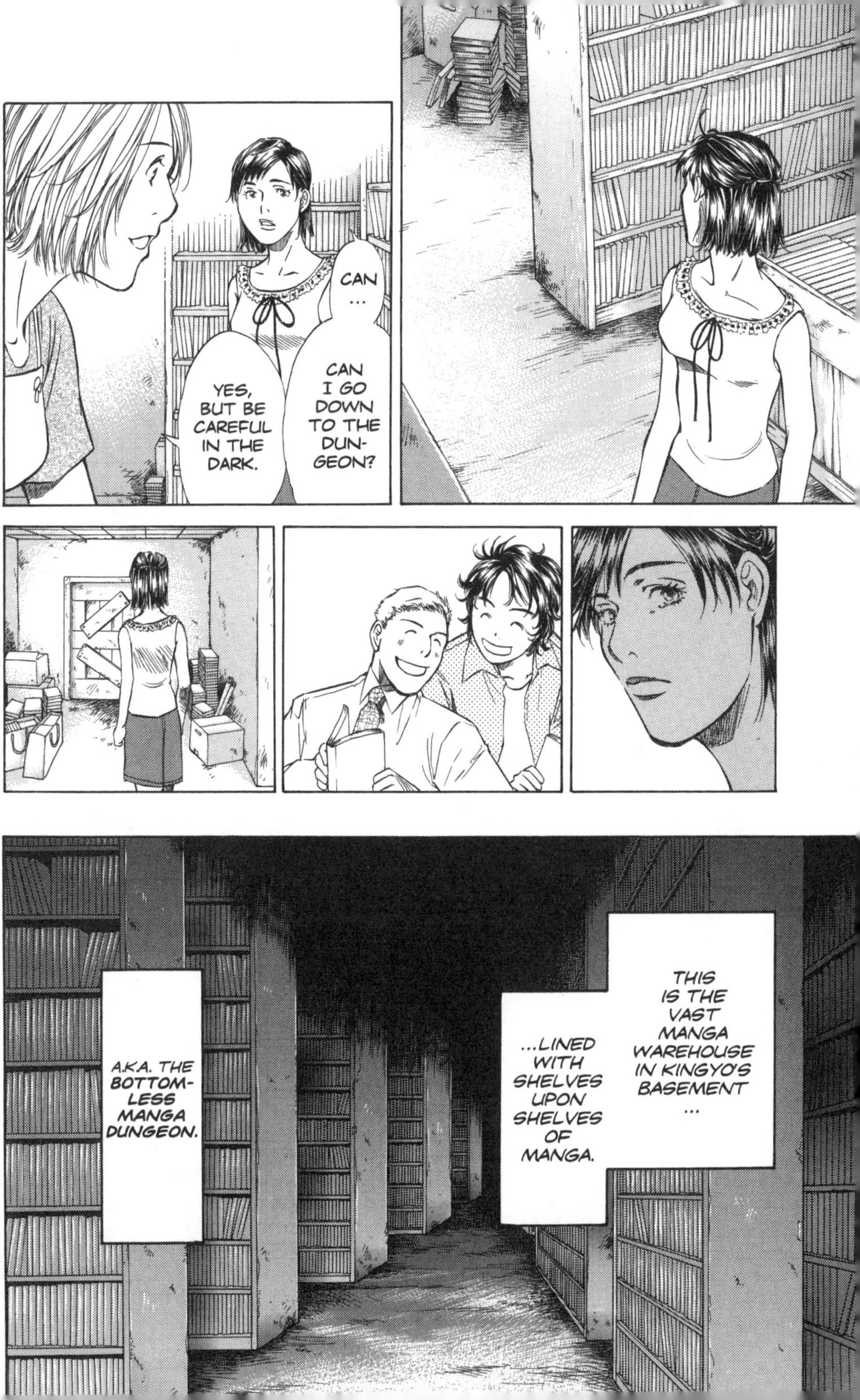
CAN ...
CAN I GO DOWN TO THE DUN-GEON?
YES, BUT BE CAREFUL IN THE DARK.
THIS IS THE VAST MANGA WAREHOUSE IN KINGYO'S BASEMENT ...
...LINED WITH SHELVES UPON SHELVES OF MANGA.
A.K.A. THE BOTTOM-LESS MANGA DUNGEON.

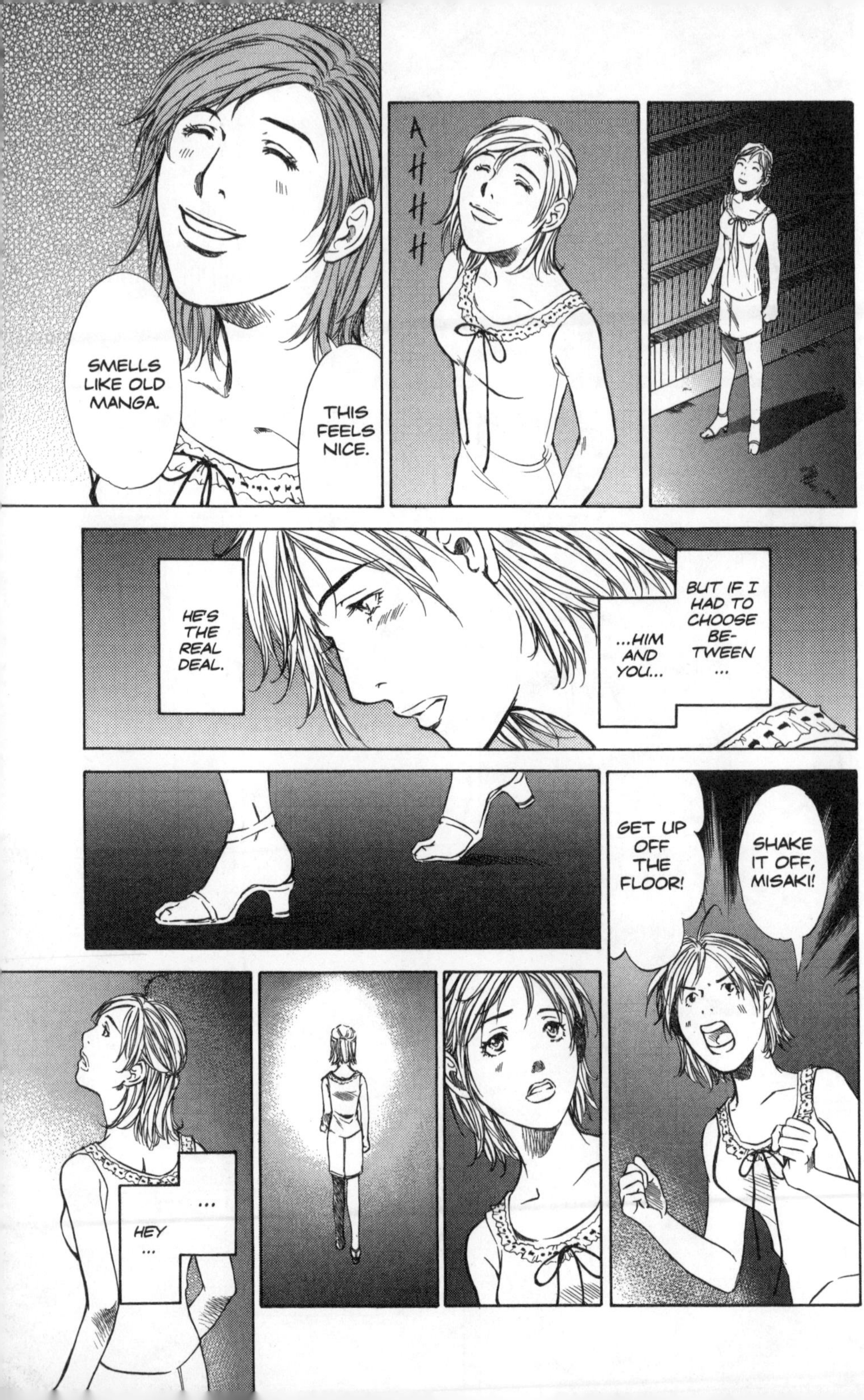
AHHH
THIS FEELS NICE.
SMELLS LIKE OLD MANGA.
BUT IF I HAD TO CHOOSE BE- TWEEN ...
...HIM AND YOU...
HE'S THE REAL DEAL.
SHAKE IT OFF, MISAKI!
GET UP OFF THE FLOOR!
...
HEY ...

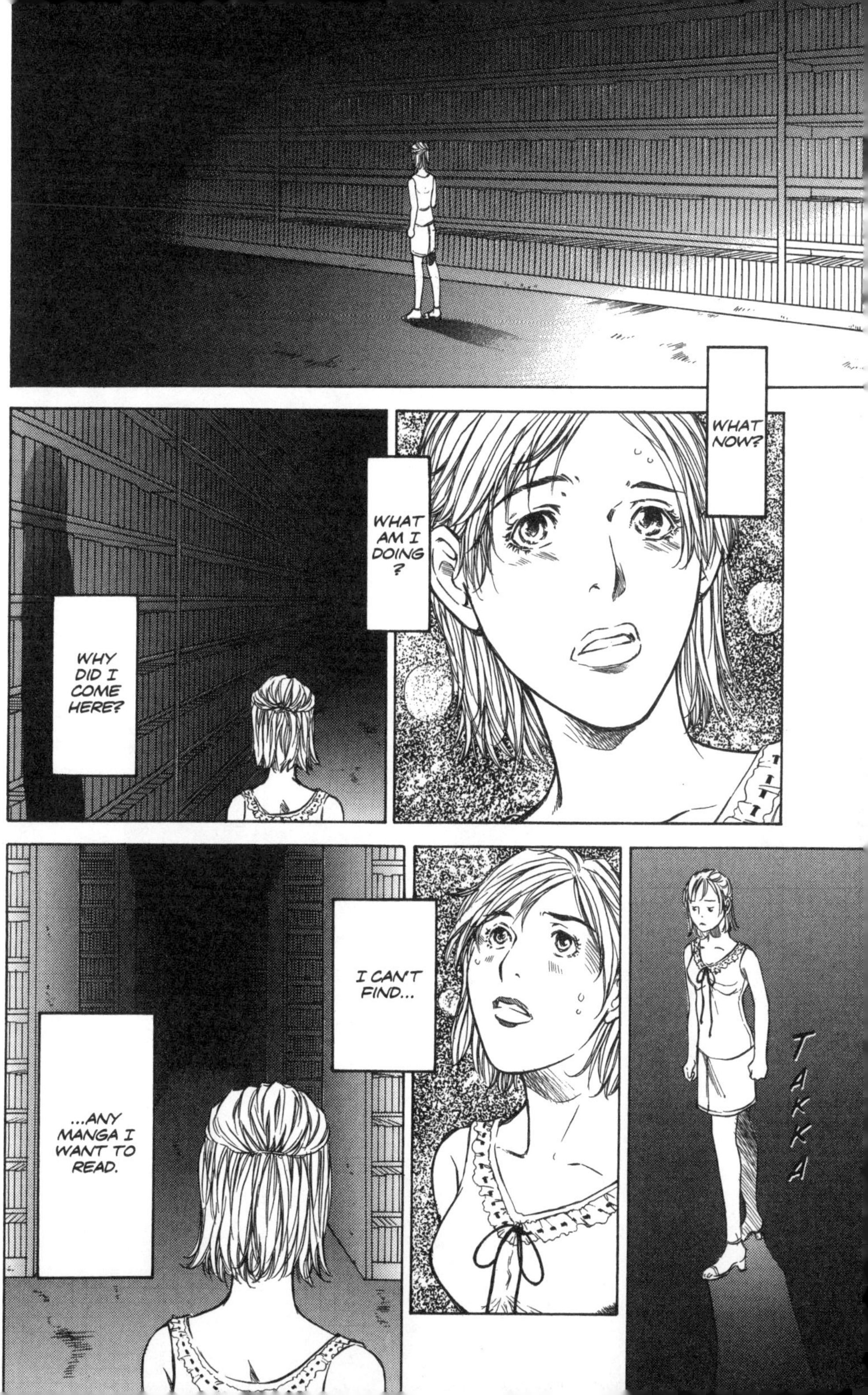
WHAT NOW?
WHAT AM I DOING ?
WHY DID I COME HERE?
TAKKA
I CAN'T FIND...
...ANY MANGA I WANT TO READ.

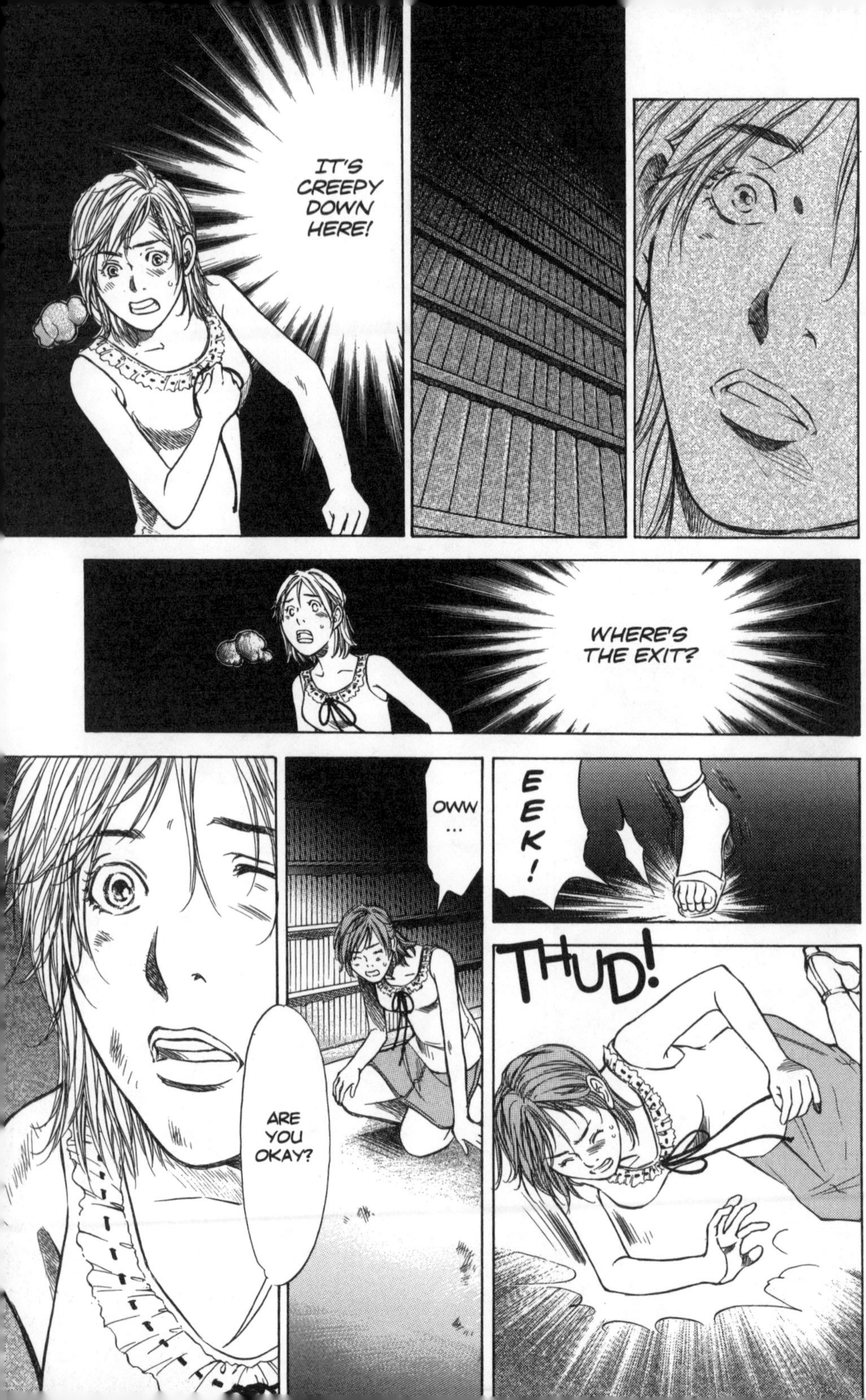
IT'S CREEPY DOWN HERE!
WHERE'S THE EXIT?
EEK!
THUD!
OWW...
ARE YOU OKAY?

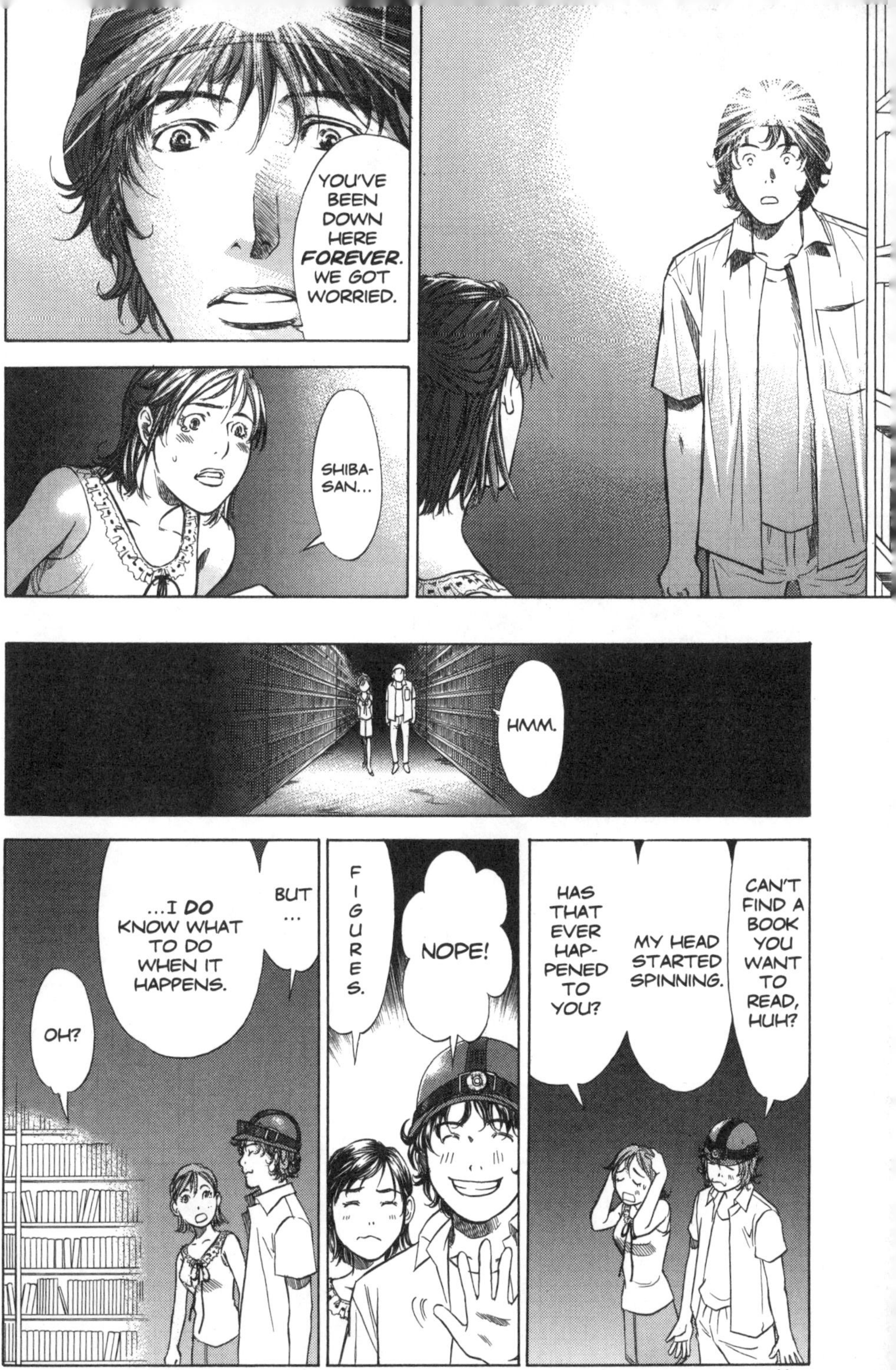
YOU'VE BEEN DOWN HERE FOREVER. WE GOT WORRIED.
SHIBA-SAN...
HMM.
CAN'T FIND A BOOK YOU WANT TO READ, HUH?
MY HEAD STARTED SPINNING.
HAS THAT EVER HAP-PENED TO YOU?
NOPE!
FIGURES.
BUT...
...I DO KNOW WHAT TO DO WHEN IT HAPPENS.
OH?

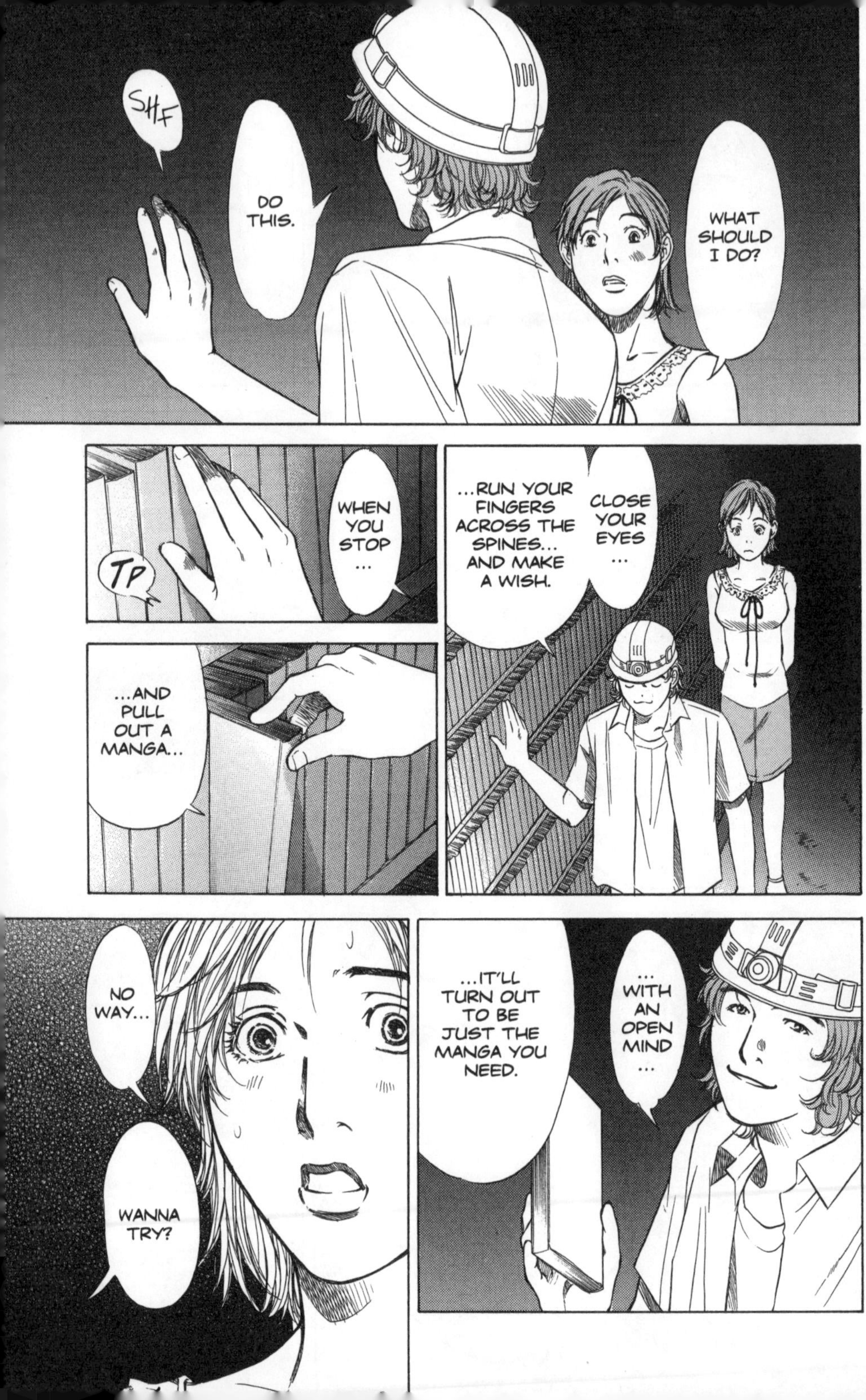
WHAT SHOULD I DO?
DO THIS.
SHF
CLOSE YOUR EYES ...
...RUN YOUR FINGERS ACROSS THE SPINES... AND MAKE A WISH.
WHEN YOU STOP ...
TP
...AND PULL OUT A MANGA...
... WITH AN OPEN MIND ...
...IT'LL TURN OUT TO BE JUST THE MANGA YOU NEED.
NO WAY...
WANNA TRY?

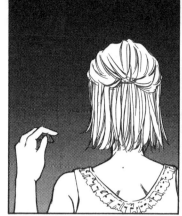
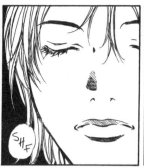
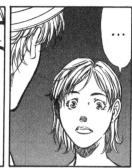

...

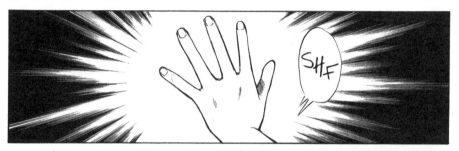

SHF

SHF

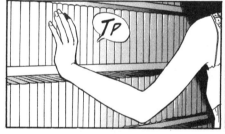

TP

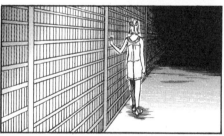

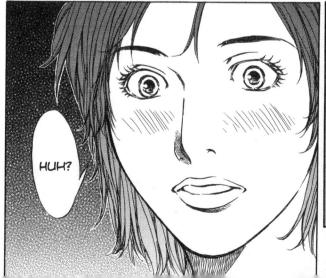

HUH?

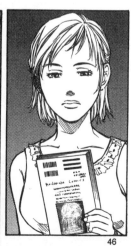

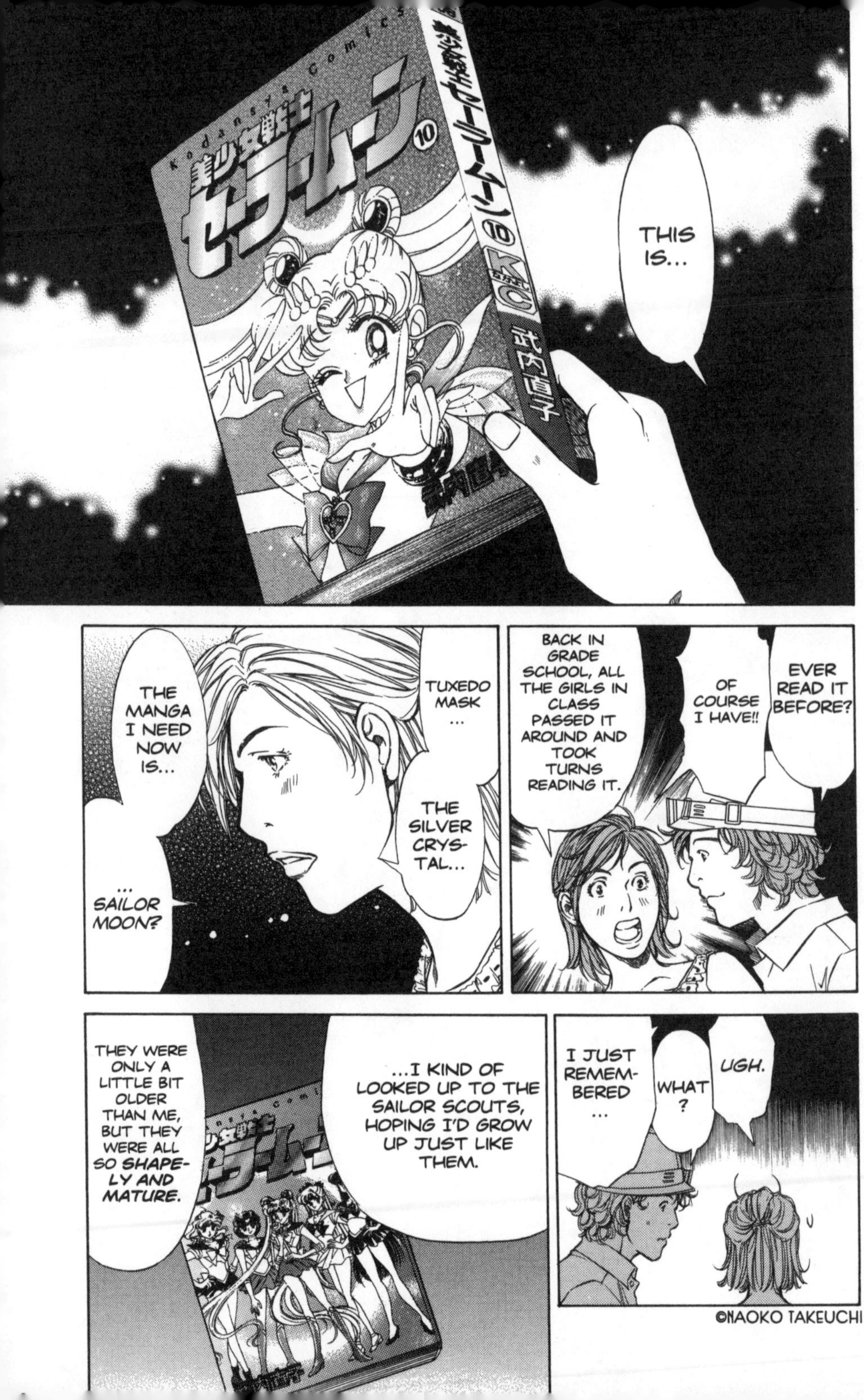
美少女戦士セーラームーン 10
武内直子
THIS IS...
EVER READ IT BEFORE?
OF COURSE I HAVE!!
BACK IN GRADE SCHOOL, ALL THE GIRLS IN CLASS PASSED IT AROUND AND TOOK TURNS READING IT.
TUXEDO MASK ...
THE SILVER CRYSTAL...
THE MANGA I NEED NOW IS...
... SAILOR MOON?
UGH.
WHAT?
I JUST REMEMBERED ...
...I KIND OF LOOKED UP TO THE SAILOR SCOUTS, HOPING I'D GROW UP JUST LIKE THEM.
THEY WERE ONLY A LITTLE BIT OLDER THAN ME, BUT THEY WERE ALL SO *SHAPELY AND MATURE.*

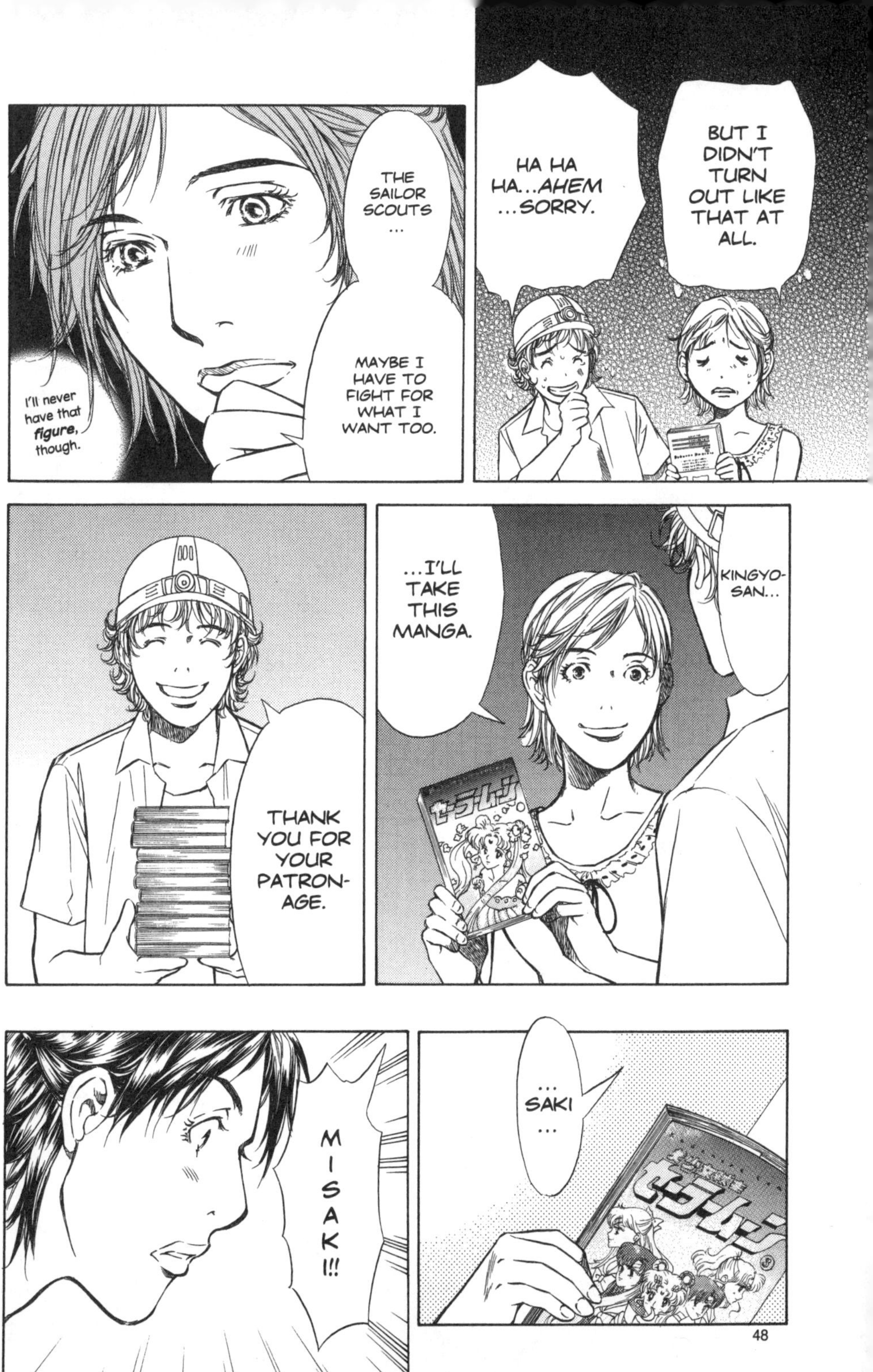
BUT I DIDN'T TURN OUT LIKE THAT AT ALL.
HA HA HA...*AHEM* ...SORRY.
THE SAILOR SCOUTS ...
MAYBE I HAVE TO FIGHT FOR WHAT I WANT TOO.
I'll never have that **figure**, though.
KINGYO-SAN...
...I'LL TAKE THIS MANGA.
THANK YOU FOR YOUR PATRON-AGE.
... SAKI ...
MISAKI!!!

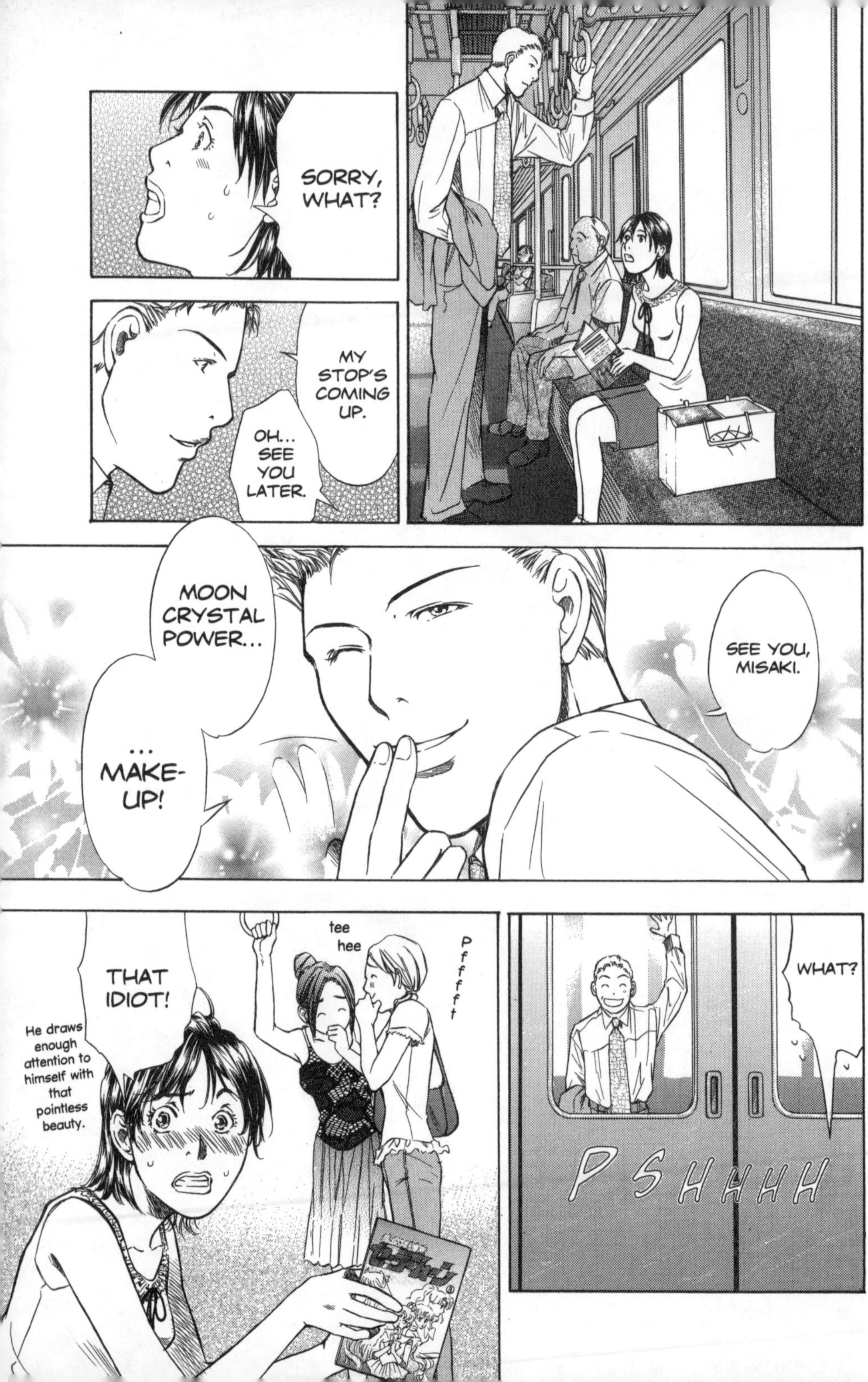
SORRY, WHAT?
MY STOP'S COMING UP.
OH... SEE YOU LATER.
SEE YOU, MISAKI.
MOON CRYSTAL POWER...
... MAKE-UP!
WHAT?
PSHHHH
Pfffft
tee hee
THAT IDIOT!
He draws enough attention to himself with that pointless beauty.

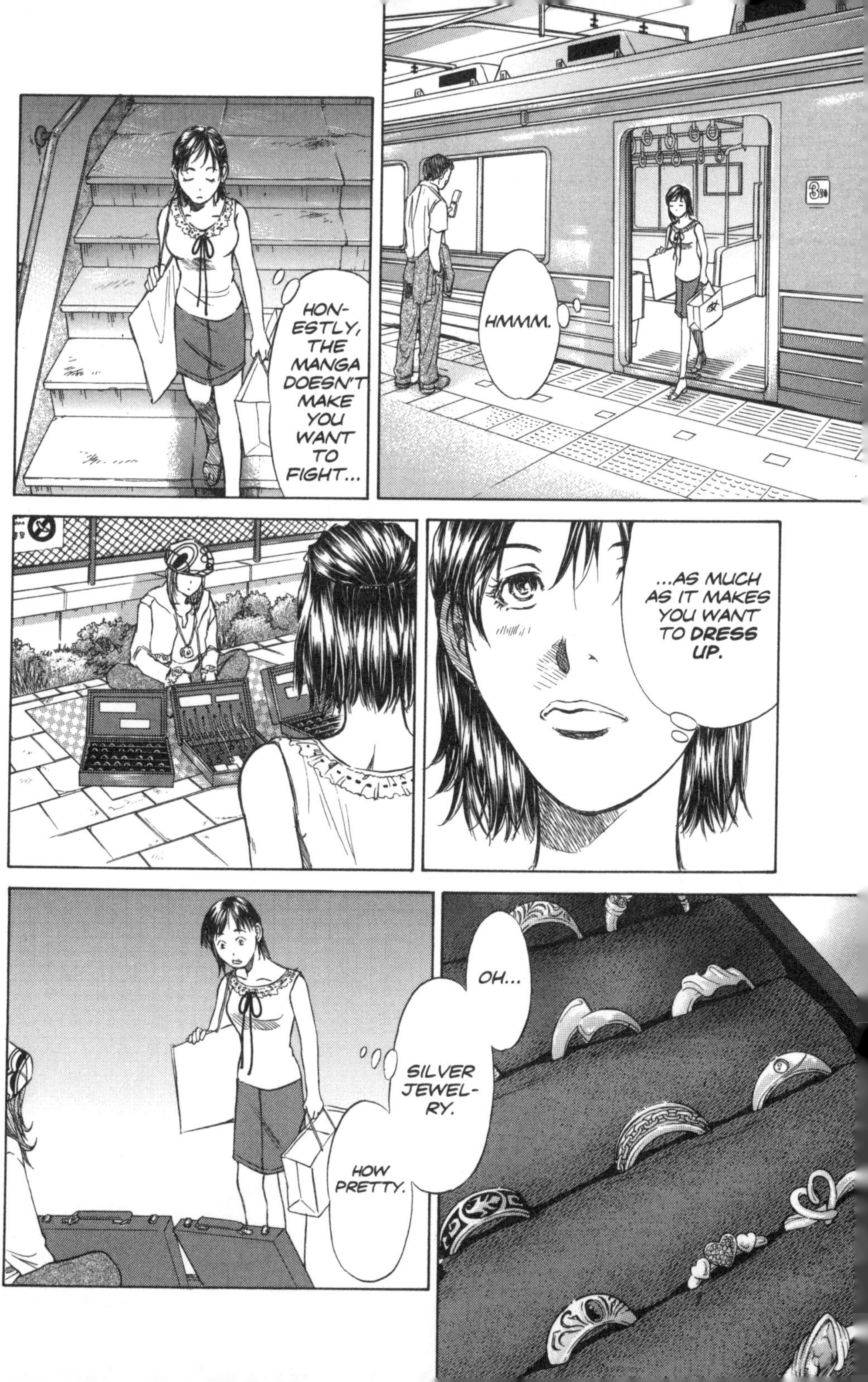
HMMM.
HON-ESTLY, THE MANGA DOESN'T MAKE YOU WANT TO FIGHT...
...AS MUCH AS IT MAKES YOU WANT TO **DRESS UP.**
OH...
SILVER JEWEL-RY.
HOW PRETTY.

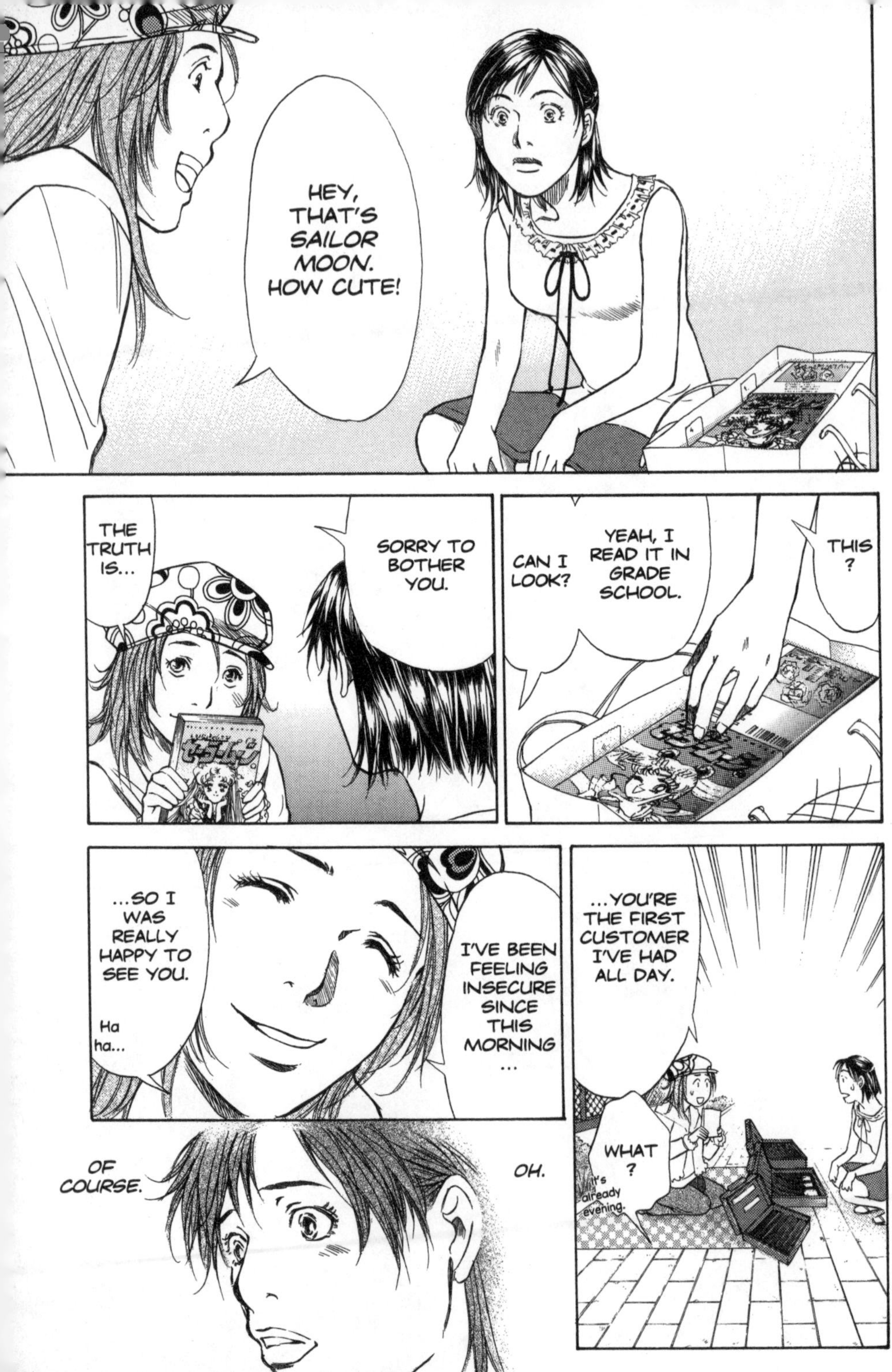
HEY, THAT'S SAILOR MOON. HOW CUTE!
THIS?
YEAH, I READ IT IN GRADE SCHOOL.
CAN I LOOK?
SORRY TO BOTHER YOU.
THE TRUTH IS...
...YOU'RE THE FIRST CUSTOMER I'VE HAD ALL DAY.
WHAT?
It's already evening.
I'VE BEEN FEELING INSECURE SINCE THIS MORNING...
...SO I WAS REALLY HAPPY TO SEE YOU.
Ha ha...
OH.
OF COURSE.

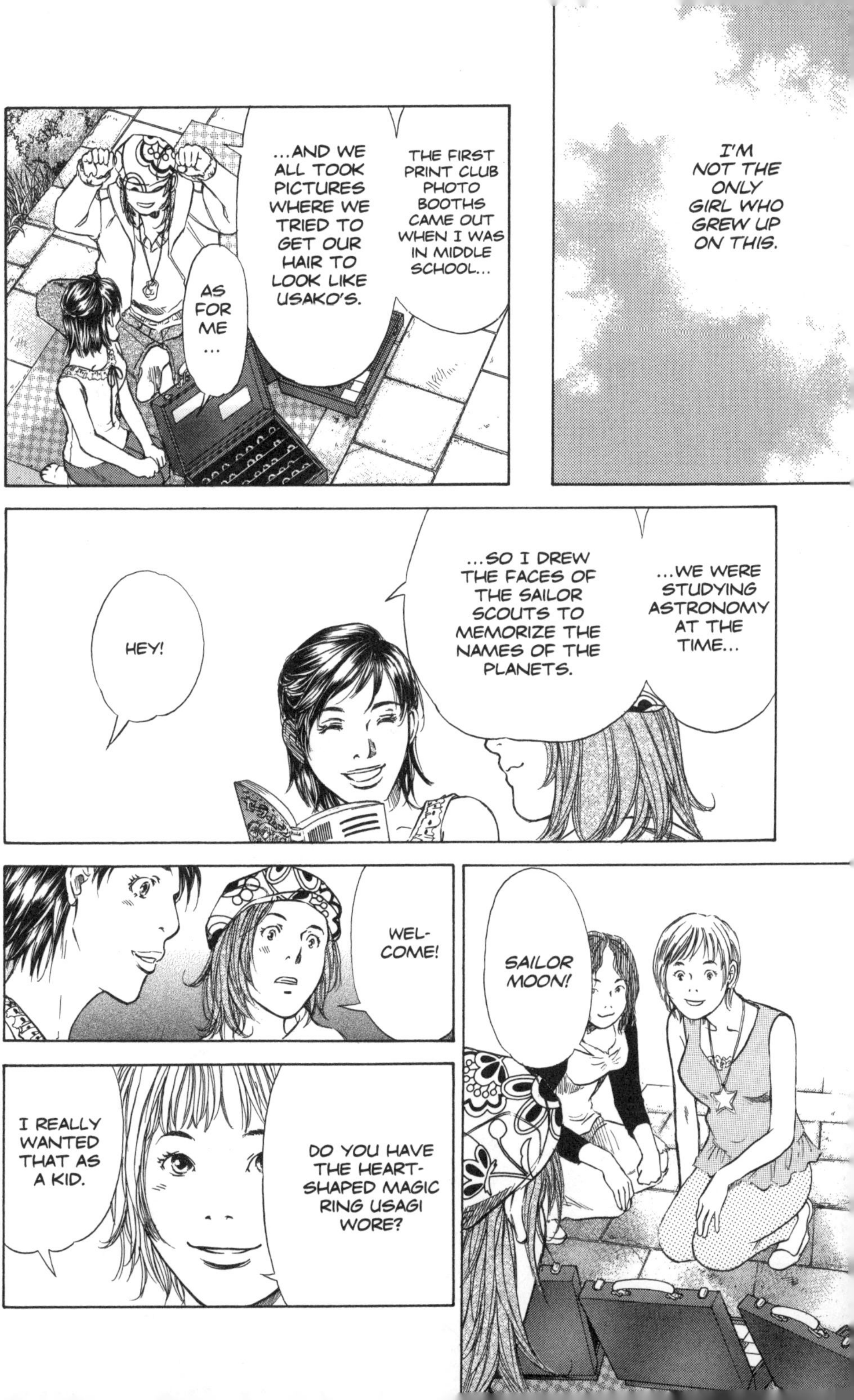
I'M NOT THE ONLY GIRL WHO GREW UP ON THIS.
THE FIRST PRINT CLUB PHOTO BOOTHS CAME OUT WHEN I WAS IN MIDDLE SCHOOL...
...AND WE ALL TOOK PICTURES WHERE WE TRIED TO GET OUR HAIR TO LOOK LIKE USAKO'S.
AS FOR ME...
...WE WERE STUDYING ASTRONOMY AT THE TIME...
...SO I DREW THE FACES OF THE SAILOR SCOUTS TO MEMORIZE THE NAMES OF THE PLANETS.
HEY!
SAILOR MOON!
WEL-COME!
DO YOU HAVE THE HEART-SHAPED MAGIC RING USAGI WORE?
I REALLY WANTED THAT AS A KID.

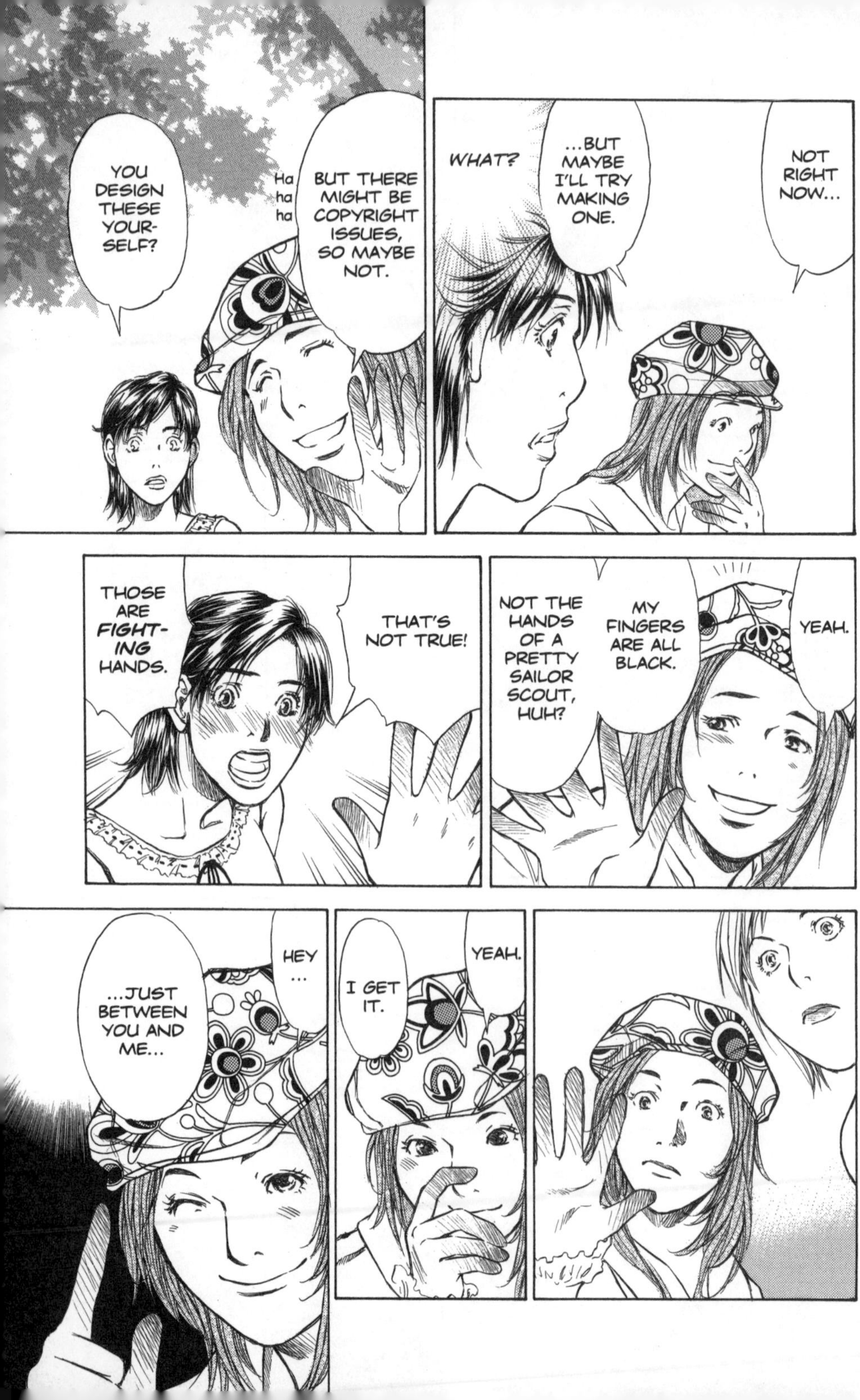
NOT RIGHT NOW...
...BUT MAYBE I'LL TRY MAKING ONE.
WHAT?
BUT THERE MIGHT BE COPYRIGHT ISSUES, SO MAYBE NOT.
Ha ha ha
YOU DESIGN THESE YOURSELF?
YEAH.
MY FINGERS ARE ALL BLACK.
NOT THE HANDS OF A PRETTY SAILOR SCOUT, HUH?
THAT'S NOT TRUE!
THOSE ARE *FIGHTING* HANDS.
YEAH.
I GET IT.
HEY...
...JUST BETWEEN YOU AND ME...

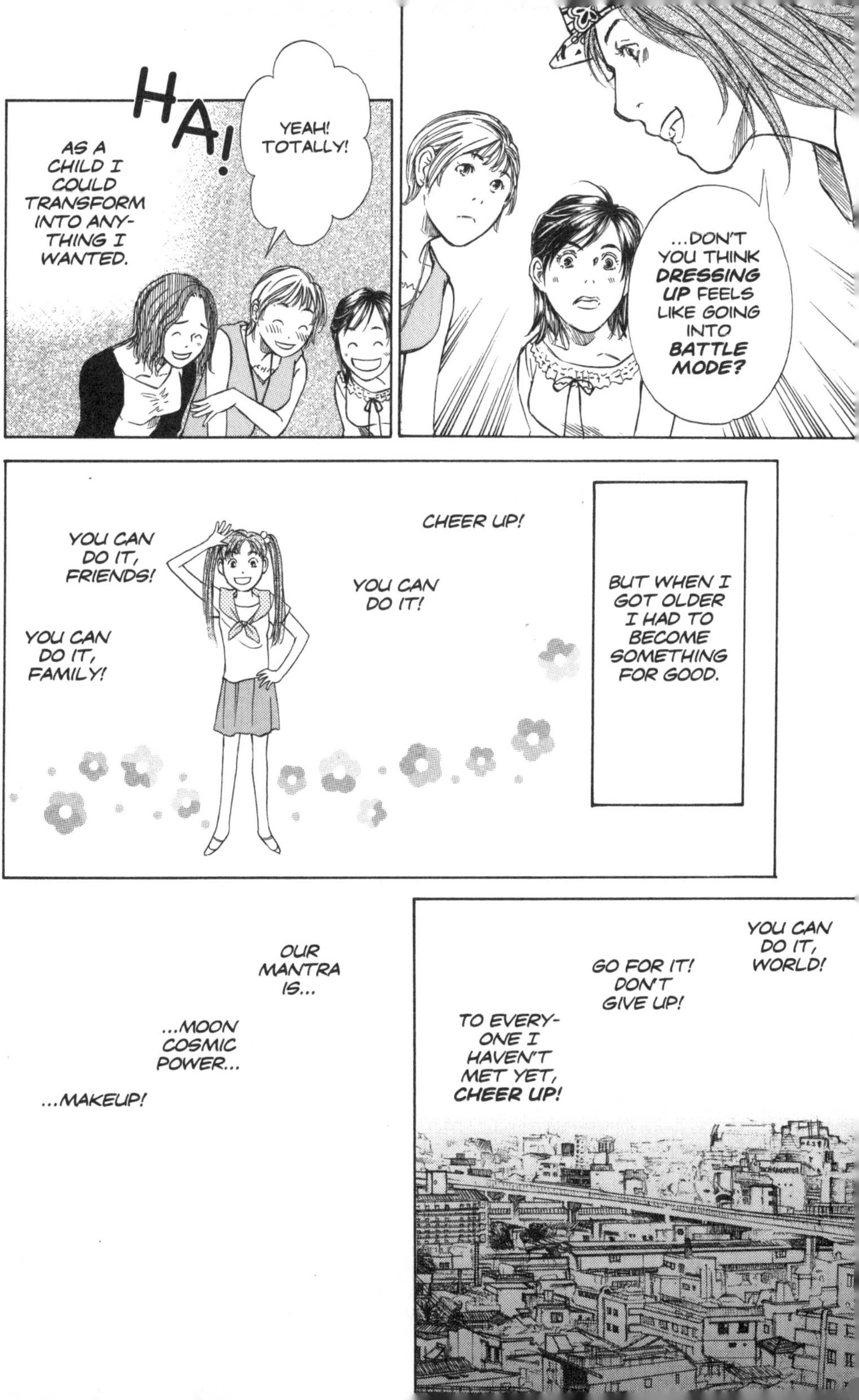
...DON'T YOU THINK DRESSING UP FEELS LIKE GOING INTO BATTLE MODE?
YEAH! TOTALLY!
HA!
AS A CHILD I COULD TRANSFORM INTO ANYTHING I WANTED.
BUT WHEN I GOT OLDER I HAD TO BECOME SOMETHING FOR GOOD.
CHEER UP!
YOU CAN DO IT!
YOU CAN DO IT, FRIENDS!
YOU CAN DO IT, FAMILY!
YOU CAN DO IT, WORLD!
GO FOR IT! DON'T GIVE UP!
TO EVERYONE I HAVEN'T MET YET, CHEER UP!
OUR MANTRA IS...
...MOON COSMIC POWER...
...MAKEUP!

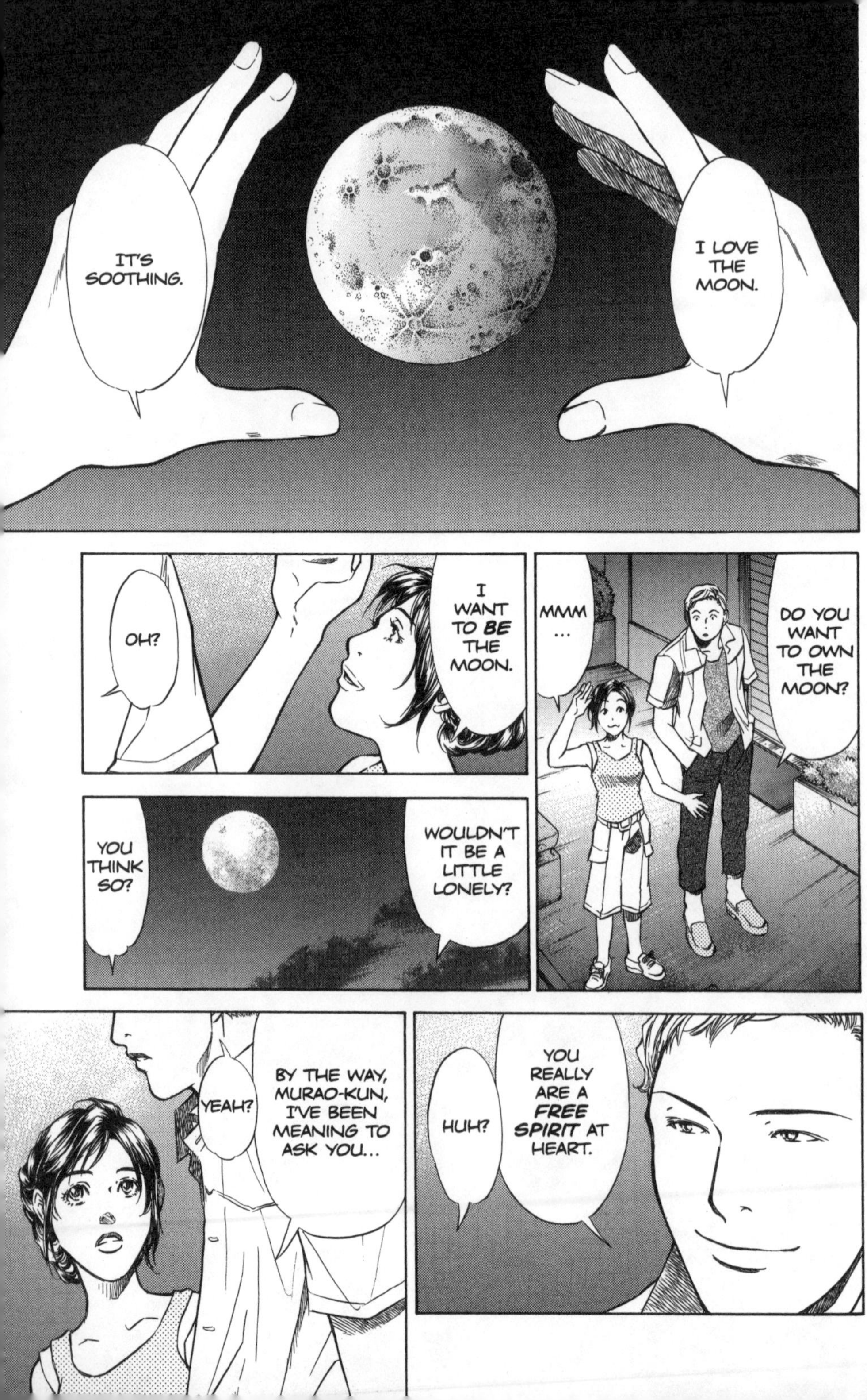
I LOVE THE MOON.
IT'S SOOTHING.
DO YOU WANT TO OWN THE MOON?
MMM...
I WANT TO **BE** THE MOON.
OH?
WOULDN'T IT BE A LITTLE LONELY?
YOU THINK SO?
YOU REALLY ARE A **FREE SPIRIT** AT HEART.
HUH?
BY THE WAY, MURAO-KUN, I'VE BEEN MEANING TO ASK YOU...
YEAH?

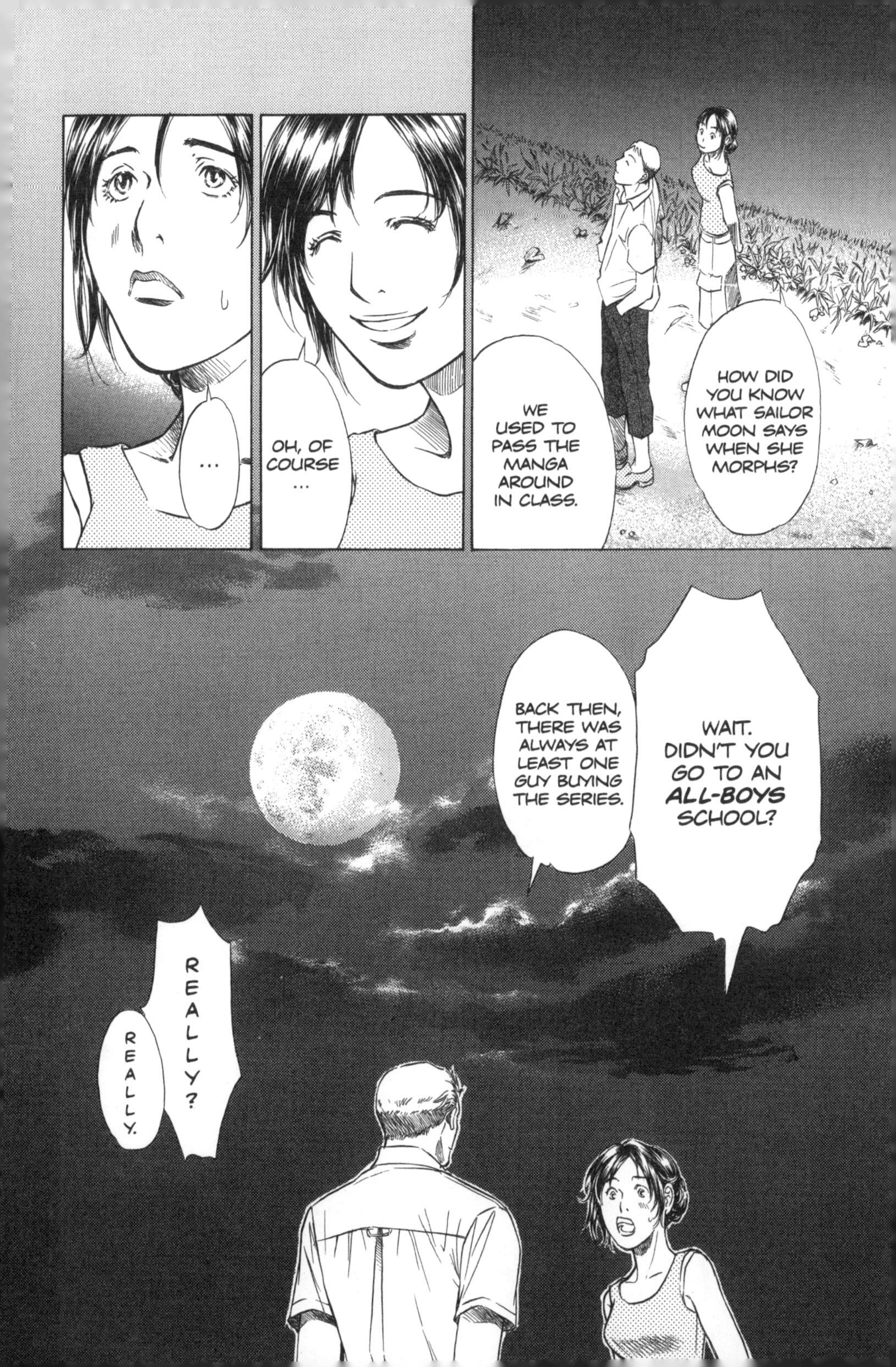
HOW DID YOU KNOW WHAT SAILOR MOON SAYS WHEN SHE MORPHS?
WE USED TO PASS THE MANGA AROUND IN CLASS.
OH, OF COURSE ...
...
WAIT. DIDN'T YOU GO TO AN ALL-BOYS SCHOOL?
BACK THEN, THERE WAS ALWAYS AT LEAST ONE GUY BUYING THE SERIES.
REALLY?
REALLY.

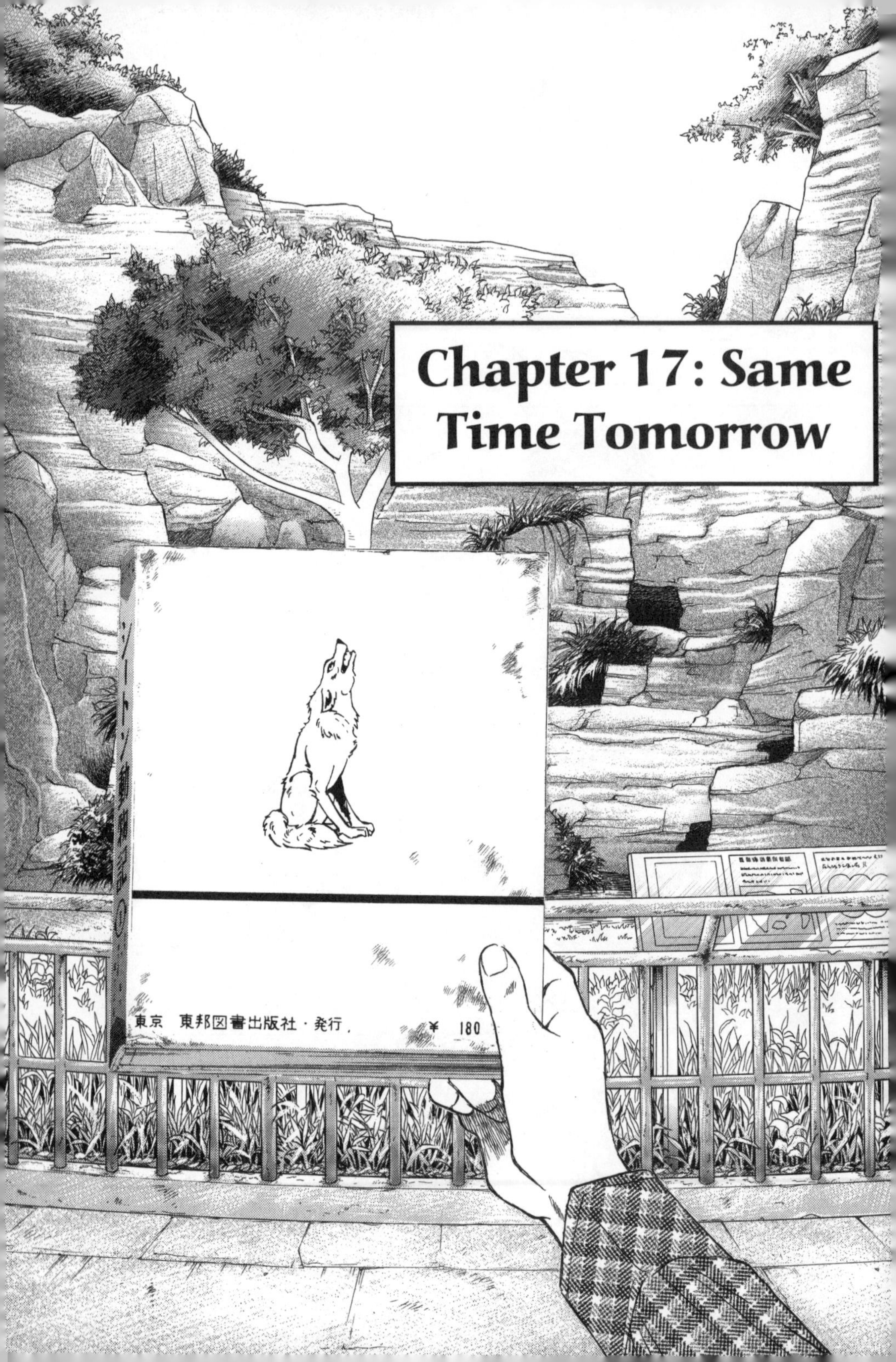
Chapter 17: Same Time Tomorrow
東京　東邦図書出版社・発行
¥ 180

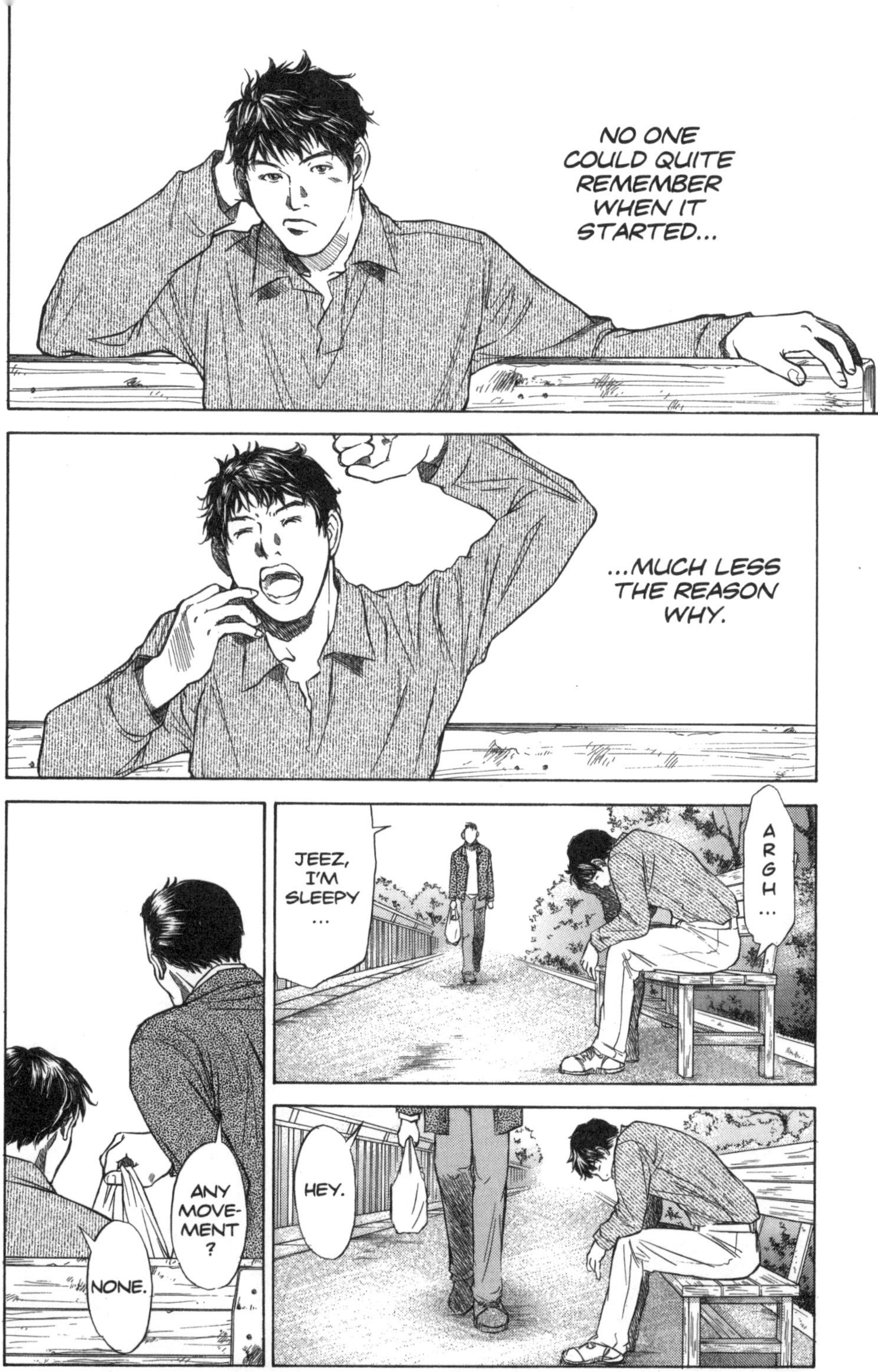
NO ONE COULD QUITE REMEMBER WHEN IT STARTED...
...MUCH LESS THE REASON WHY.
ARGH...
JEEZ, I'M SLEEPY...
HEY.
ANY MOVEMENT?
NONE.

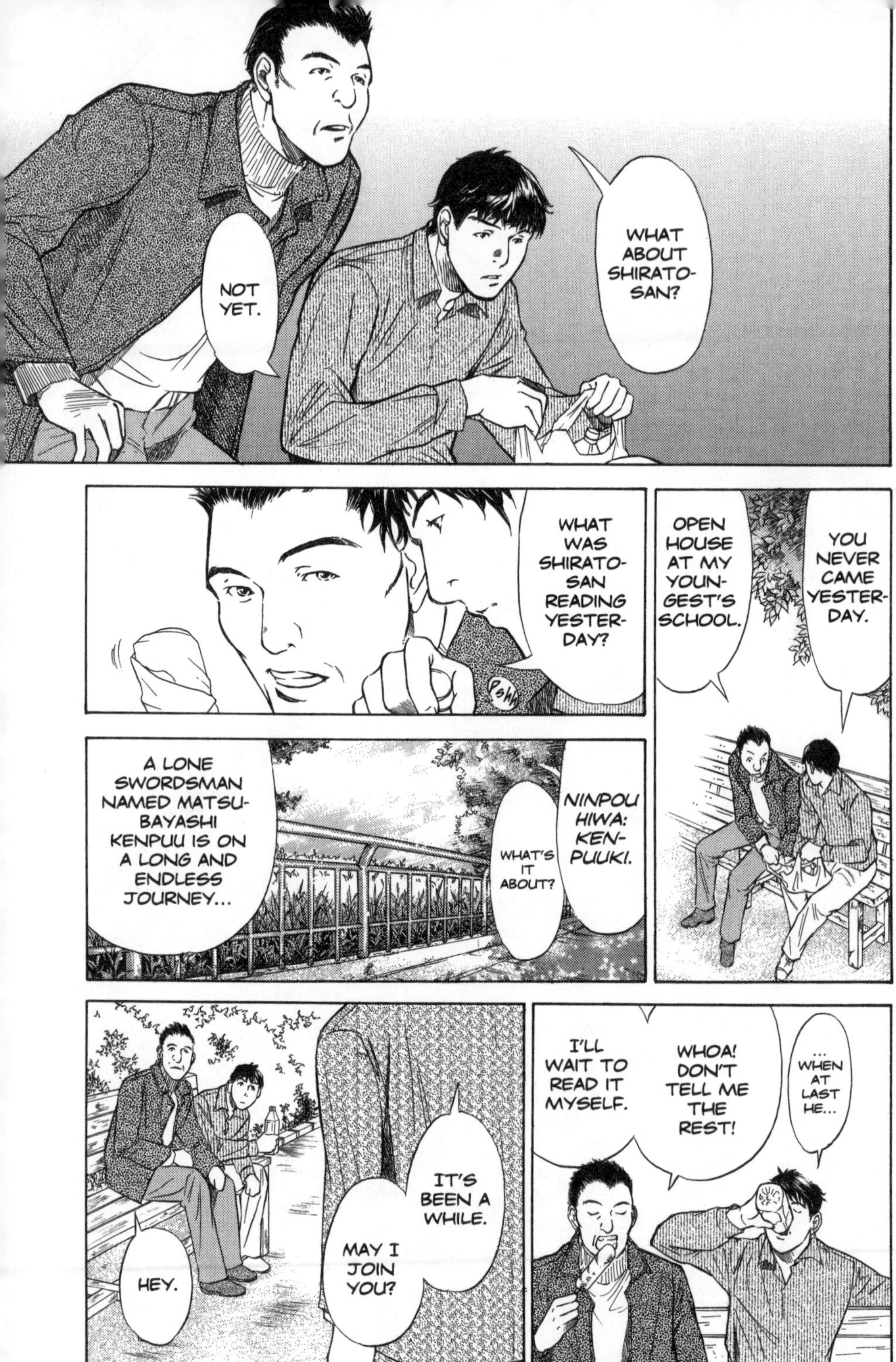
WHAT ABOUT SHIRATO-SAN?
NOT YET.
YOU NEVER CAME YESTERDAY.
OPEN HOUSE AT MY YOUNGEST'S SCHOOL.
WHAT WAS SHIRATO-SAN READING YESTERDAY?
PSHH
NINPOU HIWA: KENPUUKI.
WHAT'S IT ABOUT?
A LONE SWORDSMAN NAMED MATSUBAYASHI KENPUU IS ON A LONG AND ENDLESS JOURNEY...
...WHEN AT LAST HE...
WHOA! DON'T TELL ME THE REST!
I'LL WAIT TO READ IT MYSELF.
IT'S BEEN A WHILE.
MAY I JOIN YOU?
HEY.

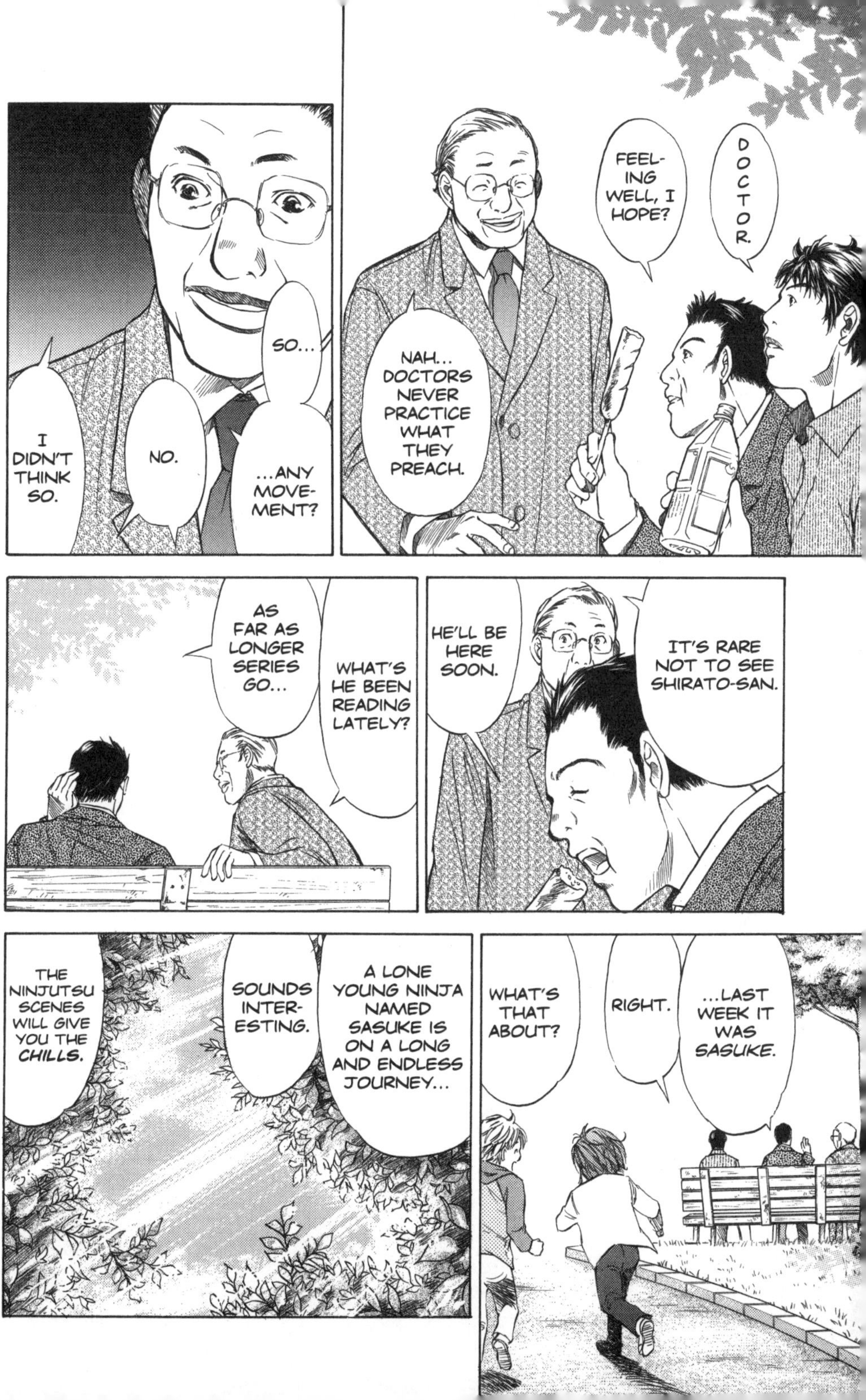
DOCTOR.
FEELING WELL, I HOPE?
NAH... DOCTORS NEVER PRACTICE WHAT THEY PREACH.
SO...
...ANY MOVEMENT?
NO.
I DIDN'T THINK SO.
IT'S RARE NOT TO SEE SHIRATO-SAN.
HE'LL BE HERE SOON.
WHAT'S HE BEEN READING LATELY?
AS FAR AS LONGER SERIES GO...
...LAST WEEK IT WAS SASUKE.
RIGHT.
WHAT'S THAT ABOUT?
A LONE YOUNG NINJA NAMED SASUKE IS ON A LONG AND ENDLESS JOURNEY...
SOUNDS INTERESTING.
THE NINJUTSU SCENES WILL GIVE YOU THE *CHILLS.*

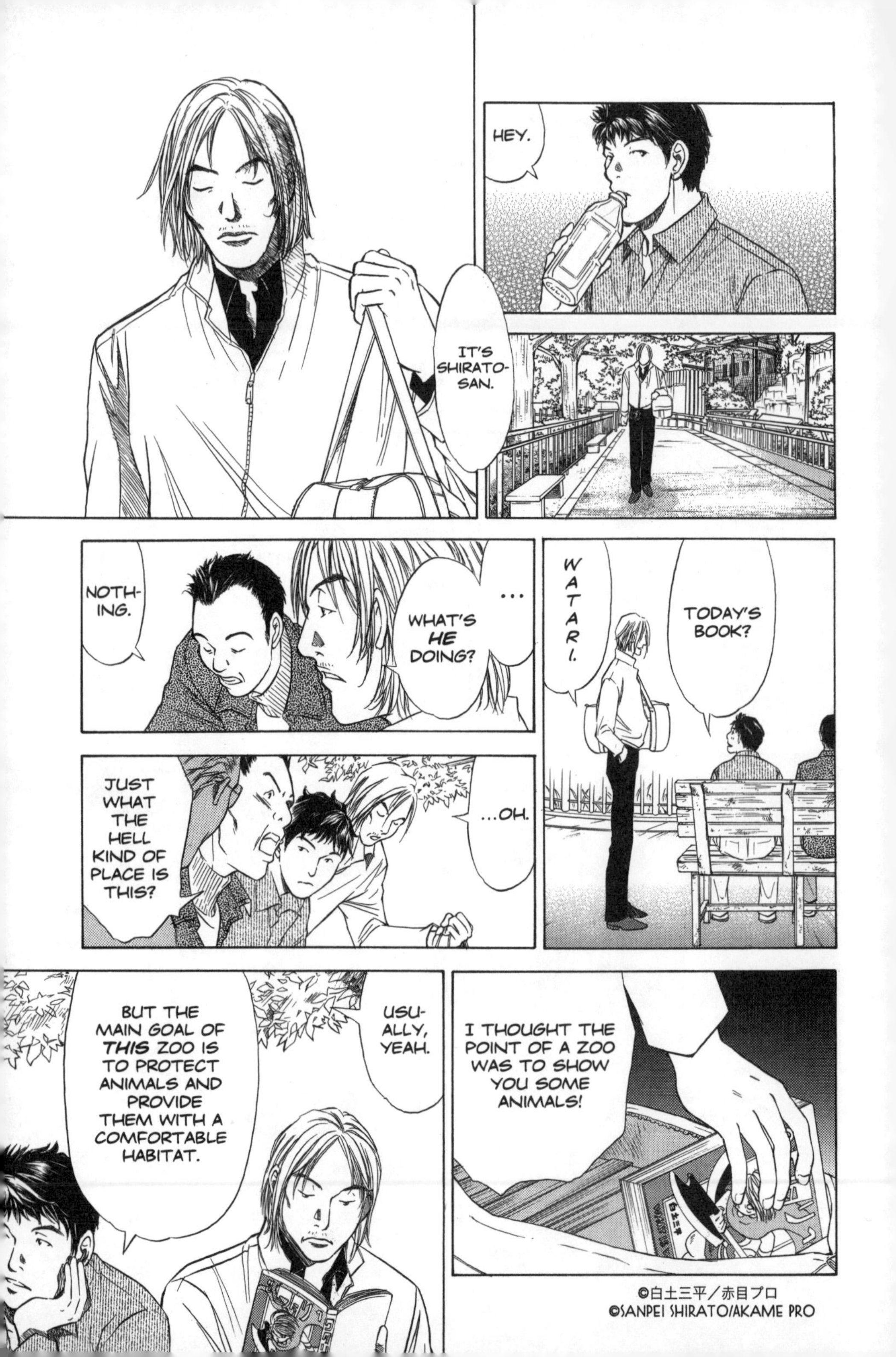
HEY.
IT'S SHIRATO-SAN.
TODAY'S BOOK?
WATARI.
...
WHAT'S **HE** DOING?
NOTHING.
...OH.
JUST WHAT THE HELL KIND OF PLACE IS THIS?
I THOUGHT THE POINT OF A ZOO WAS TO SHOW YOU SOME ANIMALS!
USUALLY, YEAH.
BUT THE MAIN GOAL OF **THIS** ZOO IS TO PROTECT ANIMALS AND PROVIDE THEM WITH A COMFORTABLE HABITAT.

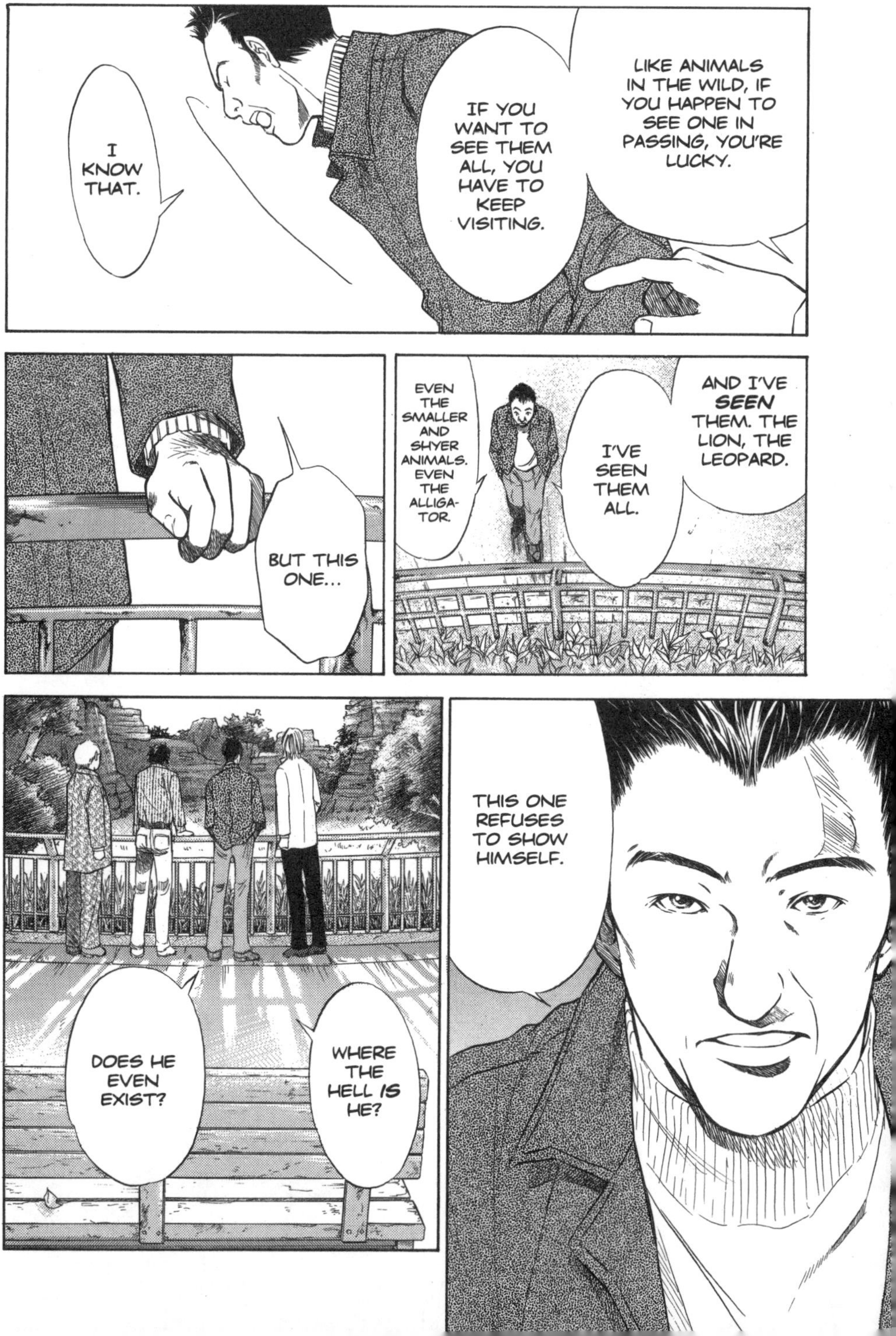
LIKE ANIMALS IN THE WILD, IF YOU HAPPEN TO SEE ONE IN PASSING, YOU'RE LUCKY.
IF YOU WANT TO SEE THEM ALL, YOU HAVE TO KEEP VISITING.
I KNOW THAT.
AND I'VE *SEEN* THEM. THE LION, THE LEOPARD.
I'VE SEEN THEM ALL.
EVEN THE SMALLER AND SHYER ANIMALS. EVEN THE ALLIGATOR.
BUT THIS ONE...
THIS ONE REFUSES TO SHOW HIMSELF.
WHERE THE HELL *IS* HE?
DOES HE EVEN EXIST?

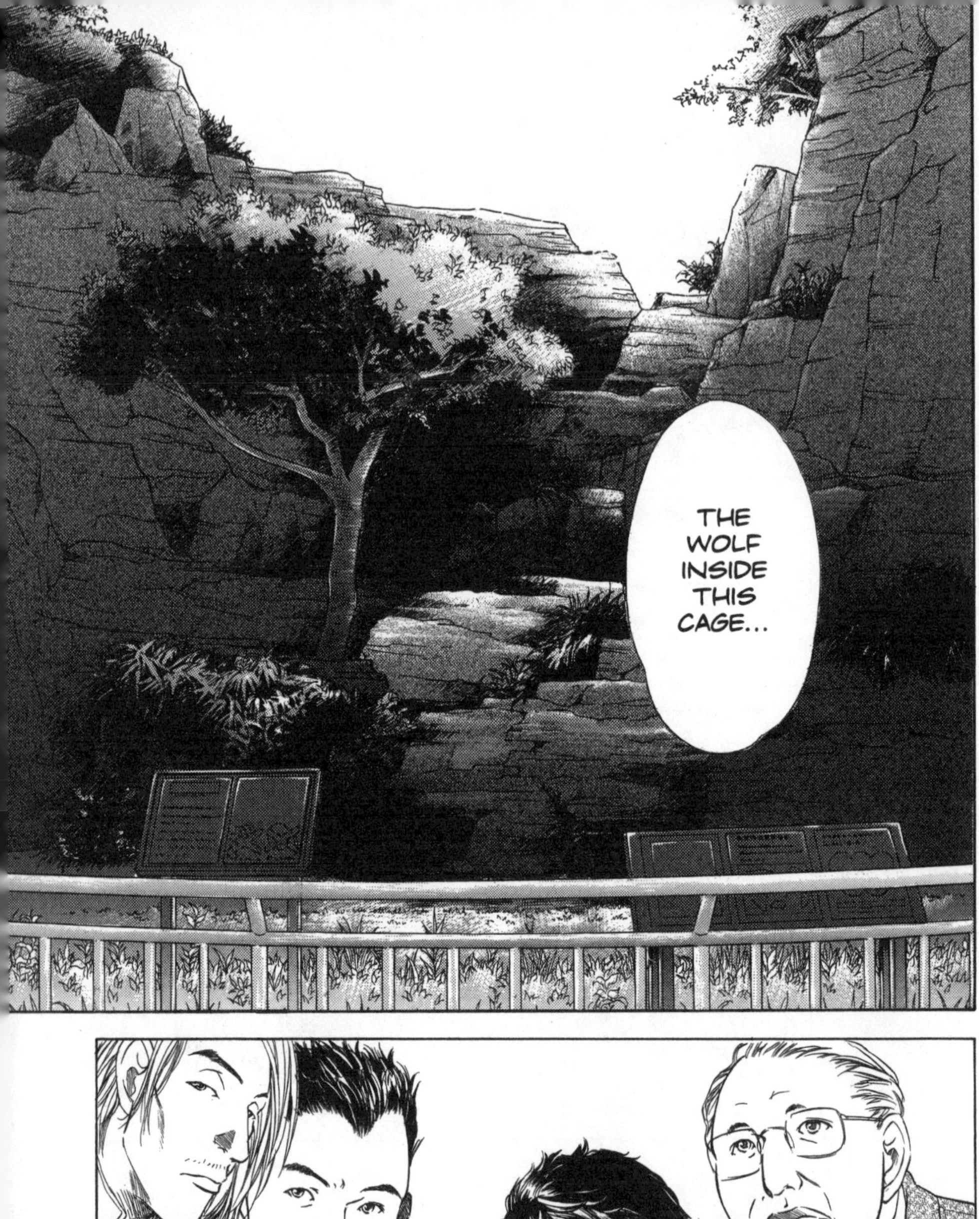
THE WOLF INSIDE THIS CAGE...

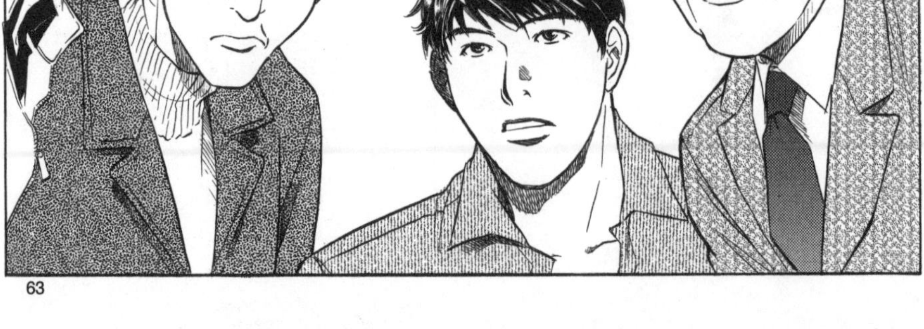

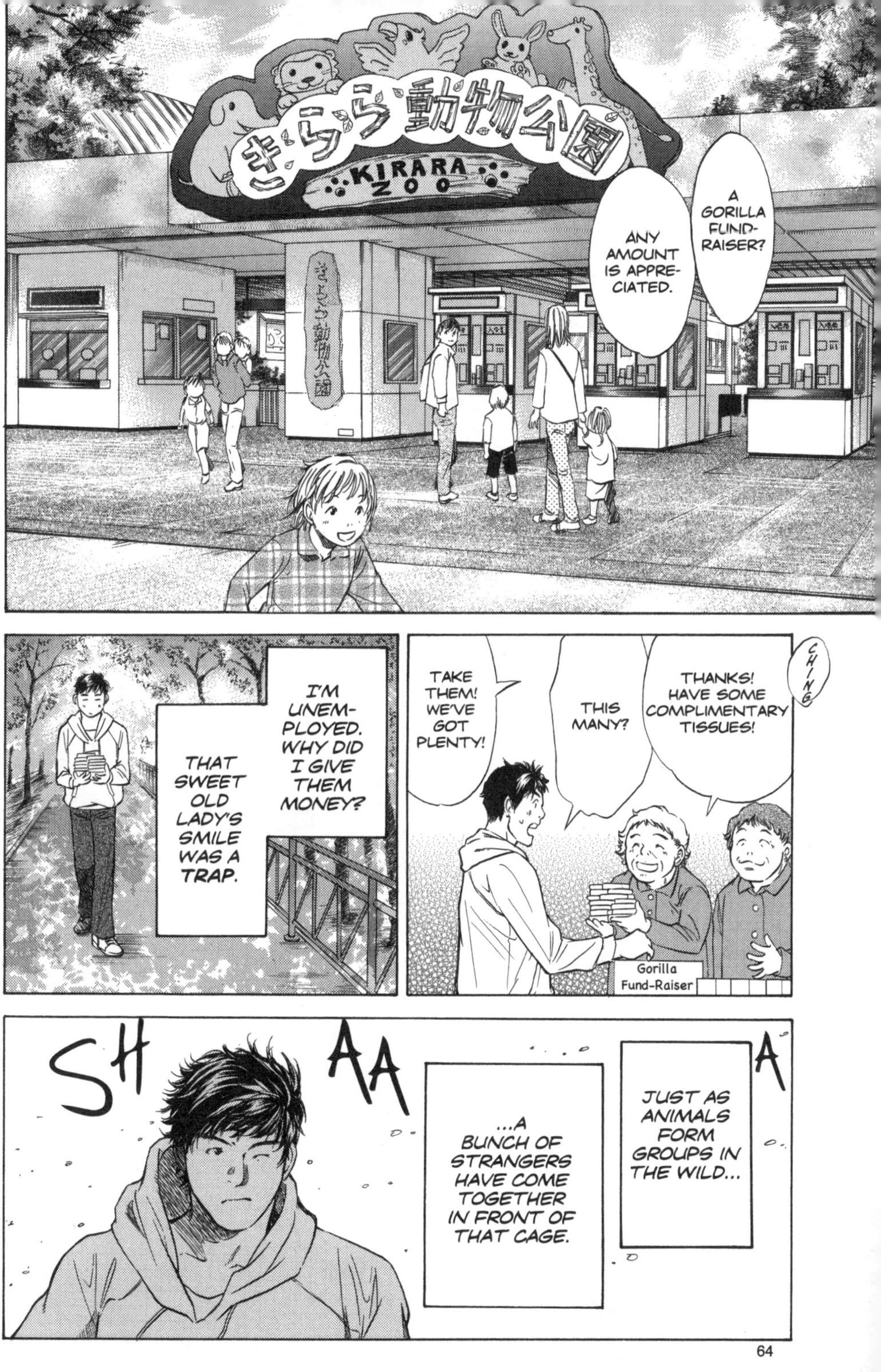
きらら動物公園
KIRARA ZOO
A GORILLA FUND-RAISER?
ANY AMOUNT IS APPRECIATED.
CHING
THANKS! HAVE SOME COMPLIMENTARY TISSUES!
THIS MANY?
TAKE THEM! WE'VE GOT PLENTY!
Gorilla Fund-Raiser
I'M UNEMPLOYED. WHY DID I GIVE THEM MONEY?
THAT SWEET OLD LADY'S SMILE WAS A TRAP.
SHAAA
JUST AS ANIMALS FORM GROUPS IN THE WILD...
...A BUNCH OF STRANGERS HAVE COME TOGETHER IN FRONT OF THAT CAGE.

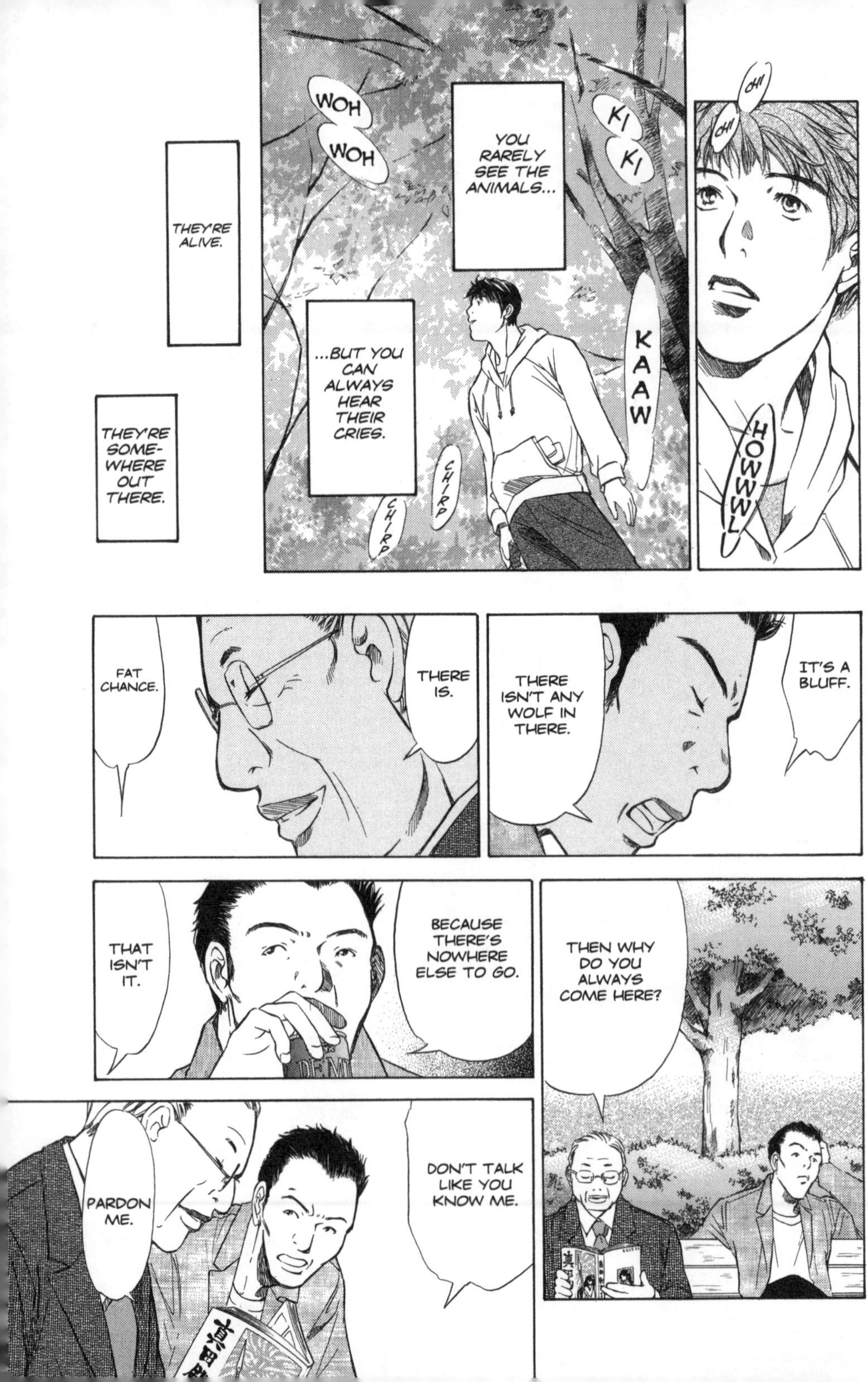
CHI
CHI
HOWWWL
KI
KI
YOU RARELY SEE THE ANIMALS...
WOH
WOH
KAAW
...BUT YOU CAN ALWAYS HEAR THEIR CRIES.
CHIRP
CHIRP
THEY'RE ALIVE.
THEY'RE SOMEWHERE OUT THERE.
IT'S A BLUFF.
THERE ISN'T ANY WOLF IN THERE.
THERE IS.
FAT CHANCE.
THEN WHY DO YOU ALWAYS COME HERE?
BECAUSE THERE'S NOWHERE ELSE TO GO.
THAT ISN'T IT.
DON'T TALK LIKE YOU KNOW ME.
PARDON ME.

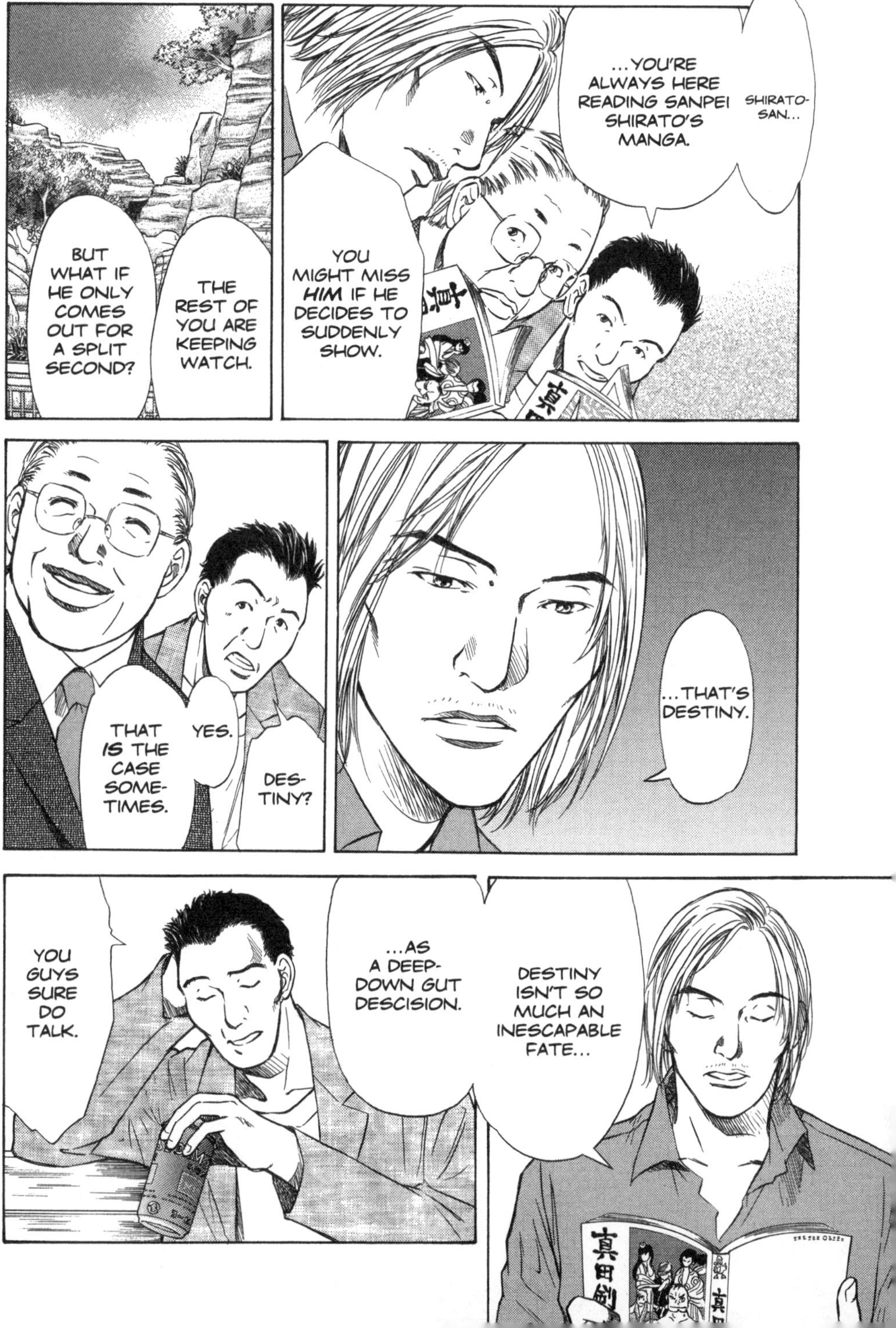
SHIRATO-SAN...
...YOU'RE ALWAYS HERE READING SANPEI SHIRATO'S MANGA.
YOU MIGHT MISS *HIM* IF HE DECIDES TO SUDDENLY SHOW.
THE REST OF YOU ARE KEEPING WATCH.
BUT WHAT IF HE ONLY COMES OUT FOR A SPLIT SECOND?
...THAT'S DESTINY.
DESTINY?
YES.
THAT *IS* THE CASE SOMETIMES.
DESTINY ISN'T SO MUCH AN INESCAPABLE FATE...
...AS A DEEP-DOWN GUT DESCISION.
YOU GUYS SURE DO TALK.

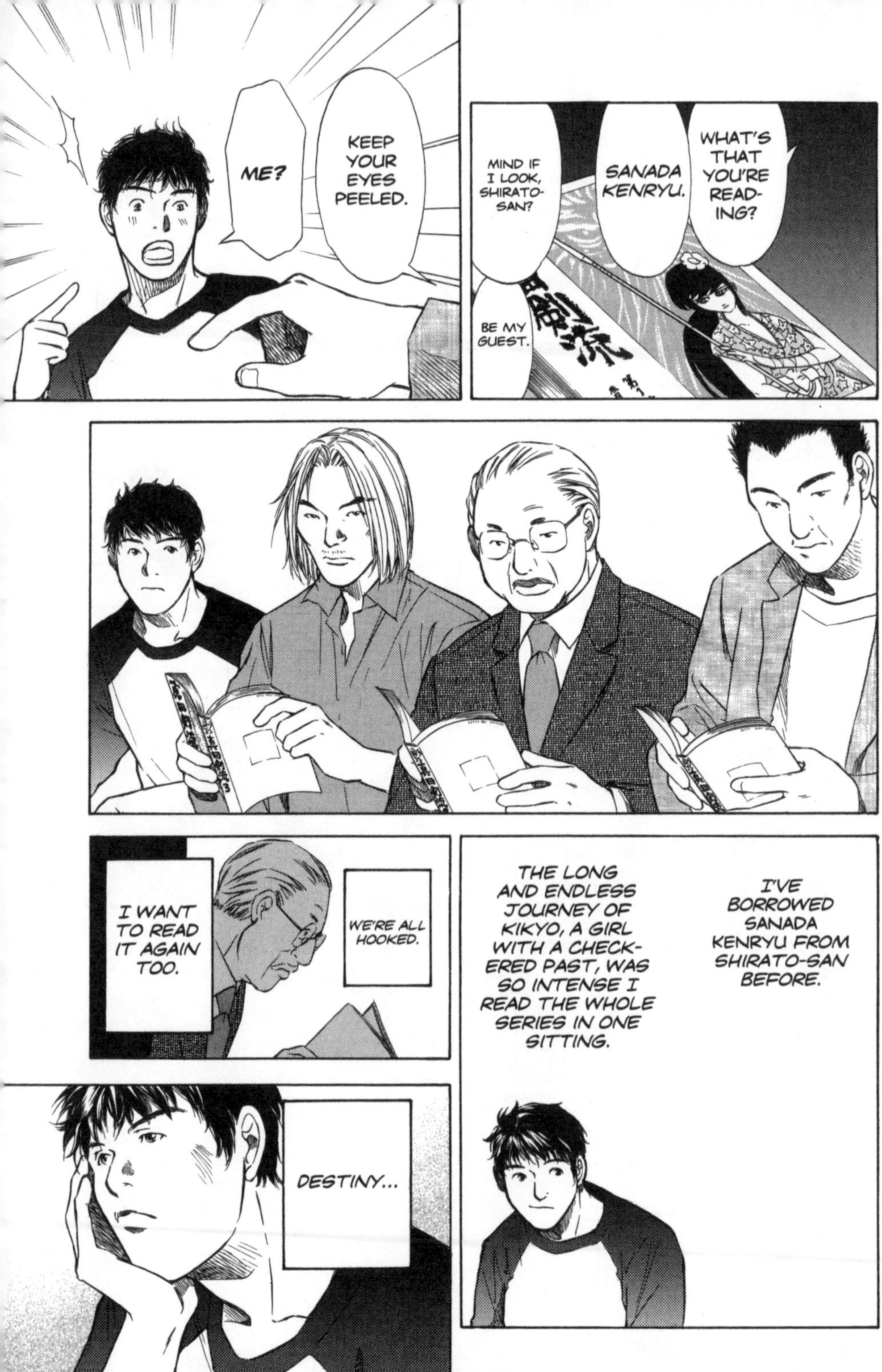
WHAT'S THAT YOU'RE READ-ING?
SANADA KENRYU.
MIND IF I LOOK, SHIRATO-SAN?
BE MY GUEST.
KEEP YOUR EYES PEELED.
ME?
I'VE BORROWED SANADA KENRYU FROM SHIRATO-SAN BEFORE.
THE LONG AND ENDLESS JOURNEY OF KIKYO, A GIRL WITH A CHECK-ERED PAST, WAS SO INTENSE I READ THE WHOLE SERIES IN ONE SITTING.
WE'RE ALL HOOKED.
I WANT TO READ IT AGAIN TOO.
DESTINY...

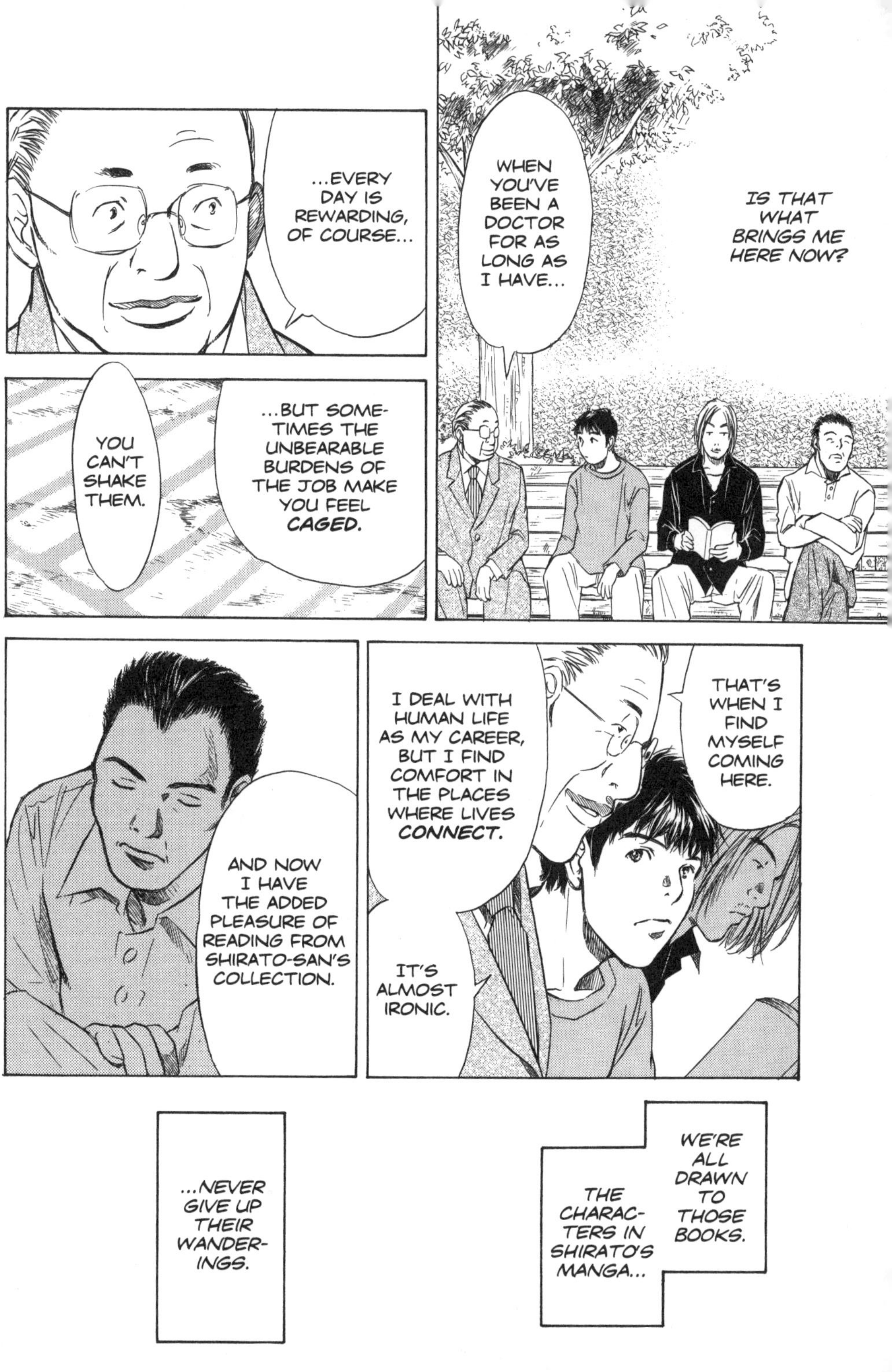
IS THAT WHAT BRINGS ME HERE NOW?
WHEN YOU'VE BEEN A DOCTOR FOR AS LONG AS I HAVE...
...EVERY DAY IS REWARDING, OF COURSE...
...BUT SOMETIMES THE UNBEARABLE BURDENS OF THE JOB MAKE YOU FEEL **CAGED.**
YOU CAN'T SHAKE THEM.
THAT'S WHEN I FIND MYSELF COMING HERE.
I DEAL WITH HUMAN LIFE AS MY CAREER, BUT I FIND COMFORT IN THE PLACES WHERE LIVES **CONNECT.**
IT'S ALMOST IRONIC.
AND NOW I HAVE THE ADDED PLEASURE OF READING FROM SHIRATO-SAN'S COLLECTION.
WE'RE ALL DRAWN TO THOSE BOOKS.
THE CHARACTERS IN SHIRATO'S MANGA...
...NEVER GIVE UP THEIR WANDERINGS.

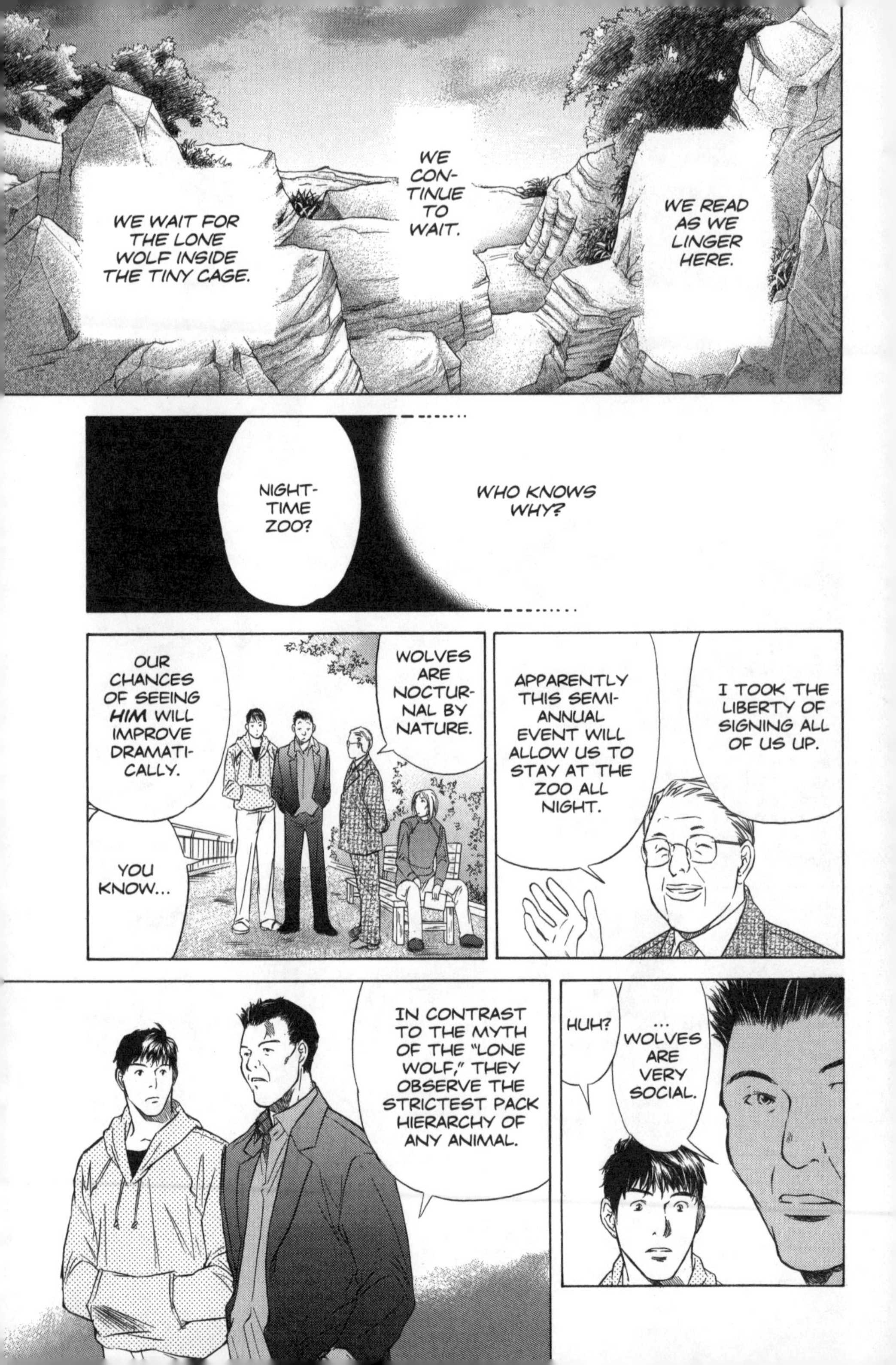
WE READ AS WE LINGER HERE.
WE CONTINUE TO WAIT.
WE WAIT FOR THE LONE WOLF INSIDE THE TINY CAGE.
WHO KNOWS WHY?
NIGHT-TIME ZOO?
I TOOK THE LIBERTY OF SIGNING ALL OF US UP.
APPARENTLY THIS SEMI-ANNUAL EVENT WILL ALLOW US TO STAY AT THE ZOO ALL NIGHT.
WOLVES ARE NOCTURNAL BY NATURE.
OUR CHANCES OF SEEING *HIM* WILL IMPROVE DRAMATICALLY.
YOU KNOW...
...WOLVES ARE VERY SOCIAL.
HUH?
IN CONTRAST TO THE MYTH OF THE "LONE WOLF," THEY OBSERVE THE STRICTEST PACK HIERARCHY OF ANY ANIMAL.

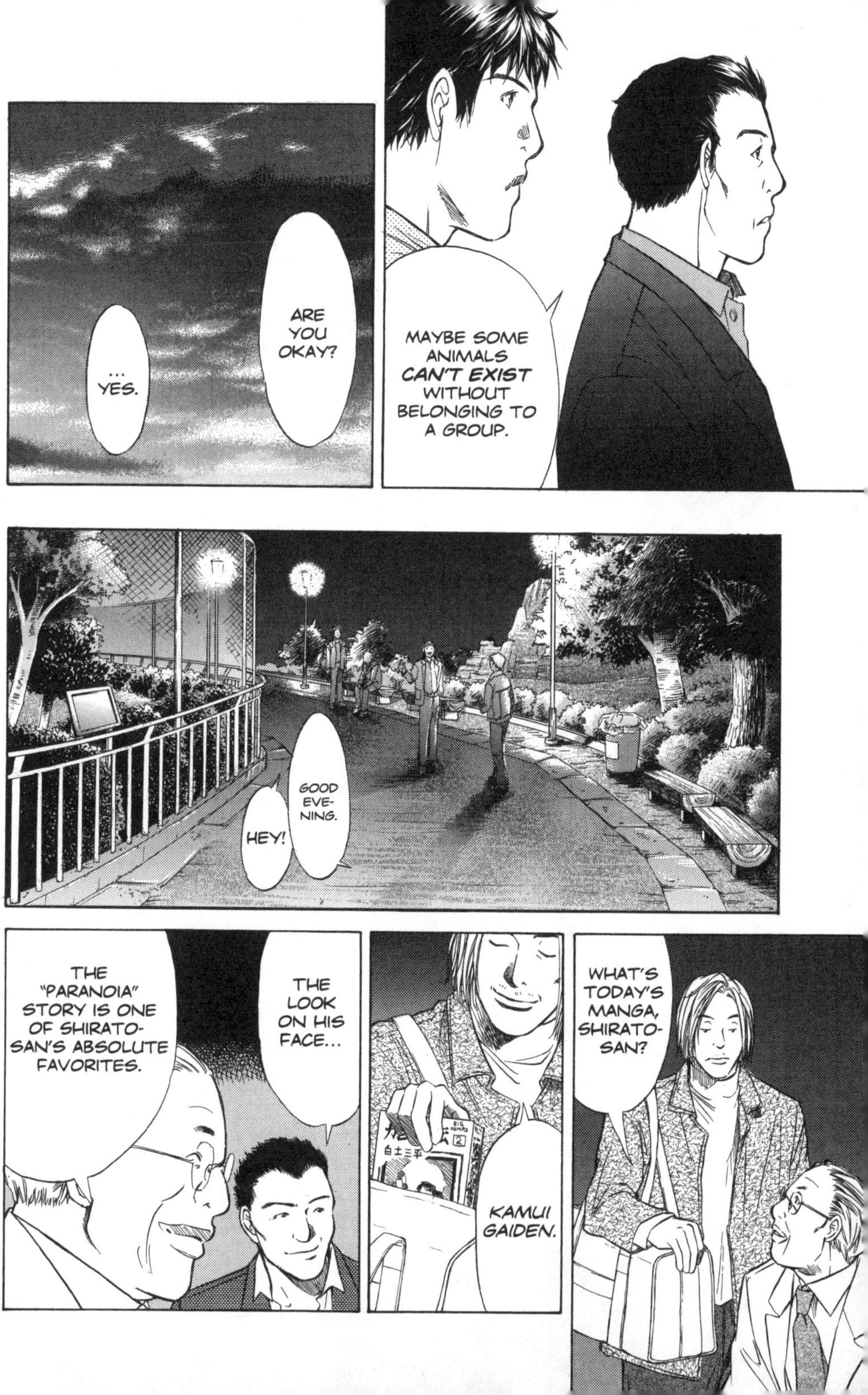
MAYBE SOME ANIMALS **CAN'T EXIST** WITHOUT BELONGING TO A GROUP.
ARE YOU OKAY?
... YES.
GOOD EVE-NING.
HEY!
WHAT'S TODAY'S MANGA, SHIRATO-SAN?
KAMUI GAIDEN.
THE LOOK ON HIS FACE...
THE "PARANOIA" STORY IS ONE OF SHIRATO-SAN'S ABSOLUTE FAVORITES.

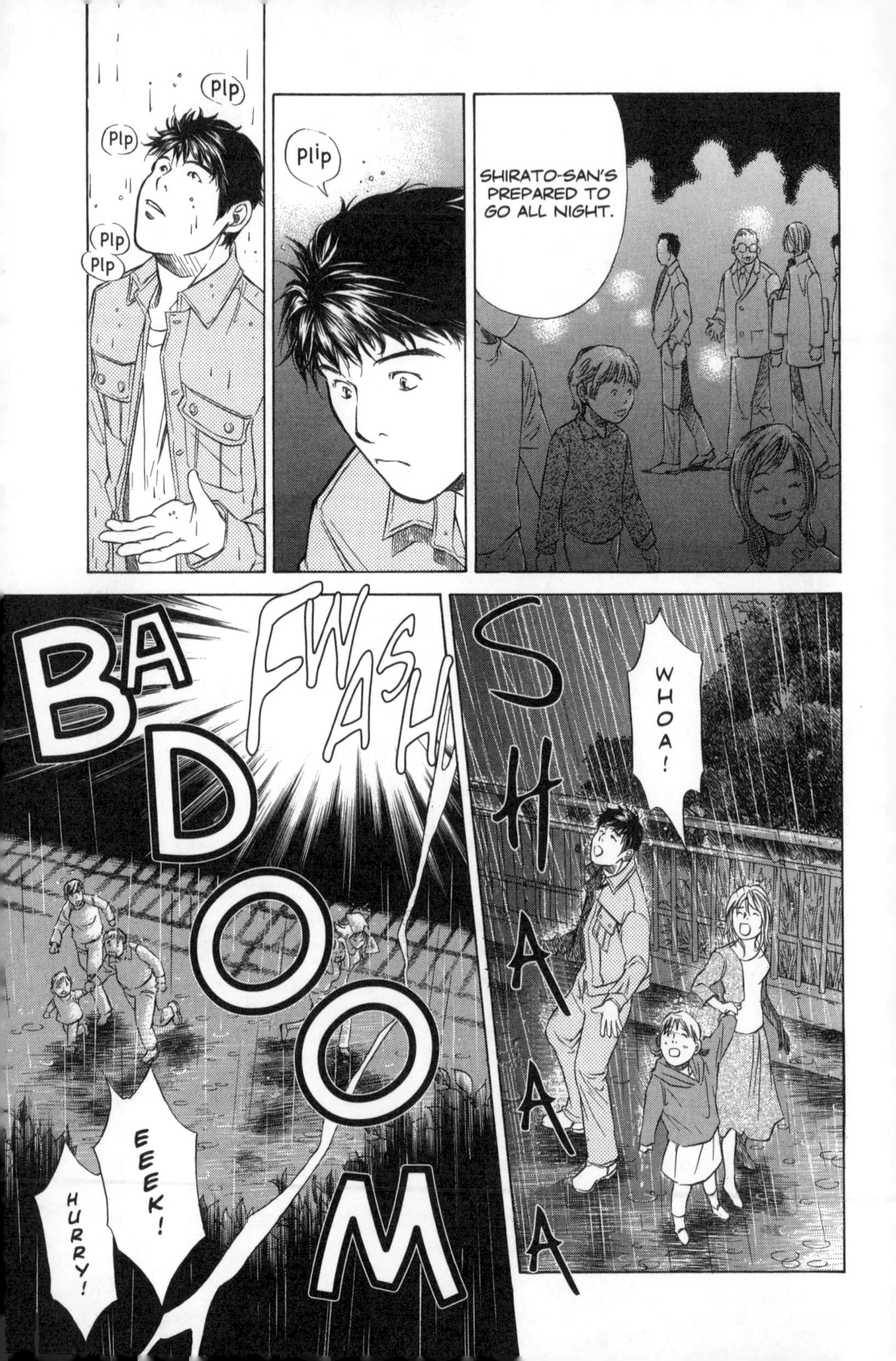
SHIRATO-SAN'S PREPARED TO GO ALL NIGHT.
plip
plip
plip
plip
plip
SHAAAA
WHOA!
FWASH
BADOOOM
EEEK!
HURRY!

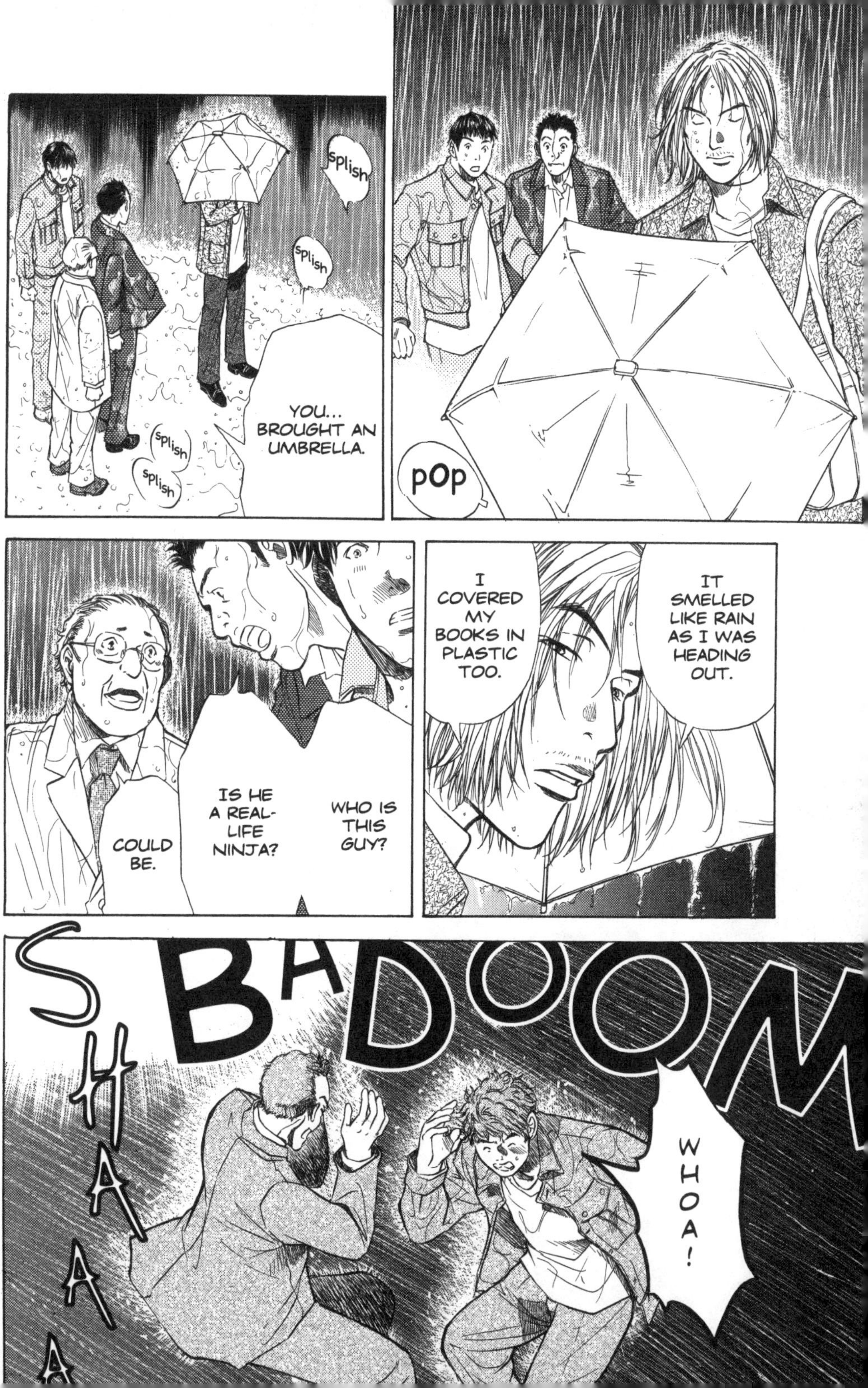
pOp
splish
splish
splish
splish
YOU... BROUGHT AN UMBRELLA.
IT SMELLED LIKE RAIN AS I WAS HEADING OUT.
I COVERED MY BOOKS IN PLASTIC TOO.
WHO IS THIS GUY?
IS HE A REAL-LIFE NINJA?
COULD BE.
SHAAA
BADOOM
WHOA!

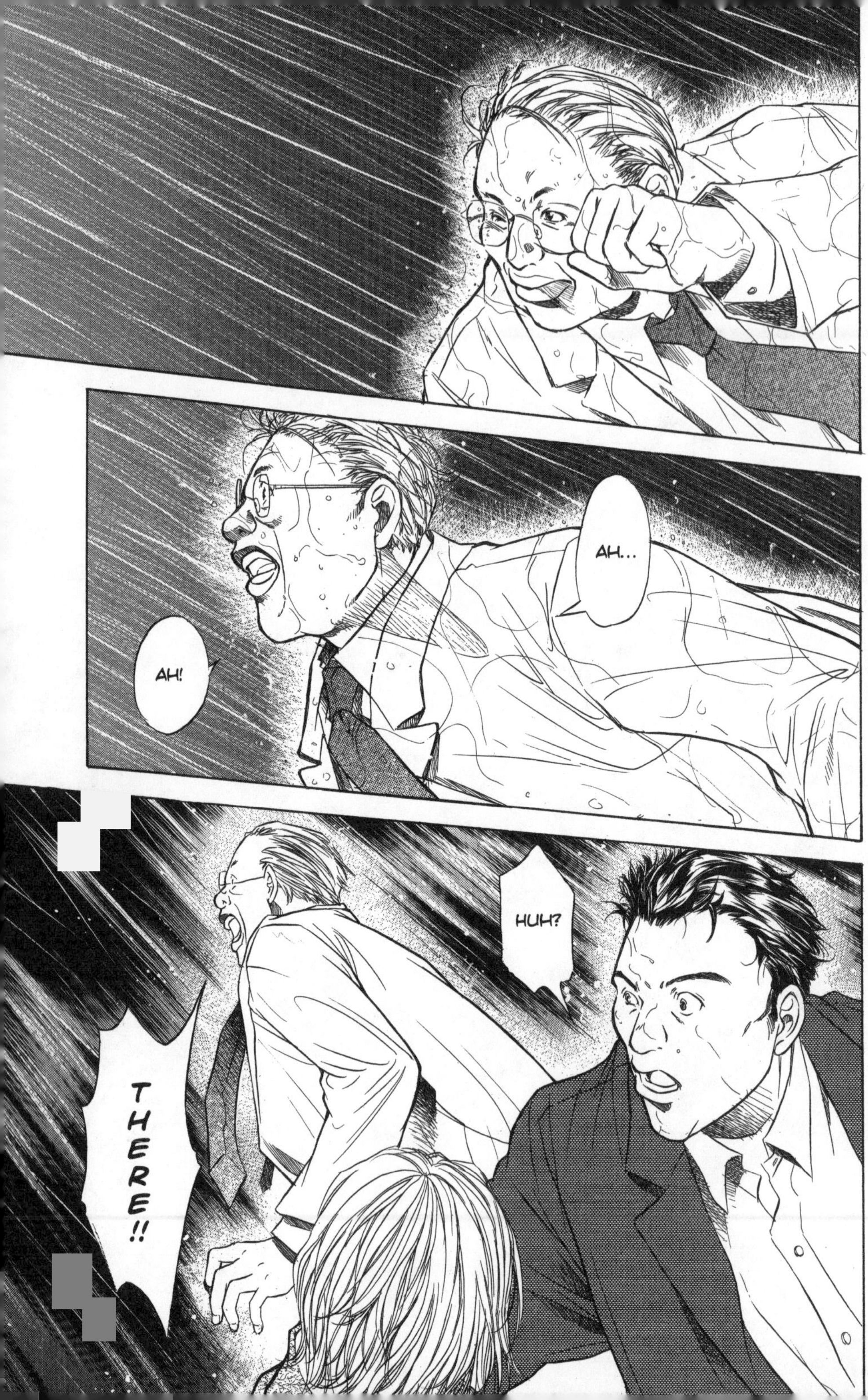
AH...
AH!
HUH?
THERE!!

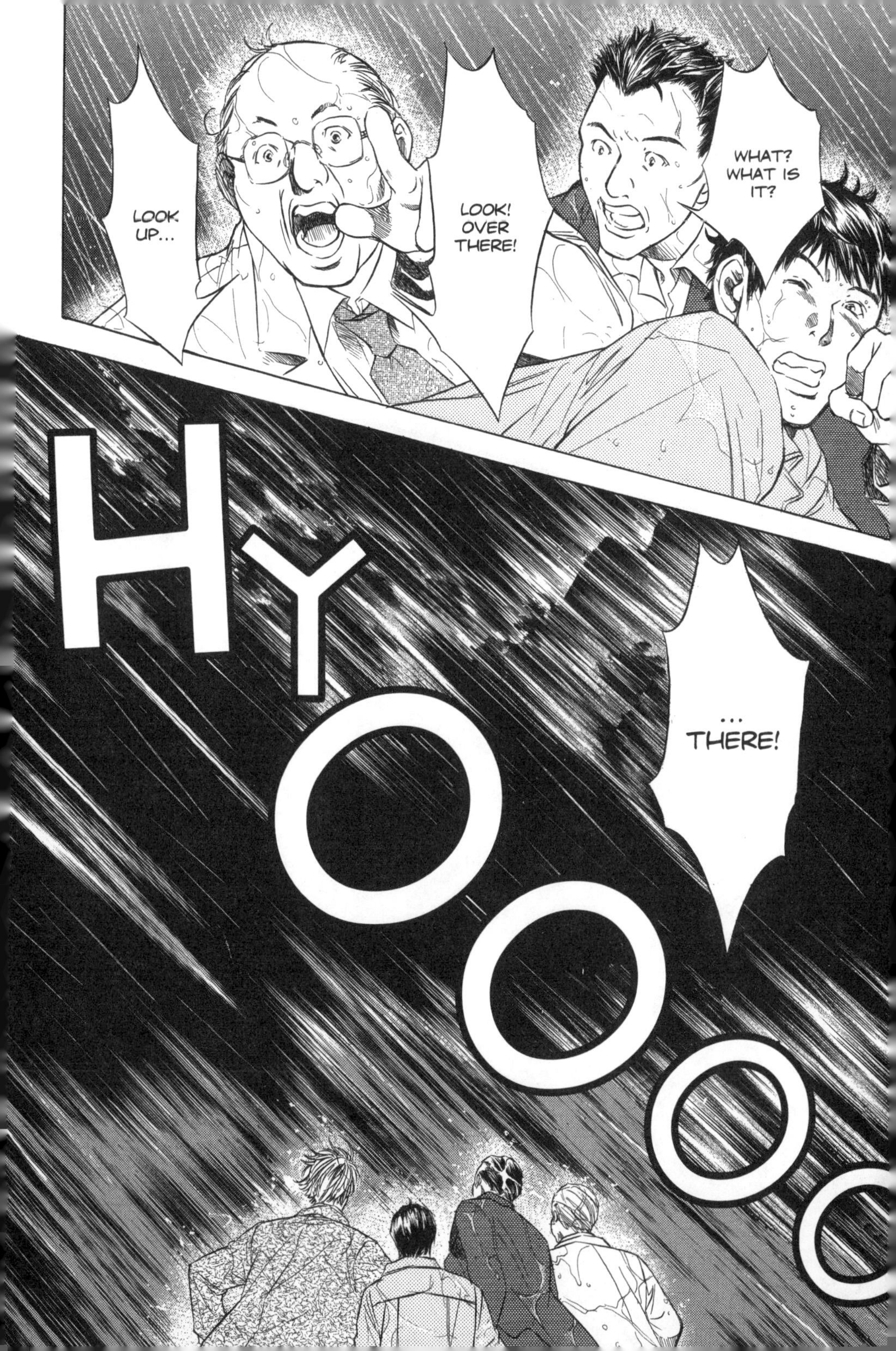
WHAT? WHAT IS IT?
LOOK! OVER THERE!
LOOK UP...
...THERE!
HYOOOOO

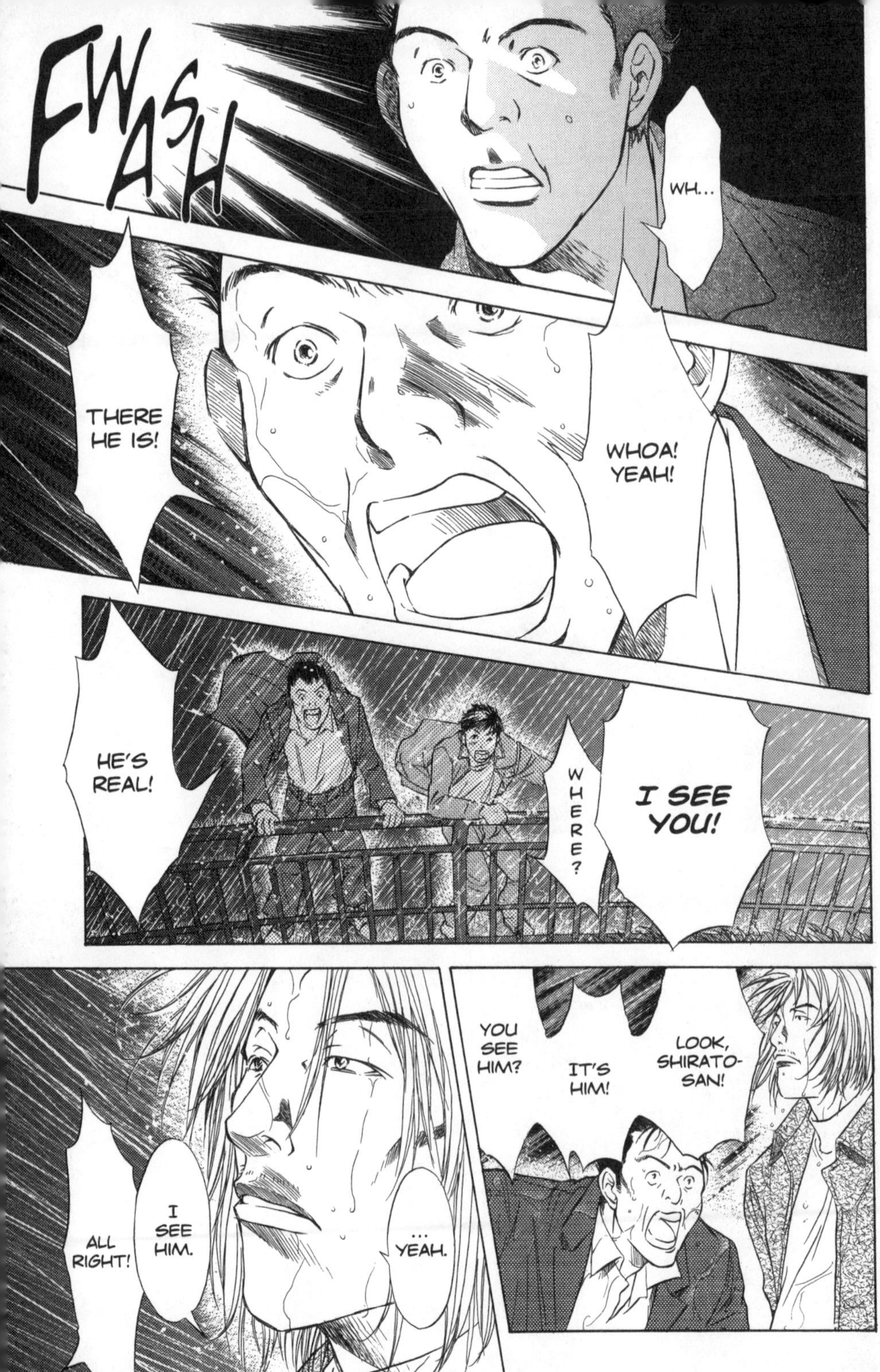
FWASH
WH...
WHOA! YEAH!
THERE HE IS!
I SEE YOU!
WHERE?
HE'S REAL!
LOOK, SHIRATO-SAN!
IT'S HIM!
YOU SEE HIM?
... YEAH.
I SEE HIM.
ALL RIGHT!

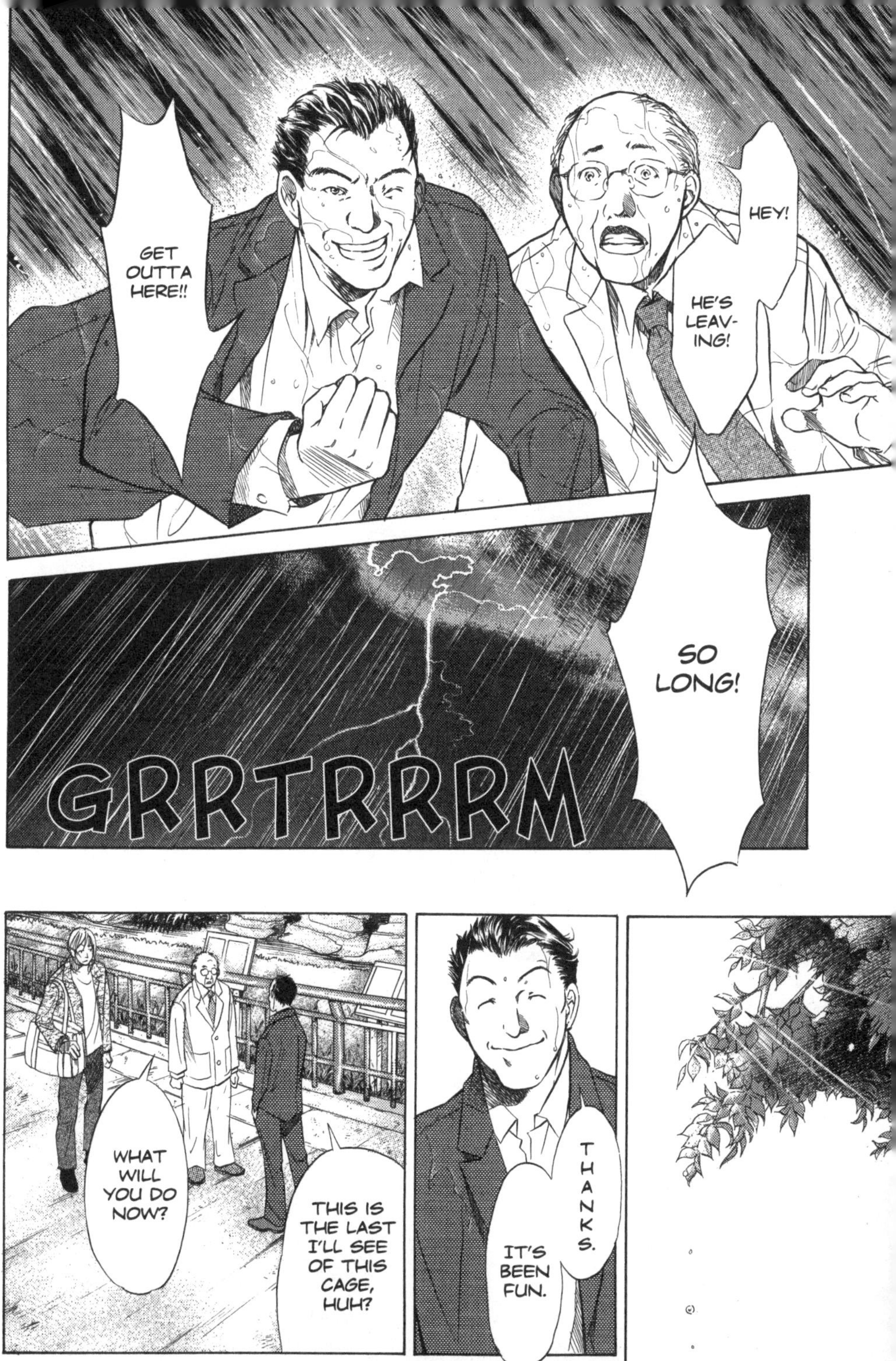
HEY!
HE'S LEAVING!
GET OUTTA HERE!!
SO LONG!
GRRTRRRM
THANKS.
IT'S BEEN FUN.
THIS IS THE LAST I'LL SEE OF THIS CAGE, HUH?
WHAT WILL YOU DO NOW?

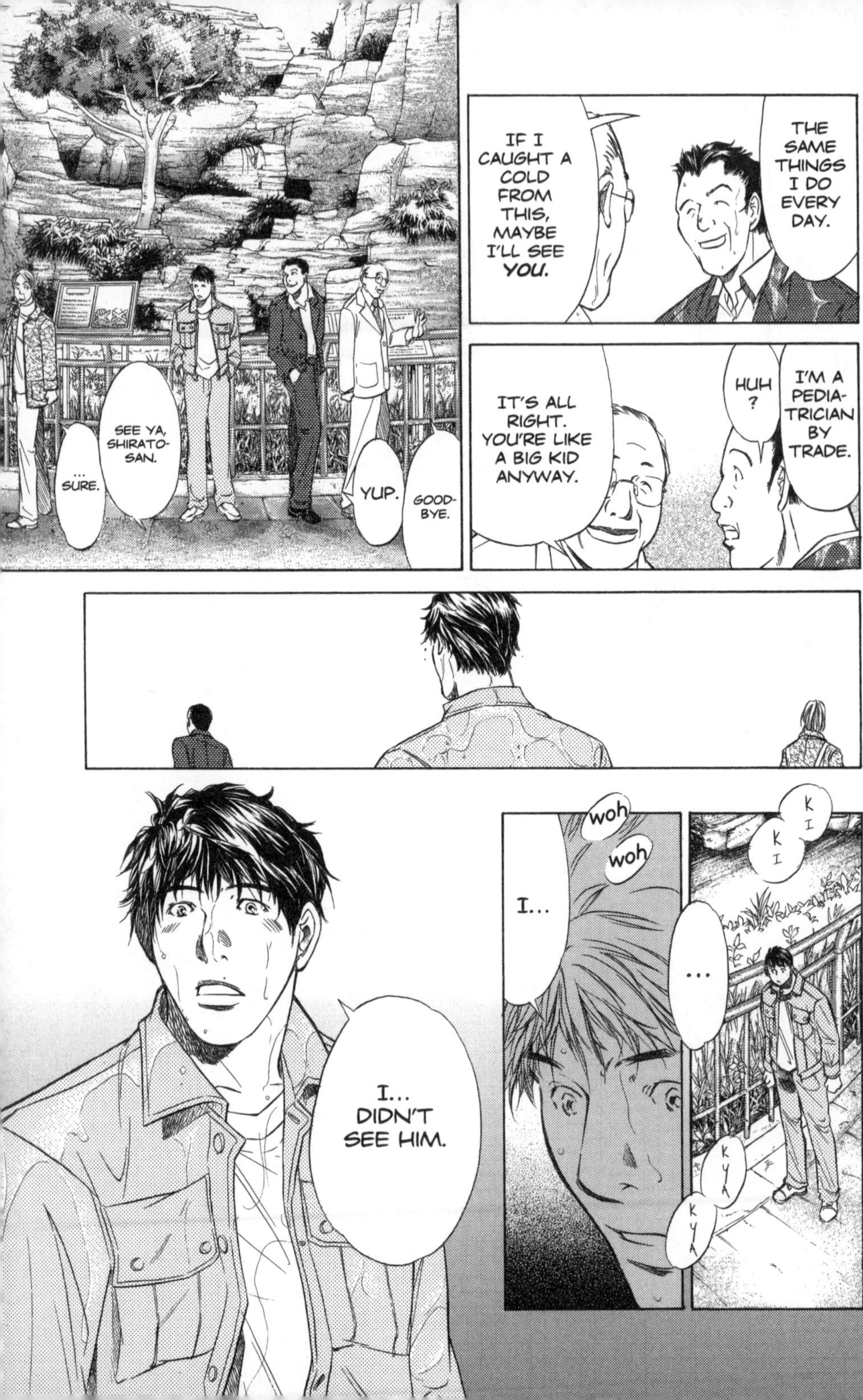
THE SAME THINGS I DO EVERY DAY.
IF I CAUGHT A COLD FROM THIS, MAYBE I'LL SEE YOU.
I'M A PEDIATRICIAN BY TRADE.
HUH?
IT'S ALL RIGHT. YOU'RE LIKE A BIG KID ANYWAY.
GOOD-BYE.
YUP.
SEE YA, SHIRATO-SAN.
... SURE.
KI KI
...
KYA KYA
woh woh
I...
I... DIDN'T SEE HIM.

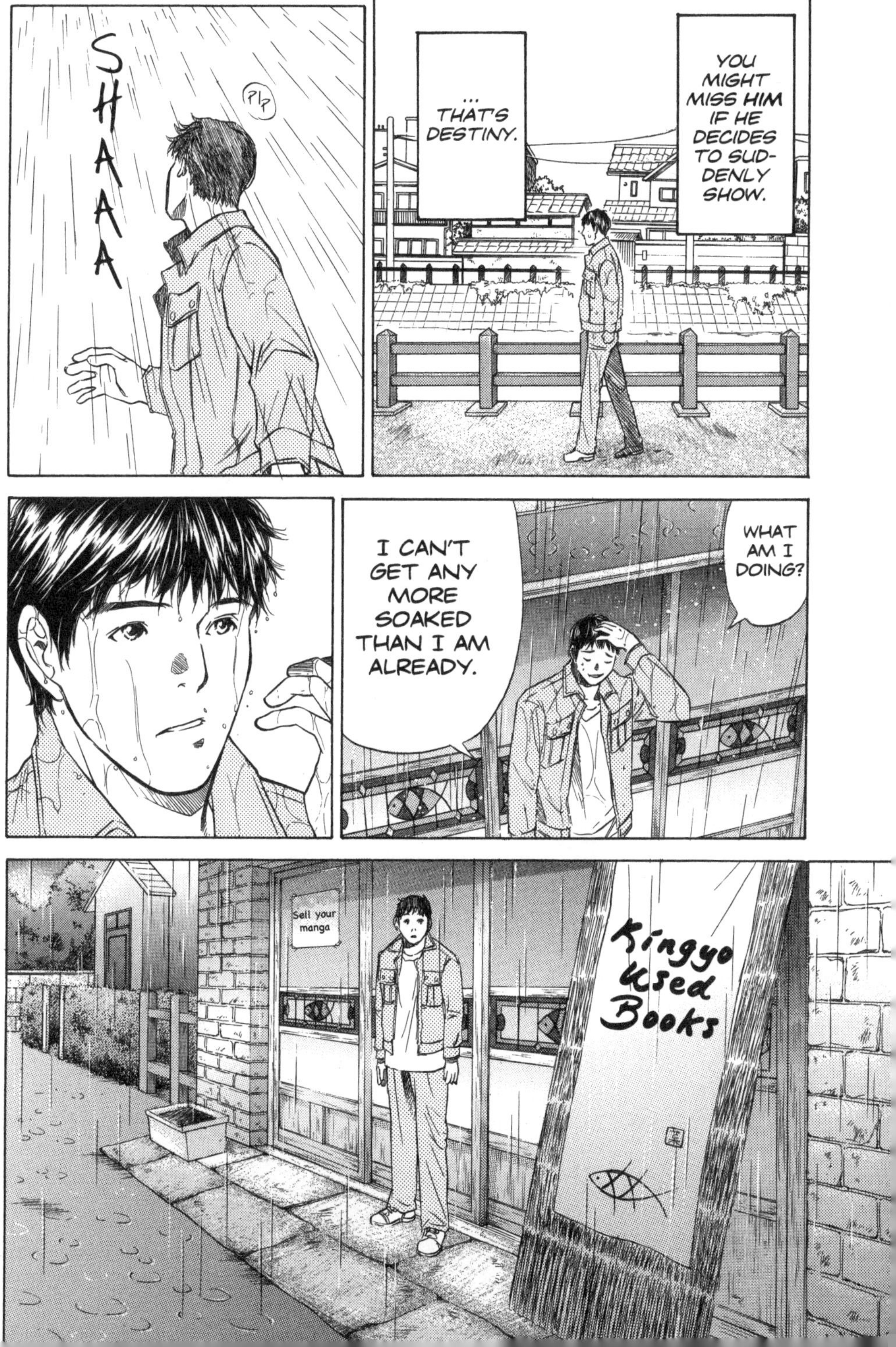
YOU MIGHT MISS HIM IF HE DECIDES TO SUDDENLY SHOW.
... THAT'S DESTINY.
SHAAA
WHAT AM I DOING?
I CAN'T GET ANY MORE SOAKED THAN I AM ALREADY.
Sell your manga
Kingyo Used Books

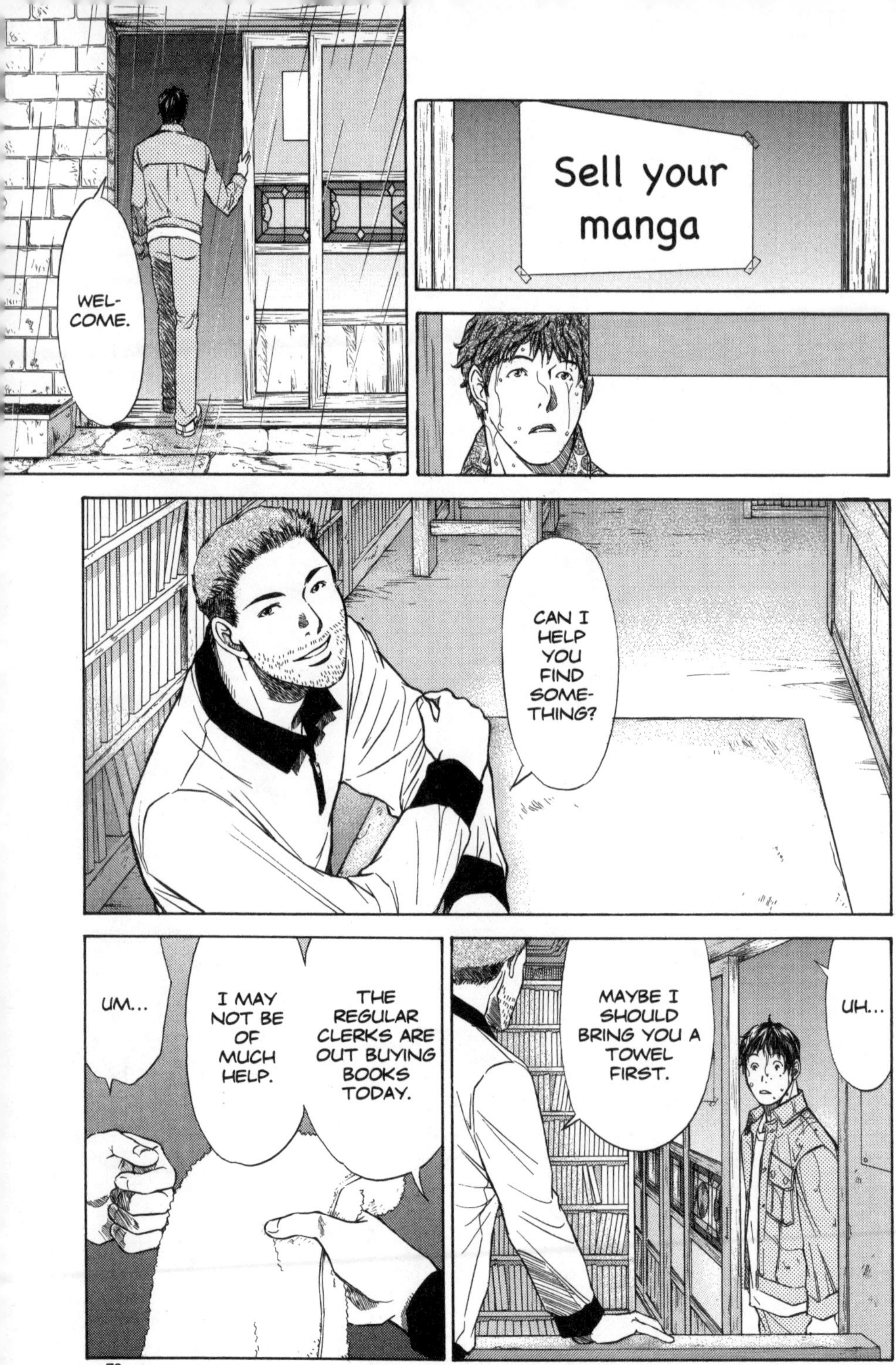
Sell your manga
WELCOME.
CAN I HELP YOU FIND SOMETHING?
UH...
MAYBE I SHOULD BRING YOU A TOWEL FIRST.
THE REGULAR CLERKS ARE OUT BUYING BOOKS TODAY.
I MAY NOT BE OF MUCH HELP.
UM...

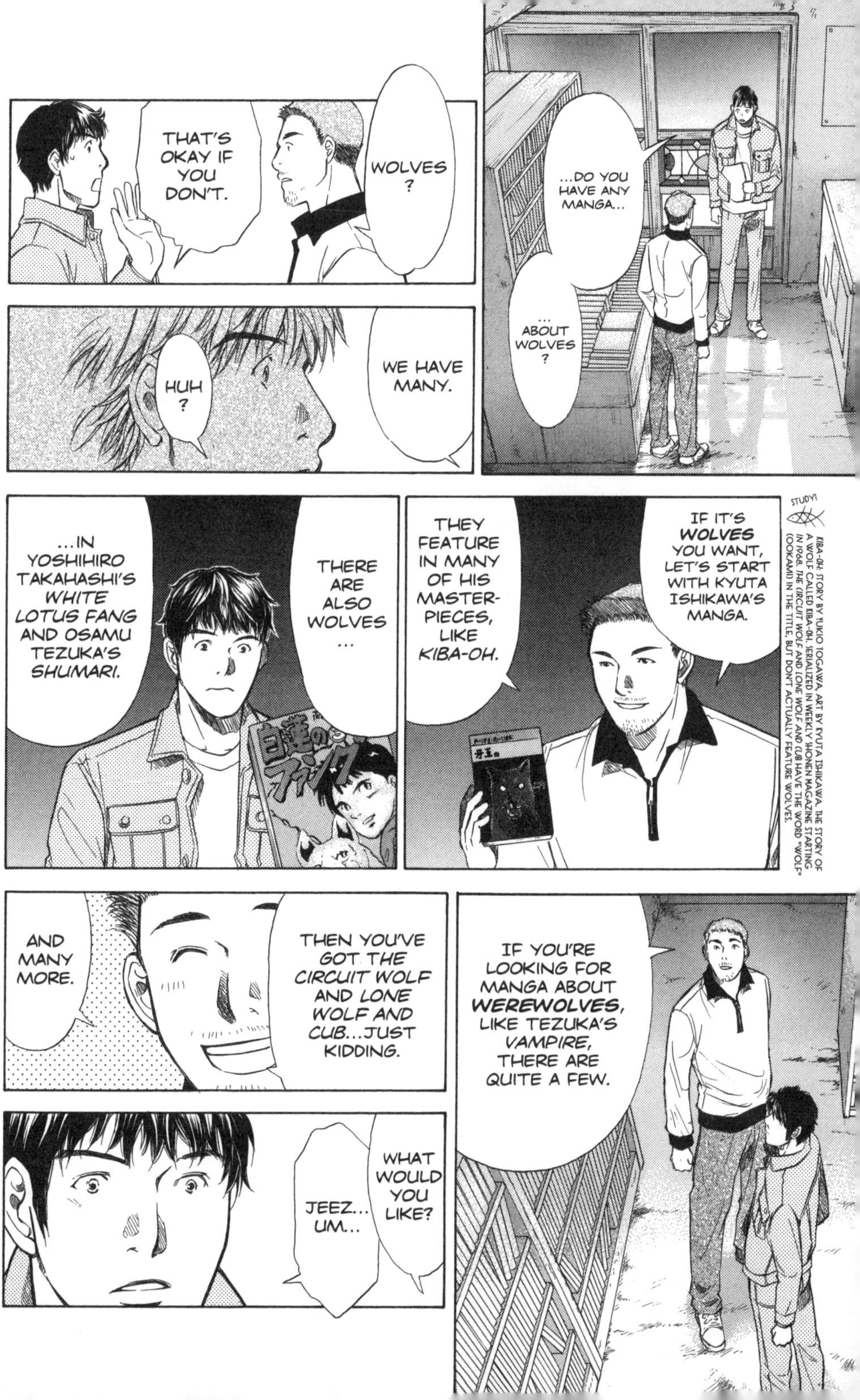
...DO YOU HAVE ANY MANGA...
...ABOUT WOLVES?
WOLVES?
THAT'S OKAY IF YOU DON'T.
WE HAVE MANY.
HUH?
IF IT'S **WOLVES** YOU WANT, LET'S START WITH KYUTA ISHIKAWA'S MANGA.
THEY FEATURE IN MANY OF HIS MASTERPIECES, LIKE *KIBA-OH*.
THERE ARE ALSO WOLVES...
...IN YOSHIHIRO TAKAHASHI'S *WHITE LOTUS FANG* AND OSAMU TEZUKA'S *SHUMARI*.
IF YOU'RE LOOKING FOR MANGA ABOUT **WEREWOLVES**, LIKE TEZUKA'S *VAMPIRE*, THERE ARE QUITE A FEW.
THEN YOU'VE GOT *THE CIRCUIT WOLF* AND *LONE WOLF AND CUB*...JUST KIDDING.
AND MANY MORE.
WHAT WOULD YOU LIKE?
JEEZ... UM...

STUDY!

KIBA-OH: STORY BY YUKIO TOGAWA, ART BY KYUTA ISHIKAWA. THE STORY OF A WOLF CALLED KIBA-OH. SERIALIZED IN WEEKLY SHONEN MAGAZINE STARTING IN 1968. *THE CIRCUIT WOLF* AND *LONE WOLF AND CUB* HAVE THE WORD "WOLF" (OOKAMI) IN THE TITLE, BUT DON'T ACTUALLY FEATURE WOLVES.

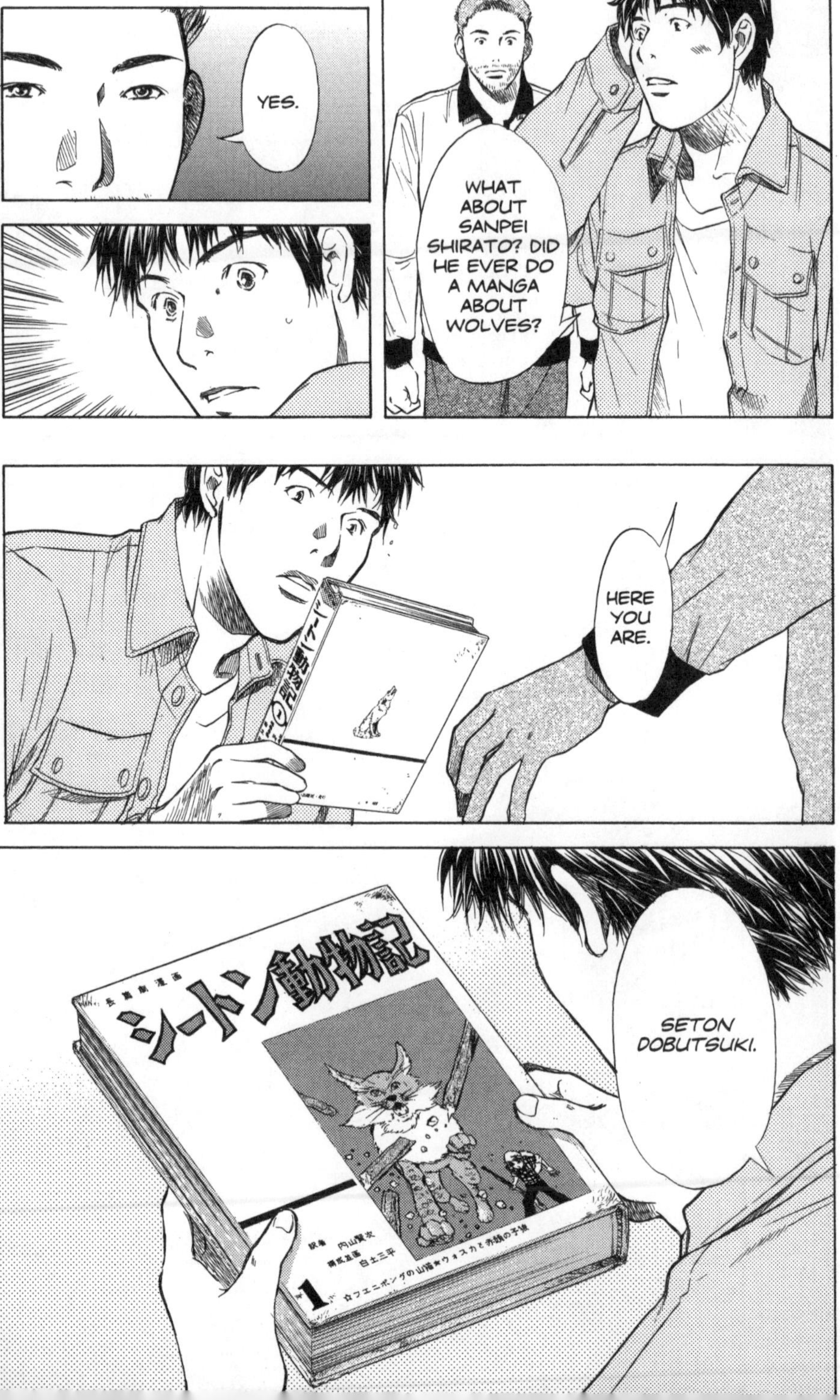
WHAT ABOUT SANPEI SHIRATO? DID HE EVER DO A MANGA ABOUT WOLVES?
YES.
HERE YOU ARE.
シートン動物記
SETON DOBUTSUKI.

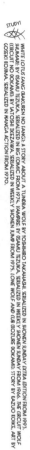

STUDY!

WHITE LOTUS FANG (*BAKUREN NO FANG*): A STORY ABOUT A TUNDRA WOLF BY YOSHIHIRO TAKAHASHI. SERIALIZED IN *SHONEN SUNDAY EXTRA EDITION* FROM 1993. *SHUMARI*: BY OSAMU TEZUKA. SERIALIZED IN *BIG COMIC* FROM 1974. *VAMPIRE*: BY OSAMU TEZUKA. SERIALIZED IN *WEEKLY SHONEN SUNDAY* FROM 1966. *THE CIRCUIT WOLF* (*CIRCUIT NO OOKAMI*): BY SATOSHI IKEZAWA. SERIALIZED IN *WEEKLY SHONEN JUMP* FROM 1975. *LONE WOLF AND CUB* (*KOZURE OOKAMI*): STORY BY KAZUO KOIKE, ART BY GOSEKI KOJIMA. SERIALIZED IN *MANGA ACTION* FROM 1970.

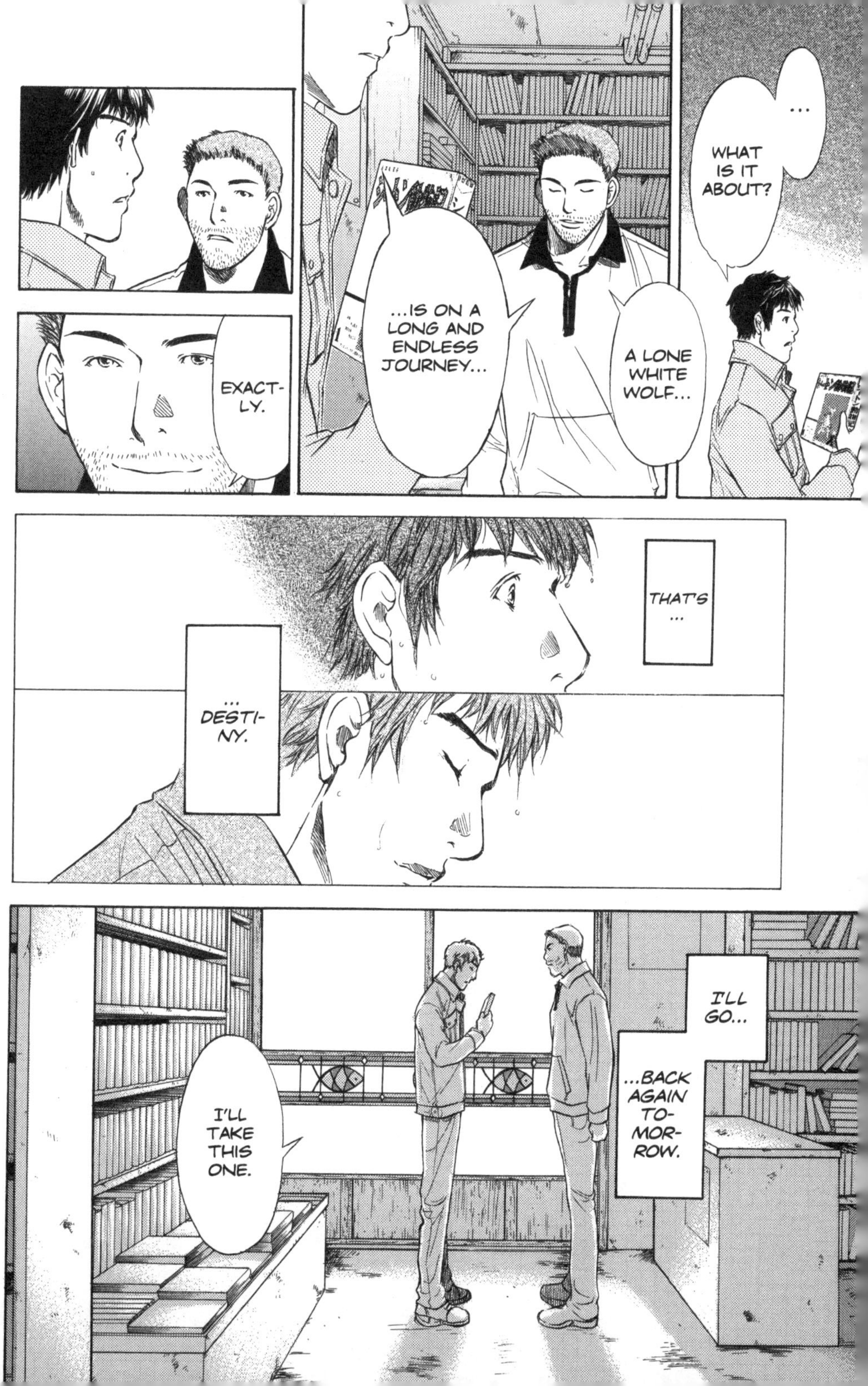
...
WHAT IS IT ABOUT?
A LONE WHITE WOLF...
...IS ON A LONG AND ENDLESS JOURNEY...
EXACT-LY.
THAT'S...
...DESTI-NY.
I'LL GO...
...BACK AGAIN TO-MOR-ROW.
I'LL TAKE THIS ONE.

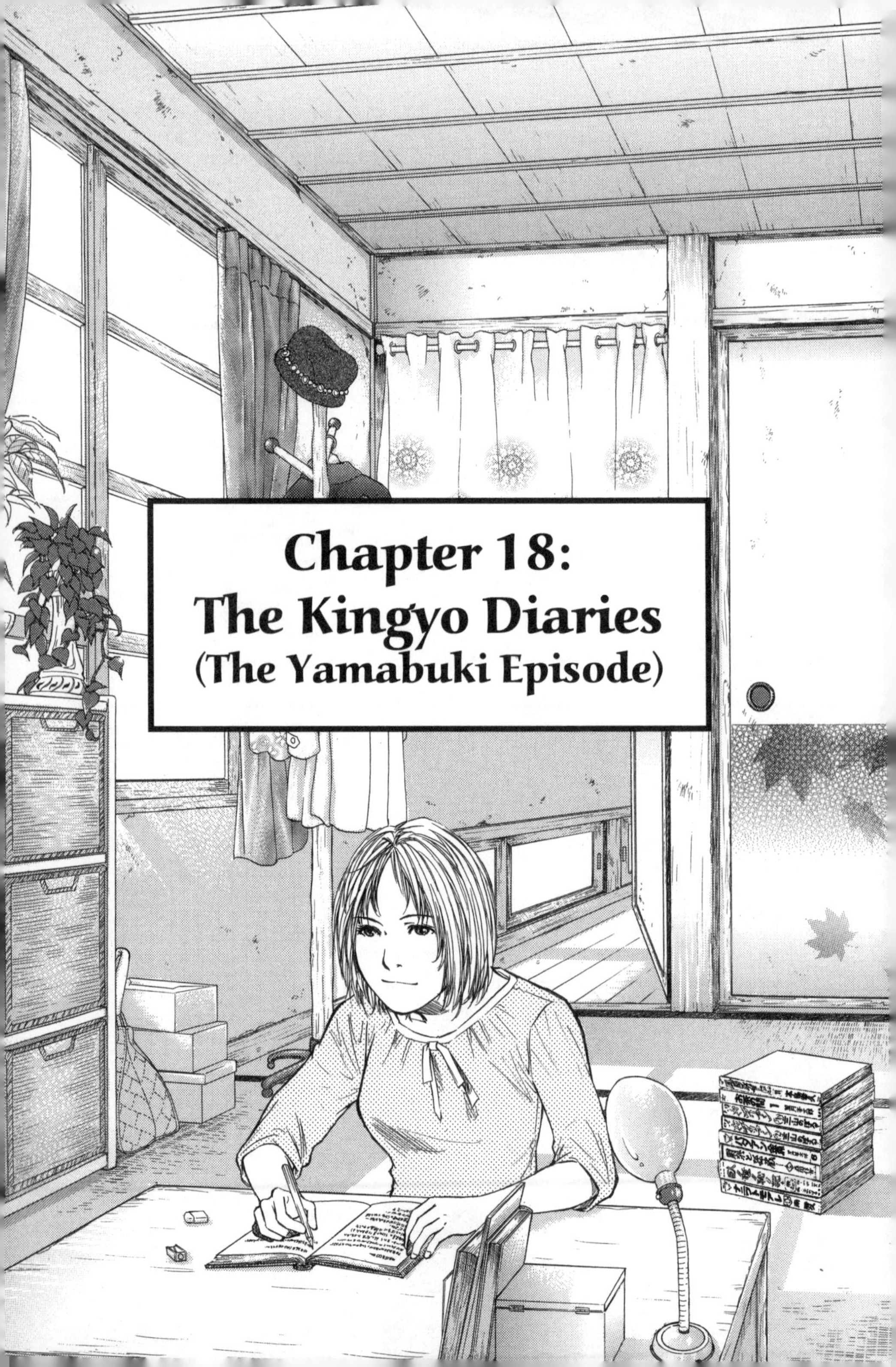
Chapter 18:
The Kingyo Diaries
(The Yamabuki Episode)

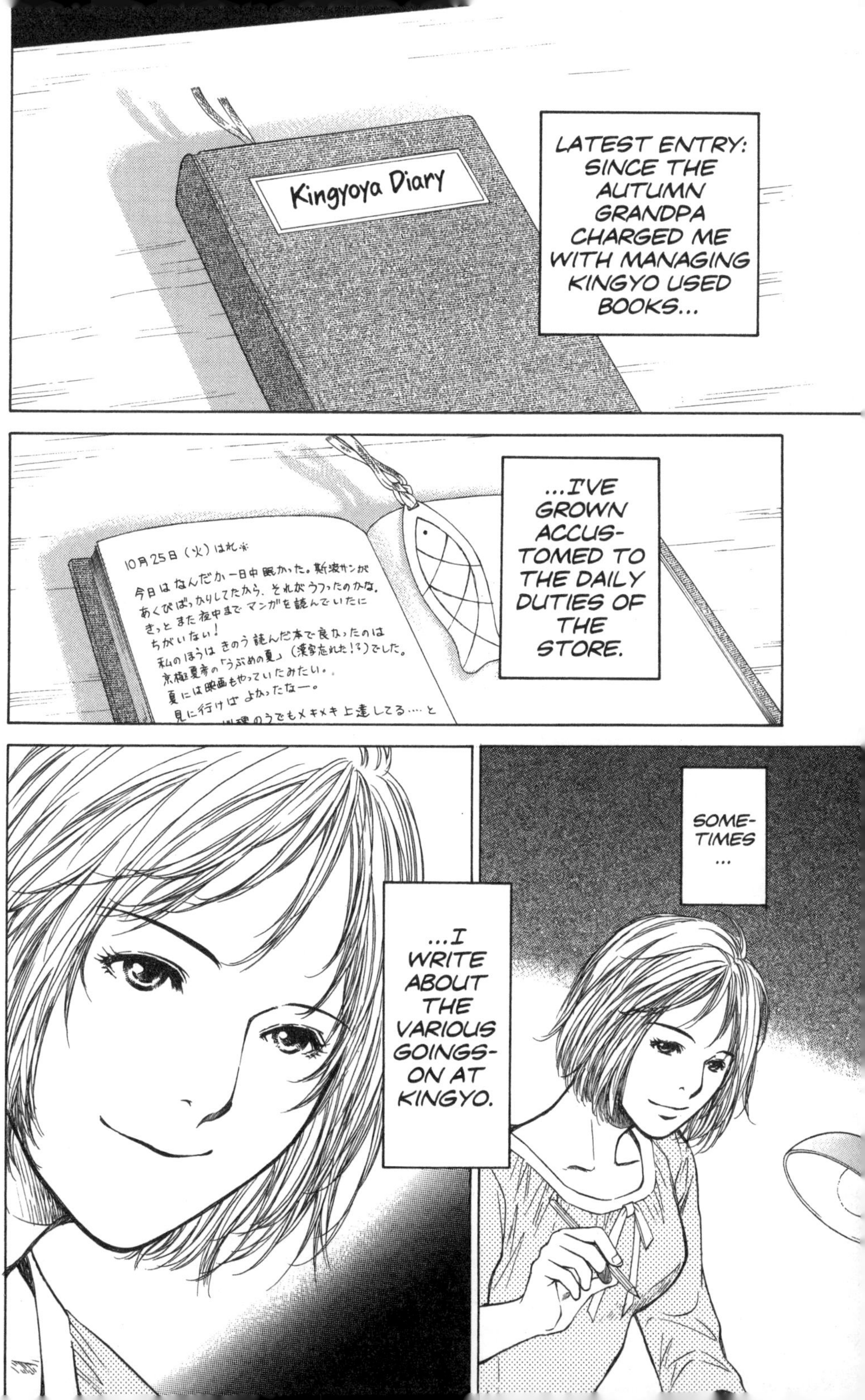
Kingyoya Diary
LATEST ENTRY: SINCE THE AUTUMN GRANDPA CHARGED ME WITH MANAGING KINGYO USED BOOKS...
10月25日（火）はれ
今日はなんだか一日中眠かった。斯波サンが
あくびばっかりしてたから、それがうつったのかな。
きっとまた夜中までマンガを読んでいたに
ちがいない！
私のほうはきのう読んだ本で良かったのは
京極夏彦の「うぶめの夏」（漢字忘れた!?）でした。
夏には映画もやっていたみたい。
見に行けばよかったなー。
でもメキメキ上達してる…と
...I'VE GROWN ACCUS-TOMED TO THE DAILY DUTIES OF THE STORE.
SOME-TIMES...
...I WRITE ABOUT THE VARIOUS GOINGS-ON AT KINGYO.

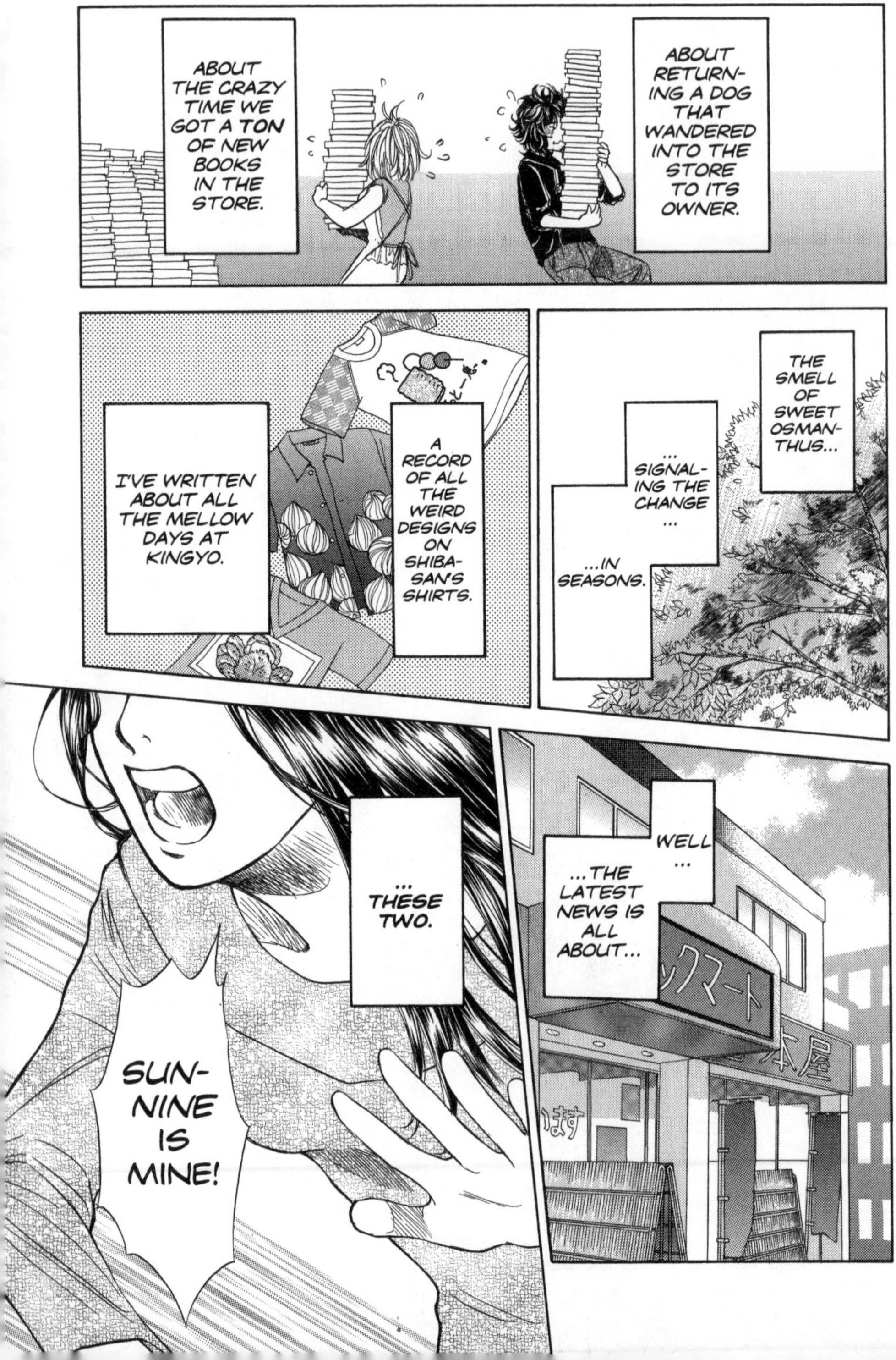
ABOUT RETURNING A DOG THAT WANDERED INTO THE STORE TO ITS OWNER.
ABOUT THE CRAZY TIME WE GOT A TON OF NEW BOOKS IN THE STORE.
THE SMELL OF SWEET OSMANTHUS...
...SIGNALING THE CHANGE...
...IN SEASONS.
A RECORD OF ALL THE WEIRD DESIGNS ON SHIBA-SAN'S SHIRTS.
I'VE WRITTEN ABOUT ALL THE MELLOW DAYS AT KINGYO.
WELL...
...THE LATEST NEWS IS ALL ABOUT...
...THESE TWO.
SUN-NINE IS MINE!

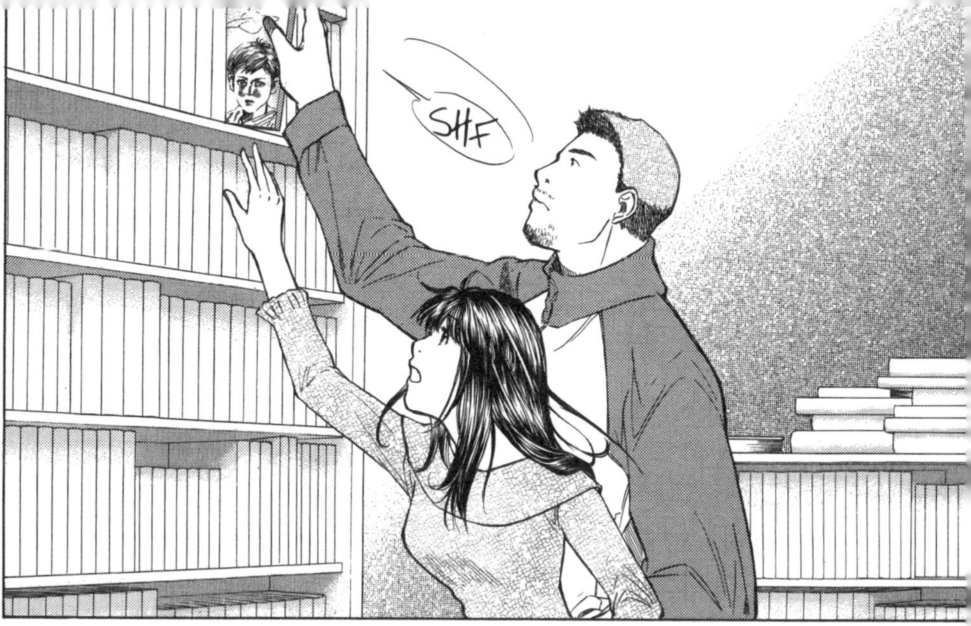
SHF

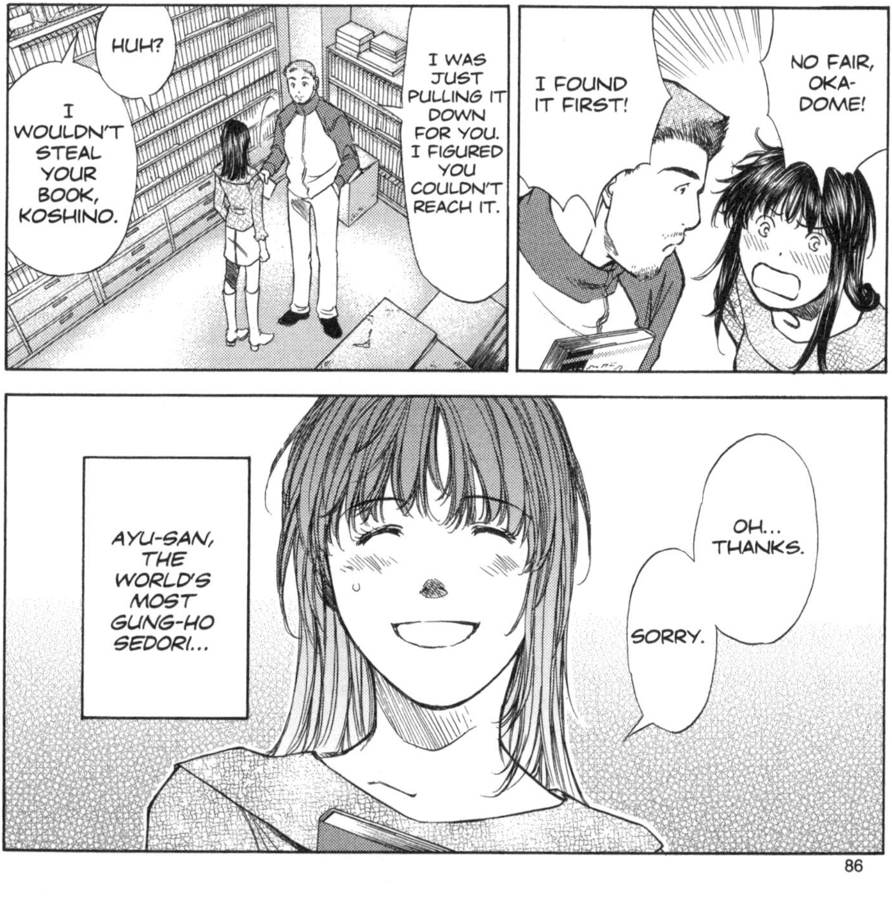
NO FAIR, OKA-DOME!
I FOUND IT FIRST!
I WAS JUST PULLING IT DOWN FOR YOU. I FIGURED YOU COULDN'T REACH IT.
HUH?
I WOULDN'T STEAL YOUR BOOK, KOSHINO.
OH... THANKS.
SORRY.
AYU-SAN, THE WORLD'S MOST GUNG-HO SEDORI...

STUDY!

Sun-Mine or *Taiyo no Ko Sun-Mine* by Soji Yamakawa. Published in three volumes under Shueisha's Compact Comics imprint beginning in 1967.

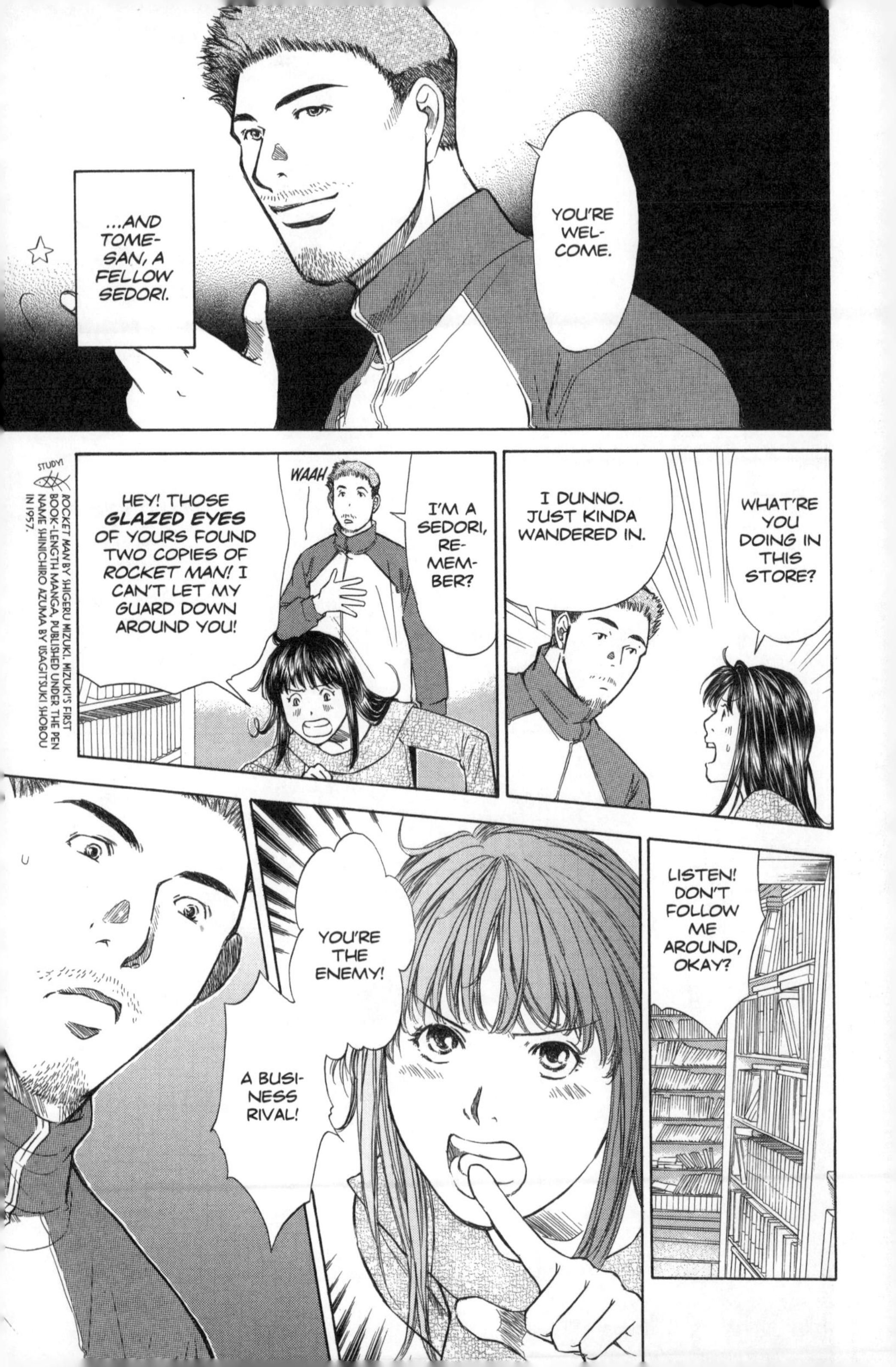
YOU'RE WEL-COME.
...AND TOME-SAN, A FELLOW SEDORI.
WHAT'RE YOU DOING IN THIS STORE?
I DUNNO. JUST KINDA WANDERED IN.
I'M A SEDORI, REMEM-BER?
WAAH
HEY! THOSE GLAZED EYES OF YOURS FOUND TWO COPIES OF ROCKET MAN! I CAN'T LET MY GUARD DOWN AROUND YOU!
LISTEN! DON'T FOLLOW ME AROUND, OKAY?
YOU'RE THE ENEMY!
A BUSI-NESS RIVAL!

STUDY!

ROCKET MAN BY SHIGERU MIZUKI. MIZUKI'S FIRST BOOK-LENGTH MANGA, PUBLISHED UNDER THE PEN NAME SHINICHIRO AZUMA BY USAGITSUKI SHOBOU IN 1957.

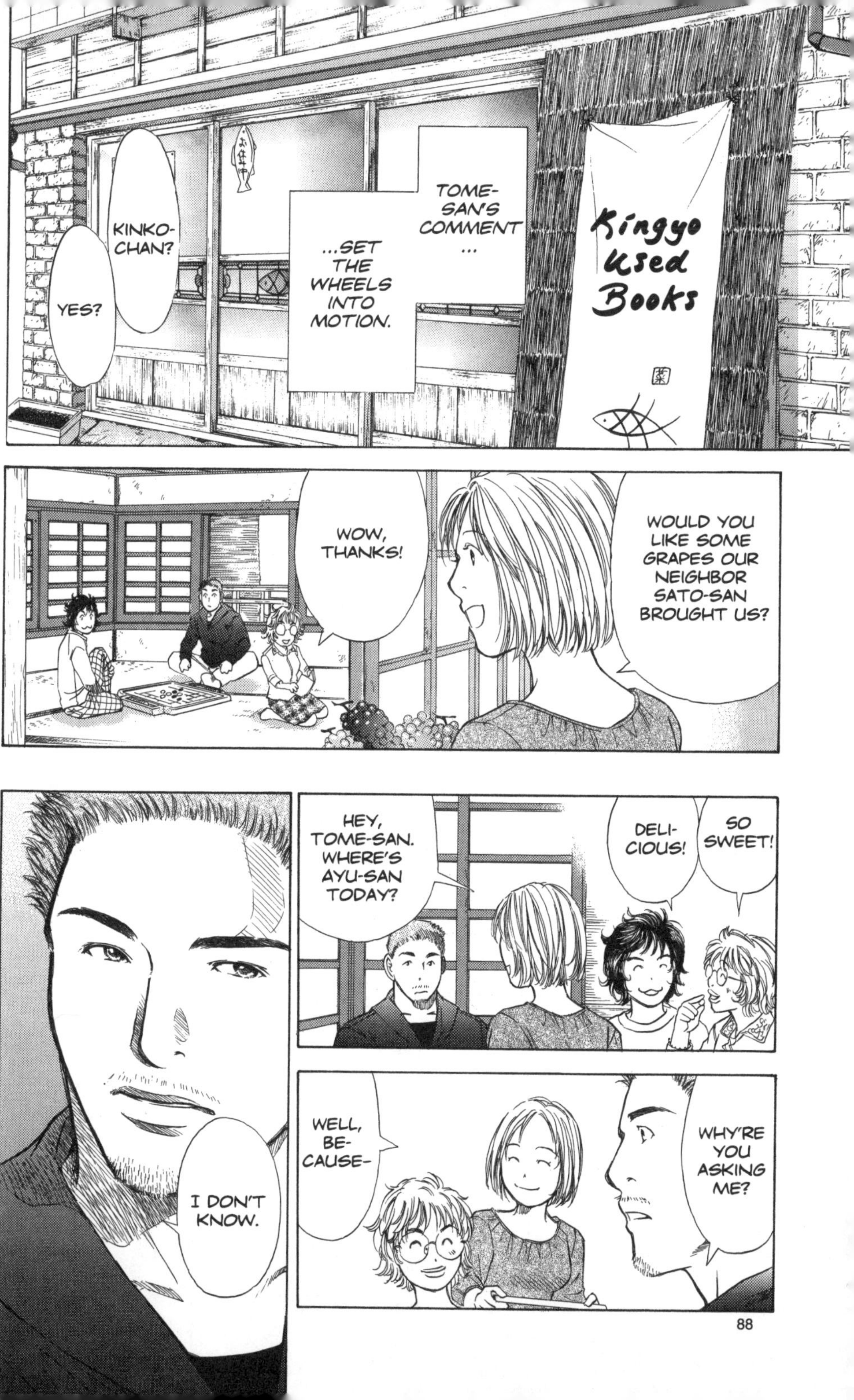
Kingyo Used Books
TOME-SAN'S COMMENT ...
...SET THE WHEELS INTO MOTION.
KINKO-CHAN?
YES?
WOULD YOU LIKE SOME GRAPES OUR NEIGHBOR SATO-SAN BROUGHT US?
WOW, THANKS!
SO SWEET!
DELI-CIOUS!
HEY, TOME-SAN. WHERE'S AYU-SAN TODAY?
WHY'RE YOU ASKING ME?
WELL, BE-CAUSE-
I DON'T KNOW.

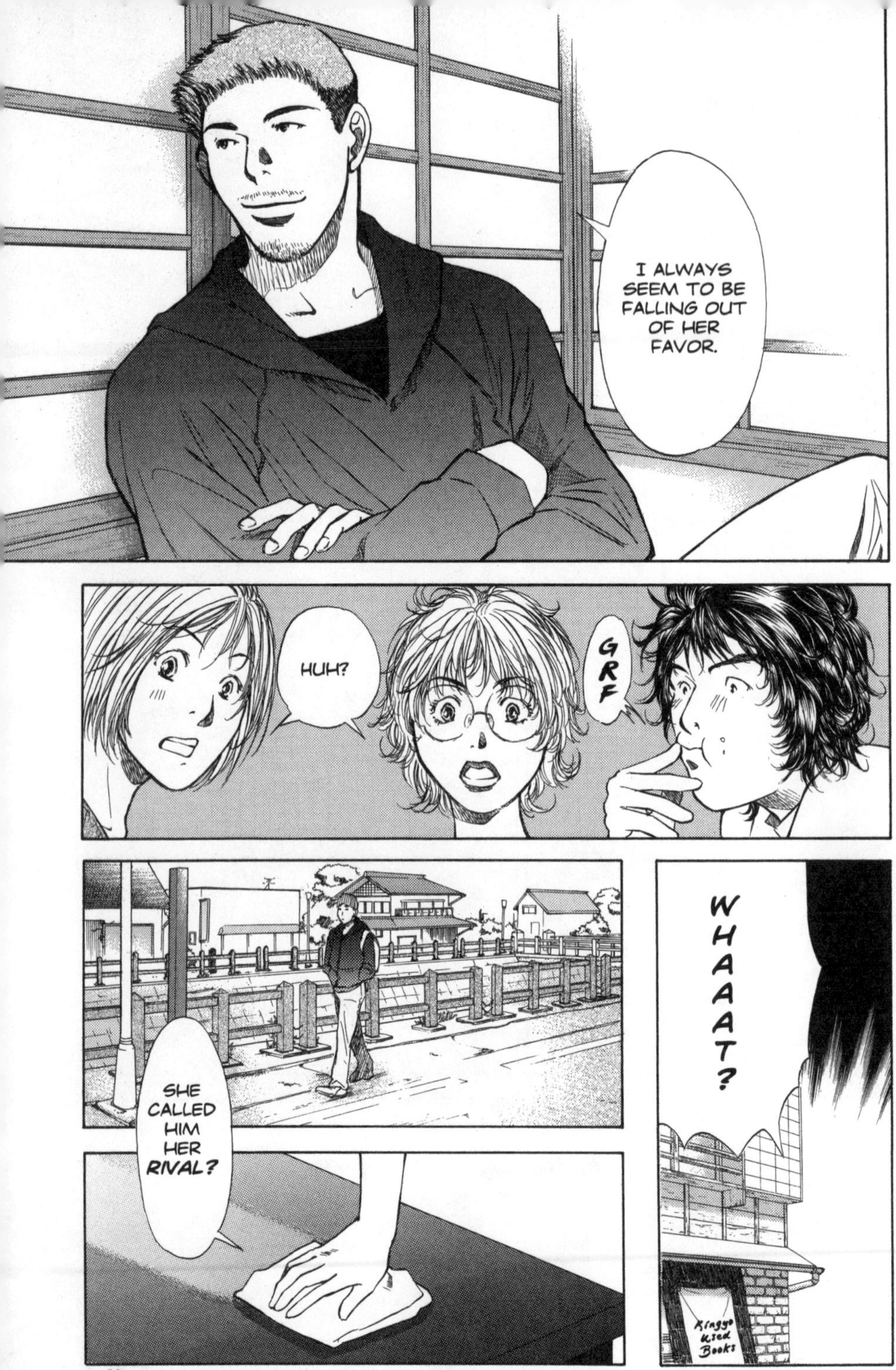
I ALWAYS SEEM TO BE FALLING OUT OF HER FAVOR.
GRF
HUH?
WHAAAAT?
Ringgo Used Books
SHE CALLED HIM HER *RIVAL?*

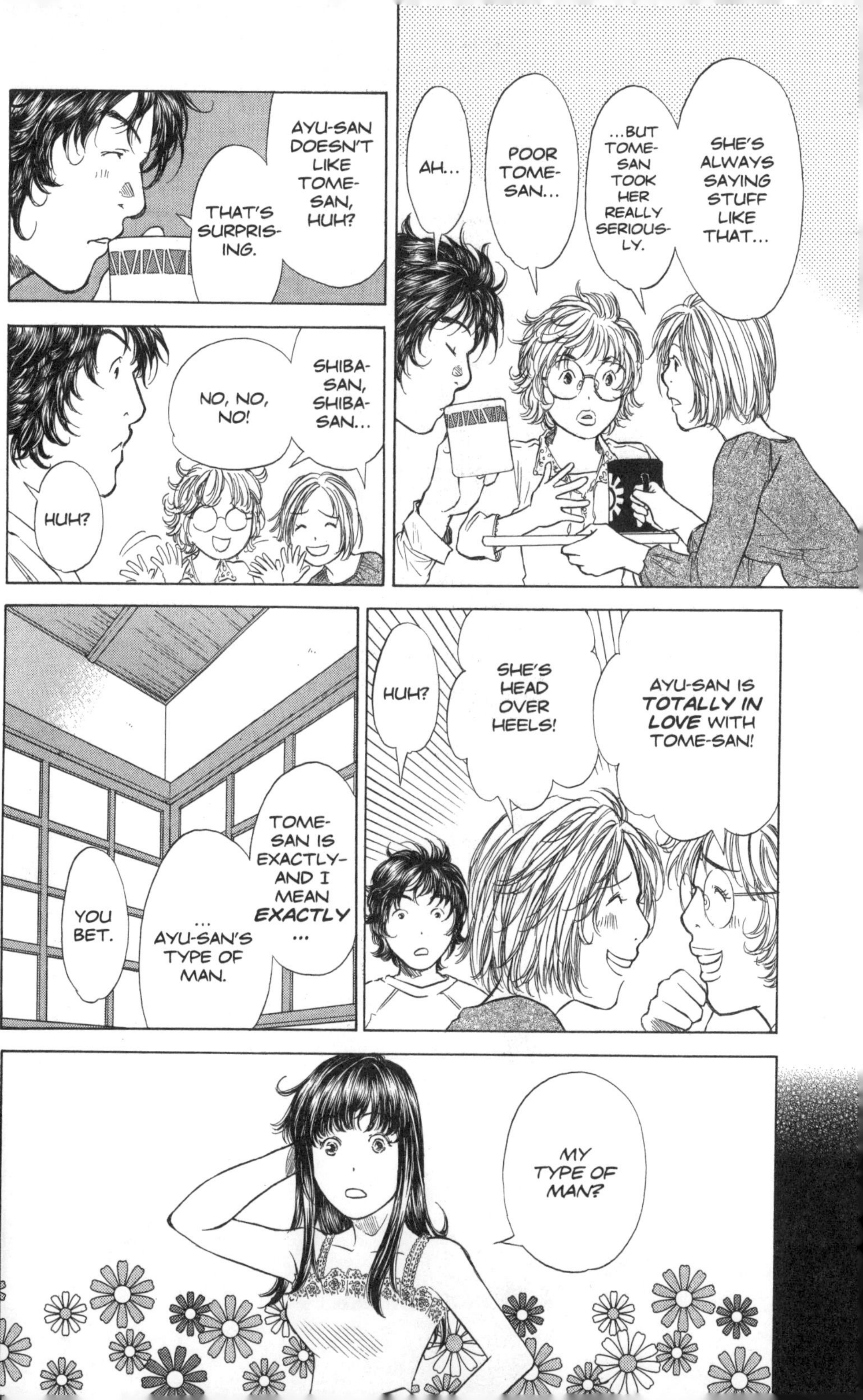
SHE'S ALWAYS SAYING STUFF LIKE THAT...
...BUT TOME-SAN TOOK HER REALLY SERIOUSLY.
POOR TOME-SAN...
AH...
AYU-SAN DOESN'T LIKE TOME-SAN, HUH?
THAT'S SURPRISING.
SHIBA-SAN, SHIBA-SAN...
NO, NO, NO!
HUH?
AYU-SAN IS ***TOTALLY IN LOVE*** WITH TOME-SAN!
SHE'S HEAD OVER HEELS!
HUH?
TOME-SAN IS EXACTLY- AND I MEAN ***EXACTLY*** ... ...AYU-SAN'S TYPE OF MAN.
YOU BET.
MY TYPE OF MAN?

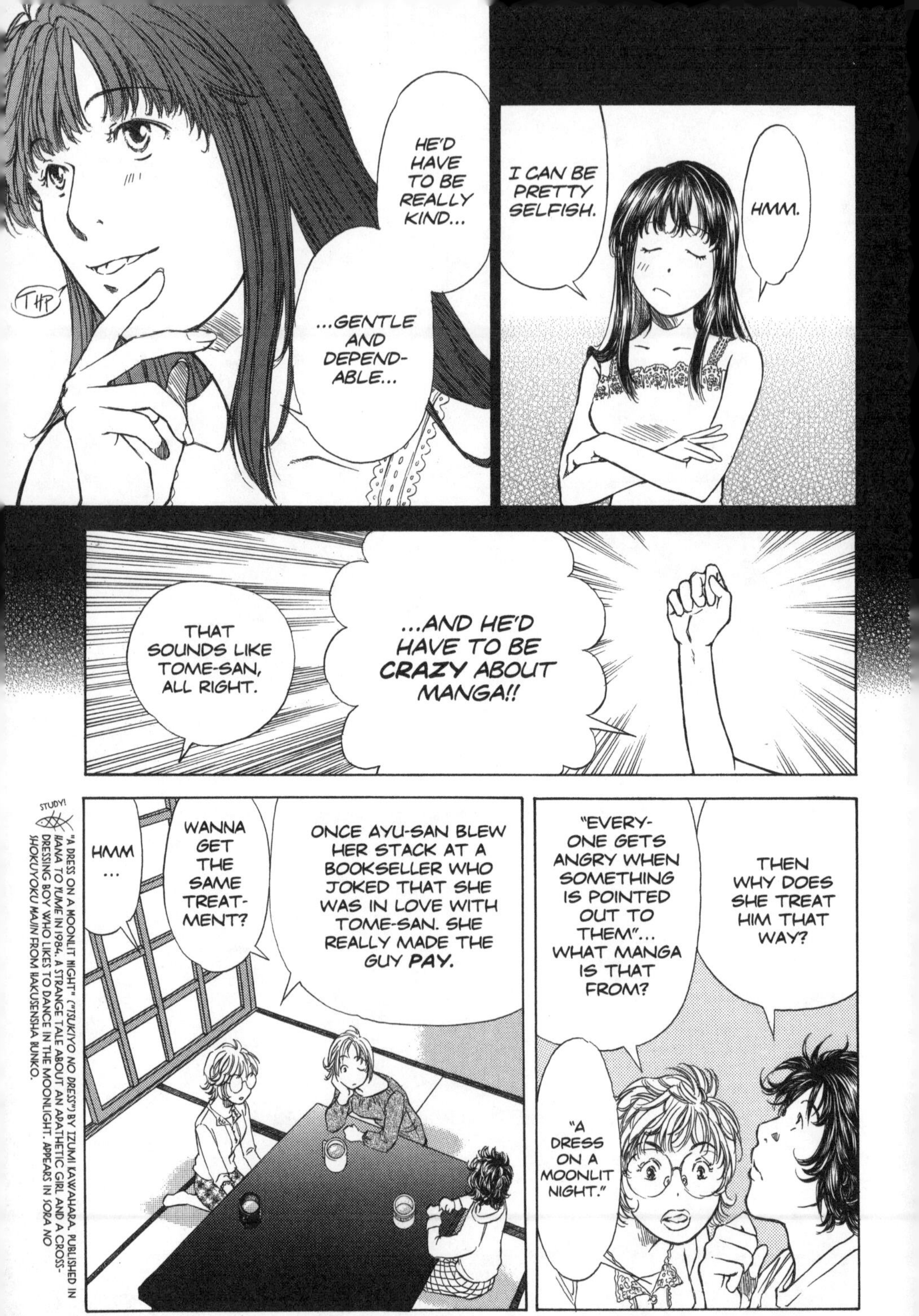
HMM.
I CAN BE PRETTY SELFISH.
HE'D HAVE TO BE REALLY KIND...
...GENTLE AND DEPEND-ABLE...
THP
...AND HE'D HAVE TO BE CRAZY ABOUT MANGA!!
THAT SOUNDS LIKE TOME-SAN, ALL RIGHT.
THEN WHY DOES SHE TREAT HIM THAT WAY?
"EVERY-ONE GETS ANGRY WHEN SOMETHING IS POINTED OUT TO THEM"... WHAT MANGA IS THAT FROM?
"A DRESS ON A MOONLIT NIGHT."
ONCE AYU-SAN BLEW HER STACK AT A BOOKSELLER WHO JOKED THAT SHE WAS IN LOVE WITH TOME-SAN. SHE REALLY MADE THE GUY **PAY.**
WANNA GET THE SAME TREAT-MENT?
HMM...

STUDY!

"A DRESS ON A MOONLIT NIGHT" ("TSUKIYO NO DRESS") BY IZUMI KAWAHARA. PUBLISHED IN HANA TO YUME IN 1984. A STRANGE TALE ABOUT AN APATHETIC GIRL AND A CROSS-DRESSING BOY WHO LIKES TO DANCE IN THE MOONLIGHT. APPEARS IN SORA NO SHOKUYOKU MAJIN FROM HAKUSENSHA BUNKO.

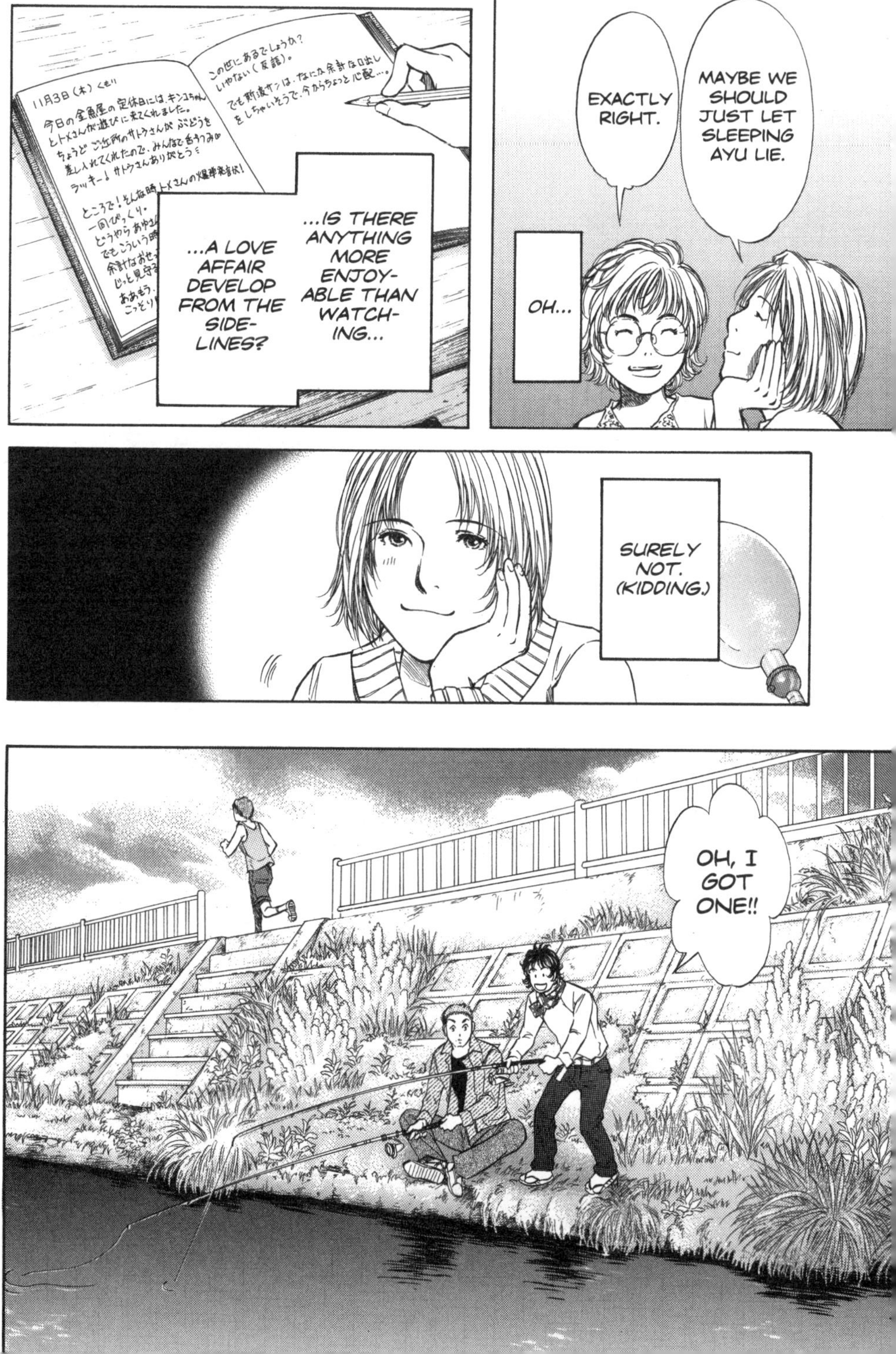
MAYBE WE SHOULD JUST LET SLEEPING AYU LIE.
EXACTLY RIGHT.
OH...
...IS THERE ANYTHING MORE ENJOY-ABLE THAN WATCH-ING...
...A LOVE AFFAIR DEVELOP FROM THE SIDE-LINES?
SURELY NOT. (KIDDING.)
OH, I GOT ONE!!

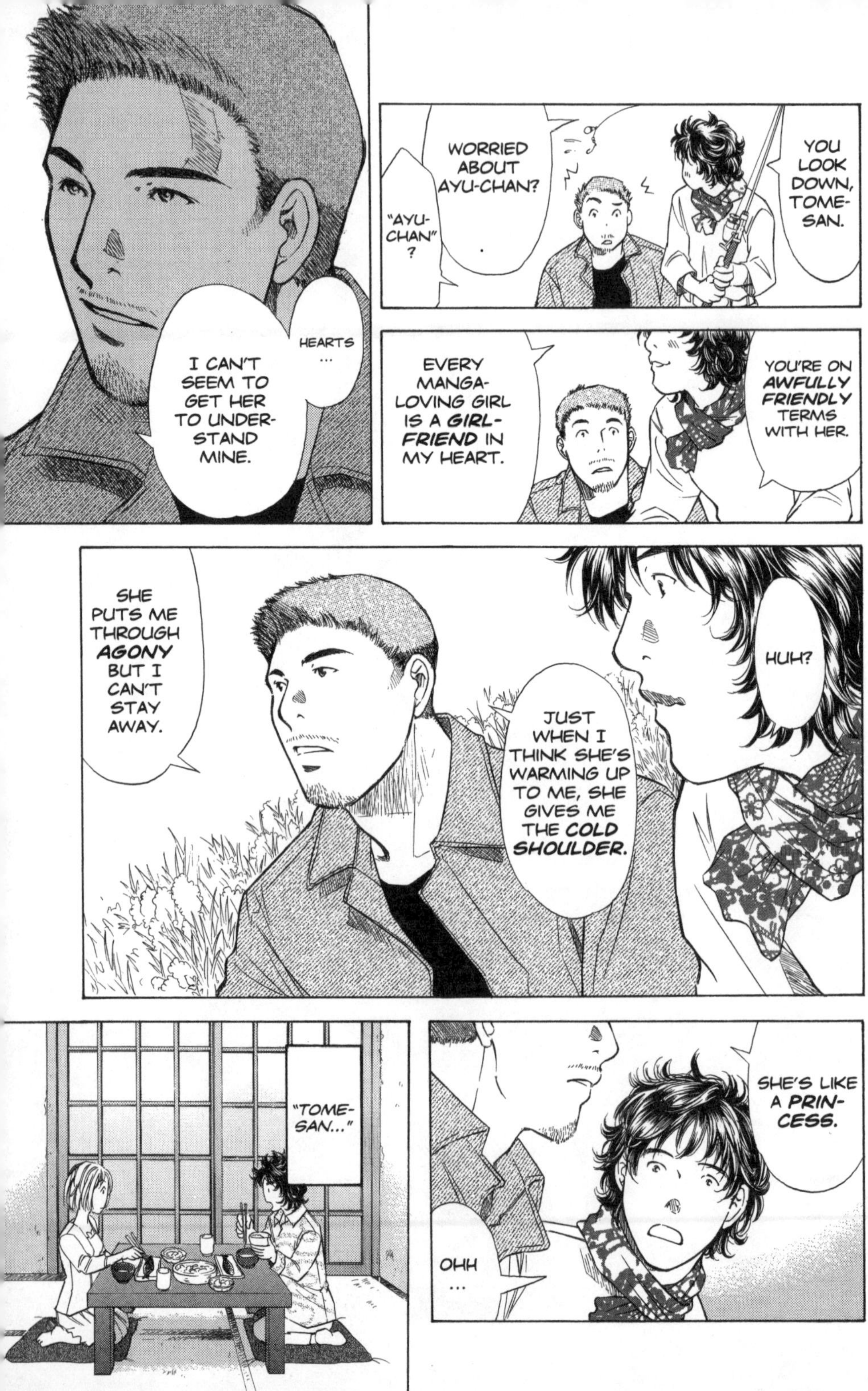
YOU LOOK DOWN, TOME-SAN.
WORRIED ABOUT AYU-CHAN?
"AYU-CHAN" ?
YOU'RE ON AWFULLY FRIENDLY TERMS WITH HER.
EVERY MANGA-LOVING GIRL IS A GIRLFRIEND IN MY HEART.
HEARTS ...
I CAN'T SEEM TO GET HER TO UNDERSTAND MINE.
HUH?
JUST WHEN I THINK SHE'S WARMING UP TO ME, SHE GIVES ME THE COLD SHOULDER.
SHE PUTS ME THROUGH AGONY BUT I CAN'T STAY AWAY.
SHE'S LIKE A PRINCESS.
OHH ...
"TOME-SAN..."

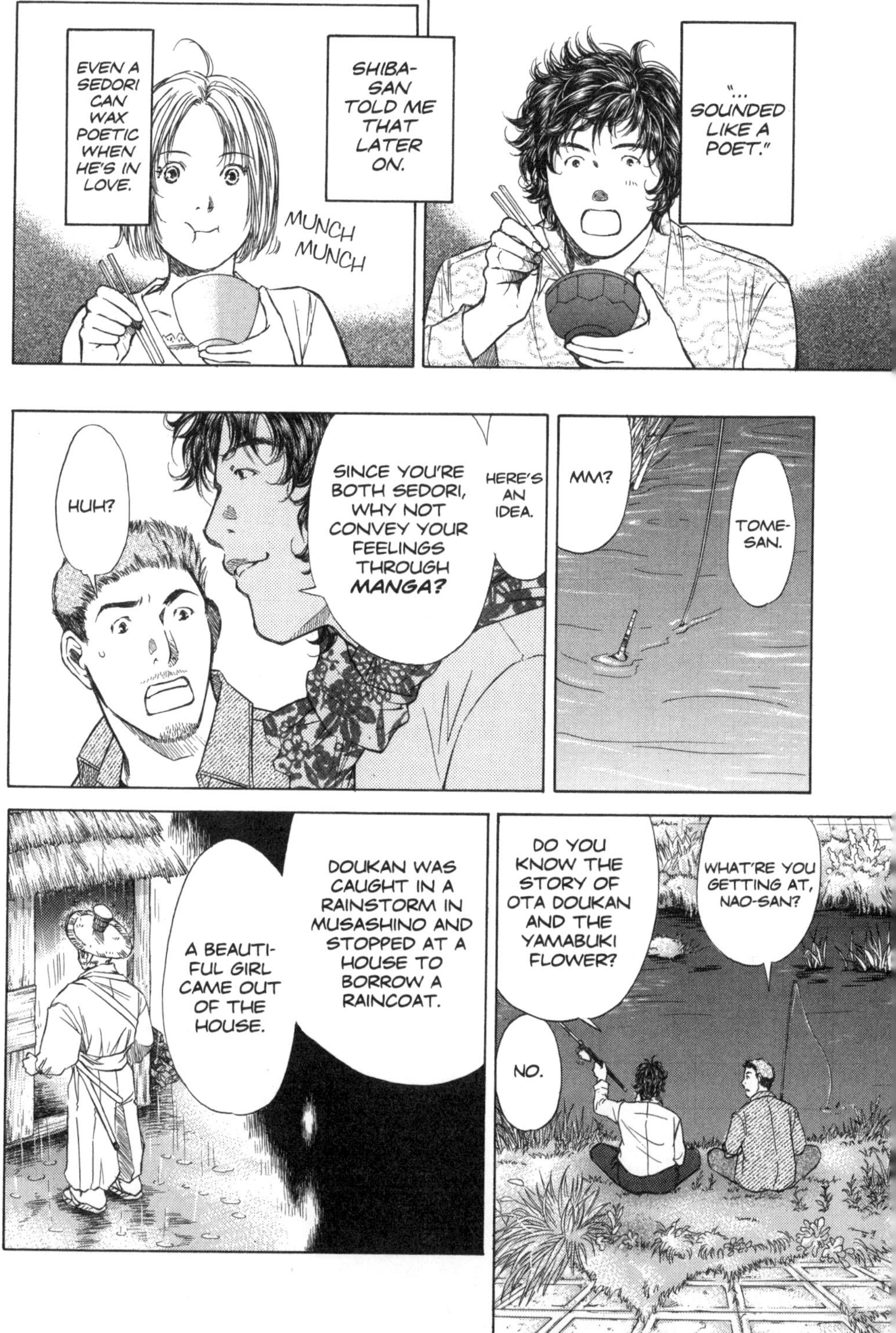
"... SOUNDED LIKE A POET."
SHIBA-SAN TOLD ME THAT LATER ON.
EVEN A SEDORI CAN WAX POETIC WHEN HE'S IN LOVE.
MUNCH MUNCH
TOME-SAN.
MM?
HERE'S AN IDEA.
SINCE YOU'RE BOTH SEDORI, WHY NOT CONVEY YOUR FEELINGS THROUGH MANGA?
HUH?
WHAT'RE YOU GETTING AT, NAO-SAN?
DO YOU KNOW THE STORY OF OTA DOUKAN AND THE YAMABUKI FLOWER?
NO.
DOUKAN WAS CAUGHT IN A RAINSTORM IN MUSASHINO AND STOPPED AT A HOUSE TO BORROW A RAINCOAT.
A BEAUTIFUL GIRL CAME OUT OF THE HOUSE.

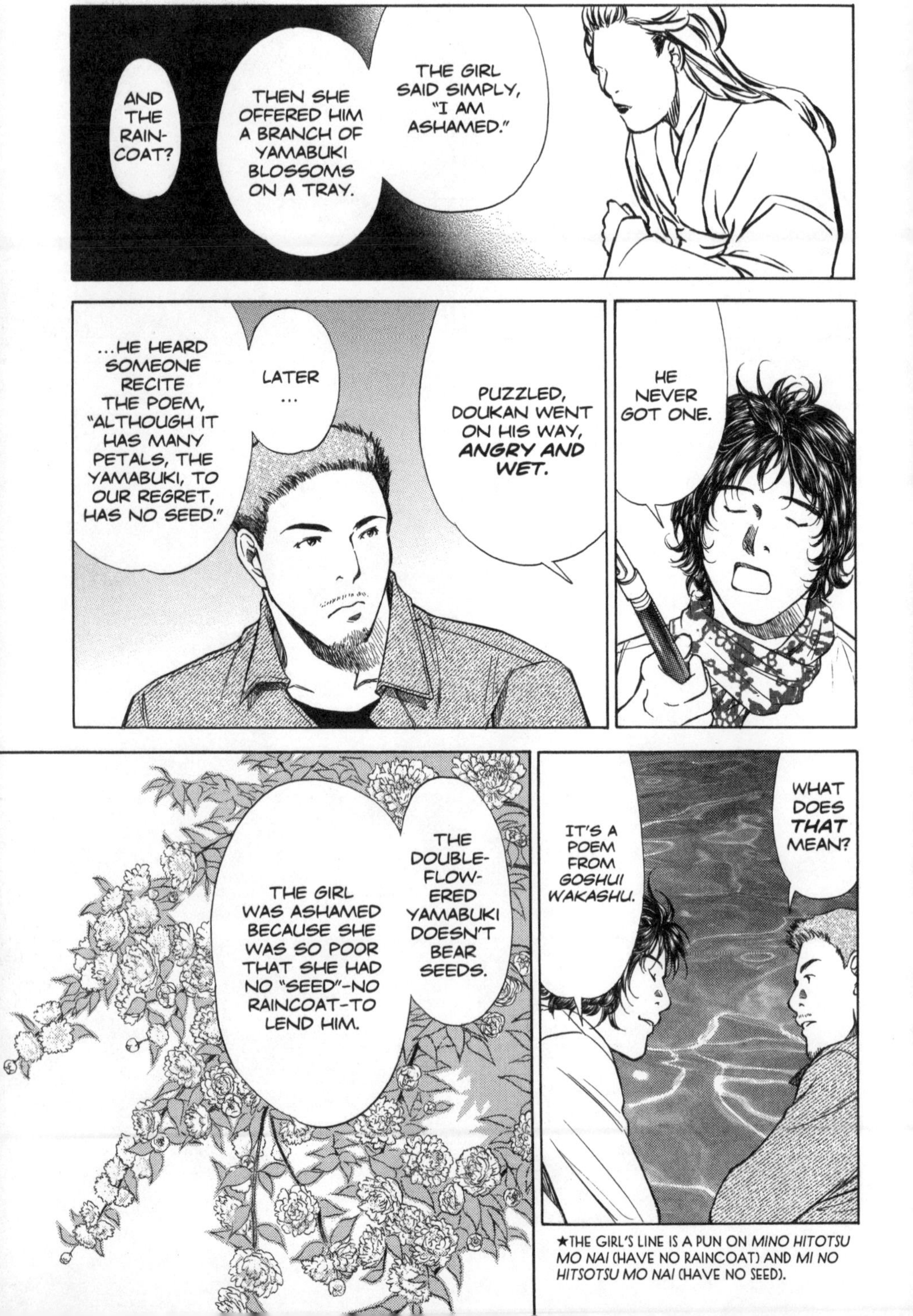
THE GIRL SAID SIMPLY, "I AM ASHAMED."
THEN SHE OFFERED HIM A BRANCH OF YAMABUKI BLOSSOMS ON A TRAY.
AND THE RAIN-COAT?
HE NEVER GOT ONE.
PUZZLED, DOUKAN WENT ON HIS WAY, ***ANGRY AND WET.***
LATER ...
...HE HEARD SOMEONE RECITE THE POEM, "ALTHOUGH IT HAS MANY PETALS, THE YAMABUKI, TO OUR REGRET, HAS NO SEED."
WHAT DOES ***THAT*** MEAN?
IT'S A POEM FROM *GOSHUI WAKASHU.*
THE DOUBLE-FLOWERED YAMABUKI DOESN'T BEAR SEEDS.
THE GIRL WAS ASHAMED BECAUSE SHE WAS SO POOR THAT SHE HAD NO "SEED"-NO RAINCOAT-TO LEND HIM.

★THE GIRL'S LINE IS A PUN ON *MINO HITOTSU MO NAI* (HAVE NO RAINCOAT) AND *MI NO HITSOTSU MO NAI* (HAVE NO SEED).

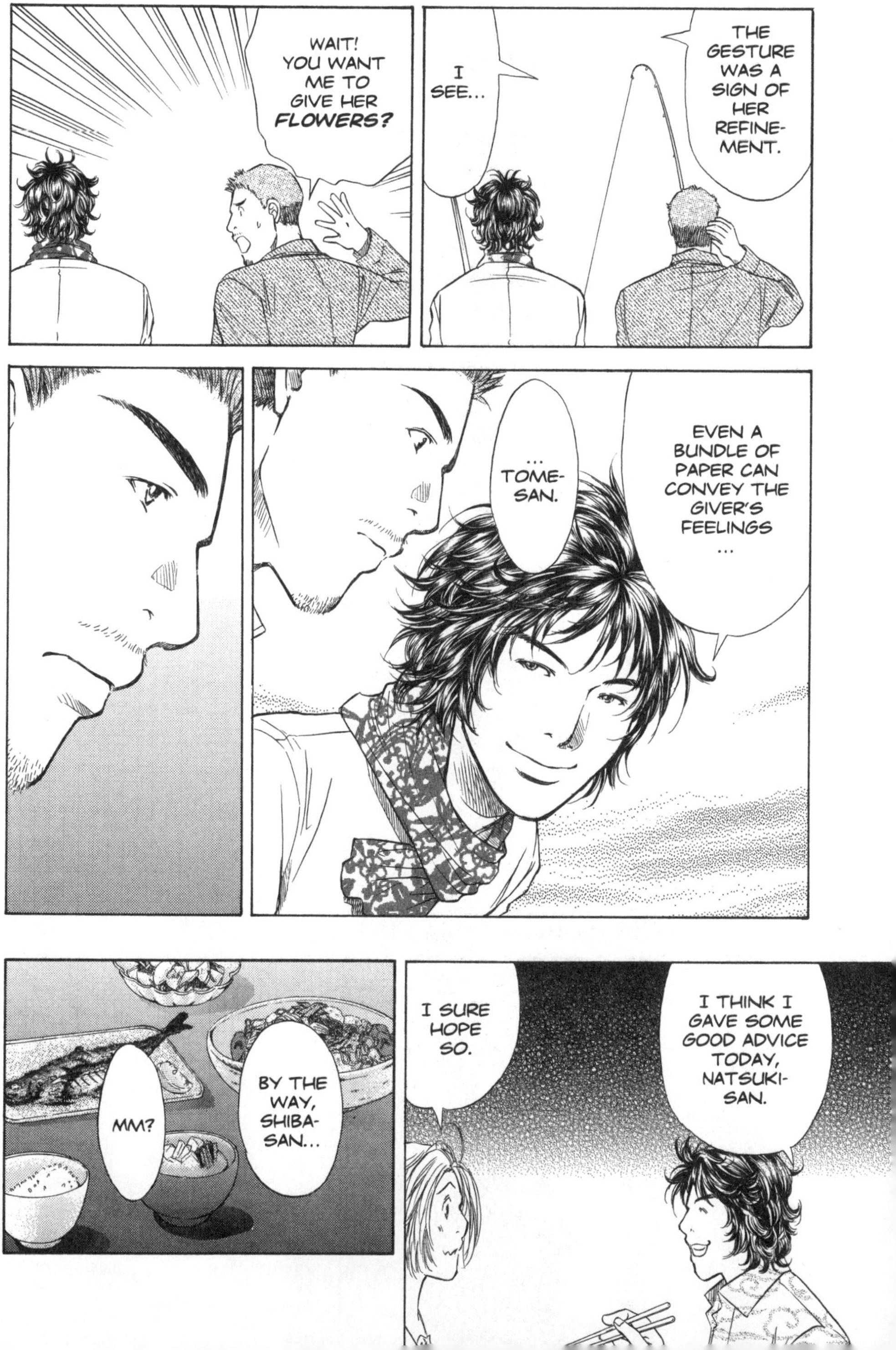
THE GESTURE WAS A SIGN OF HER REFINEMENT.
I SEE...
WAIT! YOU WANT ME TO GIVE HER *FLOWERS?*
EVEN A BUNDLE OF PAPER CAN CONVEY THE GIVER'S FEELINGS ...
... TOME-SAN.
I THINK I GAVE SOME GOOD ADVICE TODAY, NATSUKI-SAN.
I SURE HOPE SO.
BY THE WAY, SHIBA-SAN...
MM?

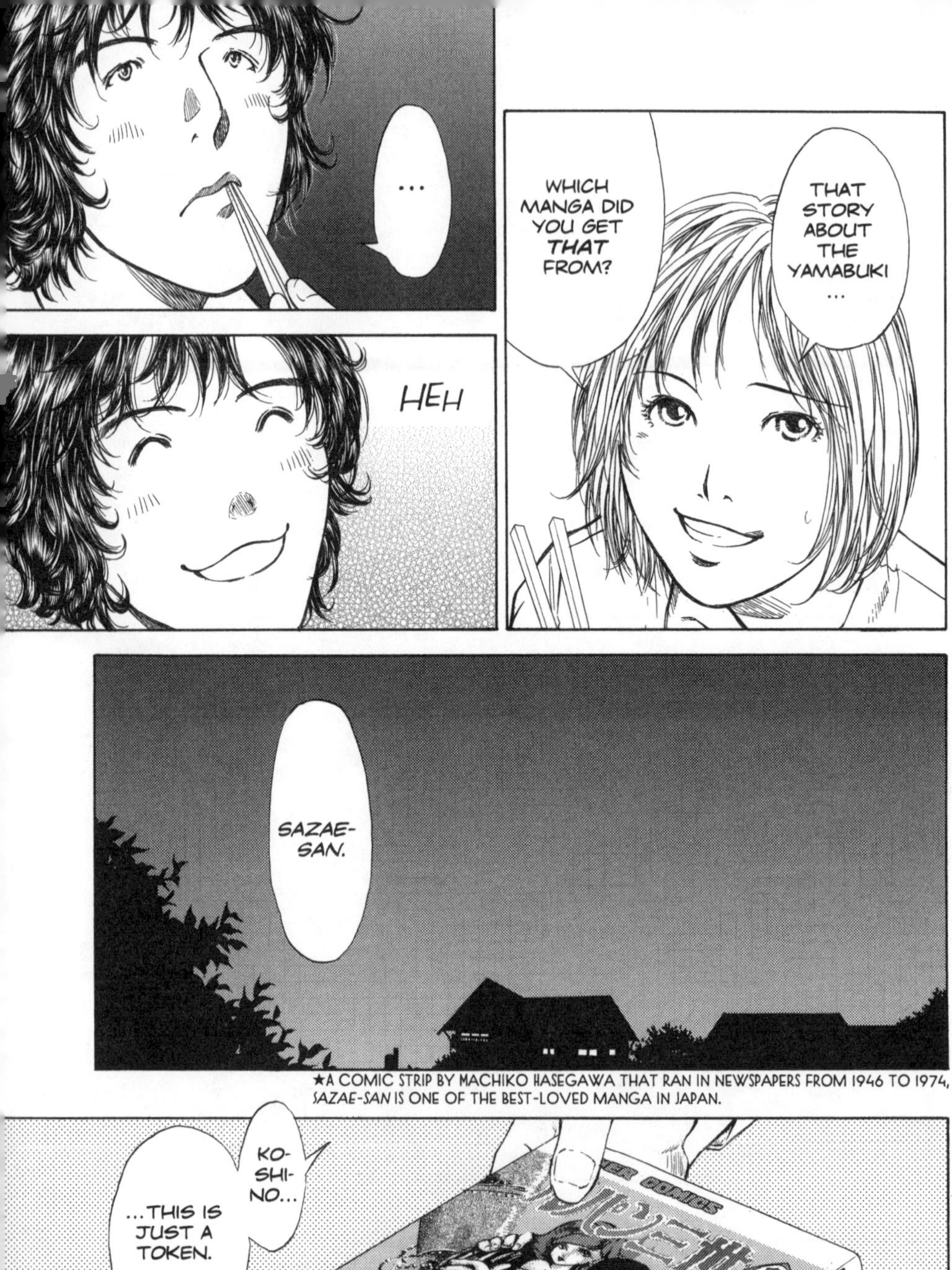
THAT STORY ABOUT THE YAMABUKI ...
WHICH MANGA DID YOU GET THAT FROM?
...
HEH
SAZAE-SAN.

★A COMIC STRIP BY MACHIKO HASEGAWA THAT RAN IN NEWSPAPERS FROM 1946 TO 1974, *SAZAE-SAN* IS ONE OF THE BEST-LOVED MANGA IN JAPAN.

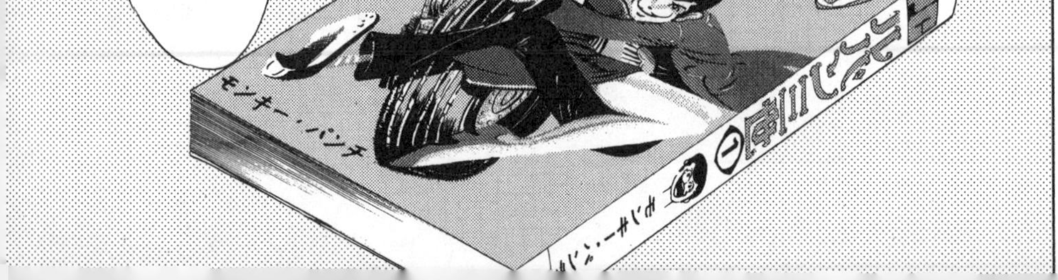
KO-SHI-NO...
...THIS IS JUST A TOKEN.

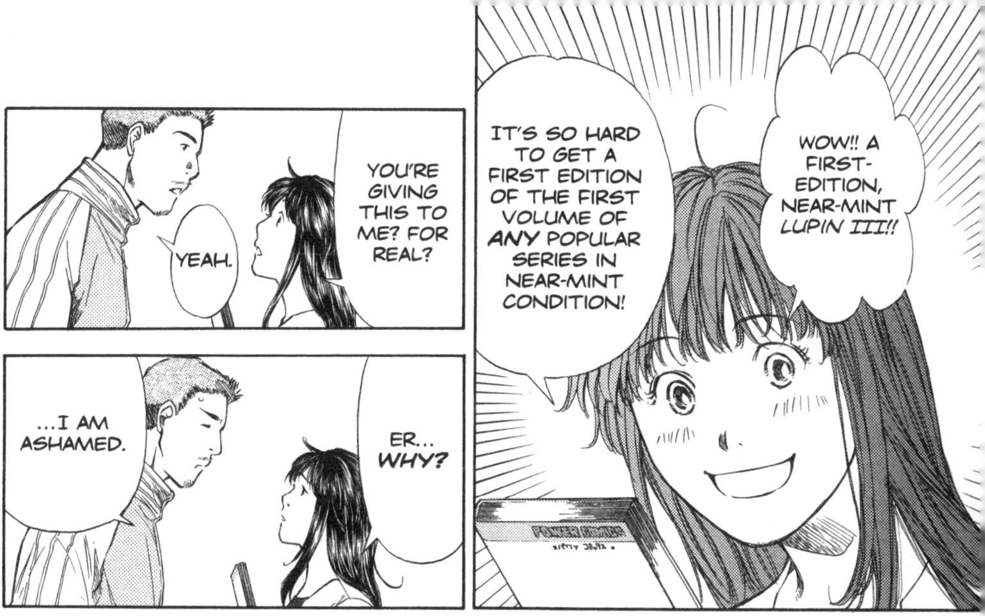
WOW!! A FIRST-EDITION, NEAR-MINT *LUPIN III*!!
IT'S SO HARD TO GET A FIRST EDITION OF THE FIRST VOLUME OF ***ANY*** POPULAR SERIES IN NEAR-MINT CONDITION!
YOU'RE GIVING THIS TO ME? FOR REAL?
YEAH.
ER... ***WHY?***
...I AM ASHAMED.

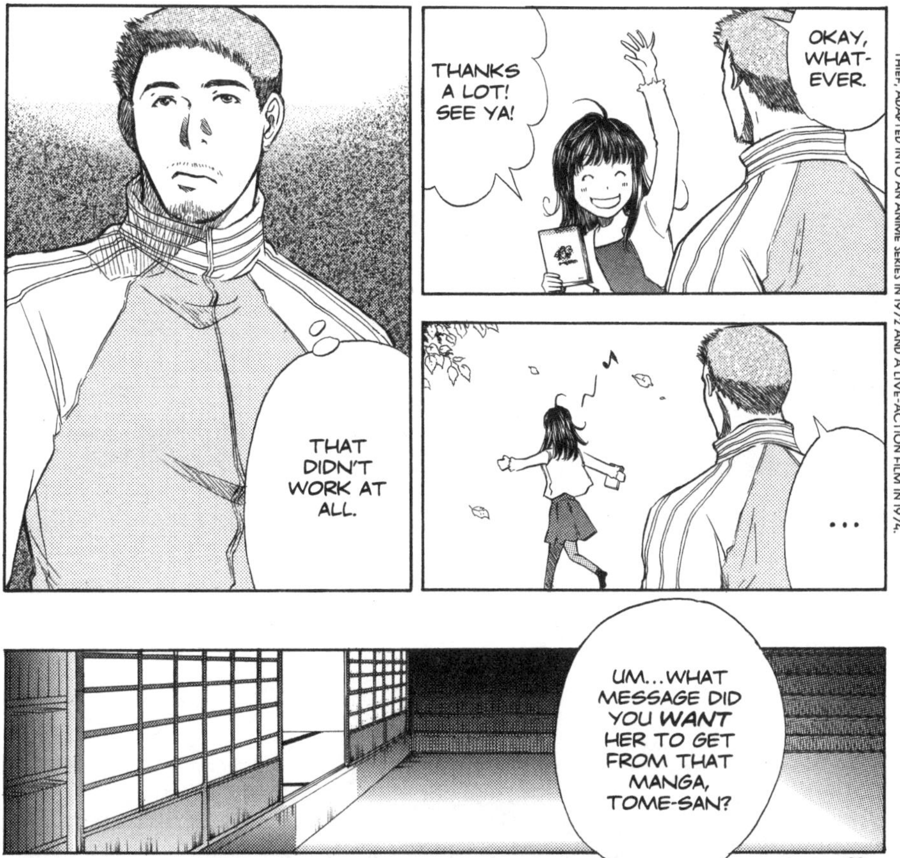
OKAY, WHAT-EVER.
THANKS A LOT! SEE YA!
...
THAT DIDN'T WORK AT ALL.
UM...WHAT MESSAGE DID YOU **WANT** HER TO GET FROM THAT MANGA, TOME-SAN?

STUDY!

LUPIN III (LUPIN SANSEI) BY MONKEY PUNCH. SERIALIZED IN THE FUTABASHA MAGAZINE *WEEKLY MANGA ACTION* FROM 1967 ONWARD. THE FIRST TANKOBON WAS PUBLISHED IN 1968. EVERYONE IN JAPAN KNOWS THIS ACTION COMEDY ABOUT AN INTERNATIONAL THIEF, ADAPTED INTO AN ANIME SERIES IN 1972 AND A LIVE-ACTION FILM IN 1974.

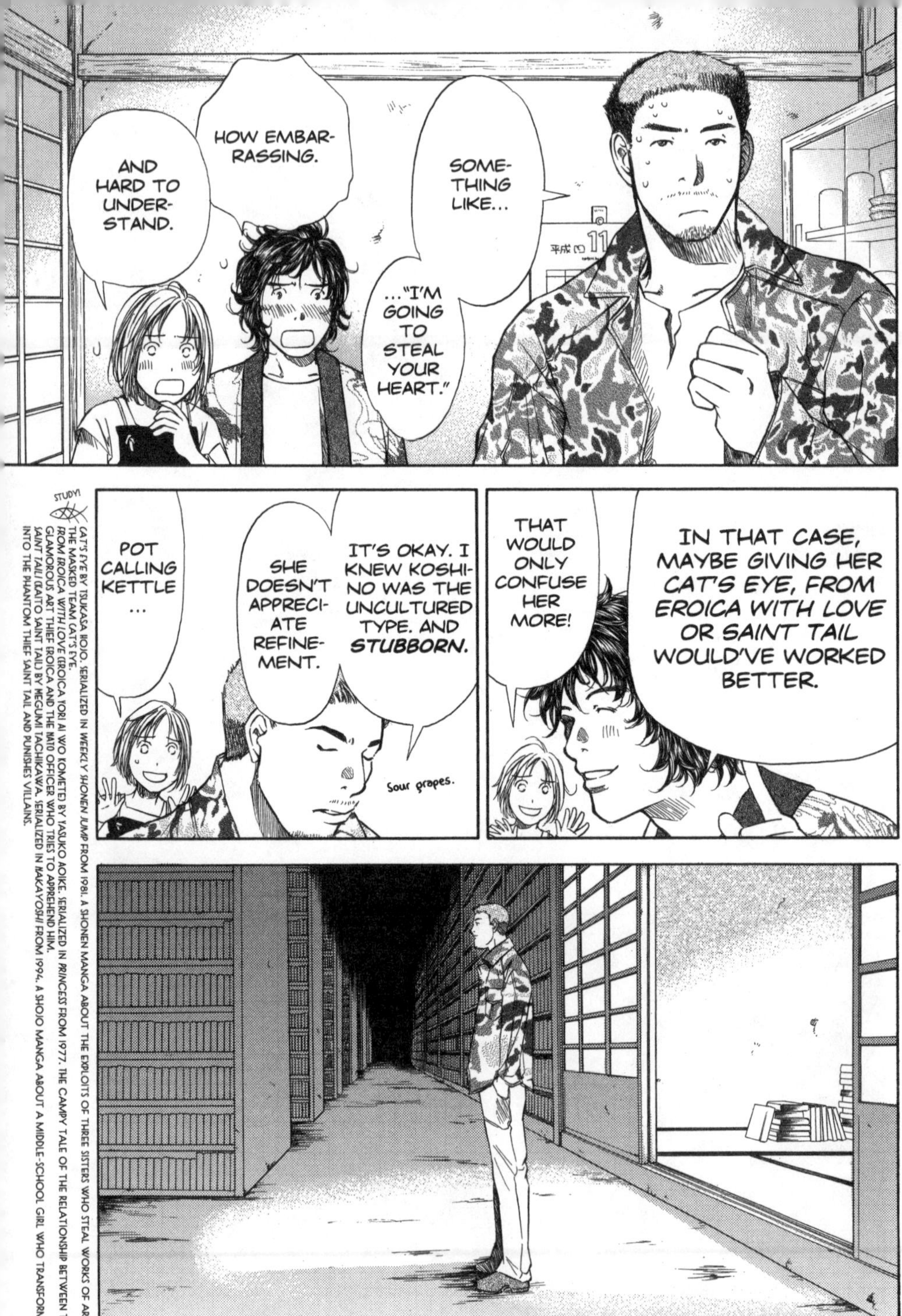
SOME-THING LIKE...
..."I'M GOING TO STEAL YOUR HEART."
HOW EMBAR-RASSING.
AND HARD TO UNDER-STAND.
IN THAT CASE, MAYBE GIVING HER CAT'S EYE, FROM EROICA WITH LOVE OR SAINT TAIL WOULD'VE WORKED BETTER.
THAT WOULD ONLY CONFUSE HER MORE!
IT'S OKAY. I KNEW KOSHI-NO WAS THE UNCULTURED TYPE. AND STUBBORN.
Sour grapes.
SHE DOESN'T APPRECI-ATE REFINE-MENT.
POT CALLING KETTLE...

STUDY!

CAT'S EYE BY TSUKASA HOJO. SERIALIZED IN *WEEKLY SHONEN JUMP* FROM 1981. A SHONEN MANGA ABOUT THE EXPLOITS OF THREE SISTERS WHO STEAL WORKS OF ART AS THE MASKED TEAM CAT'S EYE. *FROM EROICA WITH LOVE* (*EROICA YORI AI WO KOMETE*) BY YASUKO AOIKE. SERIALIZED IN *PRINCESS* FROM 1977. THE CAMPY TALE OF THE RELATIONSHIP BETWEEN THE GLAMOROUS ART THIEF EROICA AND THE NATO OFFICER WHO TRIES TO APPREHEND HIM. *SAINT TAIL* (*KAITO SAINT TAIL*) BY MEGUMI TACHIKAWA. SERIALIZED IN *NAKAYOSHI* FROM 1994. A SHOJO MANGA ABOUT A MIDDLE-SCHOOL GIRL WHO TRANSFORMS INTO THE PHANTOM THIEF SAINT TAIL AND PUNISHES VILLAINS.

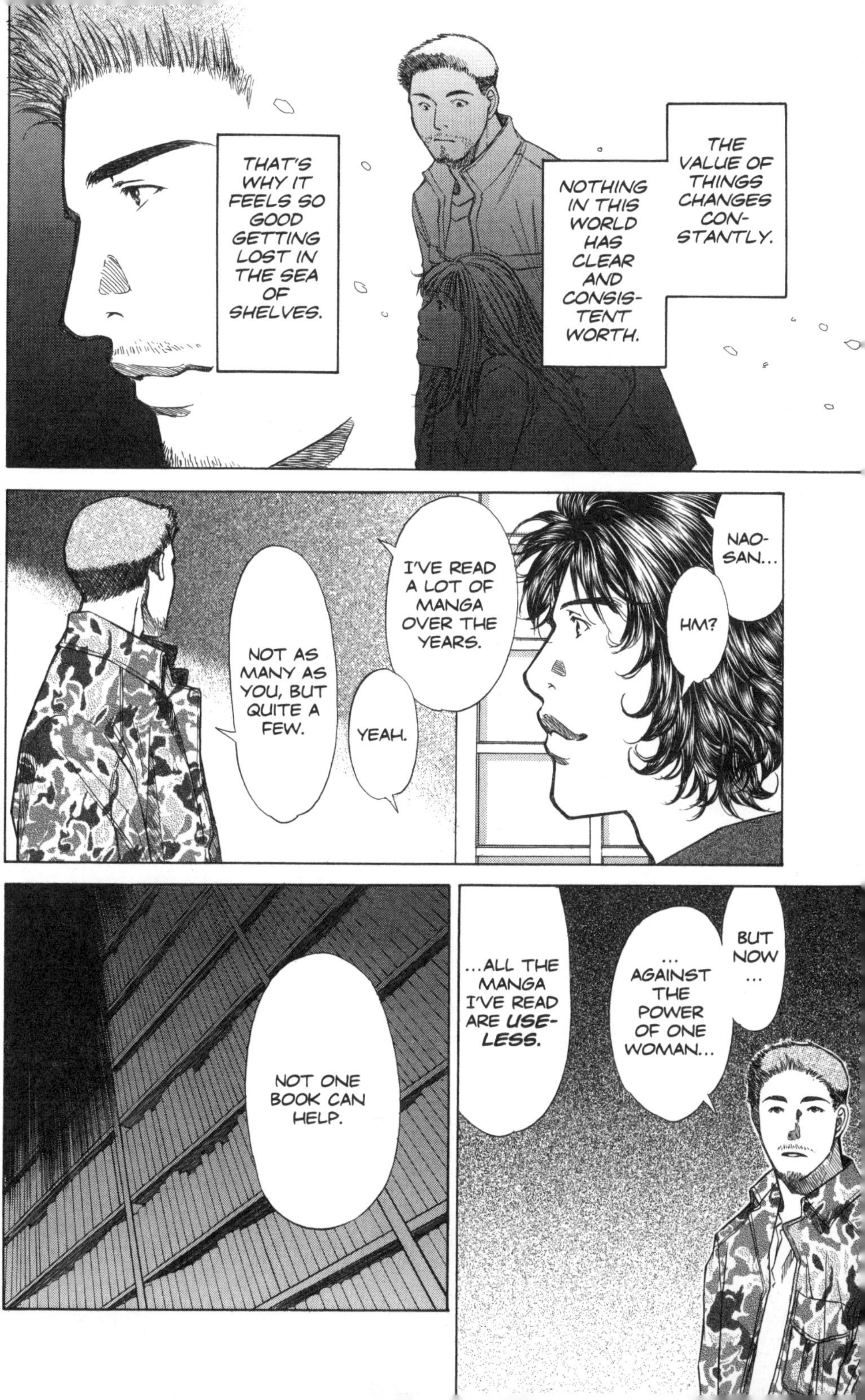
THE VALUE OF THINGS CHANGES CON-STANTLY.
NOTHING IN THIS WORLD HAS CLEAR AND CONSIS-TENT WORTH.
THAT'S WHY IT FEELS SO GOOD GETTING LOST IN THE SEA OF SHELVES.
NAO-SAN...
HM?
I'VE READ A LOT OF MANGA OVER THE YEARS.
YEAH.
NOT AS MANY AS YOU, BUT QUITE A FEW.
BUT NOW...
...AGAINST THE POWER OF ONE WOMAN...
...ALL THE MANGA I'VE READ ARE ***USE-LESS.***
NOT ONE BOOK CAN HELP.

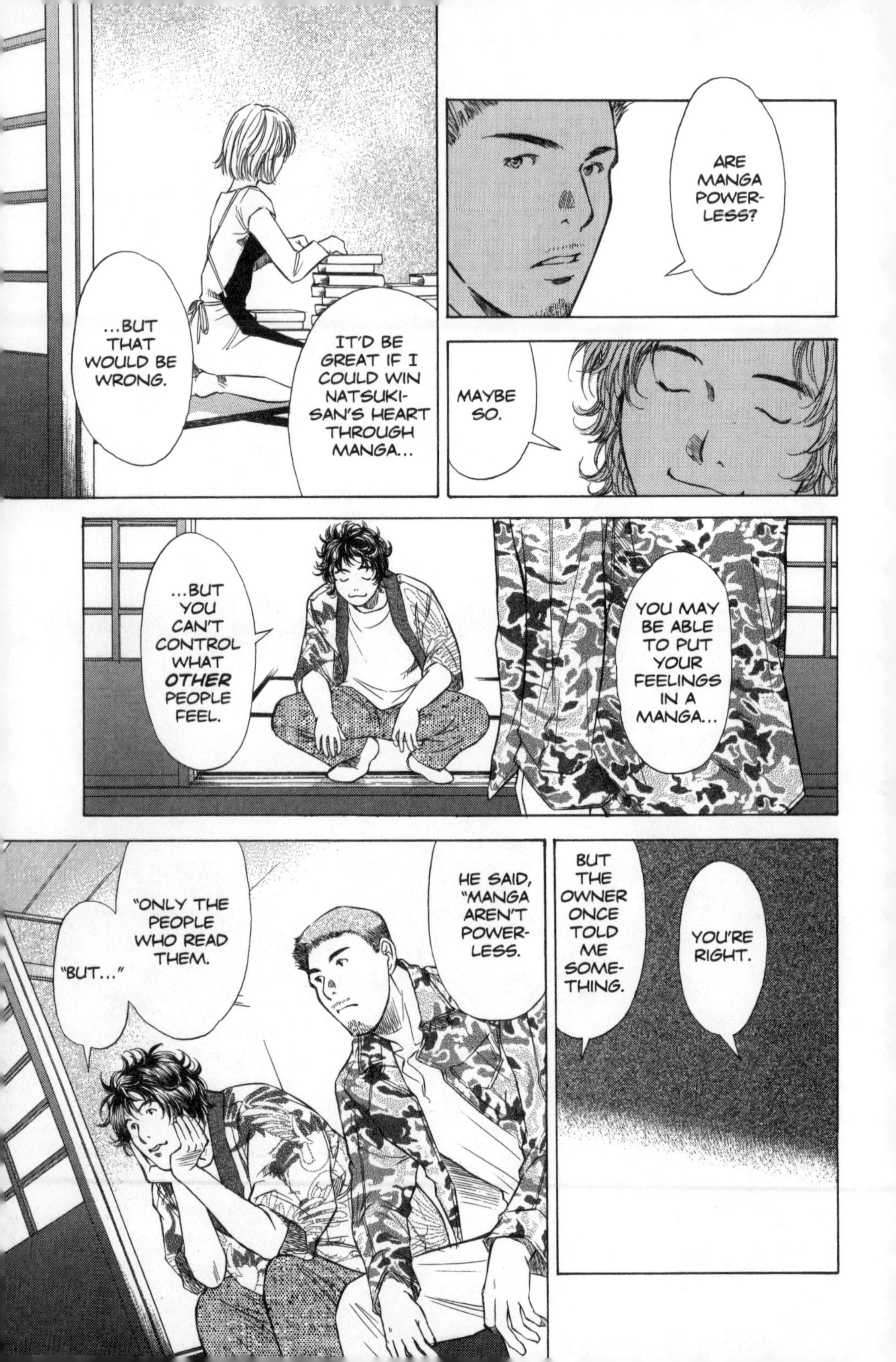
ARE MANGA POWER-LESS?
MAYBE SO.
IT'D BE GREAT IF I COULD WIN NATSUKI-SAN'S HEART THROUGH MANGA...
...BUT THAT WOULD BE WRONG.
YOU MAY BE ABLE TO PUT YOUR FEELINGS IN A MANGA...
...BUT YOU CAN'T CONTROL WHAT OTHER PEOPLE FEEL.
YOU'RE RIGHT.
BUT THE OWNER ONCE TOLD ME SOME-THING.
HE SAID, "MANGA AREN'T POWER-LESS.
"ONLY THE PEOPLE WHO READ THEM.
"BUT..."

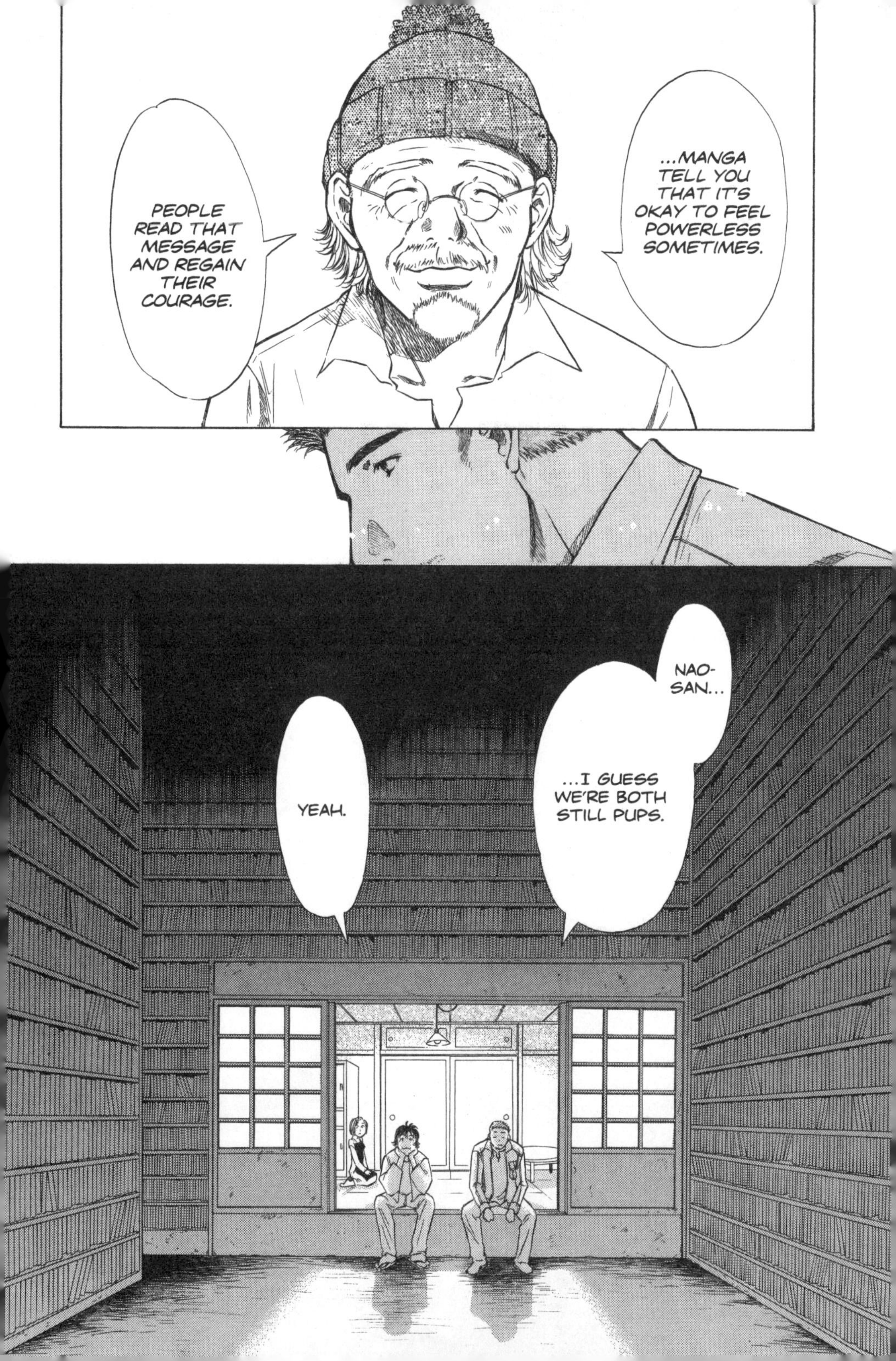
...MANGA TELL YOU THAT IT'S OKAY TO FEEL POWERLESS SOMETIMES.
PEOPLE READ THAT MESSAGE AND REGAIN THEIR COURAGE.
NAO-SAN...
...I GUESS WE'RE BOTH STILL PUPS.
YEAH.

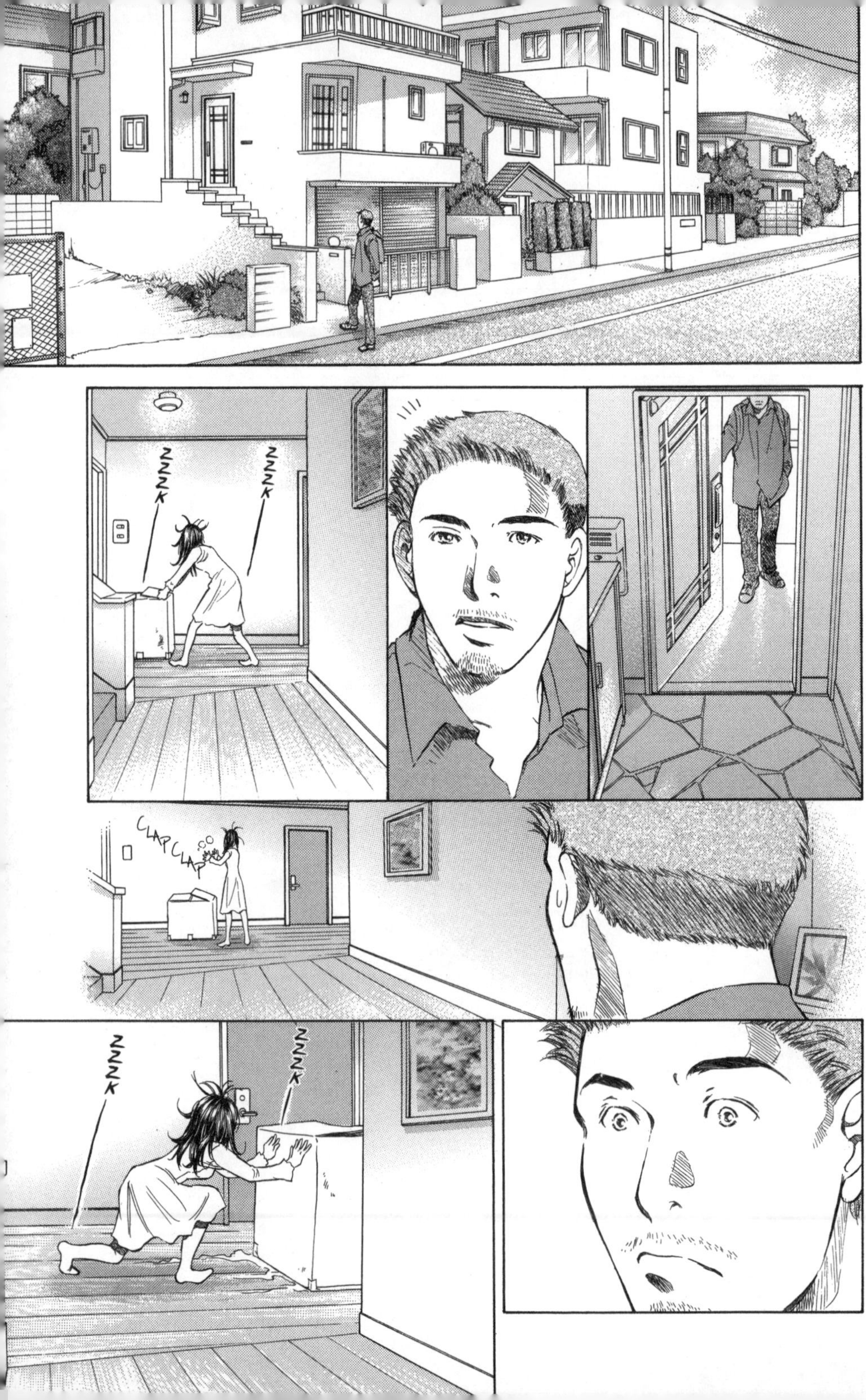
ZZZK
ZZZK
CLAP CLAP
ZZZK
ZZZK

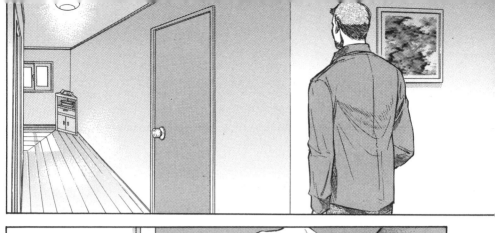

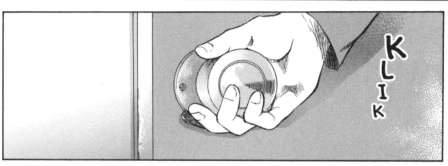

KLIK

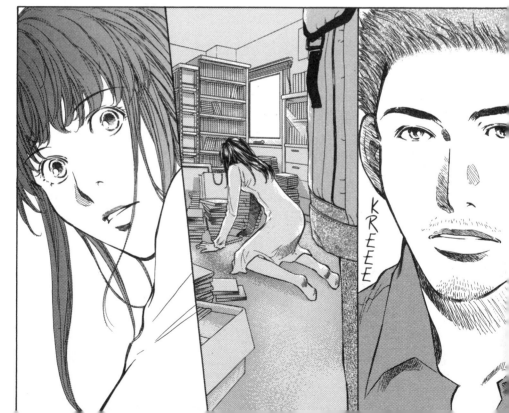

KREEE

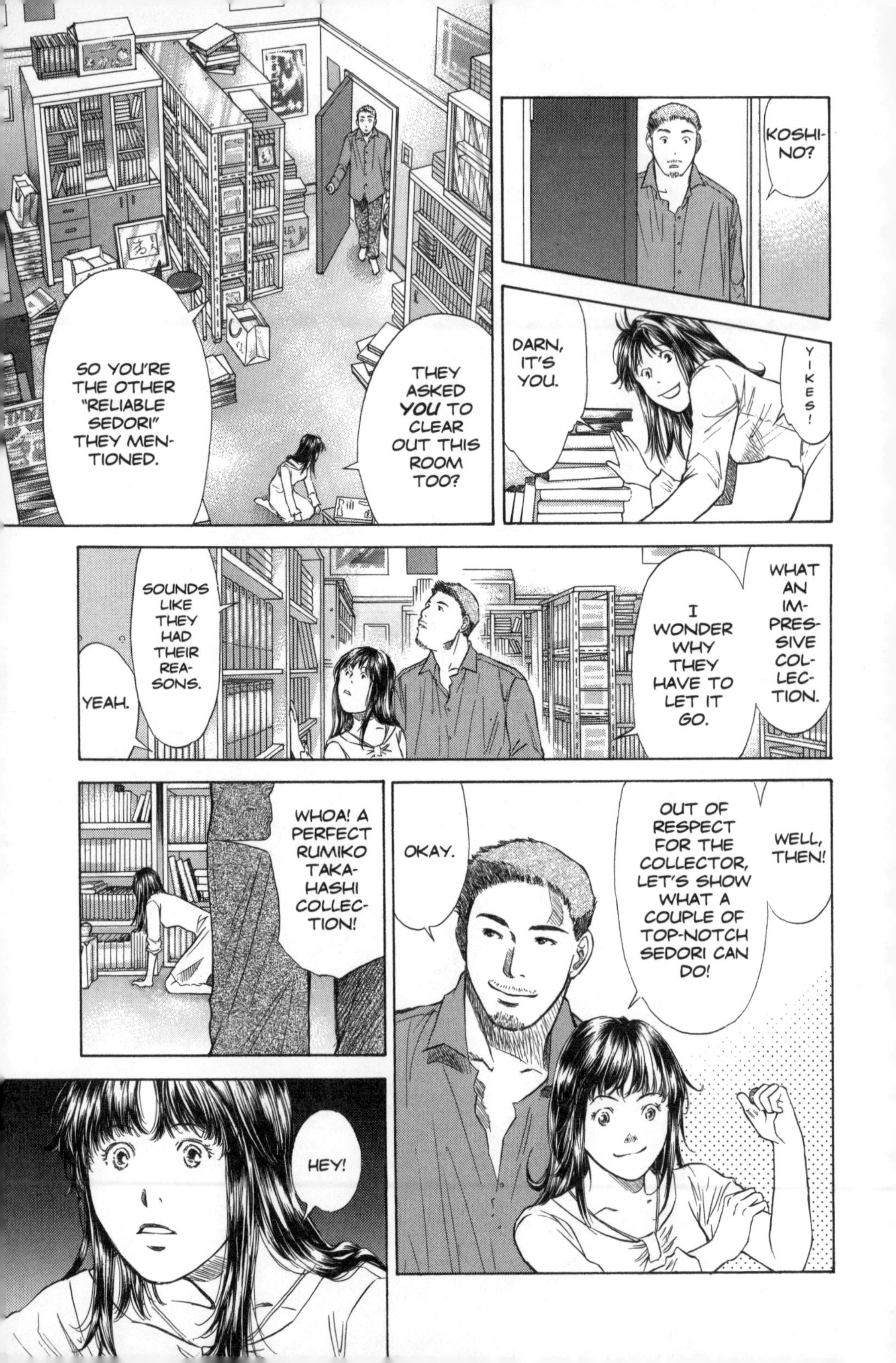
KOSHINO?
YIKES!
DARN, IT'S YOU.
THEY ASKED **YOU** TO CLEAR OUT THIS ROOM TOO?
SO YOU'RE THE OTHER "RELIABLE SEDORI" THEY MENTIONED.
WHAT AN IMPRESSIVE COLLECTION.
I WONDER WHY THEY HAVE TO LET IT GO.
SOUNDS LIKE THEY HAD THEIR REASONS.
YEAH.
WELL, THEN!
OUT OF RESPECT FOR THE COLLECTOR, LET'S SHOW WHAT A COUPLE OF TOP-NOTCH SEDORI CAN DO!
OKAY.
WHOA! A PERFECT RUMIKO TAKAHASHI COLLECTION!
HEY!

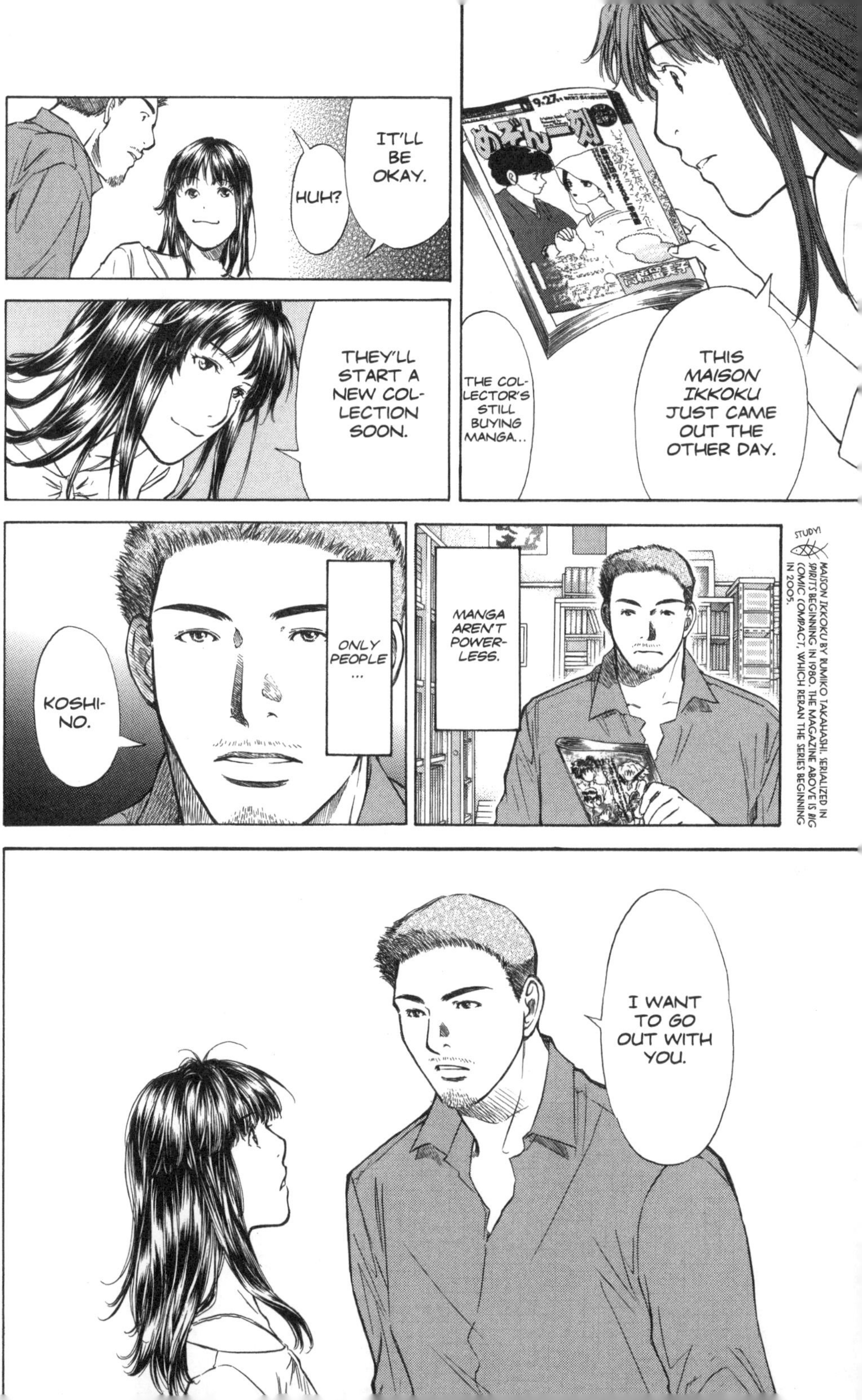
THIS MAISON IKKOKU JUST CAME OUT THE OTHER DAY.
THE COLLECTOR'S STILL BUYING MANGA...
IT'LL BE OKAY.
HUH?
THEY'LL START A NEW COLLECTION SOON.
MANGA AREN'T POWERLESS.
ONLY PEOPLE ...
KOSHINO.
I WANT TO GO OUT WITH YOU.

STUDY!
MAISON IKKOKU BY RUMIKO TAKAHASHI. SERIALIZED IN SPIRITS BEGINNING IN 1980. THE MAGAZINE ABOVE IS BIG COMIC COMPACT, WHICH RERAN THE SERIES BEGINNING IN 2005.

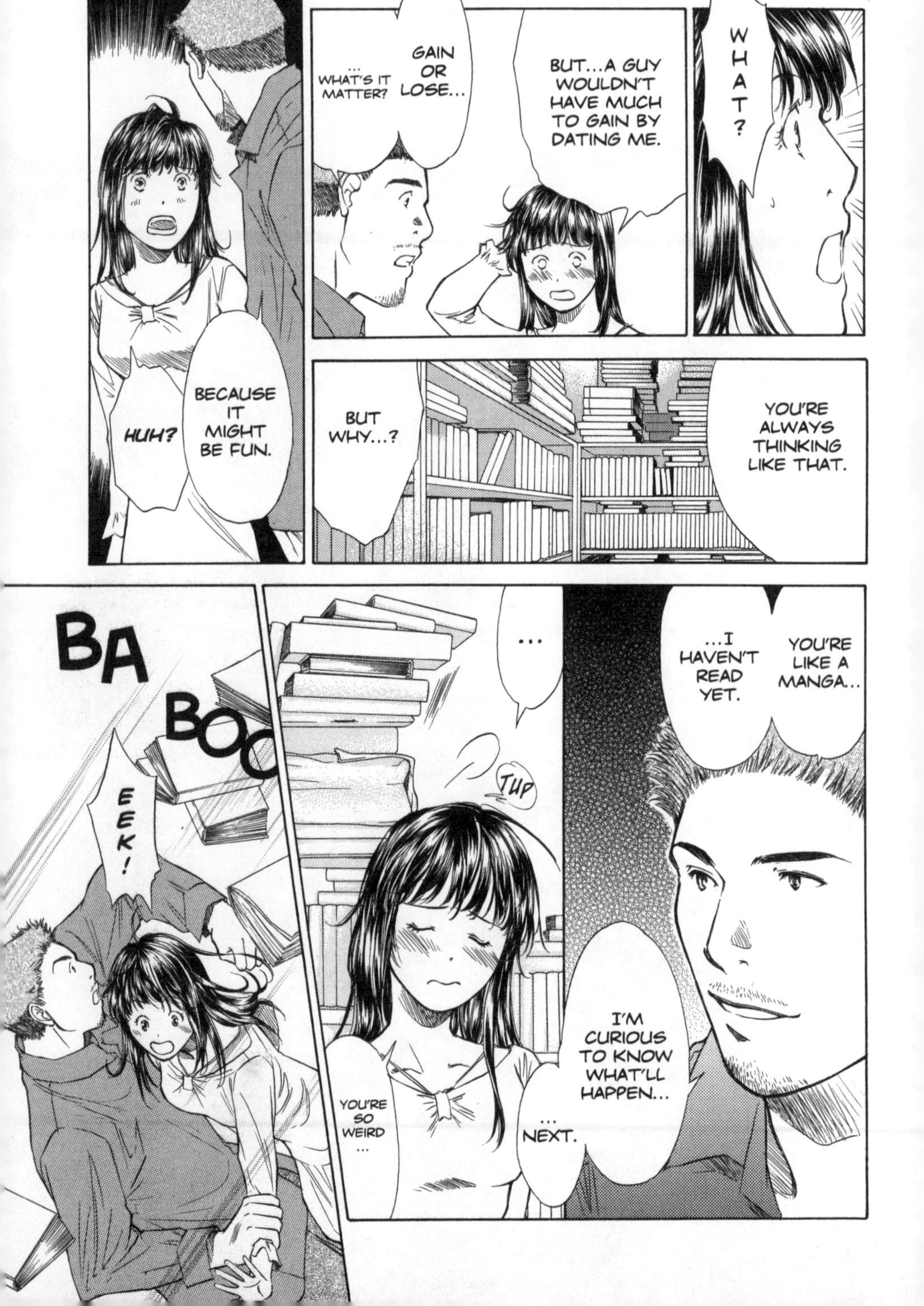
WHAT?
BUT...A GUY WOULDN'T HAVE MUCH TO GAIN BY DATING ME.
GAIN OR LOSE...
...WHAT'S IT MATTER?
YOU'RE ALWAYS THINKING LIKE THAT.
BUT WHY...?
BECAUSE IT MIGHT BE FUN.
HUH?
YOU'RE LIKE A MANGA...
...I HAVEN'T READ YET.
...
TUP
I'M CURIOUS TO KNOW WHAT'LL HAPPEN...
...NEXT.
YOU'RE SO WEIRD...
BA
BOO
EEK!

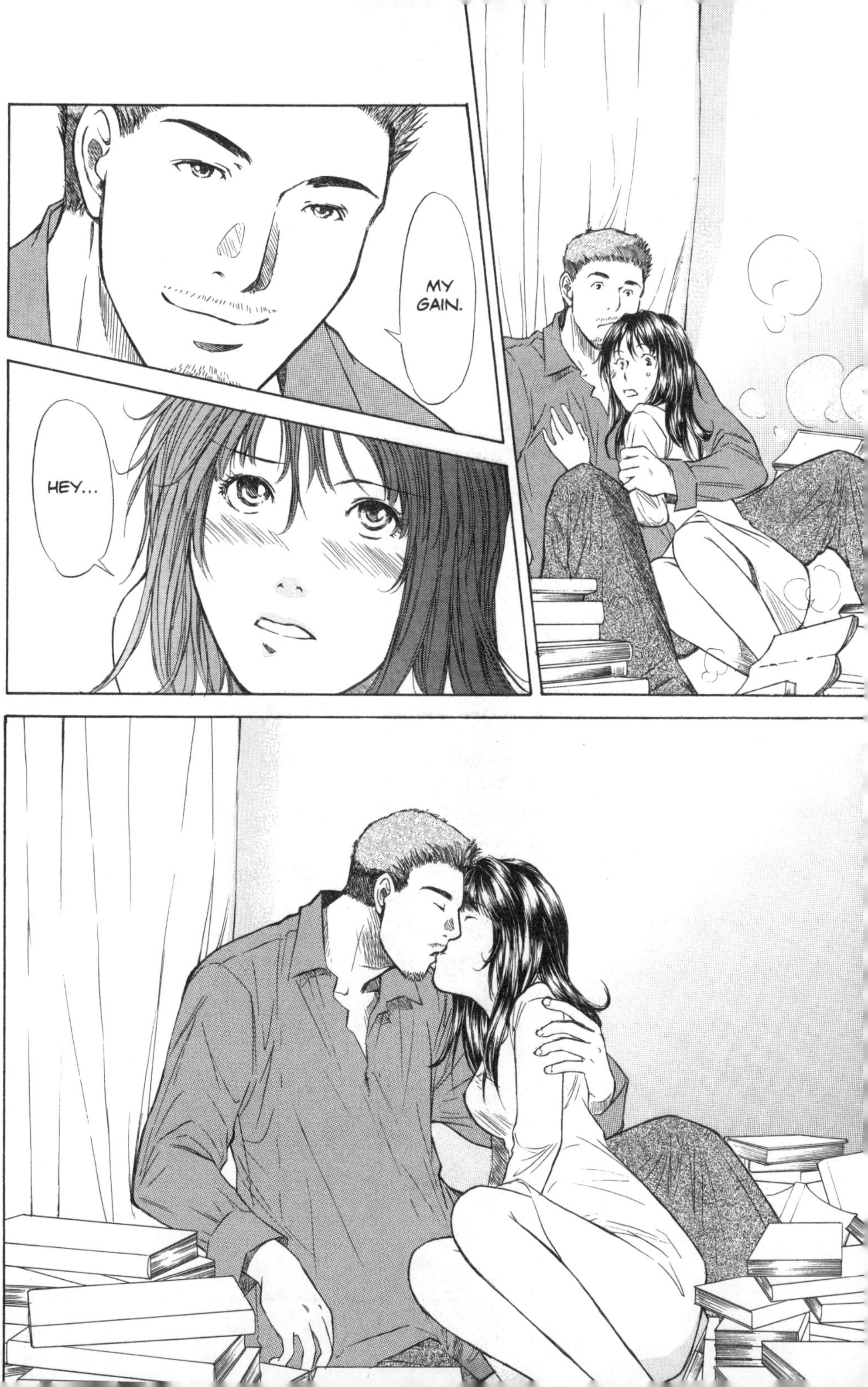
MY GAIN.
HEY...

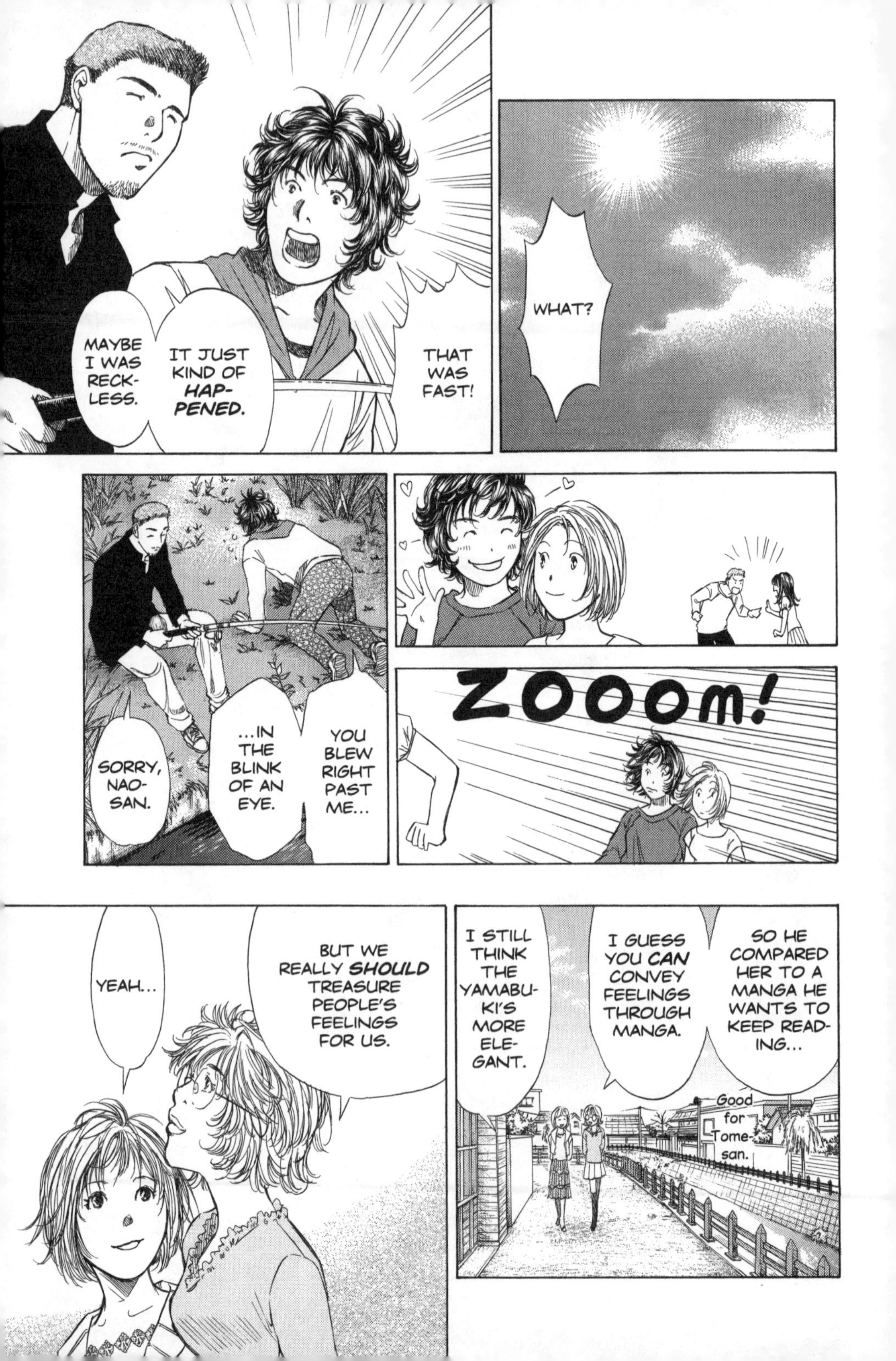
WHAT?
THAT WAS FAST!
IT JUST KIND OF HAPPENED.
MAYBE I WAS RECKLESS.
ZOOOM!
YOU BLEW RIGHT PAST ME...
...IN THE BLINK OF AN EYE.
SORRY, NAO-SAN.
SO HE COMPARED HER TO A MANGA HE WANTS TO KEEP READING...
I GUESS YOU CAN CONVEY FEELINGS THROUGH MANGA.
I STILL THINK THE YAMABUKI'S MORE ELEGANT.
Good for Tome-san.
BUT WE REALLY SHOULD TREASURE PEOPLE'S FEELINGS FOR US.
YEAH...

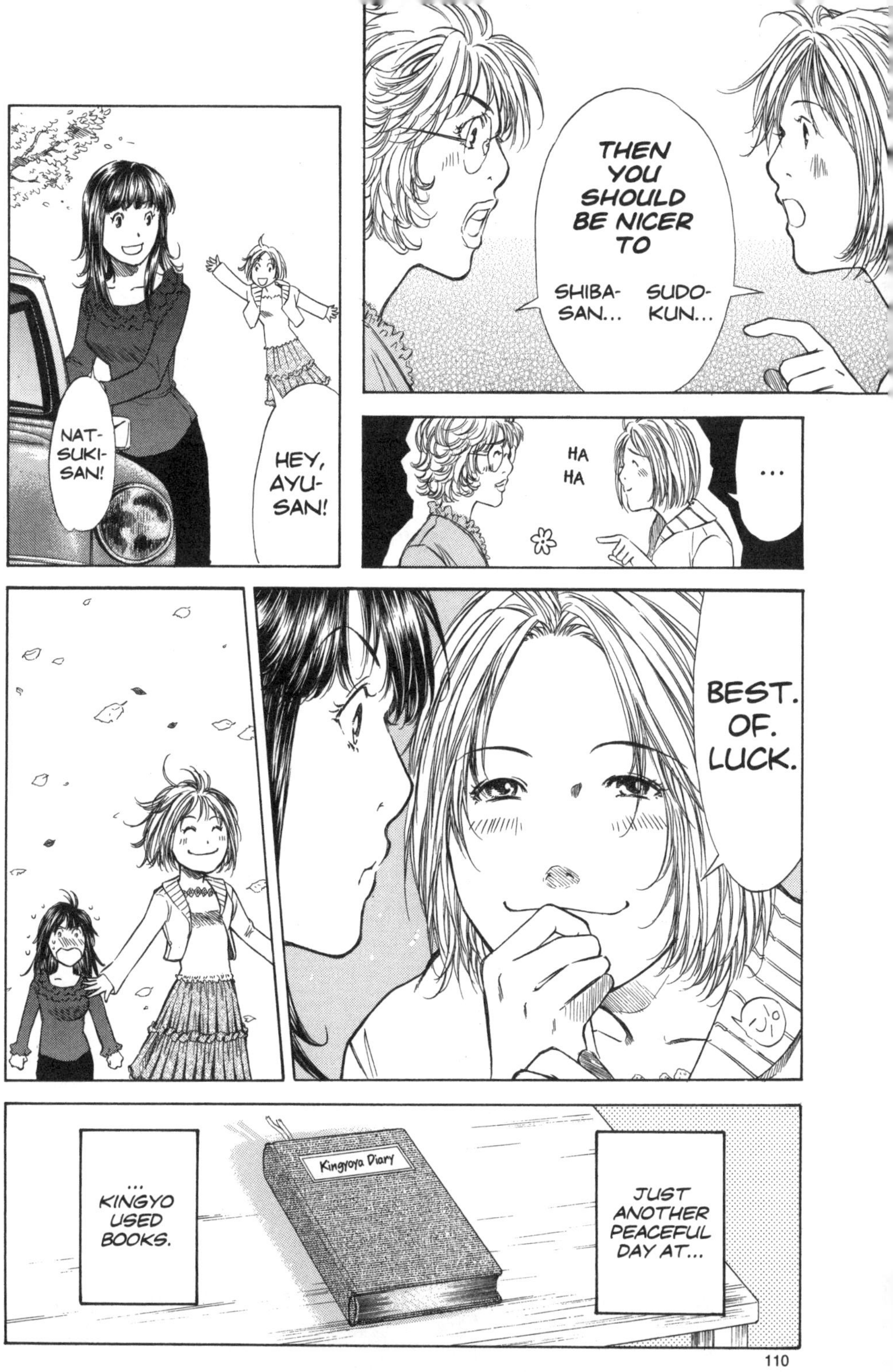
THEN YOU SHOULD BE NICER TO
SHIBA-SAN...
SUDO-KUN...
...
HA HA
HEY, AYU-SAN!
NAT-SUKI-SAN!
BEST. OF. LUCK.
JUST ANOTHER PEACEFUL DAY AT...
Kingyoya Diary
...KINGYO USED BOOKS.

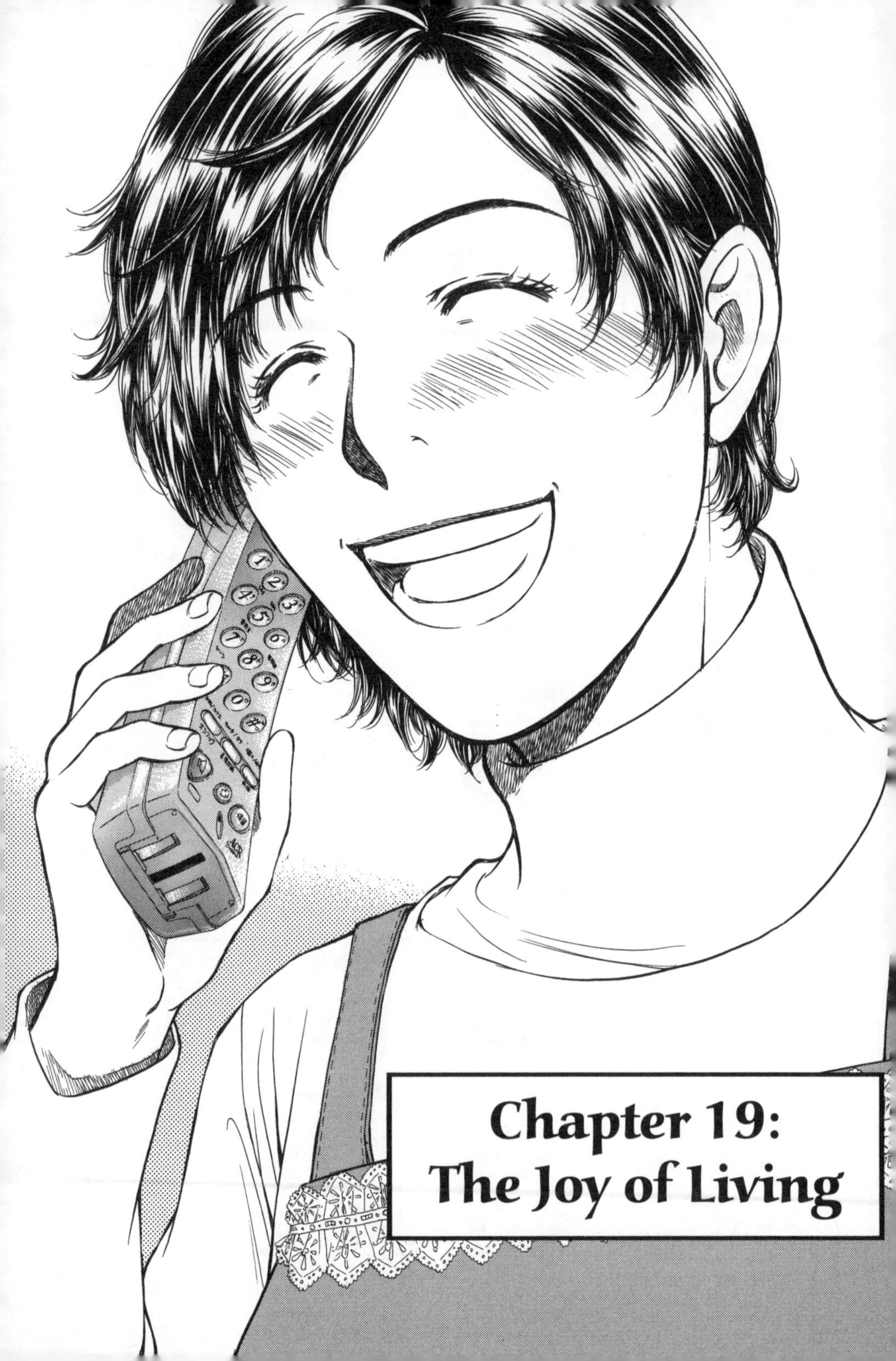

Chapter 19: The Joy of Living

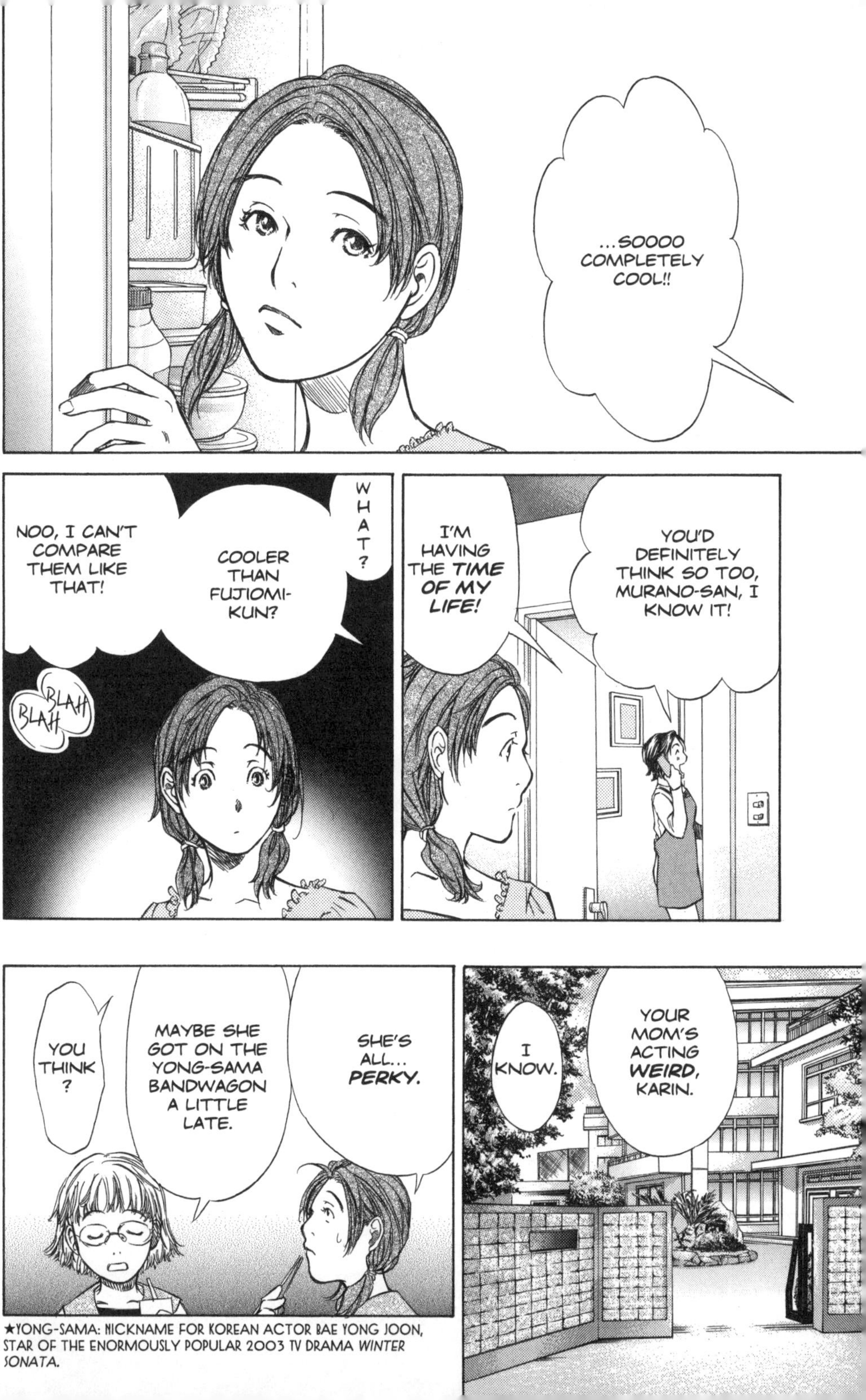
...SOOOO COMPLETELY COOL!!
YOU'D DEFINITELY THINK SO TOO, MURANO-SAN, I KNOW IT!
I'M HAVING THE *TIME OF MY LIFE!*
WHAT?
COOLER THAN FUJIOMI-KUN?
NOO, I CAN'T COMPARE THEM LIKE THAT!
BLAH BLAH
YOUR MOM'S ACTING *WEIRD,* KARIN.
I KNOW.
SHE'S ALL... *PERKY.*
MAYBE SHE GOT ON THE YONG-SAMA BANDWAGON A LITTLE LATE.
YOU THINK?

★YONG-SAMA: NICKNAME FOR KOREAN ACTOR BAE YONG JOON, STAR OF THE ENORMOUSLY POPULAR 2003 TV DRAMA *WINTER SONATA.*

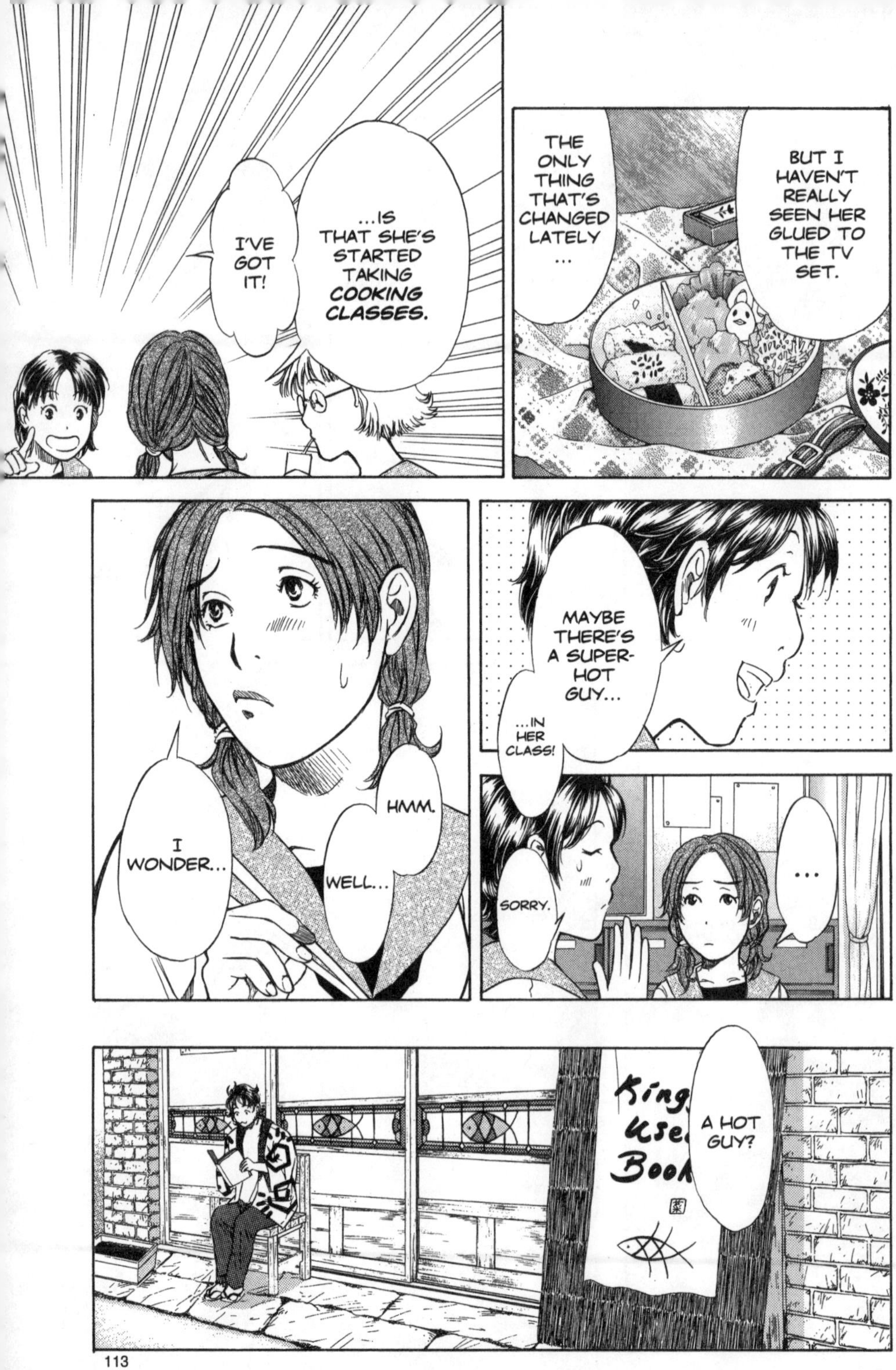
BUT I HAVEN'T REALLY SEEN HER GLUED TO THE TV SET.
THE ONLY THING THAT'S CHANGED LATELY ...
...IS THAT SHE'S STARTED TAKING **COOKING CLASSES.**
I'VE GOT IT!
MAYBE THERE'S A SUPER-HOT GUY...
...IN HER CLASS!
...
SORRY.
HMM.
WELL...
I WONDER...
A HOT GUY?

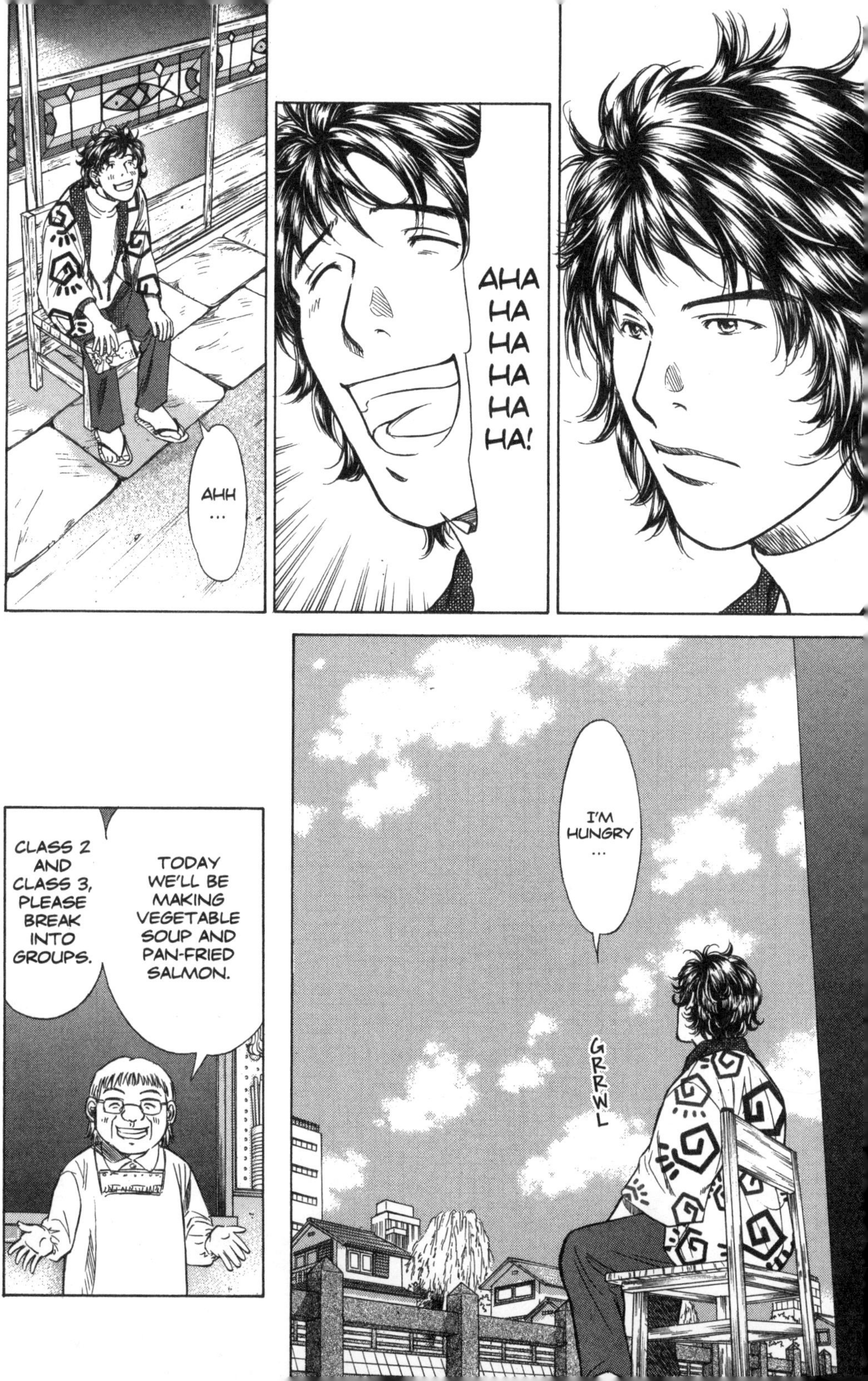
AHA HA HA HA HA HA!
AHH ...
I'M HUNGRY ...
GRRWL
TODAY WE'LL BE MAKING VEGETABLE SOUP AND PAN-FRIED SALMON.
CLASS 2 AND CLASS 3, PLEASE BREAK INTO GROUPS.

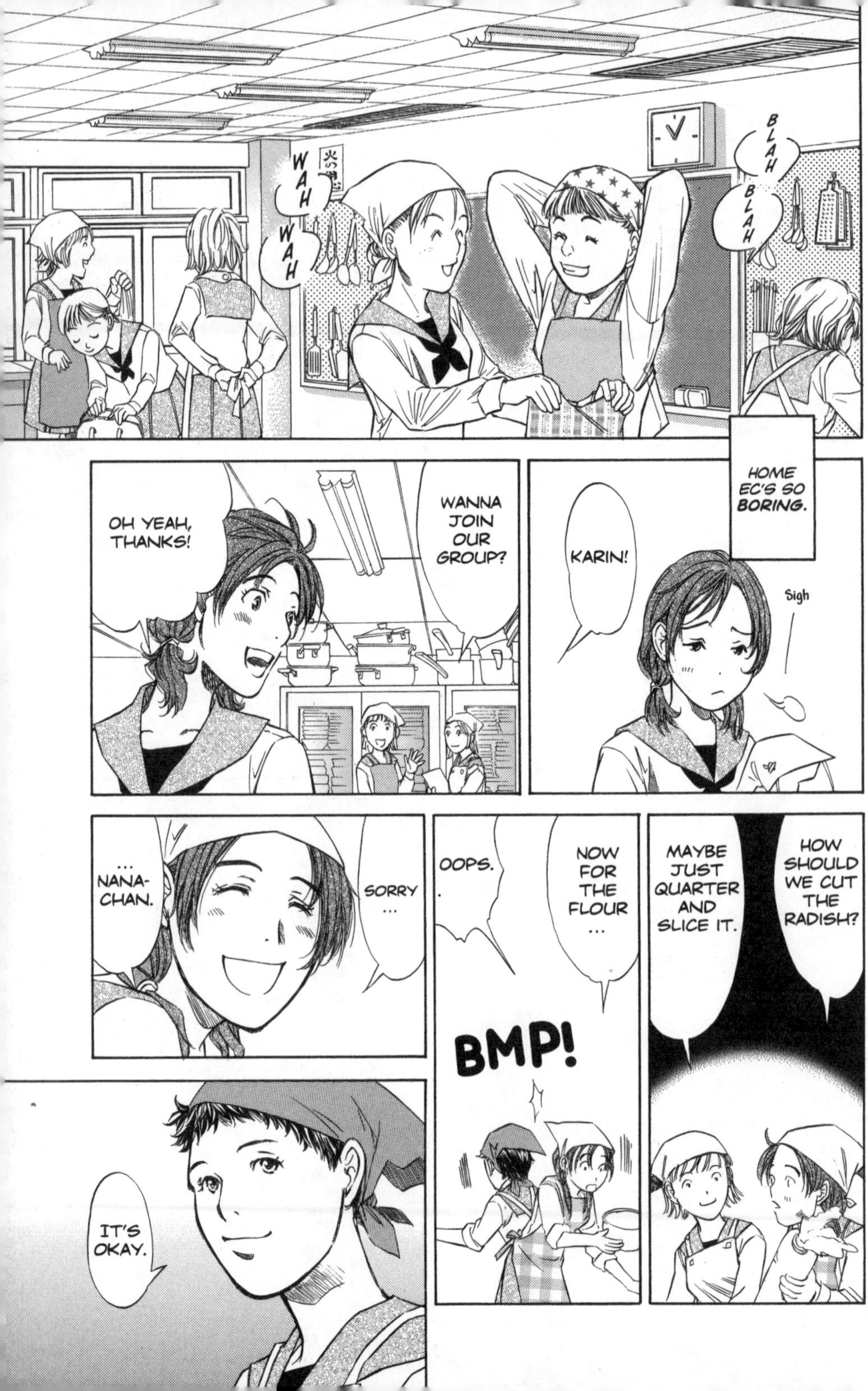
BLAH BLAH
WAH WAH
HOME EC'S SO BORING.
Sigh
KARIN!
WANNA JOIN OUR GROUP?
OH YEAH, THANKS!
HOW SHOULD WE CUT THE RADISH?
MAYBE JUST QUARTER AND SLICE IT.
NOW FOR THE FLOUR...
OOPS.
BMP!
SORRY...
... NANA-CHAN.
IT'S OKAY.

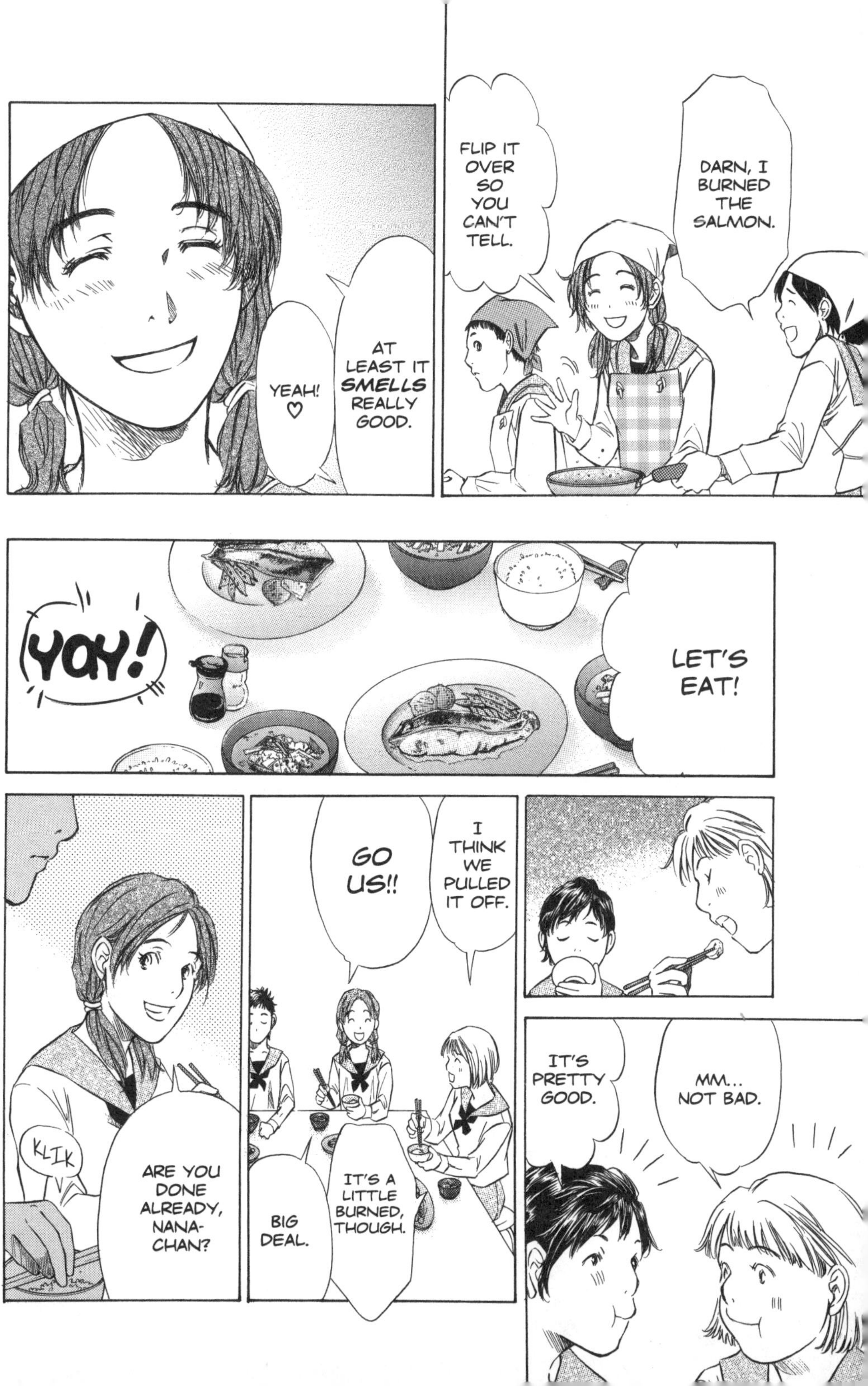
DARN, I BURNED THE SALMON.
FLIP IT OVER SO YOU CAN'T TELL.
AT LEAST IT SMELLS REALLY GOOD.
YEAH! ♡
LET'S EAT!
YAY!
MM... NOT BAD.
IT'S PRETTY GOOD.
I THINK WE PULLED IT OFF.
GO US!!
IT'S A LITTLE BURNED, THOUGH.
BIG DEAL.
ARE YOU DONE ALREADY, NANA-CHAN?
KLIK

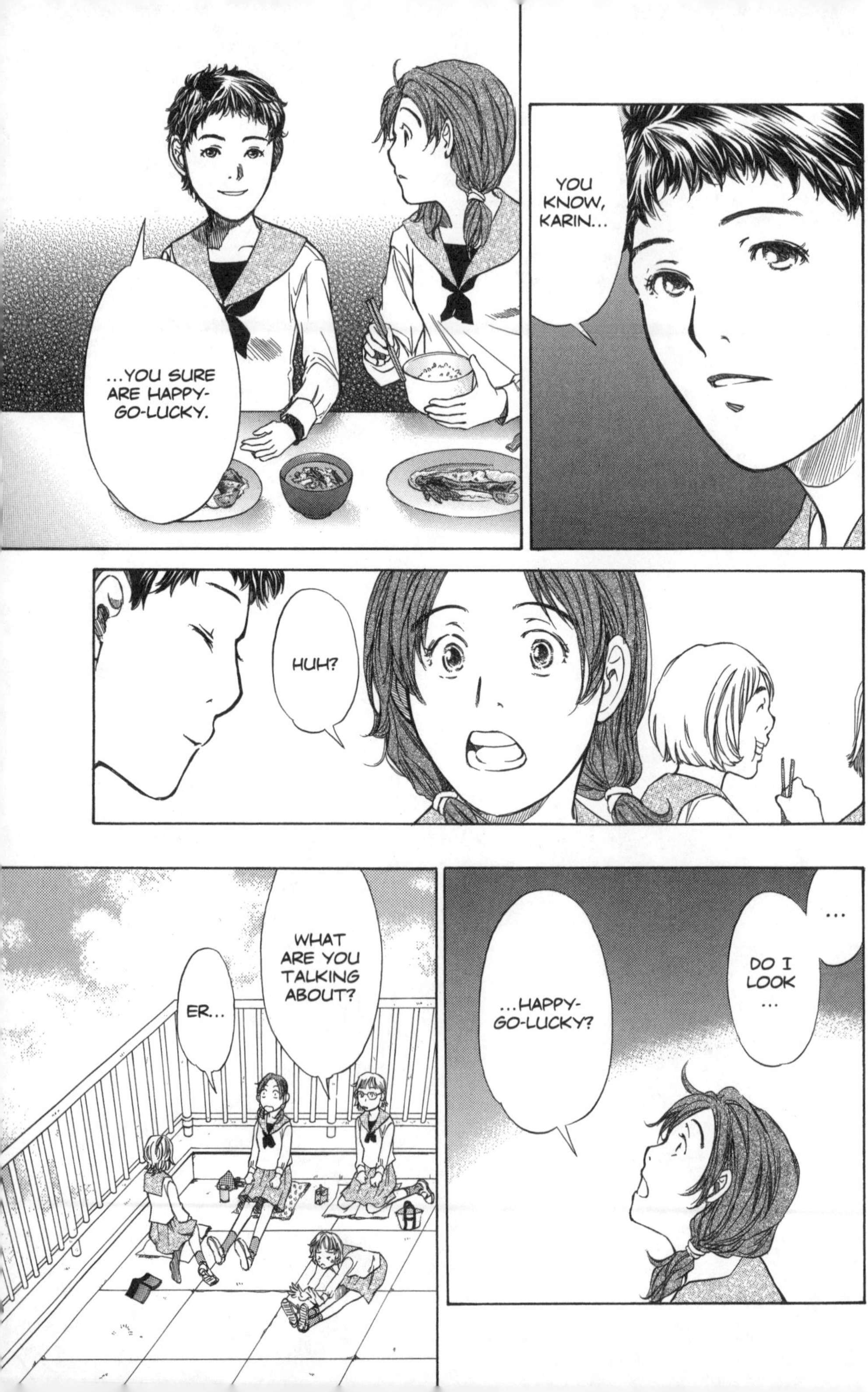
YOU KNOW, KARIN...
...YOU SURE ARE HAPPY-GO-LUCKY.
HUH?
...
DO I LOOK ...
...HAPPY-GO-LUCKY?
WHAT ARE YOU TALKING ABOUT?
ER...

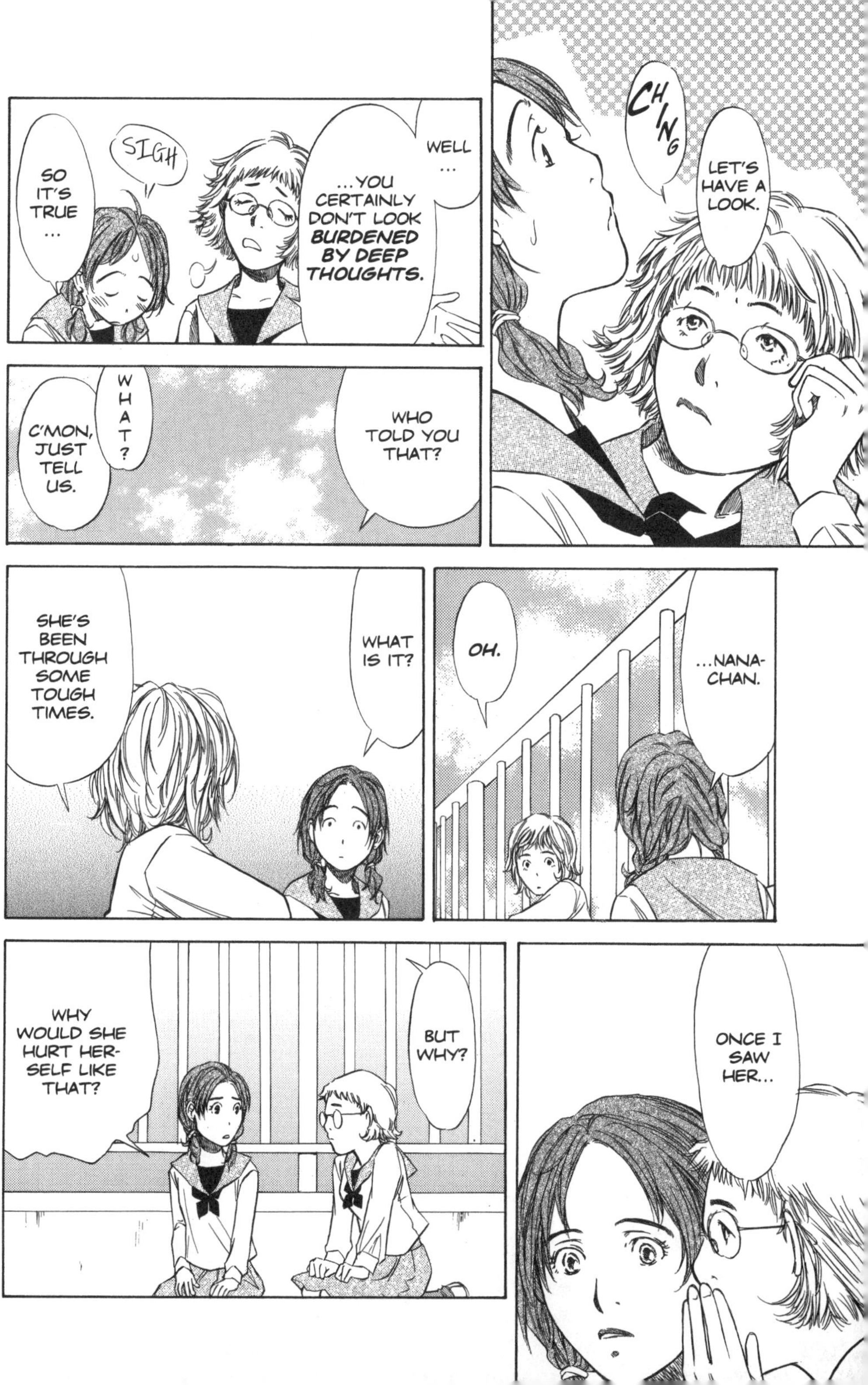
CHING
LET'S HAVE A LOOK.
WELL...
...YOU CERTAINLY DON'T LOOK **BURDENED BY DEEP THOUGHTS.**
SIGH
SO IT'S TRUE...
WHO TOLD YOU THAT?
WHAT?
C'MON, JUST TELL US.
...NANA-CHAN.
OH.
WHAT IS IT?
SHE'S BEEN THROUGH SOME TOUGH TIMES.
ONCE I SAW HER...
BUT WHY?
WHY WOULD SHE HURT HER-SELF LIKE THAT?

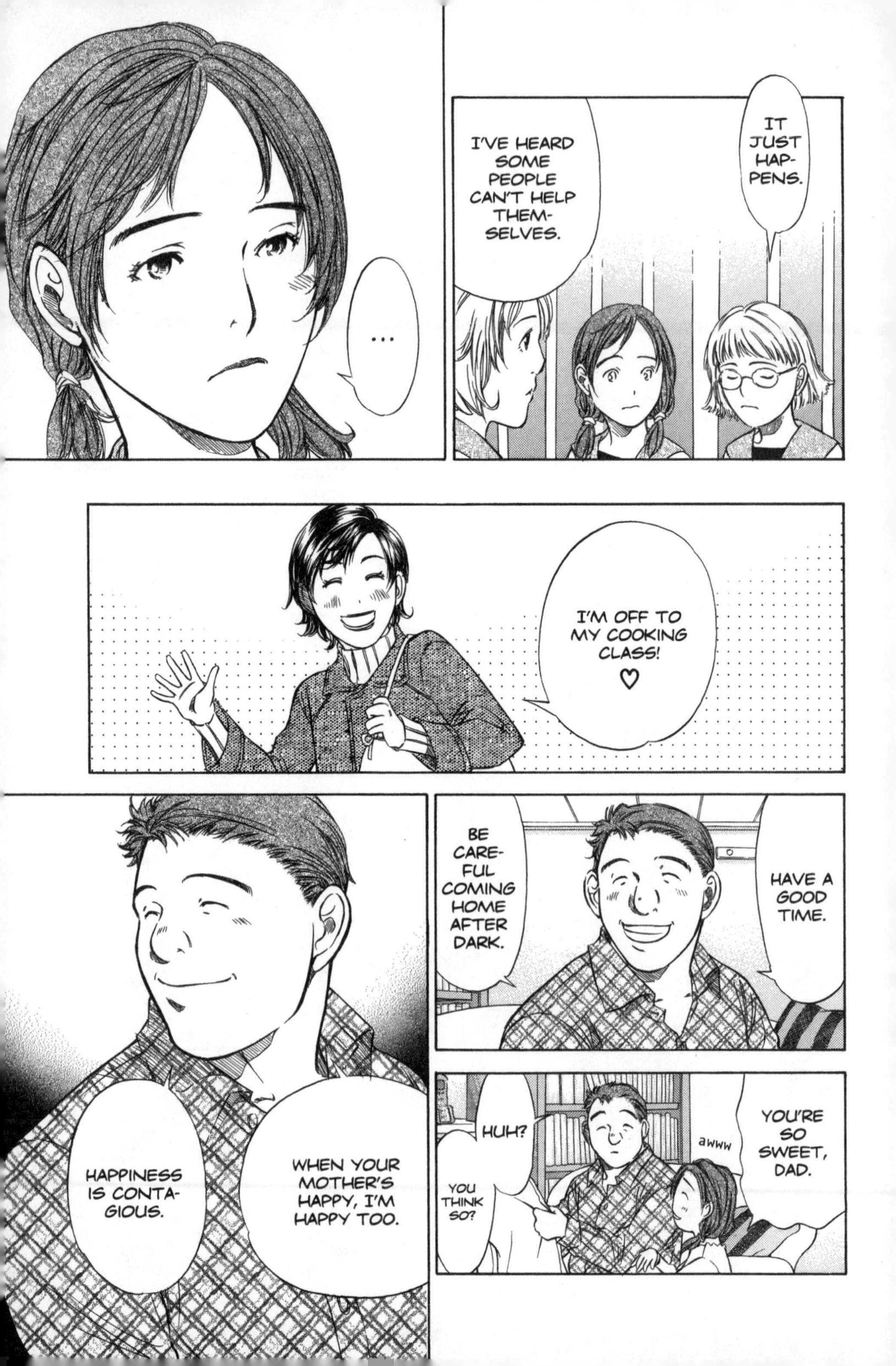
IT JUST HAP-PENS.
I'VE HEARD SOME PEOPLE CAN'T HELP THEM-SELVES.
...
I'M OFF TO MY COOKING CLASS! ♡
HAVE A GOOD TIME.
BE CARE-FUL COMING HOME AFTER DARK.
YOU'RE SO SWEET, DAD.
awww
HUH?
YOU THINK SO?
WHEN YOUR MOTHER'S HAPPY, I'M HAPPY TOO.
HAPPINESS IS CONTA-GIOUS.

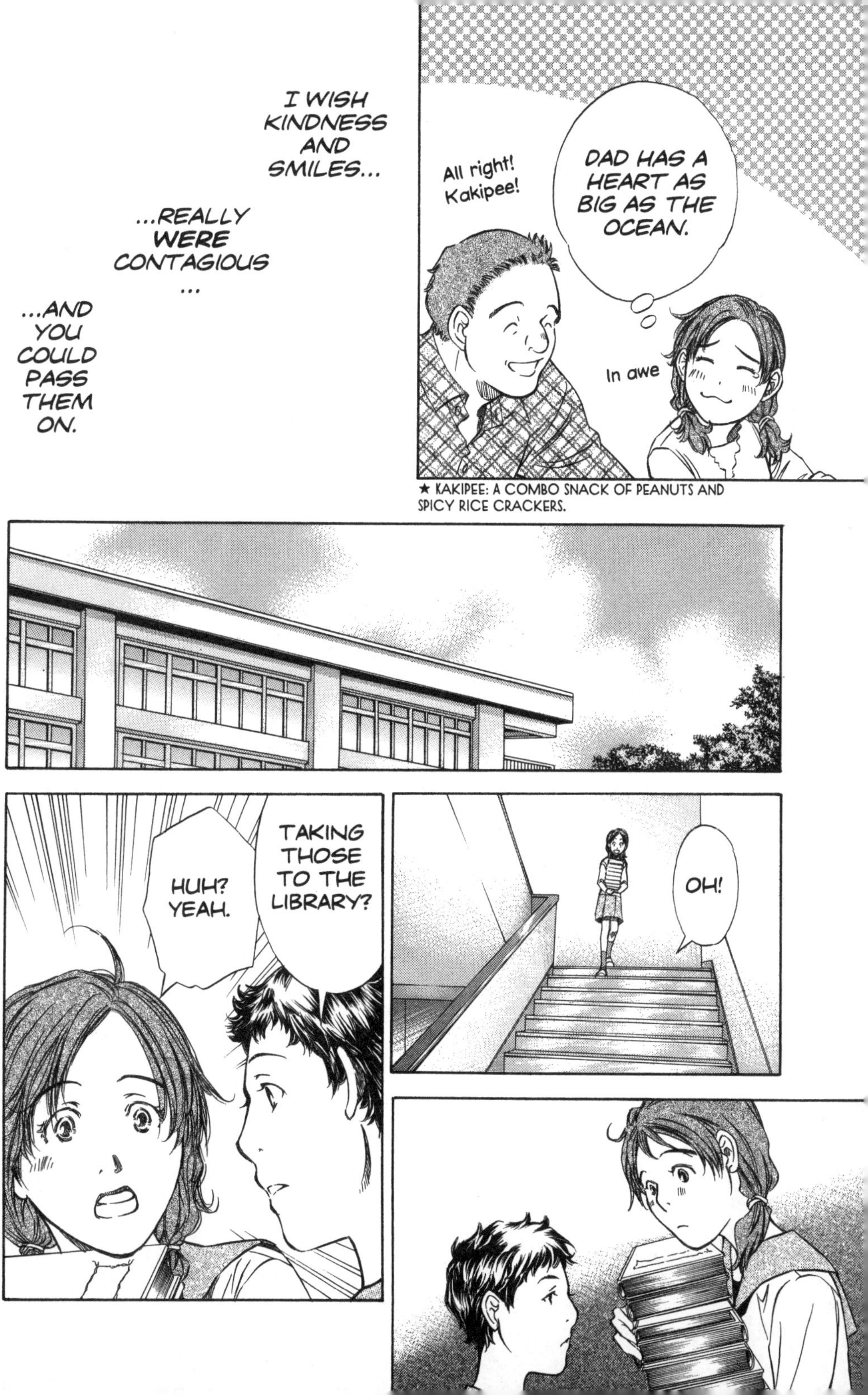
DAD HAS A HEART AS BIG AS THE OCEAN.
All right! Kakipee!
In awe
I WISH KINDNESS AND SMILES...
...REALLY WERE CONTAGIOUS ...
...AND YOU COULD PASS THEM ON.
OH!
TAKING THOSE TO THE LIBRARY?
HUH? YEAH.

★ KAKIPEE: A COMBO SNACK OF PEANUTS AND SPICY RICE CRACKERS.

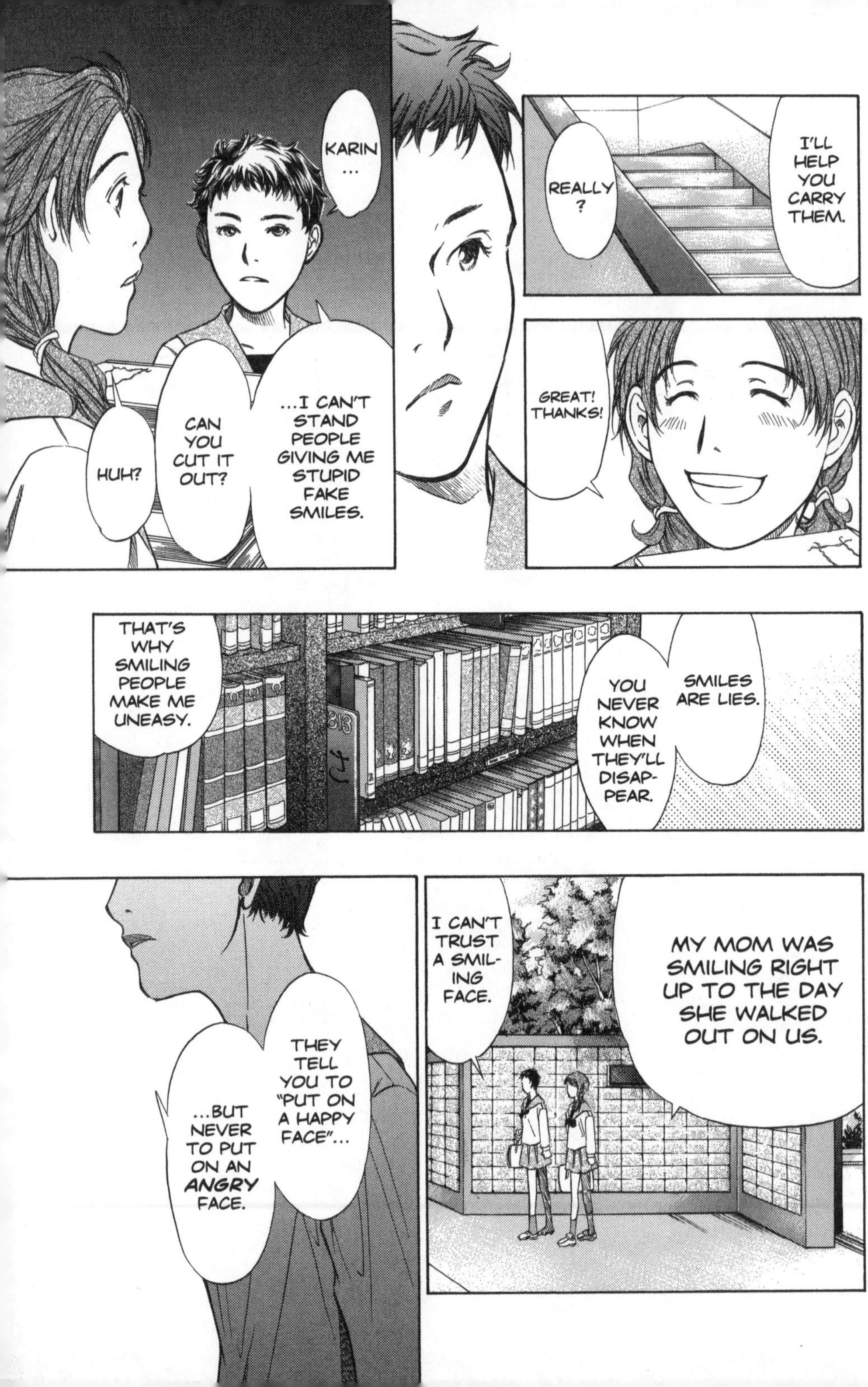
I'LL HELP YOU CARRY THEM.
REALLY?
GREAT! THANKS!
KARIN...
...I CAN'T STAND PEOPLE GIVING ME STUPID FAKE SMILES.
CAN YOU CUT IT OUT?
HUH?
SMILES ARE LIES.
YOU NEVER KNOW WHEN THEY'LL DISAPPEAR.
THAT'S WHY SMILING PEOPLE MAKE ME UNEASY.
MY MOM WAS SMILING RIGHT UP TO THE DAY SHE WALKED OUT ON US.
I CAN'T TRUST A SMILING FACE.
THEY TELL YOU TO "PUT ON A HAPPY FACE"...
...BUT NEVER TO PUT ON AN ANGRY FACE.

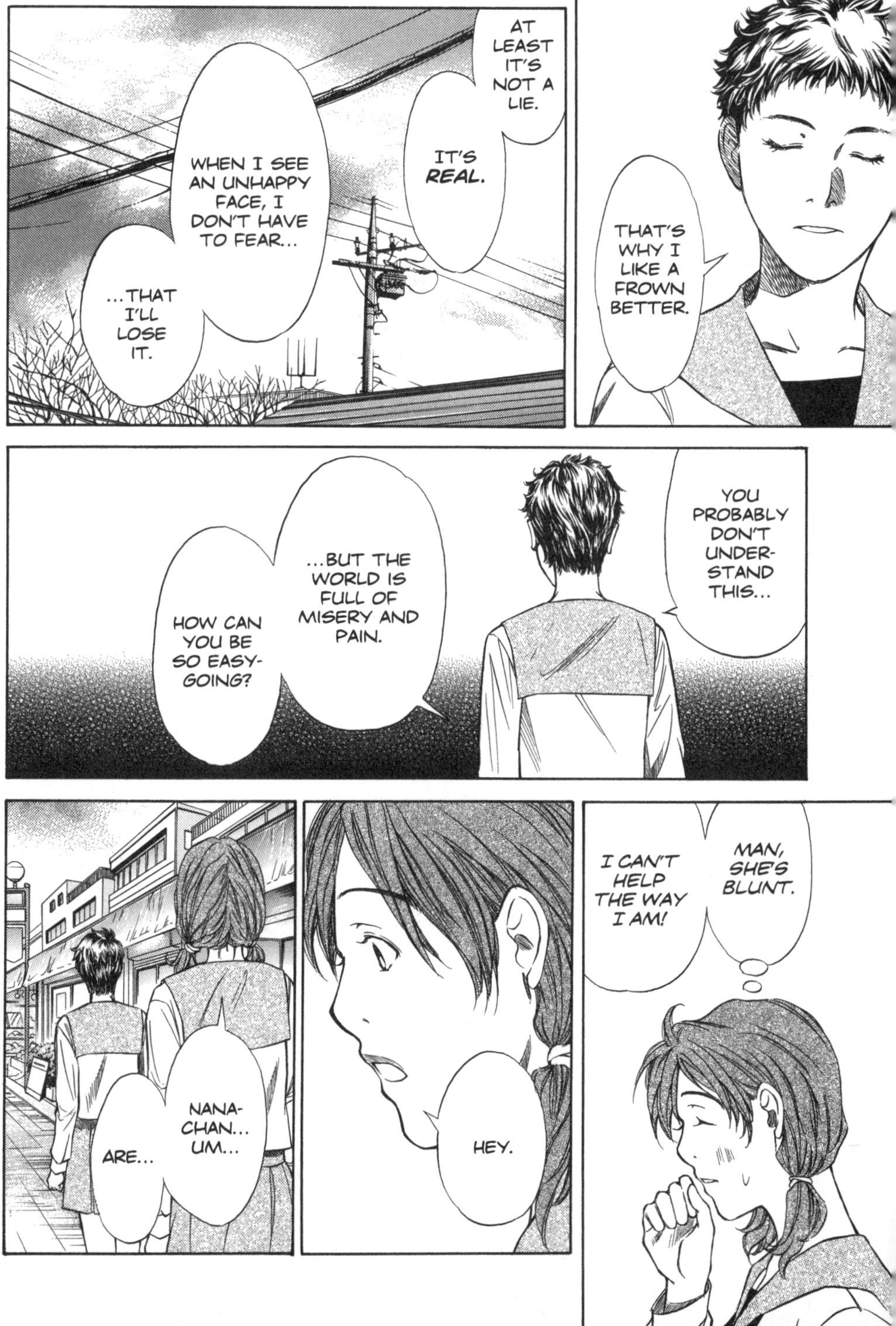
THAT'S WHY I LIKE A FROWN BETTER.
AT LEAST IT'S NOT A LIE.
IT'S **REAL.**
WHEN I SEE AN UNHAPPY FACE, I DON'T HAVE TO FEAR...
...THAT I'LL LOSE IT.
YOU PROBABLY DON'T UNDER-STAND THIS...
...BUT THE WORLD IS FULL OF MISERY AND PAIN.
HOW CAN YOU BE SO EASY-GOING?
MAN, SHE'S BLUNT.
I CAN'T HELP THE WAY I AM!
HEY.
NANA-CHAN... UM...
ARE...

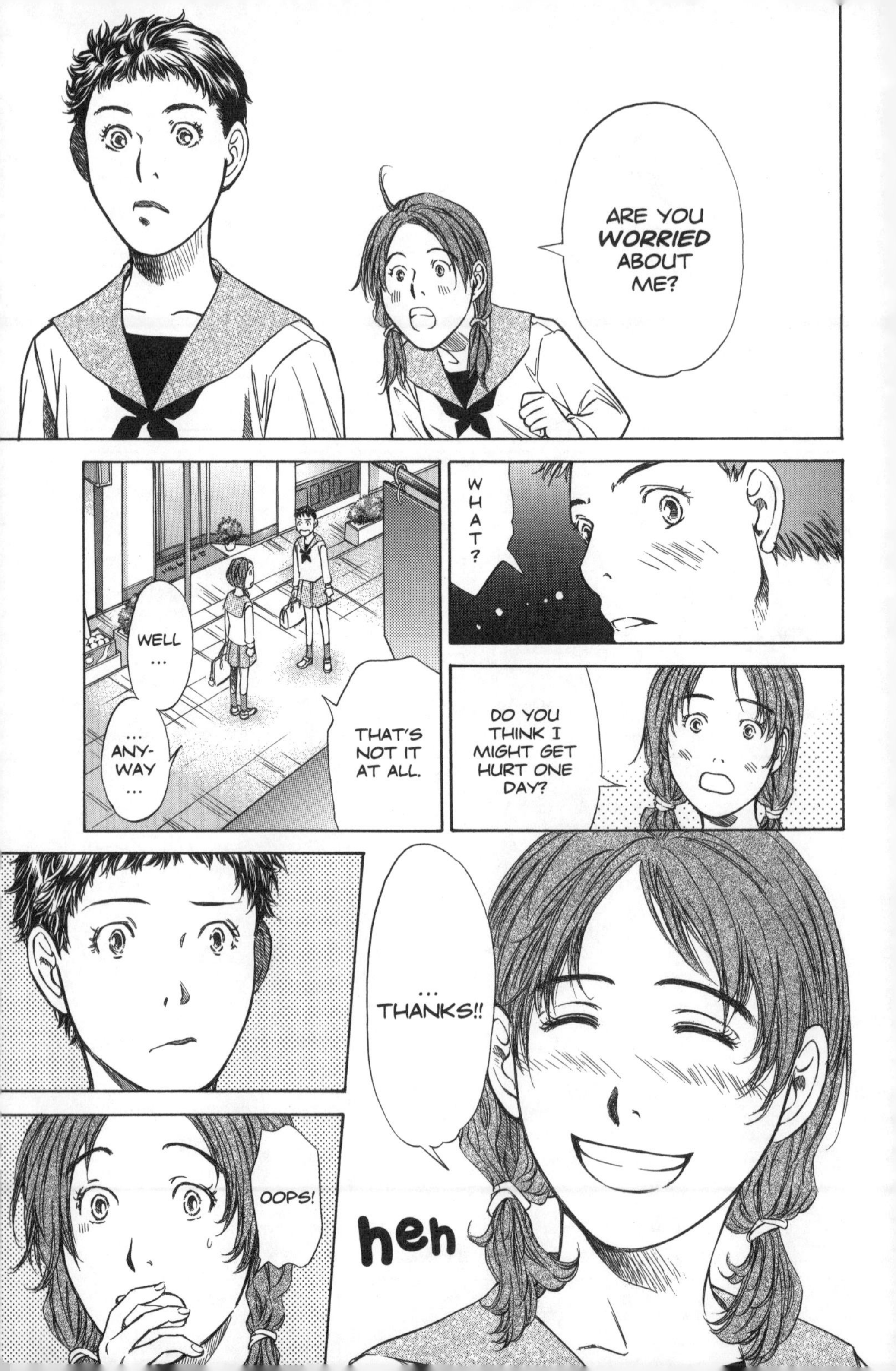
ARE YOU WORRIED ABOUT ME?
WHAT?
DO YOU THINK I MIGHT GET HURT ONE DAY?
THAT'S NOT IT AT ALL.
WELL ...
... ANY-WAY ...
... THANKS!!
heh
OOPS!

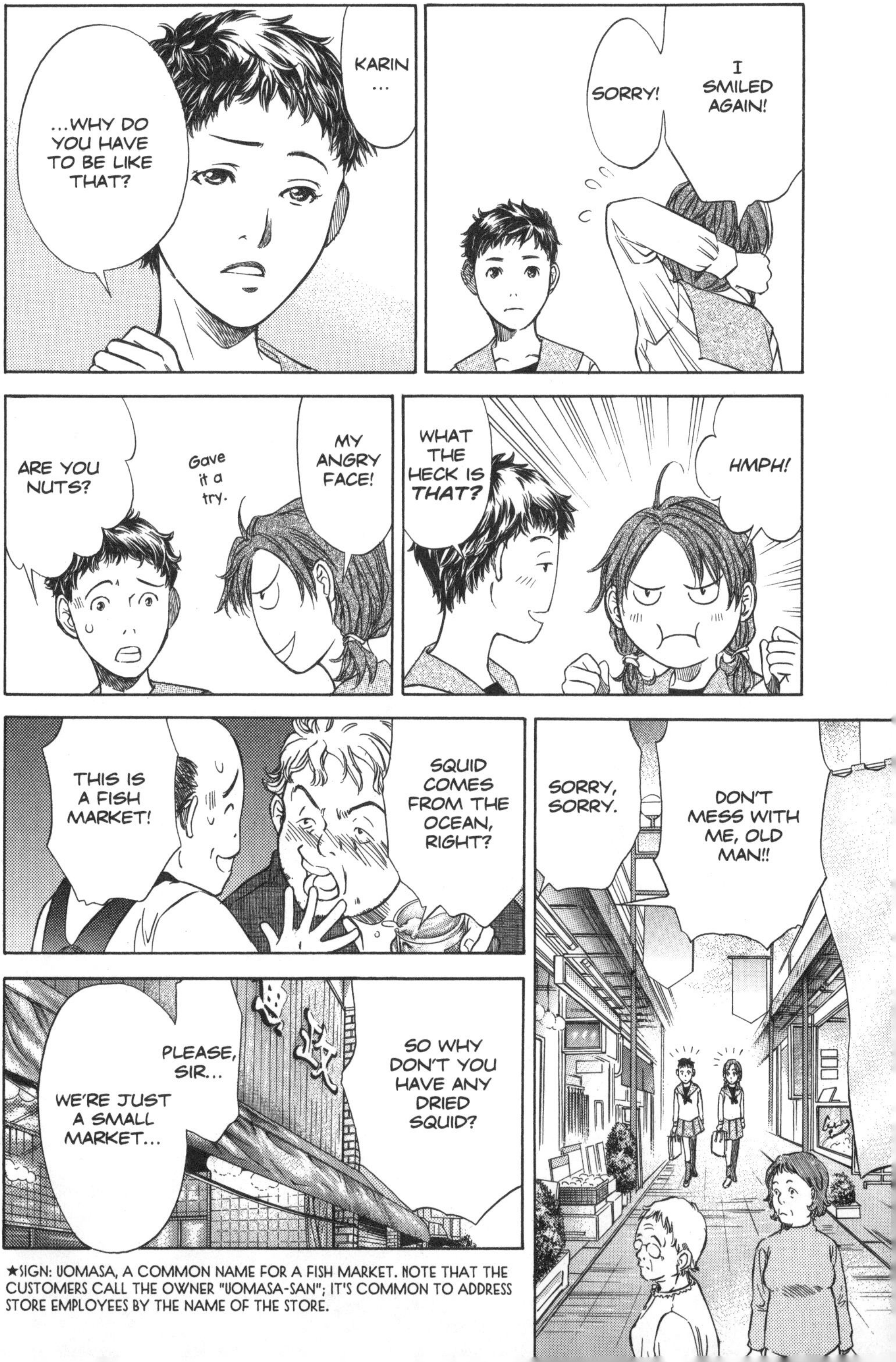
I SMILED AGAIN!
SORRY!
KARIN ...
...WHY DO YOU HAVE TO BE LIKE THAT?
HMPH!
WHAT THE HECK IS *THAT?*
MY ANGRY FACE!
Gave it a try.
ARE YOU NUTS?
DON'T MESS WITH ME, OLD MAN!!
SORRY, SORRY.
SQUID COMES FROM THE OCEAN, RIGHT?
THIS IS A FISH MARKET!
SO WHY DON'T YOU HAVE ANY DRIED SQUID?
PLEASE, SIR...
WE'RE JUST A SMALL MARKET...

★SIGN: UOMASA, A COMMON NAME FOR A FISH MARKET. NOTE THAT THE CUSTOMERS CALL THE OWNER "UOMASA-SAN"; IT'S COMMON TO ADDRESS STORE EMPLOYEES BY THE NAME OF THE STORE.

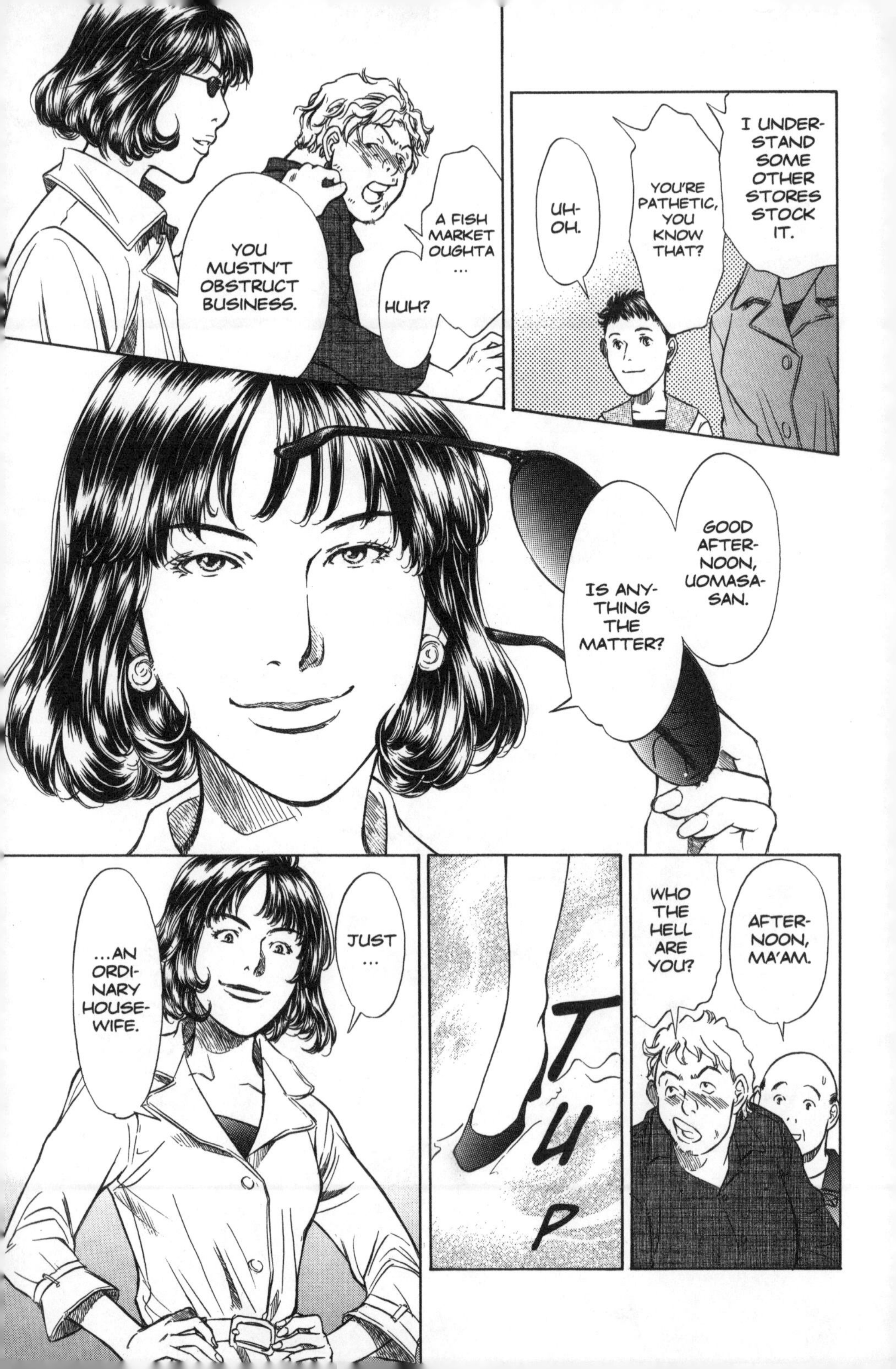
I UNDERSTAND SOME OTHER STORES STOCK IT.
YOU'RE PATHETIC, YOU KNOW THAT?
UH-OH.
A FISH MARKET OUGHTA ...
HUH?
YOU MUSTN'T OBSTRUCT BUSINESS.
GOOD AFTERNOON, UOMASA-SAN.
IS ANYTHING THE MATTER?
AFTERNOON, MA'AM.
WHO THE HELL ARE YOU?
TUP
JUST ...
...AN ORDINARY HOUSEWIFE.

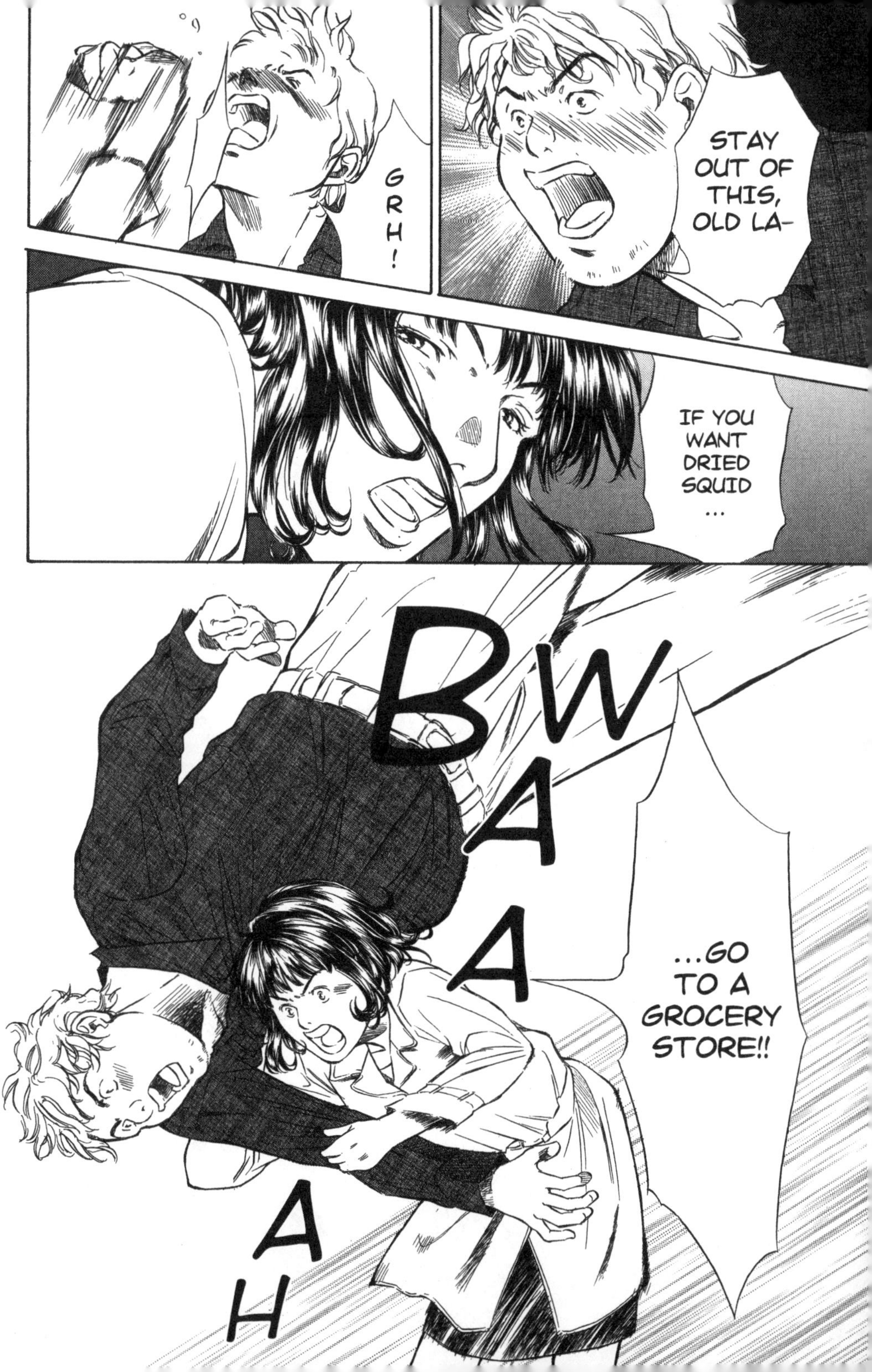
STAY OUT OF THIS, OLD LA-
GRH!
IF YOU WANT DRIED SQUID ...
...GO TO A GROCERY STORE!!
BWAAAAH

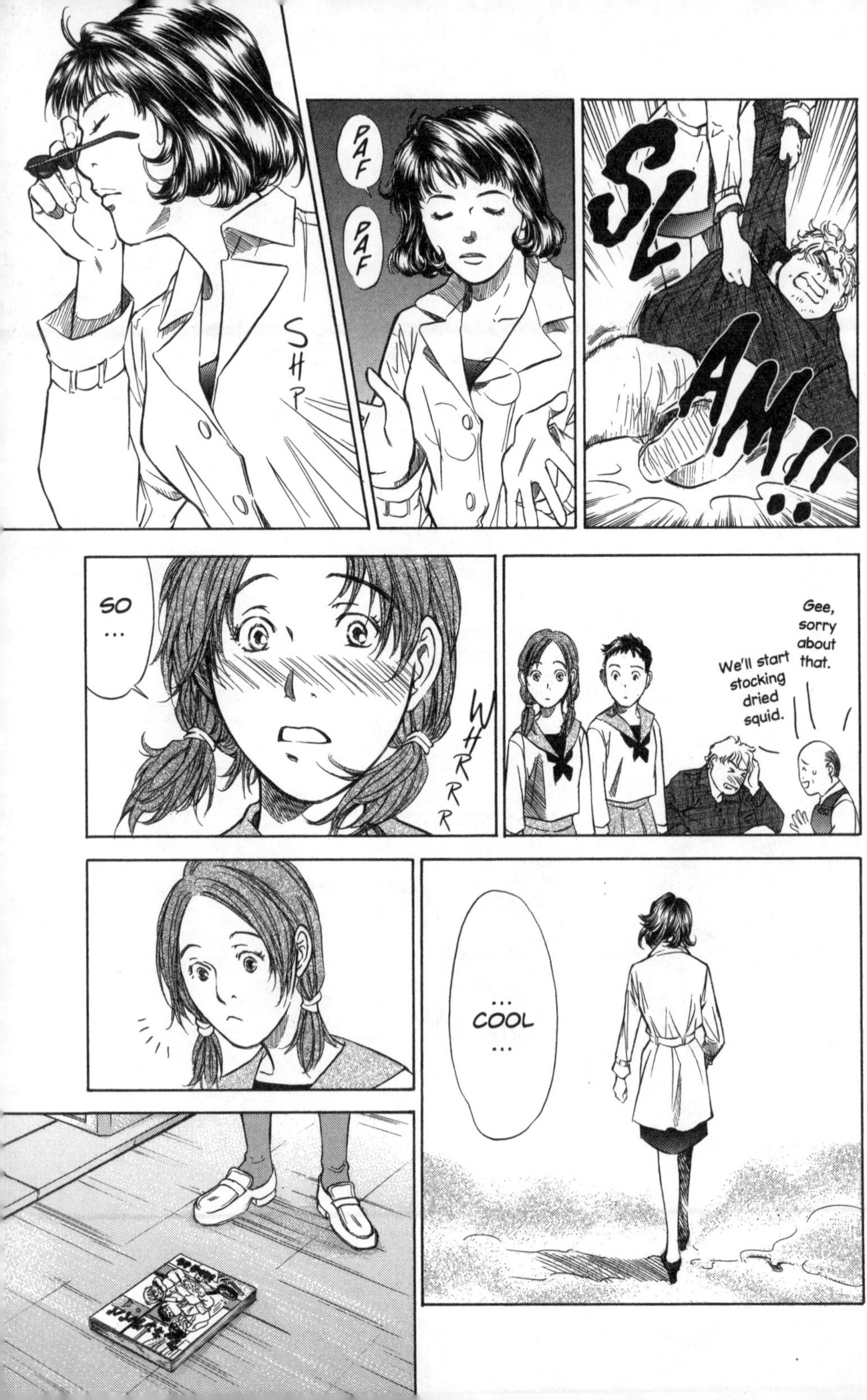
SLAM!!
PAF PAF
SHP
Gee, sorry about that.
We'll start stocking dried squid.
SO ...
WHRRRR
... COOL ...

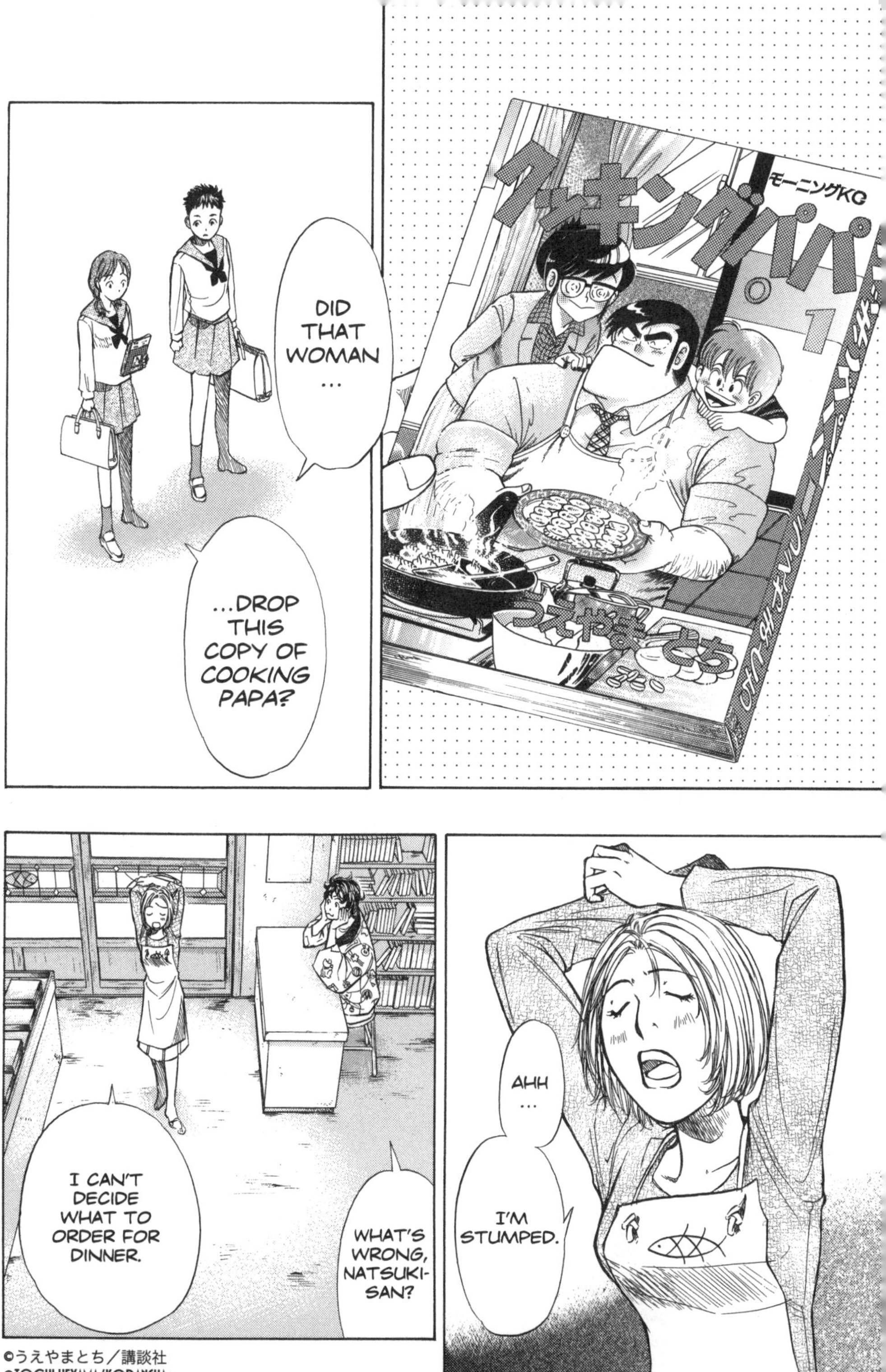
モーニングKC
DID THAT WOMAN ...
...DROP THIS COPY OF COOKING PAPA?
AHH ...
I'M STUMPED.
WHAT'S WRONG, NATSUKI-SAN?
I CAN'T DECIDE WHAT TO ORDER FOR DINNER.

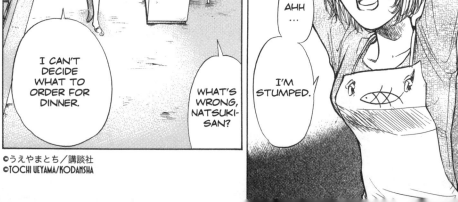

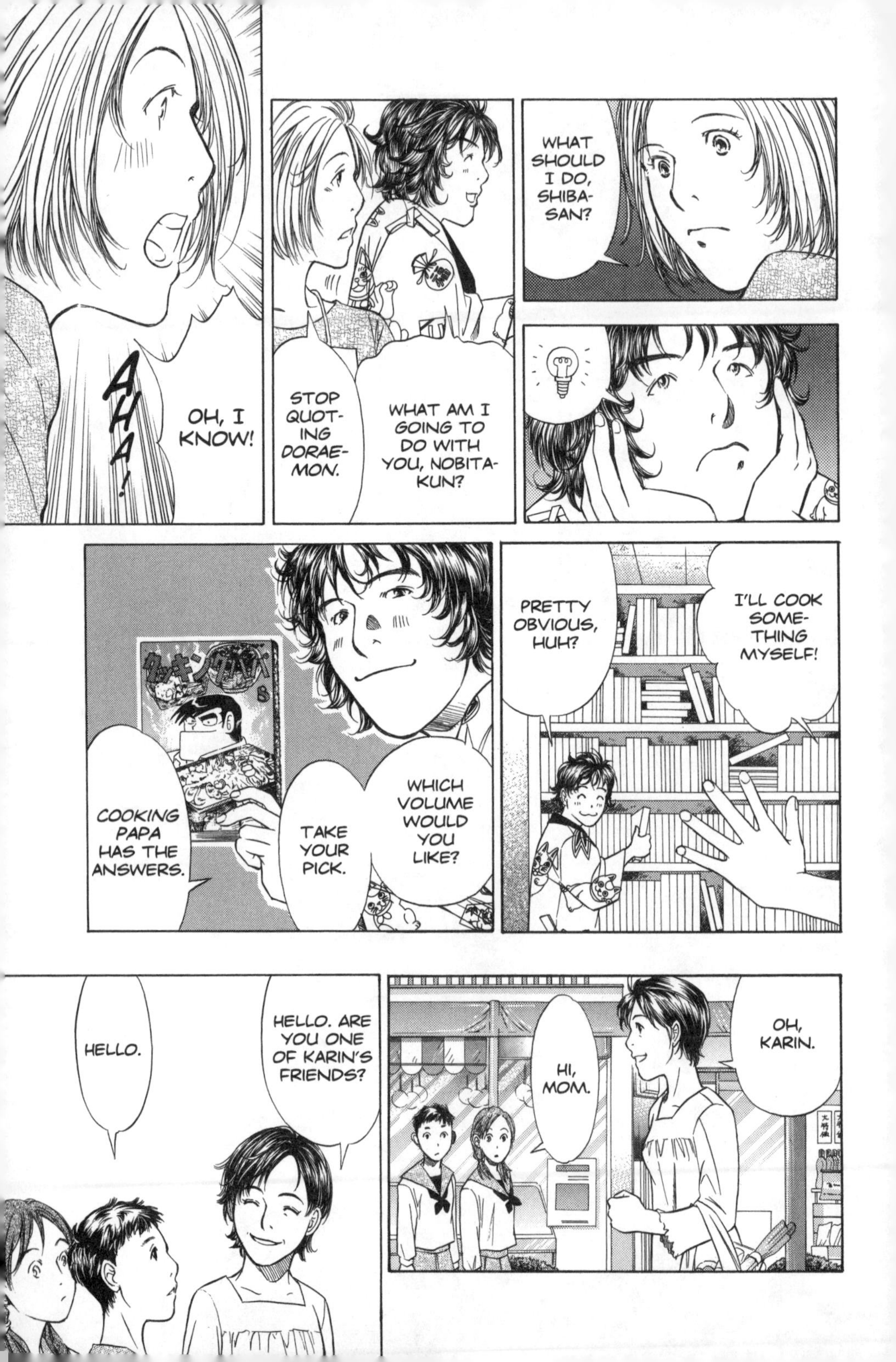
WHAT SHOULD I DO, SHIBA-SAN?
WHAT AM I GOING TO DO WITH YOU, NOBITA-KUN?
STOP QUOTING DORAEMON.
OH, I KNOW!
AHA!
I'LL COOK SOMETHING MYSELF!
PRETTY OBVIOUS, HUH?
WHICH VOLUME WOULD YOU LIKE?
TAKE YOUR PICK.
COOKING PAPA HAS THE ANSWERS.
OH, KARIN.
HI, MOM.
HELLO. ARE YOU ONE OF KARIN'S FRIENDS?
HELLO.

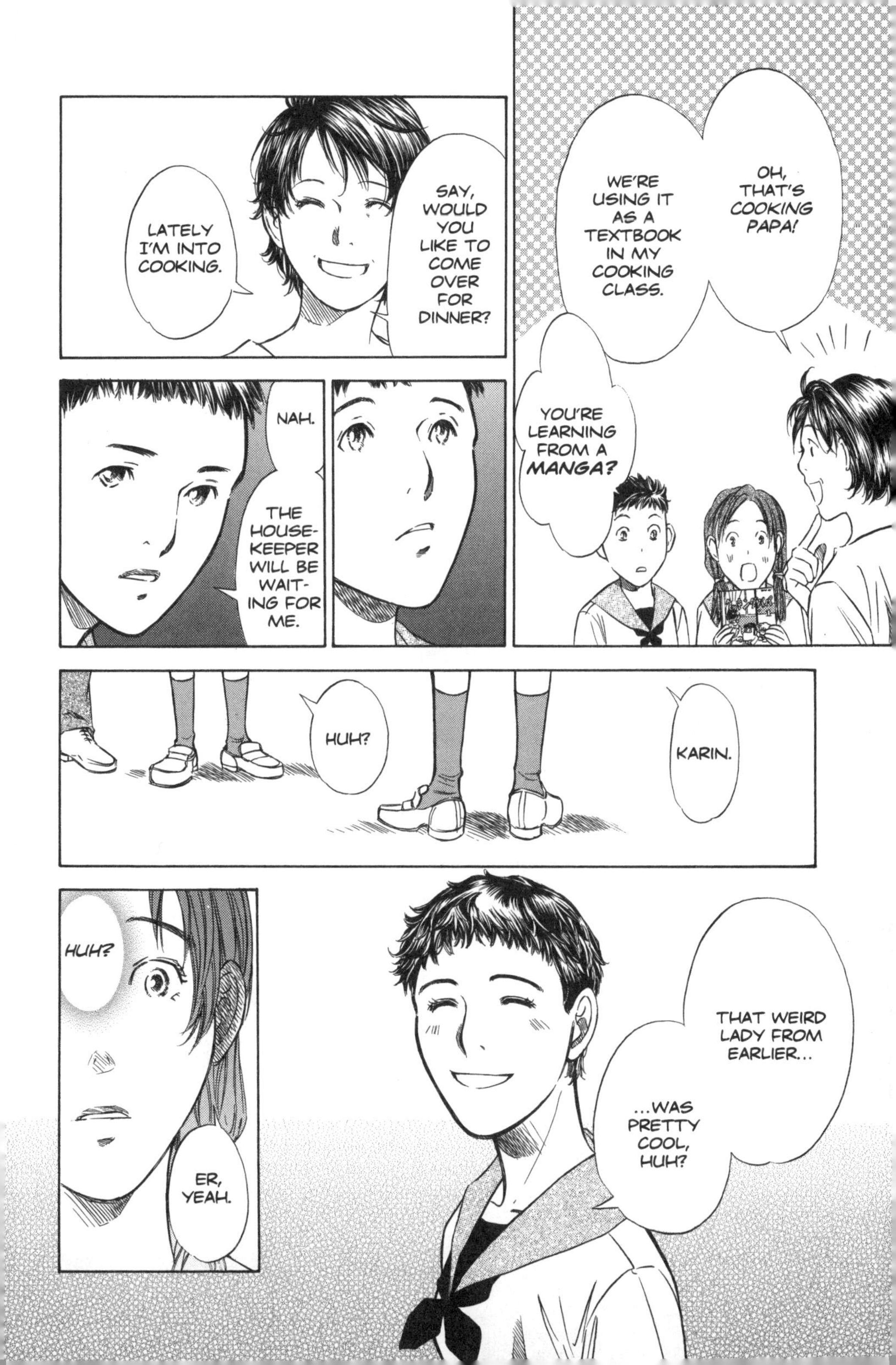
OH, THAT'S COOKING PAPA!
WE'RE USING IT AS A TEXTBOOK IN MY COOKING CLASS.
YOU'RE LEARNING FROM A *MANGA?*
SAY, WOULD YOU LIKE TO COME OVER FOR DINNER?
LATELY I'M INTO COOKING.
NAH.
THE HOUSE-KEEPER WILL BE WAIT-ING FOR ME.
KARIN.
HUH?
THAT WEIRD LADY FROM EARLIER...
...WAS PRETTY COOL, HUH?
HUH?
ER, YEAH.

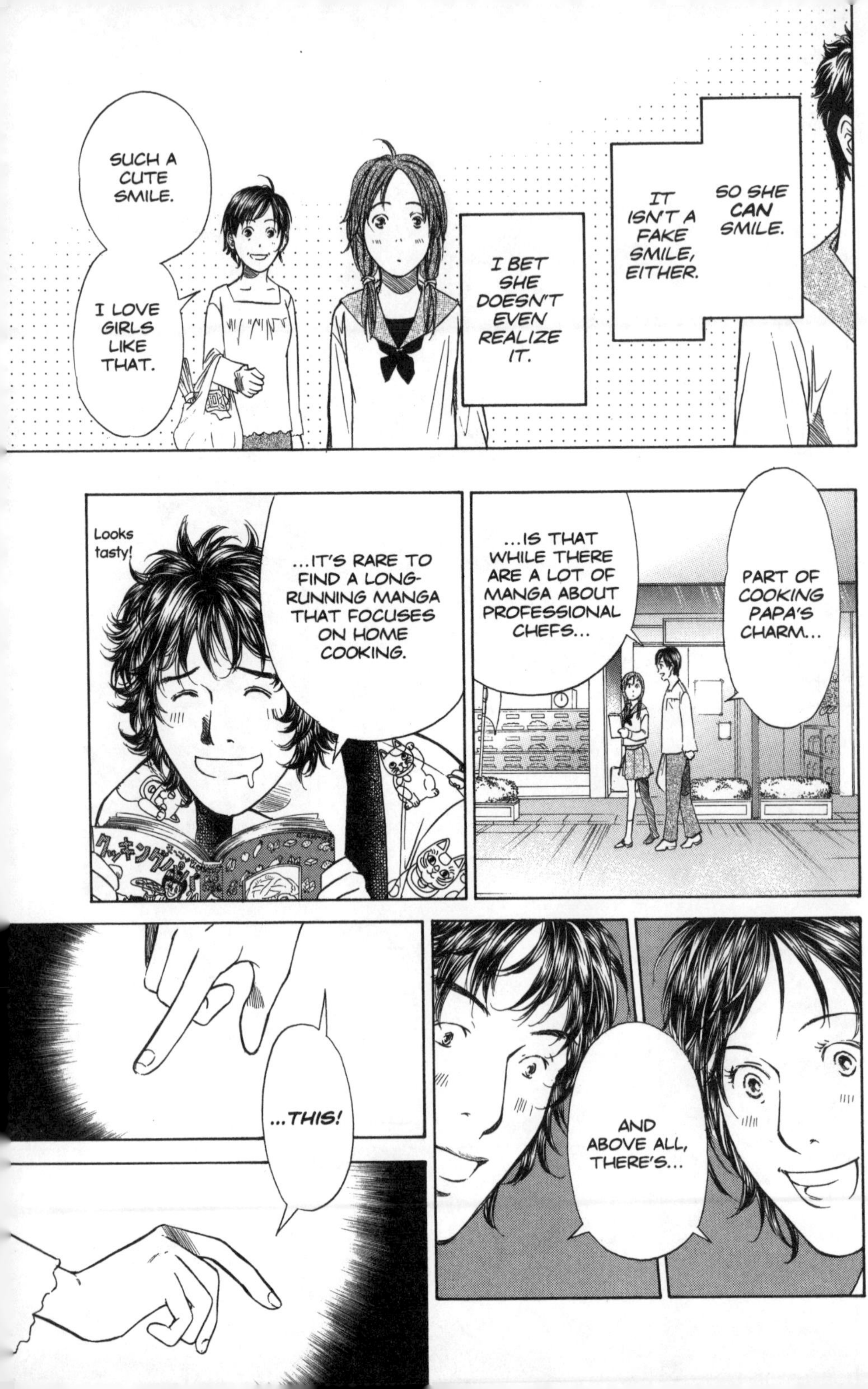
SO SHE CAN SMILE.
IT ISN'T A FAKE SMILE, EITHER.
I BET SHE DOESN'T EVEN REALIZE IT.
SUCH A CUTE SMILE.
I LOVE GIRLS LIKE THAT.
PART OF COOKING PAPA'S CHARM...
...IS THAT WHILE THERE ARE A LOT OF MANGA ABOUT PROFESSIONAL CHEFS...
...IT'S RARE TO FIND A LONG-RUNNING MANGA THAT FOCUSES ON HOME COOKING.
Looks tasty!
AND ABOVE ALL, THERE'S...
...THIS!

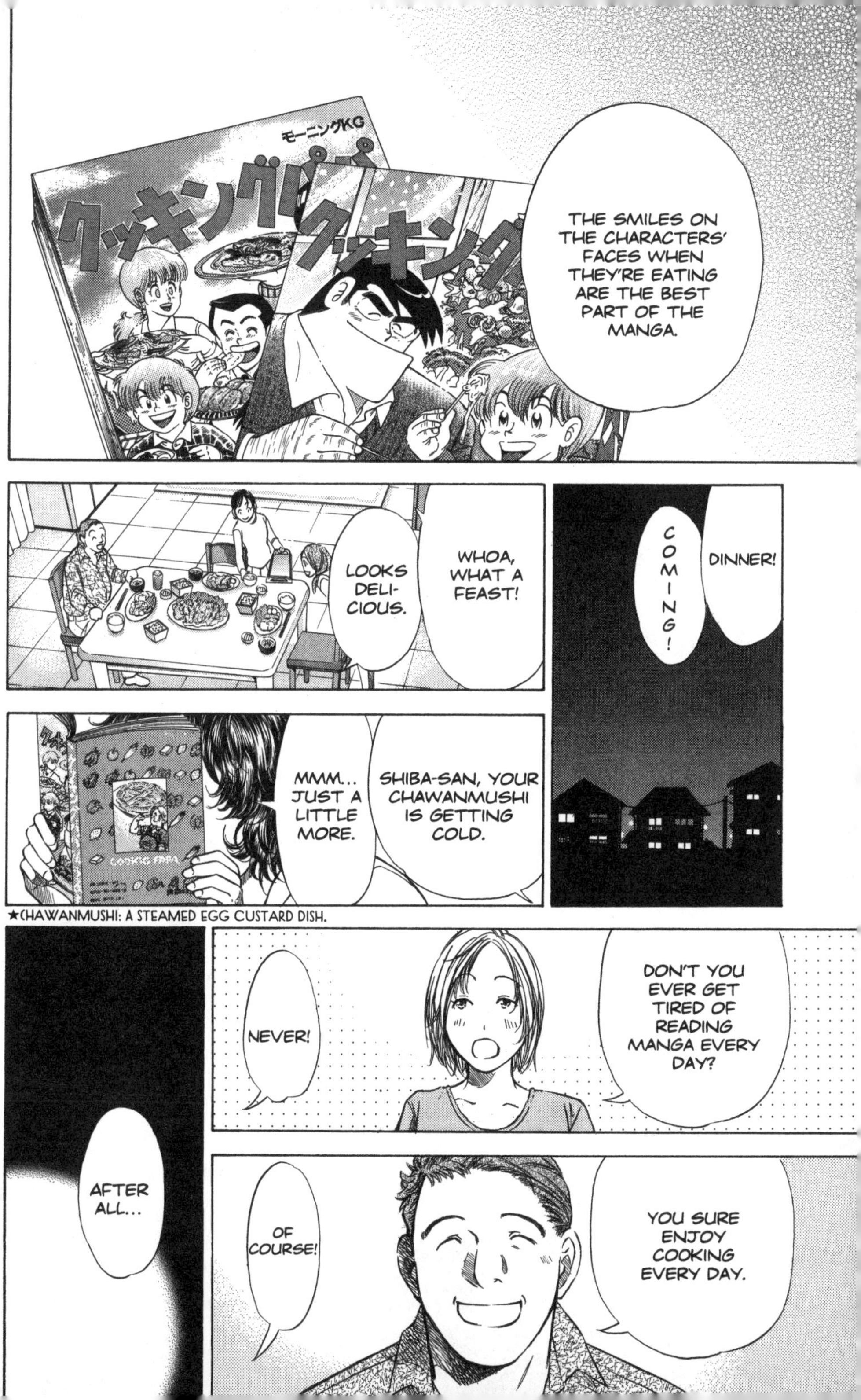
モーニングKC
THE SMILES ON THE CHARACTERS' FACES WHEN THEY'RE EATING ARE THE BEST PART OF THE MANGA.
DINNER!
COMING!
WHOA, WHAT A FEAST!
LOOKS DELI-CIOUS.
SHIBA-SAN, YOUR CHAWANMUSHI IS GETTING COLD.
MMM... JUST A LITTLE MORE.
DON'T YOU EVER GET TIRED OF READING MANGA EVERY DAY?
NEVER!
YOU SURE ENJOY COOKING EVERY DAY.
OF COURSE!
AFTER ALL...
★CHAWANMUSHI: A STEAMED EGG CUSTARD DISH.

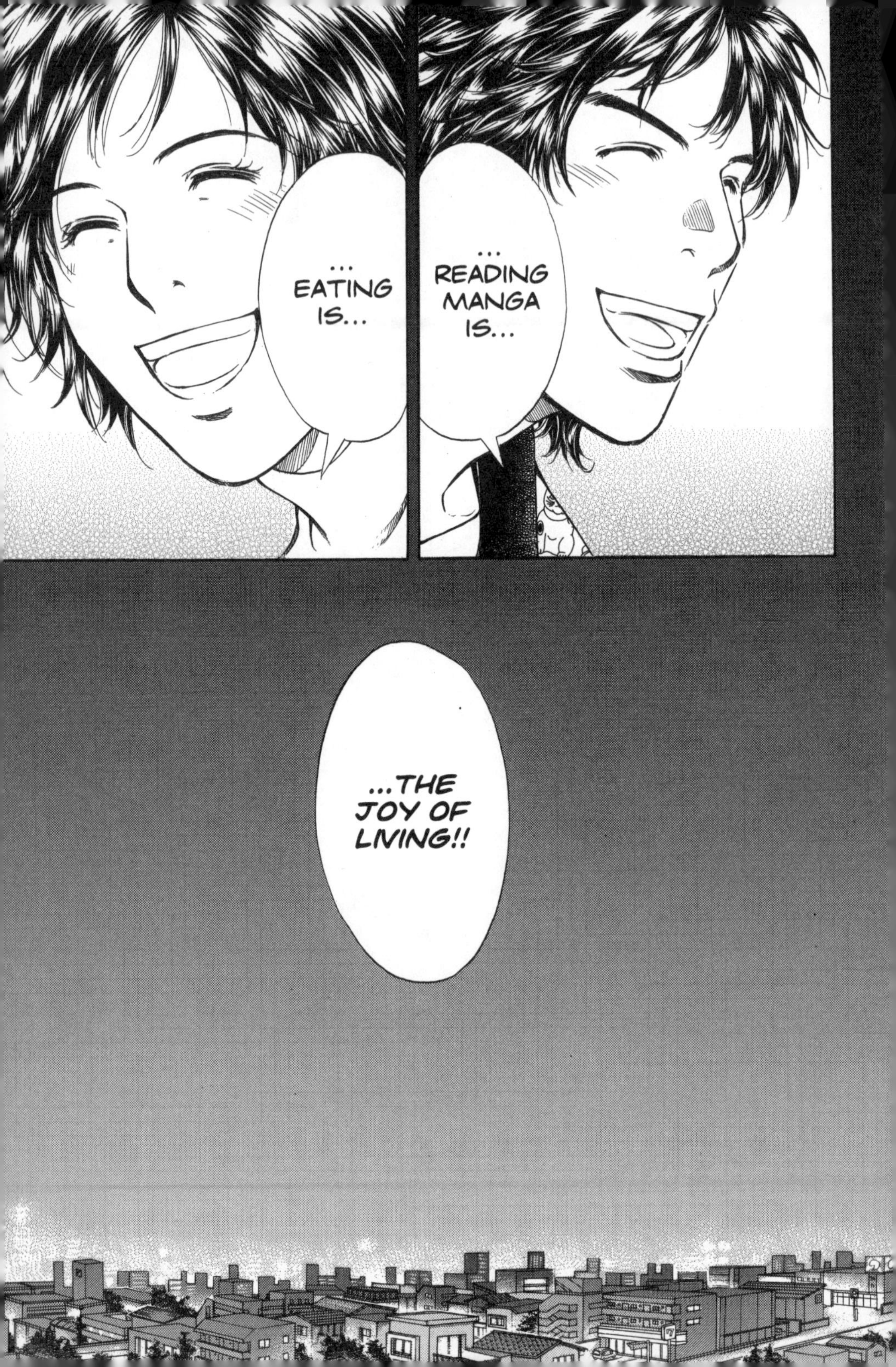
... READING MANGA IS...
... EATING IS...
...THE JOY OF LIVING!!

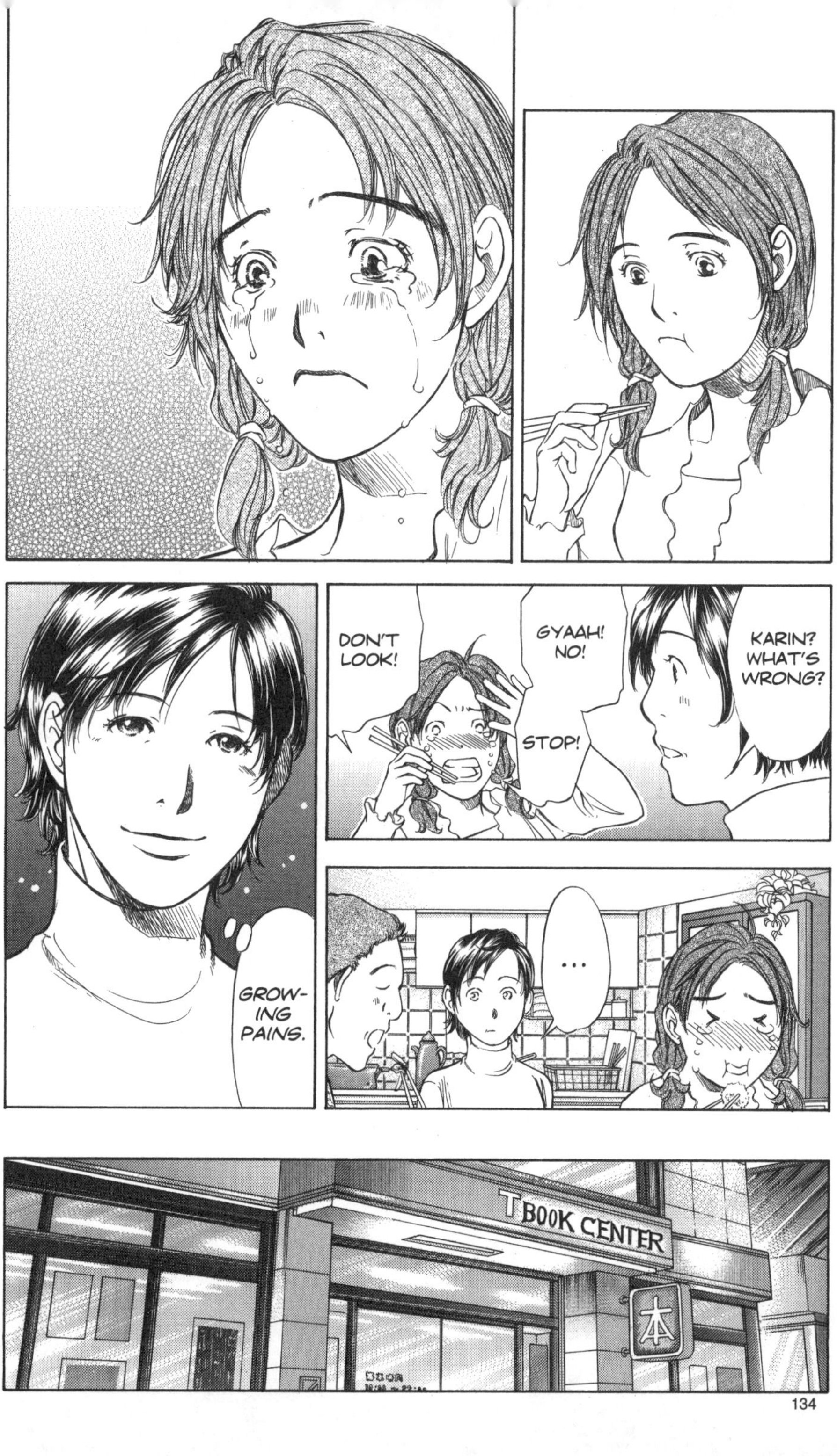
KARIN? WHAT'S WRONG?
GYAAH! NO!
STOP!
DON'T LOOK!
...
GROW-ING PAINS.
T BOOK CENTER
本

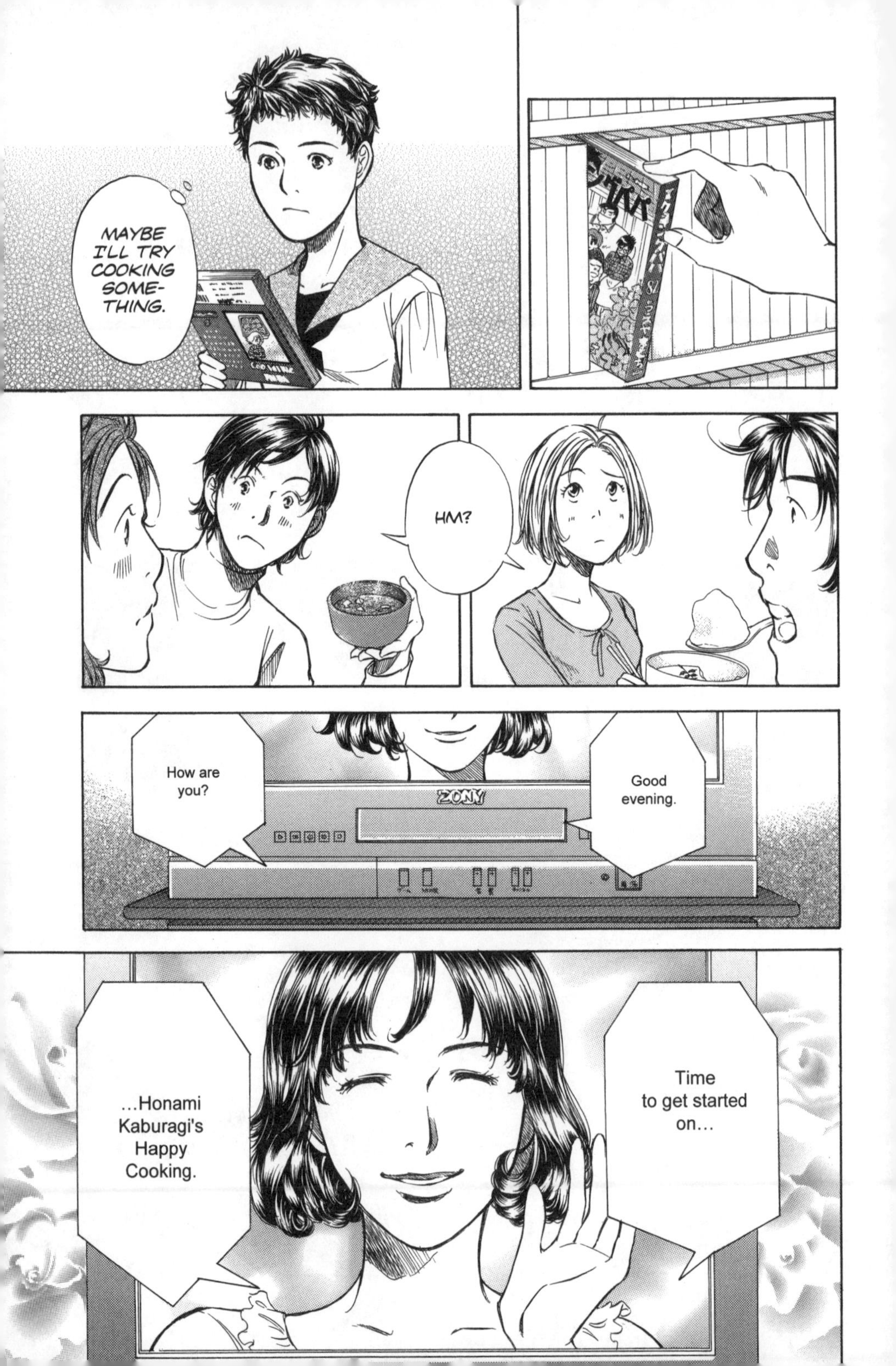
MAYBE I'LL TRY COOKING SOMETHING.
HM?
Good evening.
How are you?
Time to get started on…
…Honami Kaburagi's Happy Cooking.

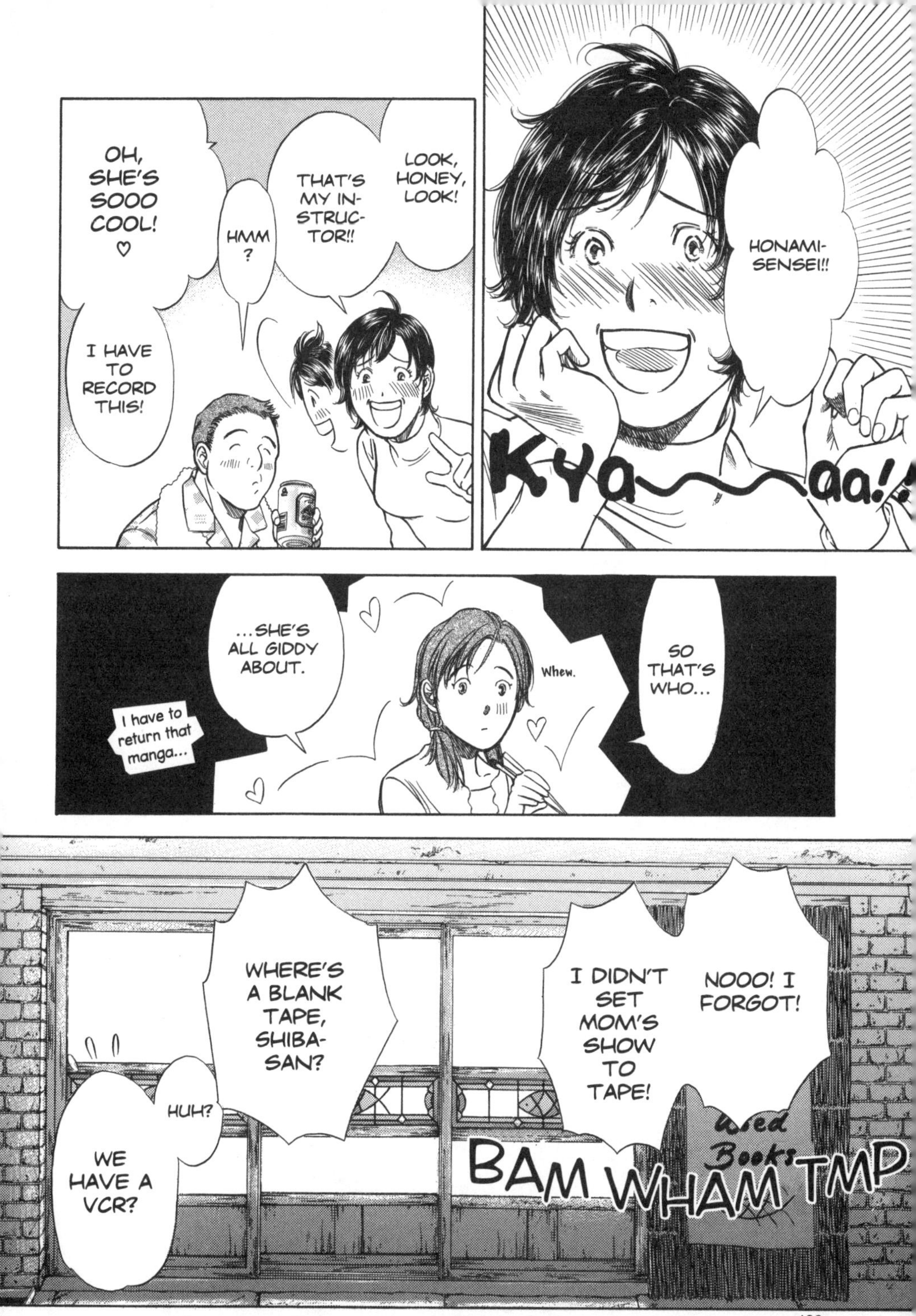
HONAMI-SENSEI!!
Kya~~aa!!
LOOK, HONEY, LOOK!
THAT'S MY INSTRUCTOR!!
HMM?
OH, SHE'S SOOO COOL! ♡
I HAVE TO RECORD THIS!
SO THAT'S WHO...
...SHE'S ALL GIDDY ABOUT.
Whew.
I have to return that manga...
NOOO! I FORGOT!
I DIDN'T SET MOM'S SHOW TO TAPE!
WHERE'S A BLANK TAPE, SHIBA-SAN?
HUH?
WE HAVE A VCR?
BAM WHAM TMP

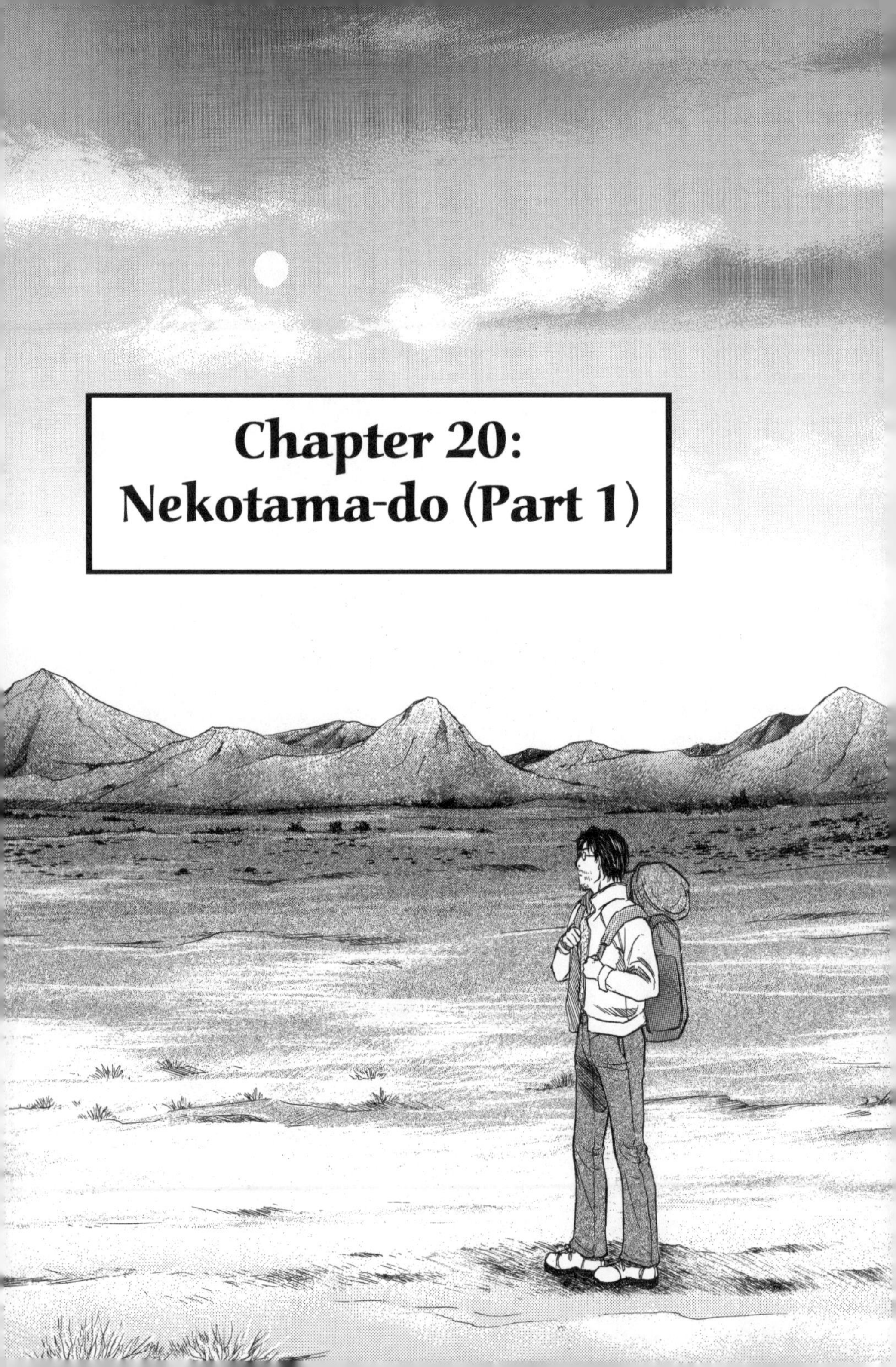
Chapter 20:
Nekotama-do (Part 1)

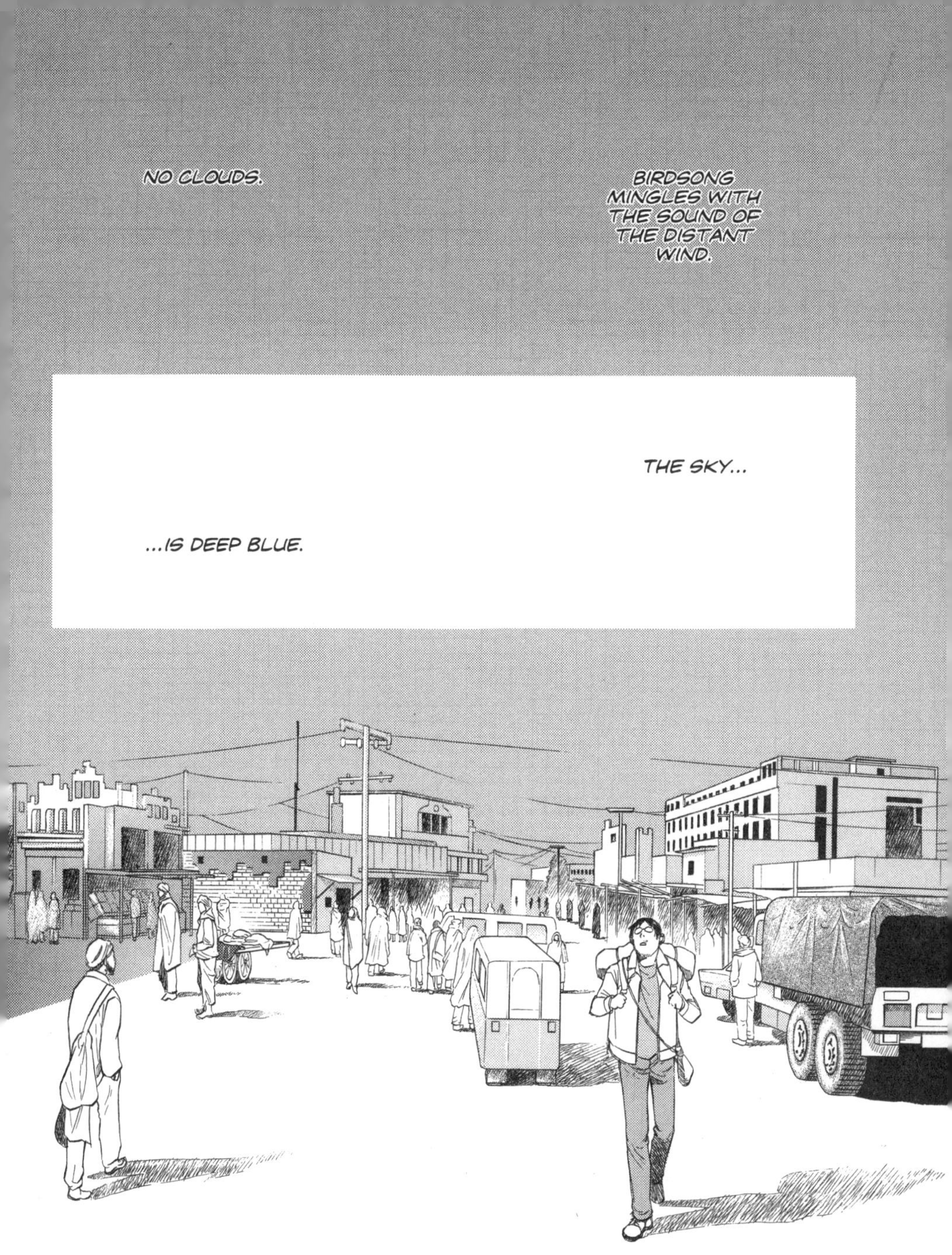
BIRDSONG MINGLES WITH THE SOUND OF THE DISTANT WIND.
NO CLOUDS.
THE SKY...
...IS DEEP BLUE.

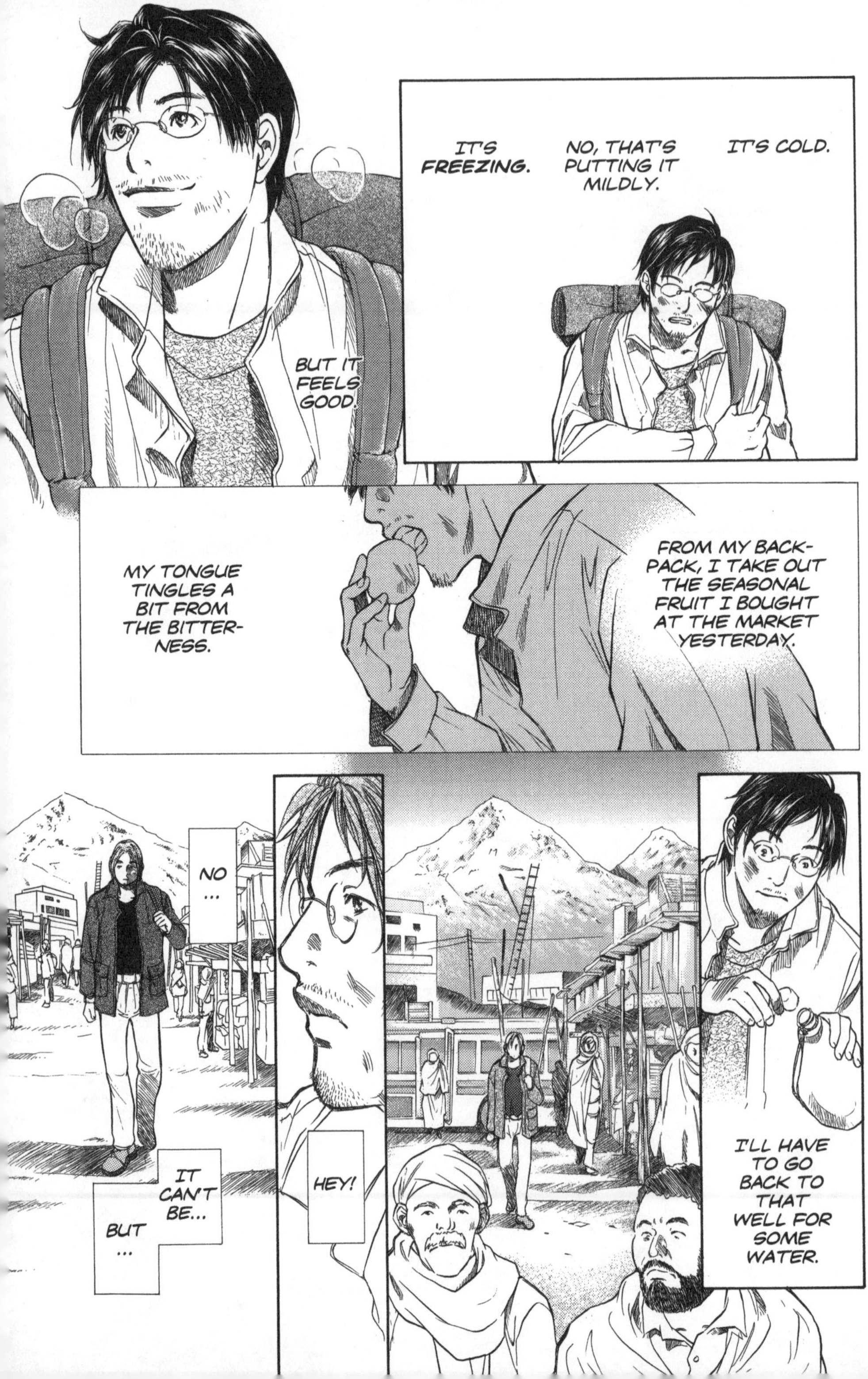
IT'S COLD.
NO, THAT'S PUTTING IT MILDLY.
IT'S FREEZING.
BUT IT FEELS GOOD.
FROM MY BACK-PACK, I TAKE OUT THE SEASONAL FRUIT I BOUGHT AT THE MARKET YESTERDAY.
MY TONGUE TINGLES A BIT FROM THE BITTER-NESS.
I'LL HAVE TO GO BACK TO THAT WELL FOR SOME WATER.
HEY!
NO ...
IT CAN'T BE...
BUT ...

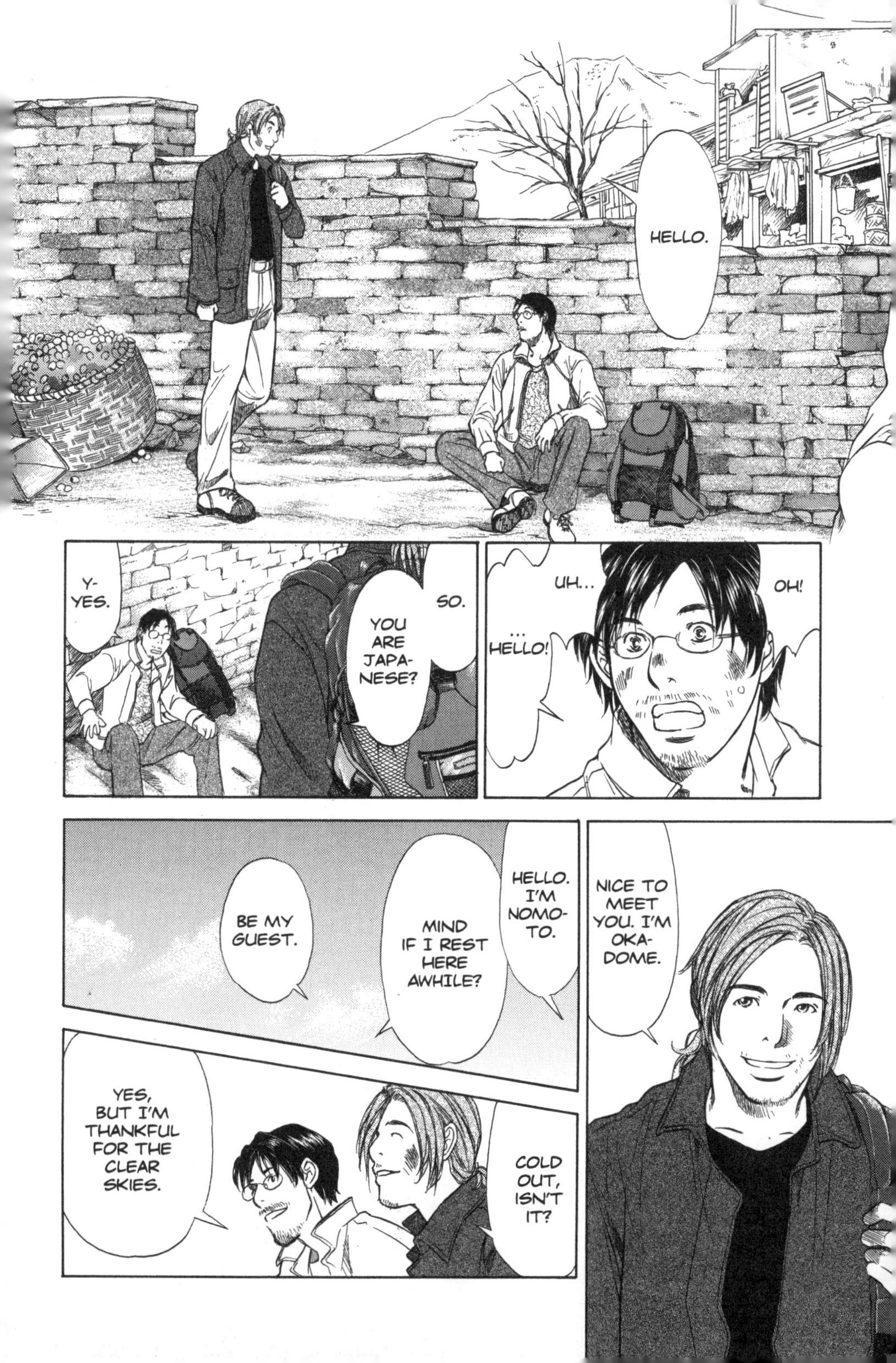
HELLO.
OH!
UH...
...HELLO!
SO.
YOU ARE JAPANESE?
Y-YES.
NICE TO MEET YOU. I'M OKADOME.
HELLO. I'M NOMOTO.
MIND IF I REST HERE AWHILE?
BE MY GUEST.
COLD OUT, ISN'T IT?
YES, BUT I'M THANKFUL FOR THE CLEAR SKIES.

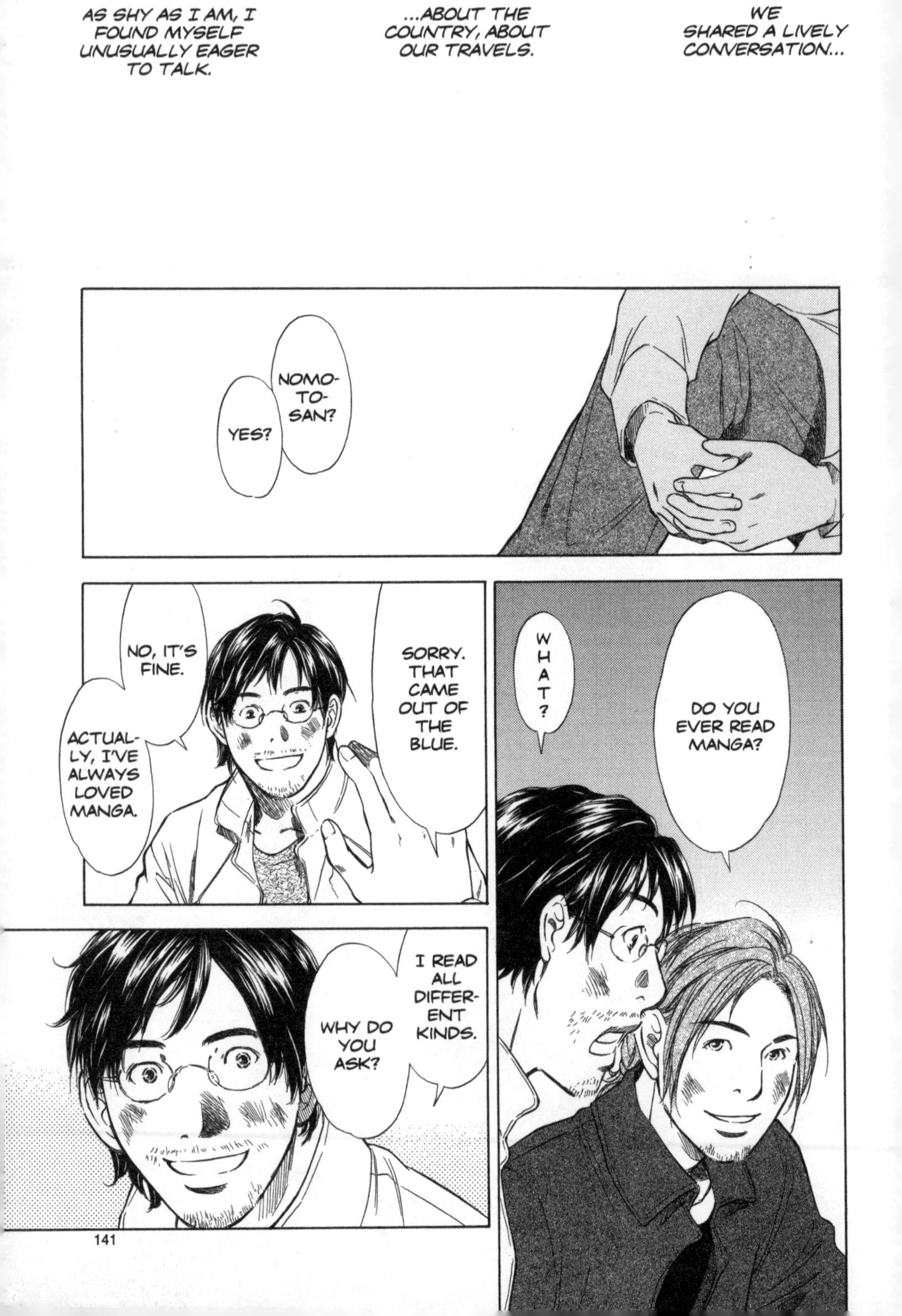
WE SHARED A LIVELY CONVERSATION...
...ABOUT THE COUNTRY, ABOUT OUR TRAVELS.
AS SHY AS I AM, I FOUND MYSELF UNUSUALLY EAGER TO TALK.
NOMO-TO-SAN?
YES?
DO YOU EVER READ MANGA?
WHAT?
SORRY. THAT CAME OUT OF THE BLUE.
NO, IT'S FINE.
ACTUAL-LY, I'VE ALWAYS LOVED MANGA.
I READ ALL DIFFER-ENT KINDS.
WHY DO YOU ASK?

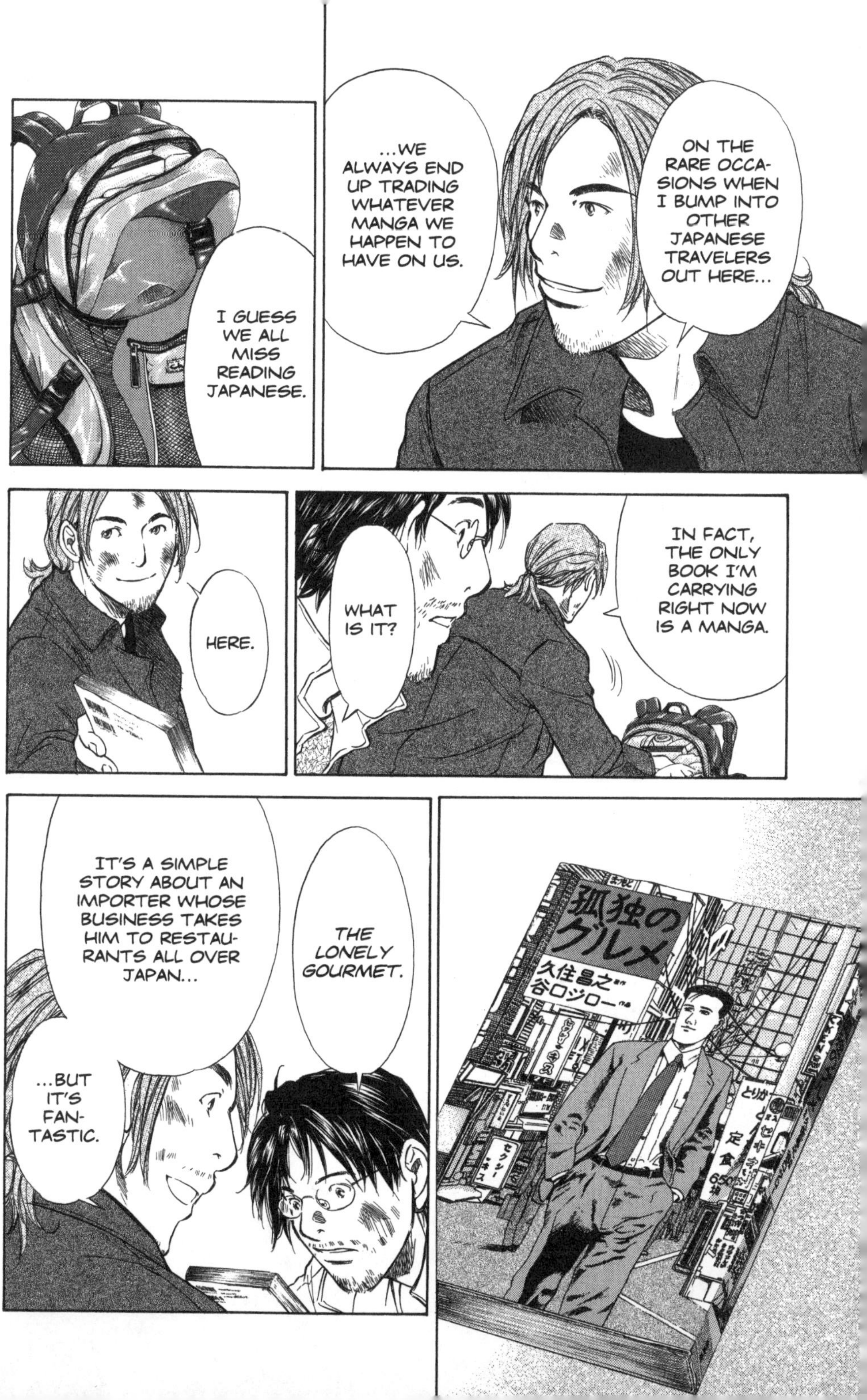
ON THE RARE OCCASIONS WHEN I BUMP INTO OTHER JAPANESE TRAVELERS OUT HERE...
...WE ALWAYS END UP TRADING WHATEVER MANGA WE HAPPEN TO HAVE ON US.
I GUESS WE ALL MISS READING JAPANESE.
IN FACT, THE ONLY BOOK I'M CARRYING RIGHT NOW IS A MANGA.
WHAT IS IT?
HERE.
孤独のグルメ
久住昌之
谷口ジロー
THE LONELY GOURMET.
IT'S A SIMPLE STORY ABOUT AN IMPORTER WHOSE BUSINESS TAKES HIM TO RESTAURANTS ALL OVER JAPAN...
...BUT IT'S FANTASTIC.

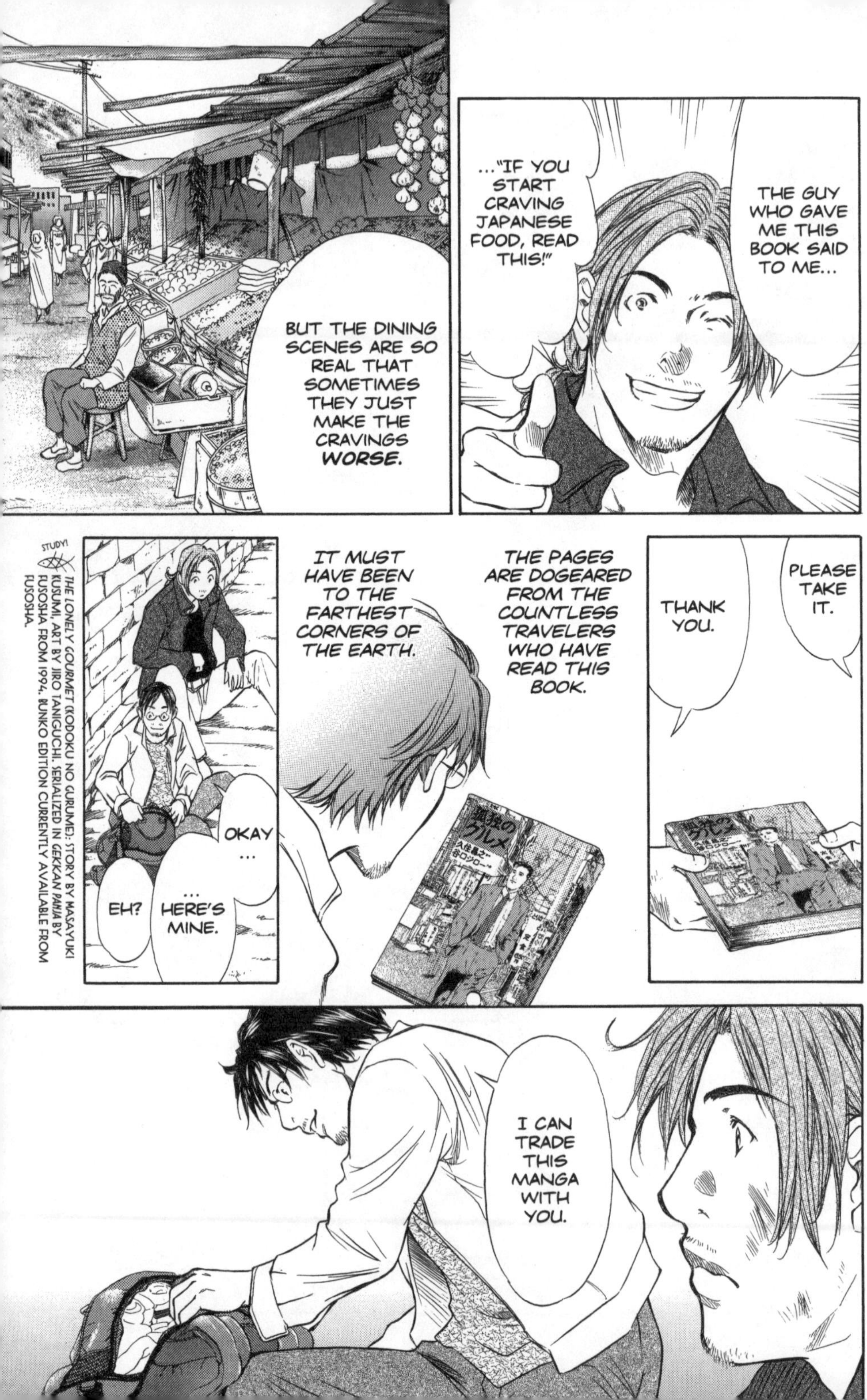
THE GUY WHO GAVE ME THIS BOOK SAID TO ME...
..."IF YOU START CRAVING JAPANESE FOOD, READ THIS!"
BUT THE DINING SCENES ARE SO REAL THAT SOMETIMES THEY JUST MAKE THE CRAVINGS WORSE.
PLEASE TAKE IT.
THANK YOU.
THE PAGES ARE DOGEARED FROM THE COUNTLESS TRAVELERS WHO HAVE READ THIS BOOK.
IT MUST HAVE BEEN TO THE FARTHEST CORNERS OF THE EARTH.
OKAY ...
... HERE'S MINE.
EH?
STUDY!
THE LONELY GOURMET (KODOKU NO GURUME): STORY BY MASAYUKI KUSUMI, ART BY JIRO TANIGUCHI. SERIALIZED IN GEKKAN PANJA BY FUSOSHA FROM 1994. BUNKO EDITION CURRENTLY AVAILABLE FROM FUSOSHA.
I CAN TRADE THIS MANGA WITH YOU.

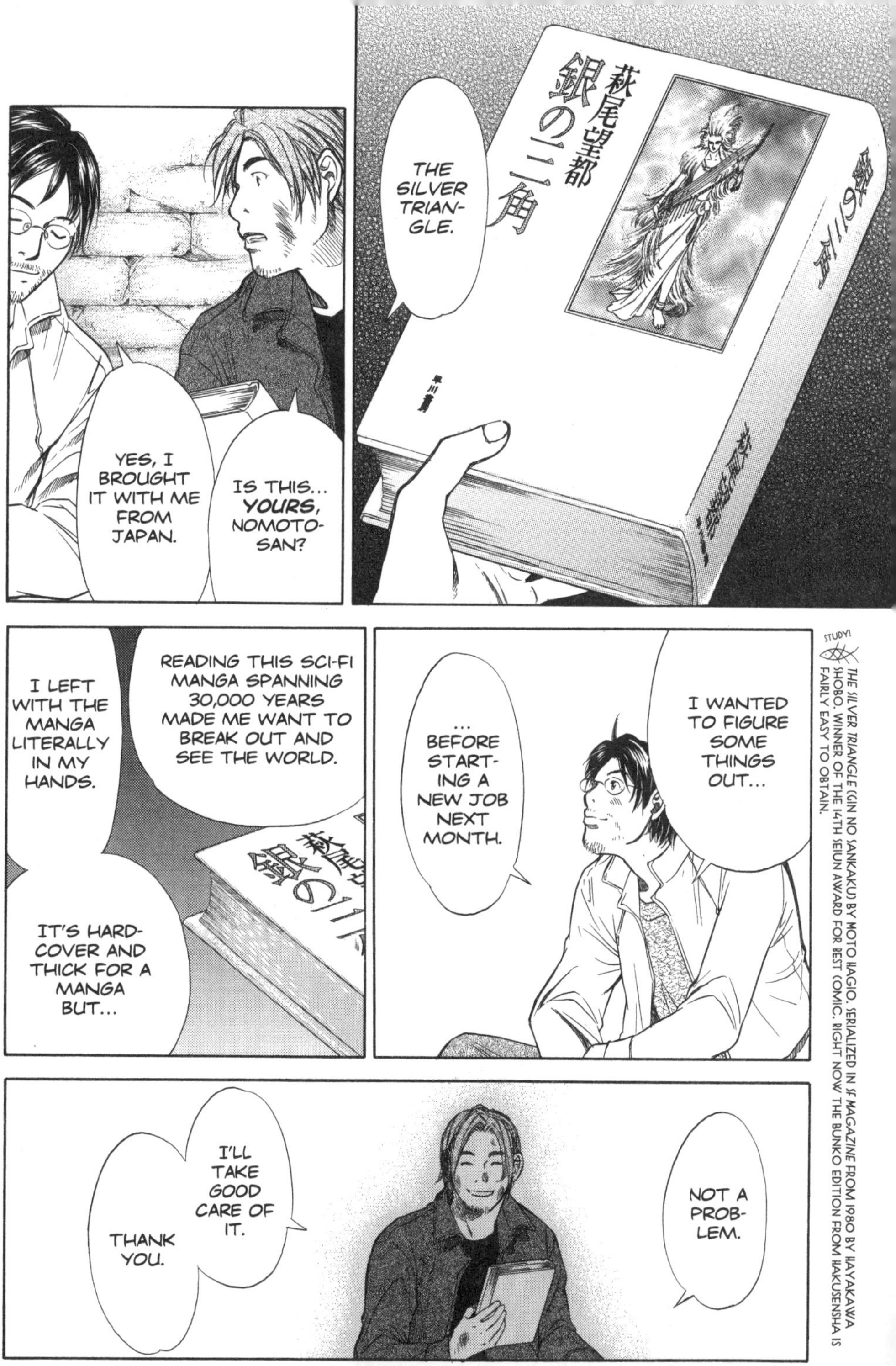
THE SILVER TRIANGLE.
IS THIS... *YOURS*, NOMOTO-SAN?
YES, I BROUGHT IT WITH ME FROM JAPAN.
I WANTED TO FIGURE SOME THINGS OUT...
...BEFORE STARTING A NEW JOB NEXT MONTH.
READING THIS SCI-FI MANGA SPANNING 30,000 YEARS MADE ME WANT TO BREAK OUT AND SEE THE WORLD.
I LEFT WITH THE MANGA LITERALLY IN MY HANDS.
IT'S HARDCOVER AND THICK FOR A MANGA BUT...
NOT A PROBLEM.
I'LL TAKE GOOD CARE OF IT.
THANK YOU.

STUDY! *THE SILVER TRIANGLE* (GIN NO SANKAKU) BY MOTO HAGIO. SERIALIZED IN SF MAGAZINE FROM 1980 BY HAYAKAWA SHOBO. WINNER OF THE 14TH SEIUN AWARD FOR BEST COMIC. RIGHT NOW THE BUNKO EDITION FROM HAKUSENSHA IS FAIRLY EASY TO OBTAIN.

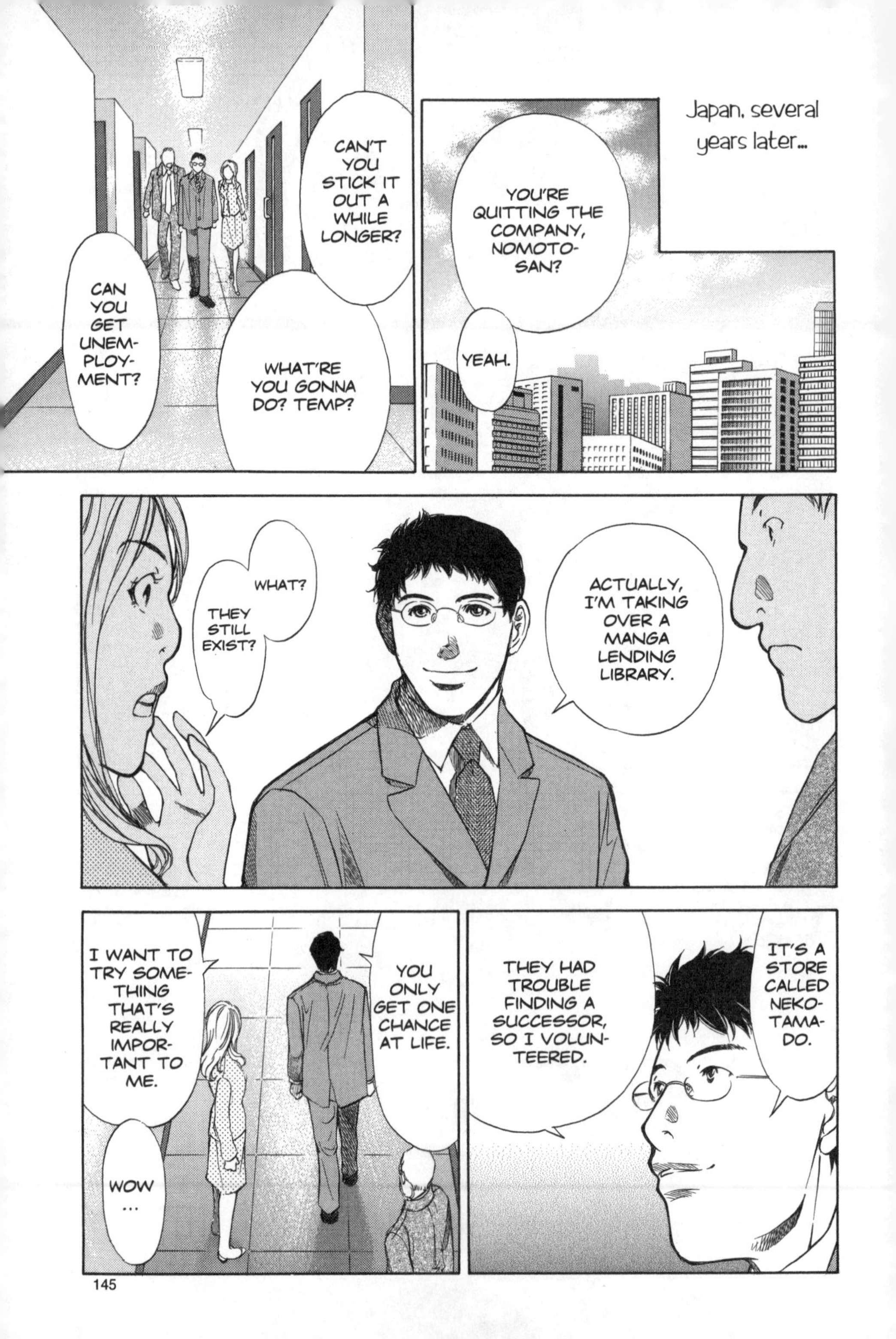
Japan, several years later...
YOU'RE QUITTING THE COMPANY, NOMOTO-SAN?
YEAH.
CAN'T YOU STICK IT OUT A WHILE LONGER?
WHAT'RE YOU GONNA DO? TEMP?
CAN YOU GET UNEMPLOYMENT?
ACTUALLY, I'M TAKING OVER A MANGA LENDING LIBRARY.
WHAT?
THEY STILL EXIST?
IT'S A STORE CALLED NEKO-TAMA-DO.
THEY HAD TROUBLE FINDING A SUCCESSOR, SO I VOLUNTEERED.
YOU ONLY GET ONE CHANCE AT LIFE.
I WANT TO TRY SOMETHING THAT'S REALLY IMPORTANT TO ME.
WOW ...

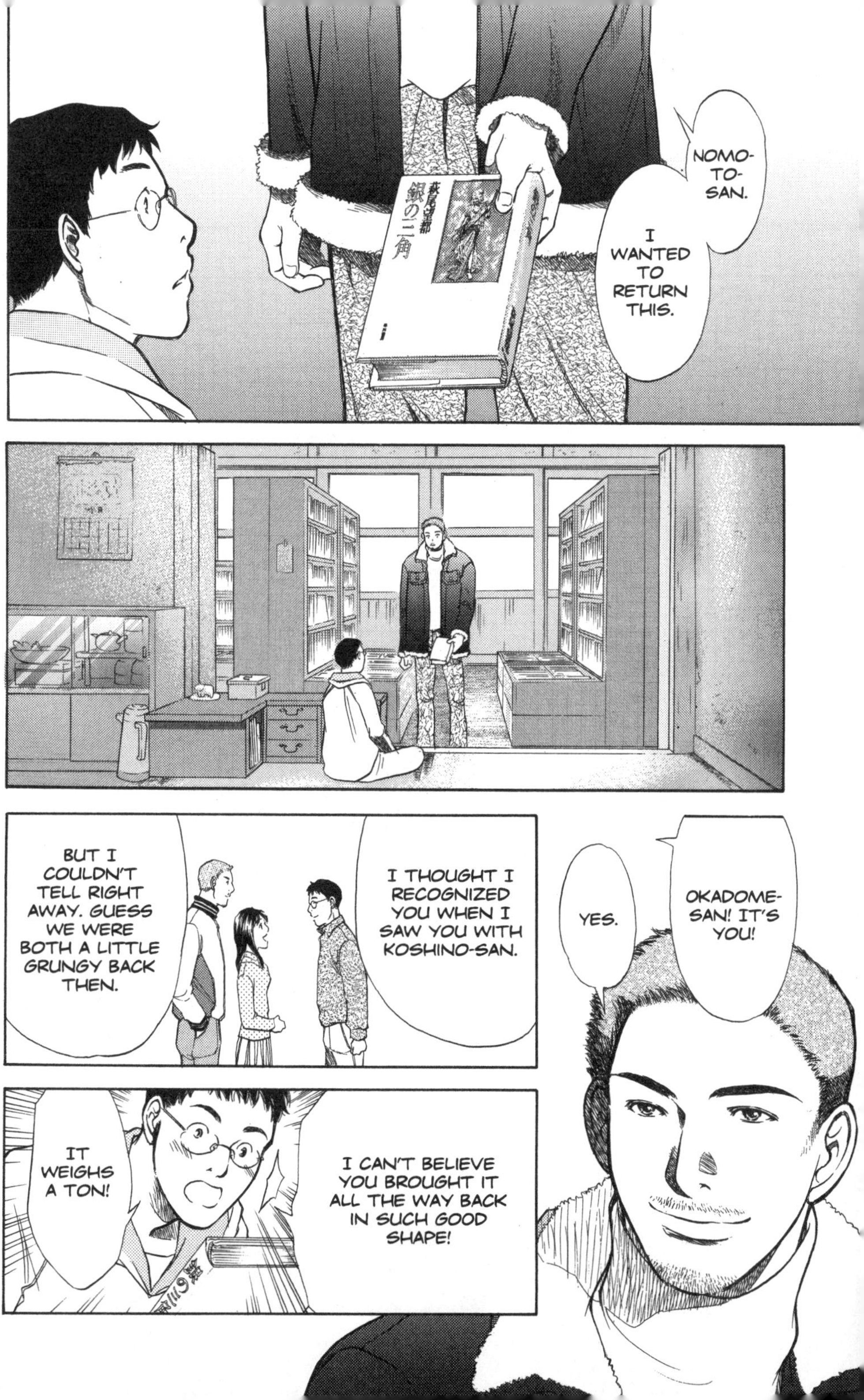
NOMO-TO-SAN.
I WANTED TO RETURN THIS.
萩尾望都
銀の三角
OKADOME-SAN! IT'S YOU!
YES.
I THOUGHT I RECOGNIZED YOU WHEN I SAW YOU WITH KOSHINO-SAN.
BUT I COULDN'T TELL RIGHT AWAY. GUESS WE WERE BOTH A LITTLE GRUNGY BACK THEN.
I CAN'T BELIEVE YOU BROUGHT IT ALL THE WAY BACK IN SUCH GOOD SHAPE!
IT WEIGHS A TON!

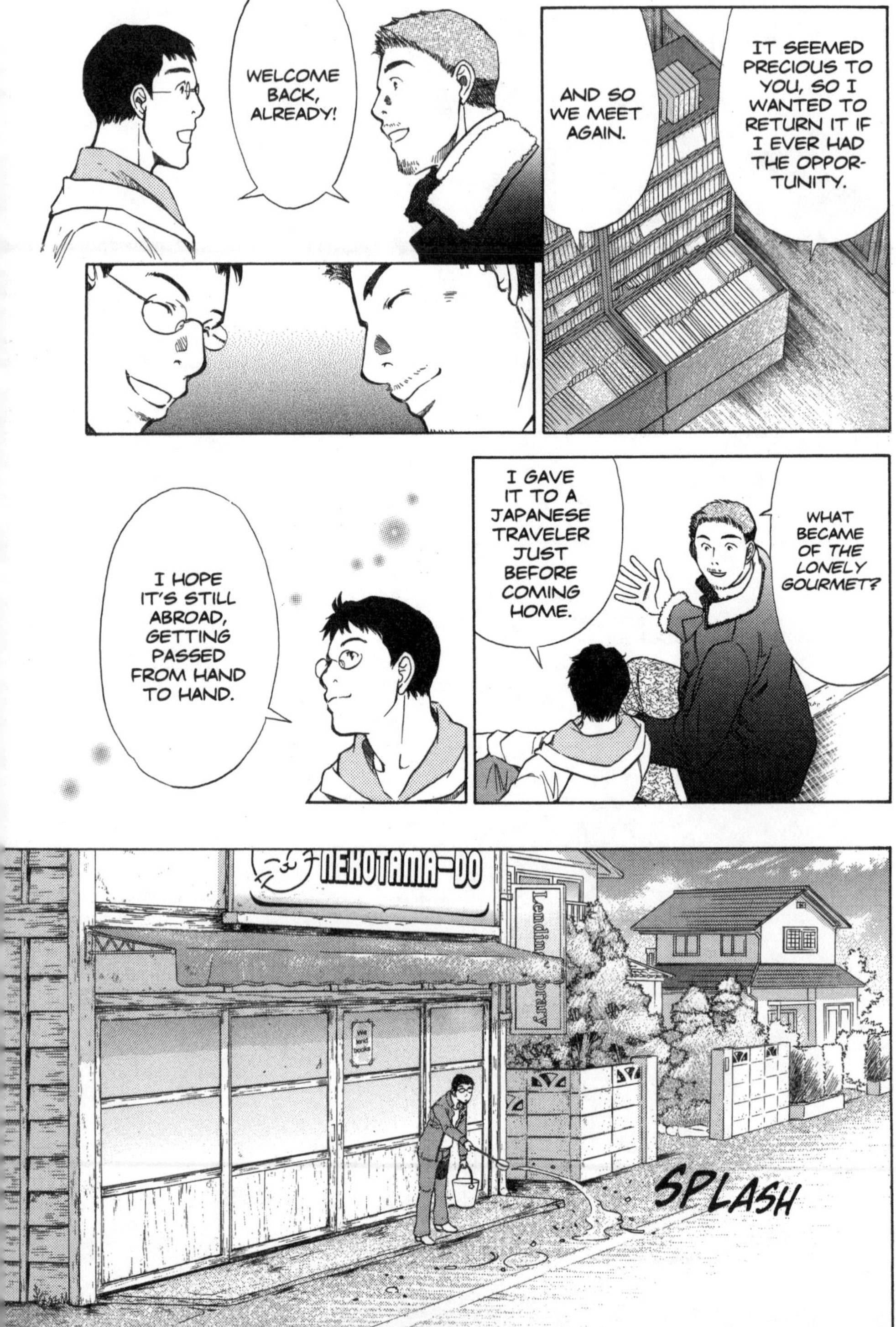
IT SEEMED PRECIOUS TO YOU, SO I WANTED TO RETURN IT IF I EVER HAD THE OPPORTUNITY.
AND SO WE MEET AGAIN.
WELCOME BACK, ALREADY!
WHAT BECAME OF THE LONELY GOURMET?
I GAVE IT TO A JAPANESE TRAVELER JUST BEFORE COMING HOME.
I HOPE IT'S STILL ABROAD, GETTING PASSED FROM HAND TO HAND.
NEKOTAMA-DO
Lending Library
We lend books
SPLASH

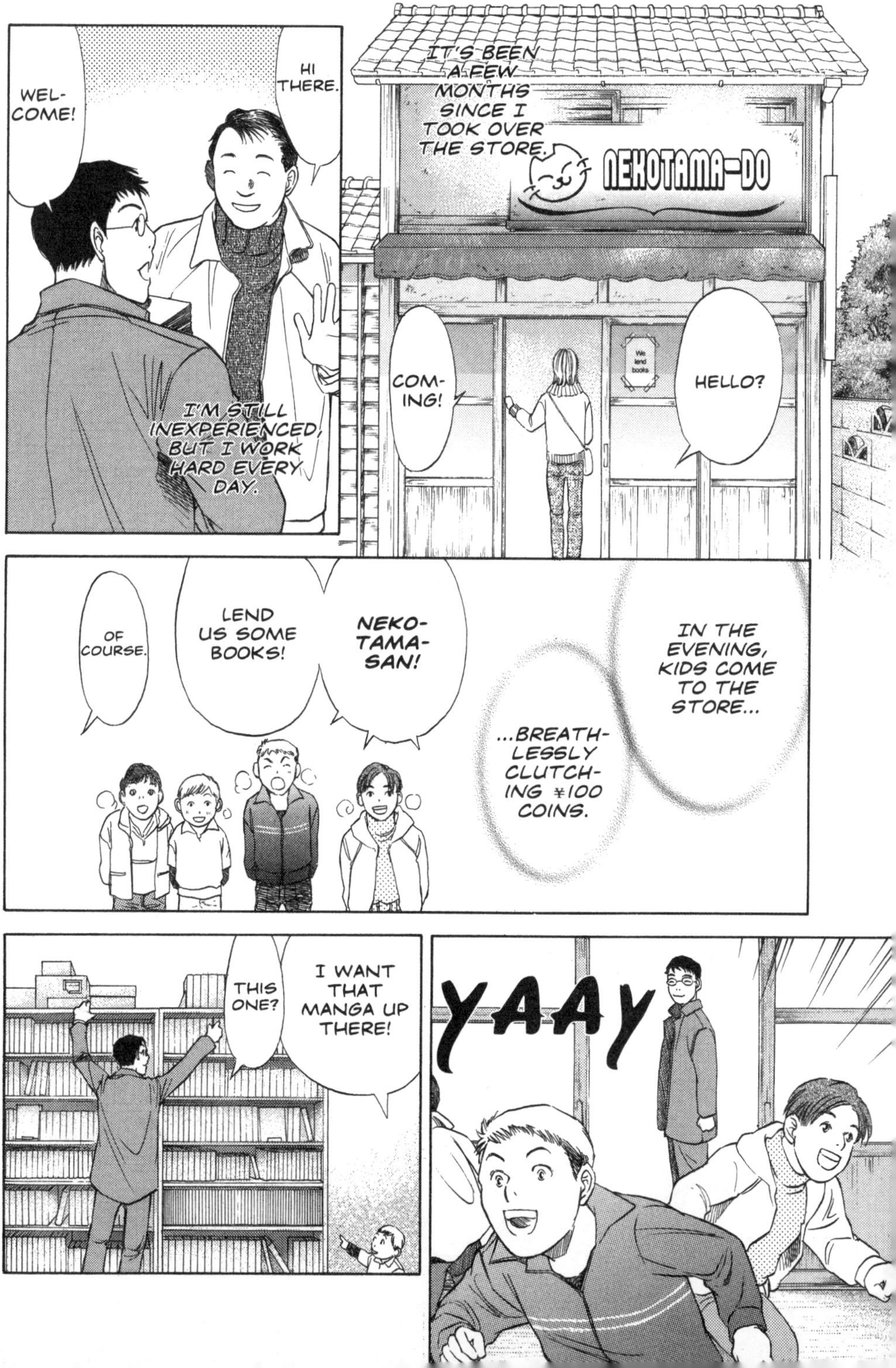
IT'S BEEN A FEW MONTHS SINCE I TOOK OVER THE STORE.
NEKOTAMA-DO
HELLO?
COM-ING!
HI THERE.
WEL-COME!
I'M STILL INEXPERIENCED, BUT I WORK HARD EVERY DAY.
IN THE EVENING, KIDS COME TO THE STORE...
...BREATH-LESSLY CLUTCH-ING ¥100 COINS.
NEKO-TAMA-SAN!
LEND US SOME BOOKS!
OF COURSE.
YAAY
I WANT THAT MANGA UP THERE!
THIS ONE?

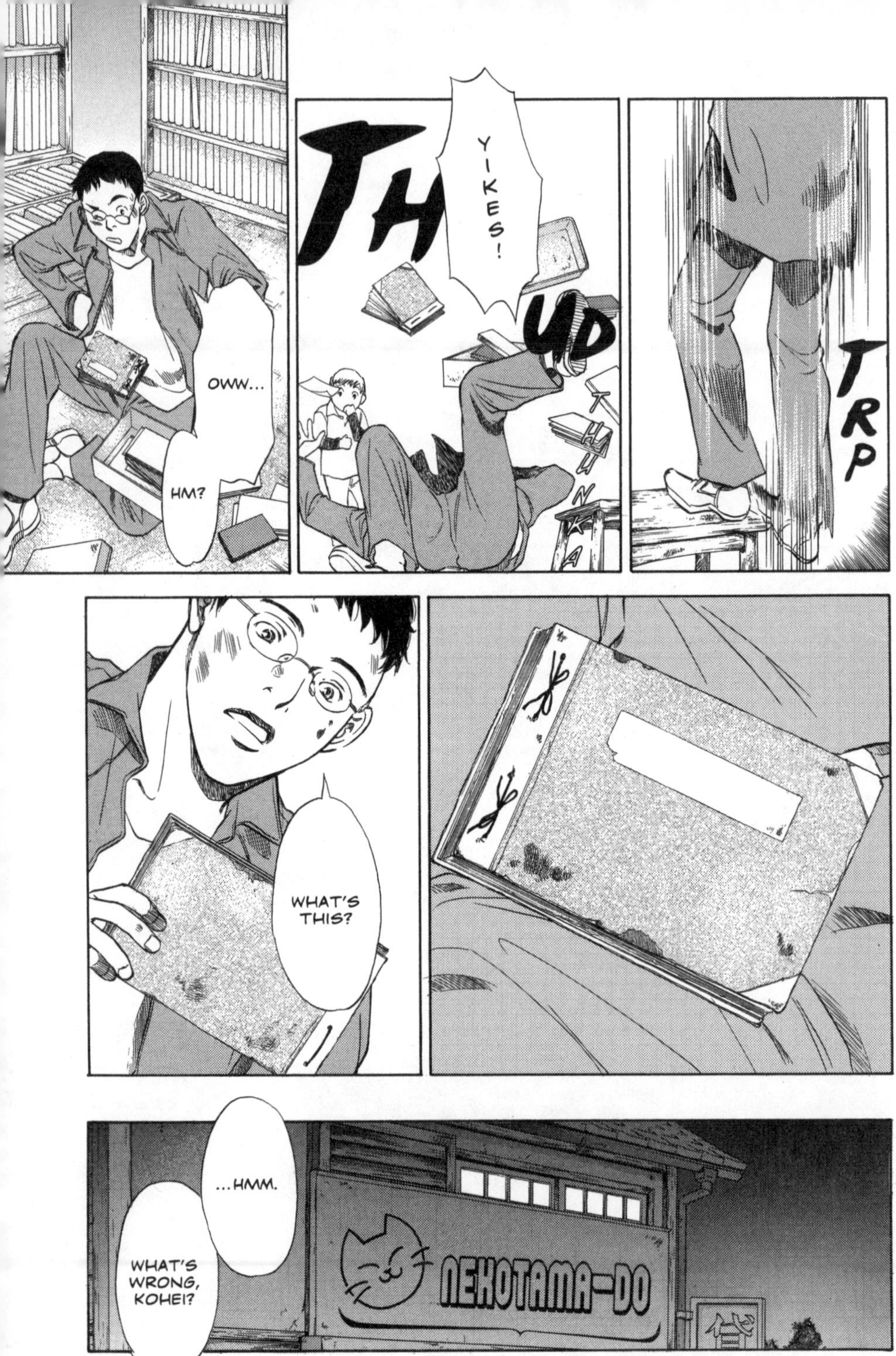
TRP
THUD
YIKES!
THUNKA
OWW...
HM?
WHAT'S THIS?
...HMM.
WHAT'S WRONG, KOHEI?
NEKOTAMA-DO

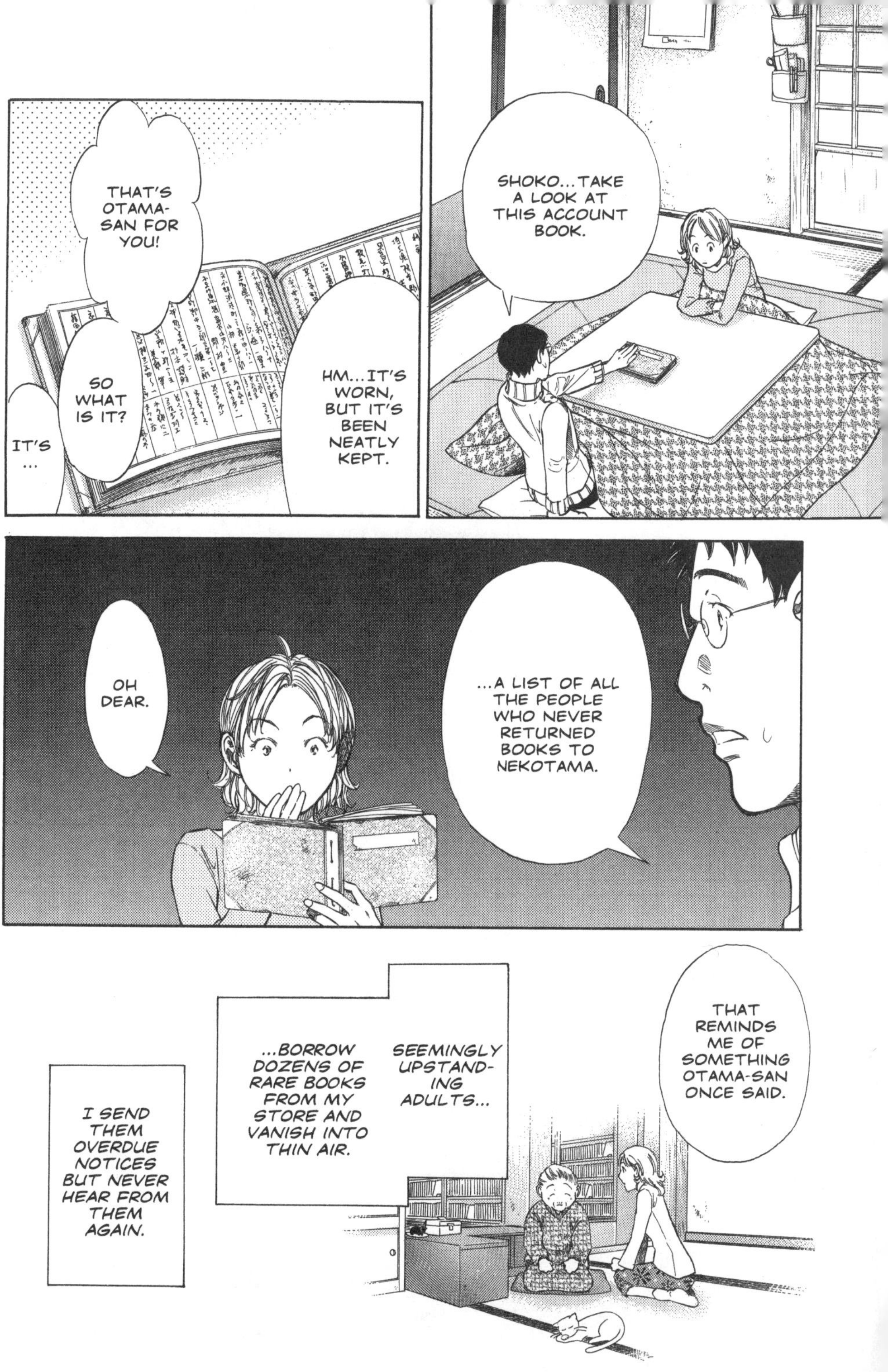
SHOKO...TAKE A LOOK AT THIS ACCOUNT BOOK.
HM...IT'S WORN, BUT IT'S BEEN NEATLY KEPT.
THAT'S OTAMA-SAN FOR YOU!
SO WHAT IS IT?
IT'S ...
...A LIST OF ALL THE PEOPLE WHO NEVER RETURNED BOOKS TO NEKOTAMA.
OH DEAR.
THAT REMINDS ME OF SOMETHING OTAMA-SAN ONCE SAID.
SEEMINGLY UPSTANDING ADULTS...
...BORROW DOZENS OF RARE BOOKS FROM MY STORE AND VANISH INTO THIN AIR.
I SEND THEM OVERDUE NOTICES BUT NEVER HEAR FROM THEM AGAIN.

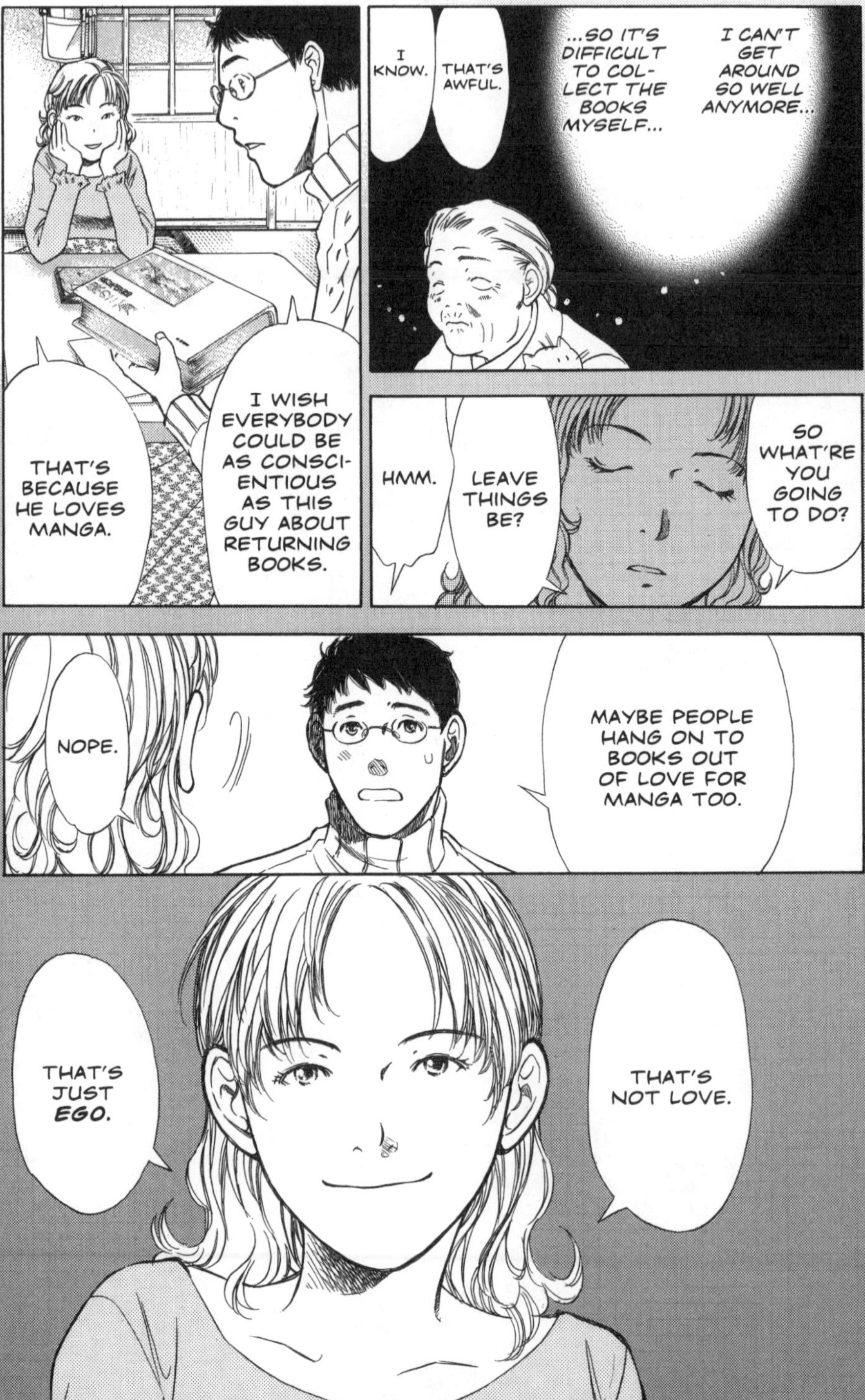
I CAN'T GET AROUND SO WELL ANYMORE...
...SO IT'S DIFFICULT TO COL-LECT THE BOOKS MYSELF...
THAT'S AWFUL.
I KNOW.
SO WHAT'RE YOU GOING TO DO?
LEAVE THINGS BE?
HMM.
I WISH EVERYBODY COULD BE AS CONSCI-ENTIOUS AS THIS GUY ABOUT RETURNING BOOKS.
THAT'S BECAUSE HE LOVES MANGA.
MAYBE PEOPLE HANG ON TO BOOKS OUT OF LOVE FOR MANGA TOO.
NOPE.
THAT'S NOT LOVE.
THAT'S JUST EGO.

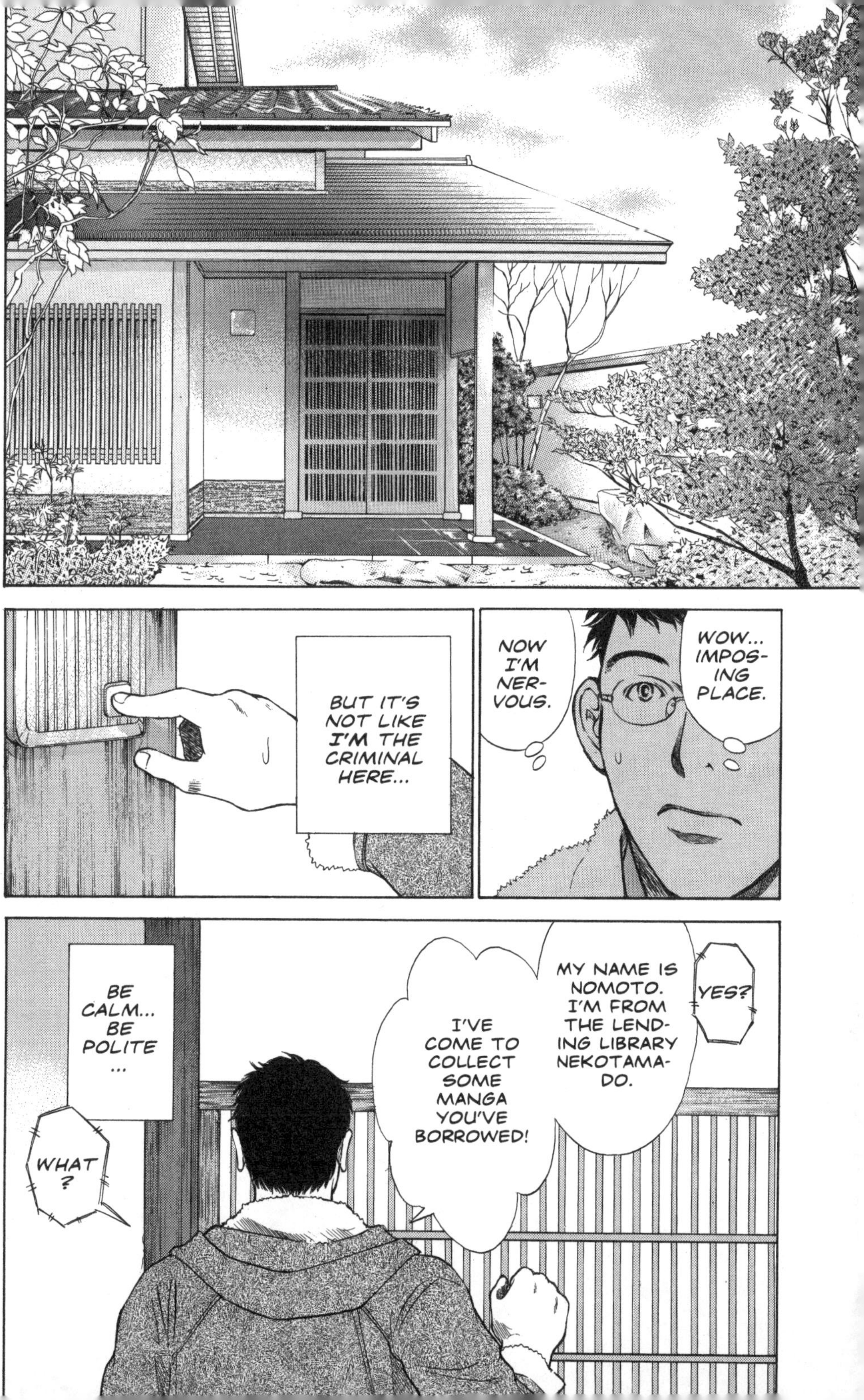
WOW... IMPOSING PLACE.
NOW I'M NERVOUS.
BUT IT'S NOT LIKE I'M THE CRIMINAL HERE...
YES?
MY NAME IS NOMOTO. I'M FROM THE LENDING LIBRARY NEKOTAMA-DO.
I'VE COME TO COLLECT SOME MANGA YOU'VE BORROWED!
BE CALM... BE POLITE...
WHAT?

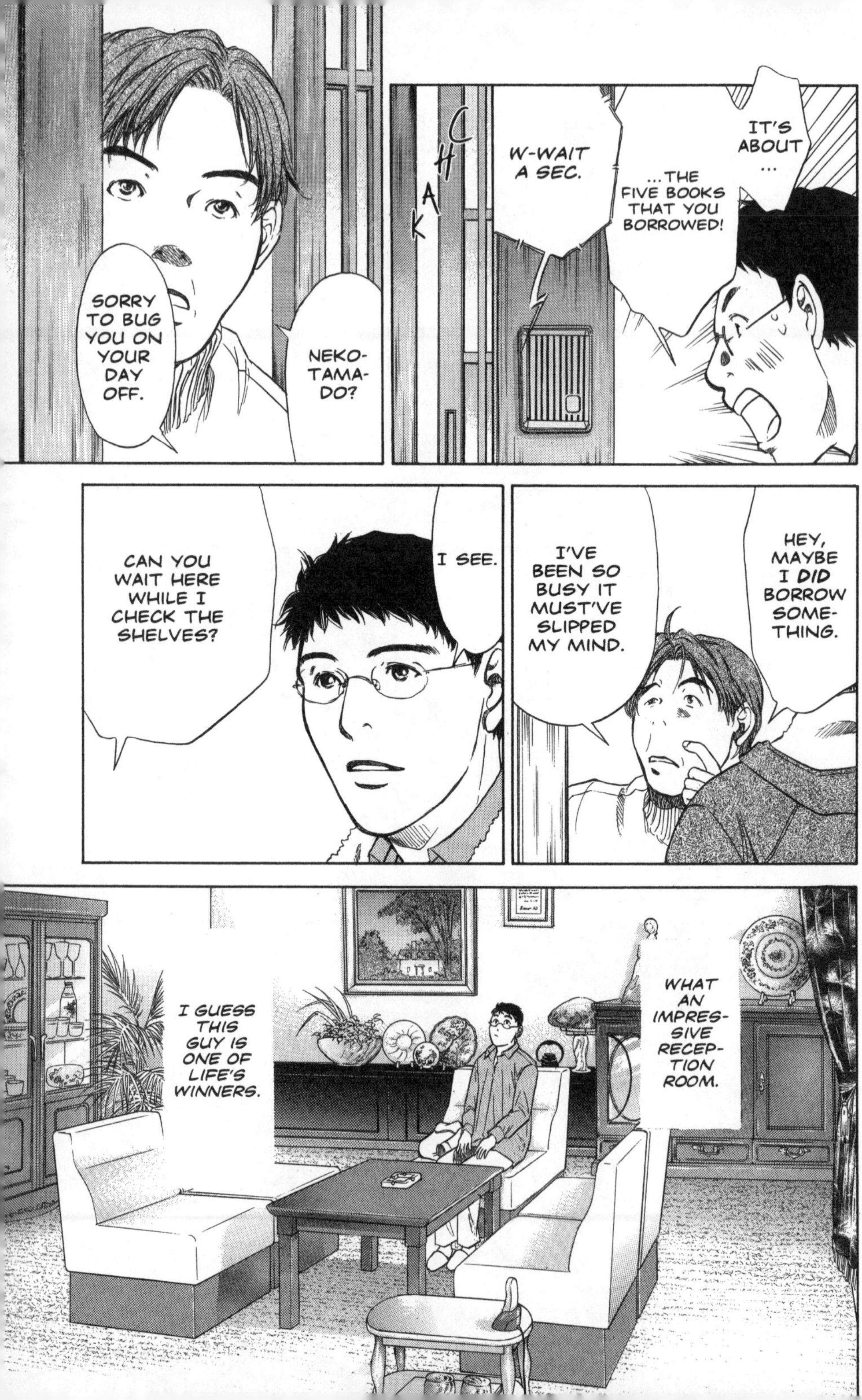
IT'S ABOUT ...
...THE FIVE BOOKS THAT YOU BORROWED!
W-WAIT A SEC.
KACH
NEKO-TAMA-DO?
SORRY TO BUG YOU ON YOUR DAY OFF.
HEY, MAYBE I *DID* BORROW SOME-THING.
I'VE BEEN SO BUSY IT MUST'VE SLIPPED MY MIND.
I SEE.
CAN YOU WAIT HERE WHILE I CHECK THE SHELVES?
WHAT AN IMPRESSIVE RECEPTION ROOM.
I GUESS THIS GUY IS ONE OF LIFE'S WINNERS.

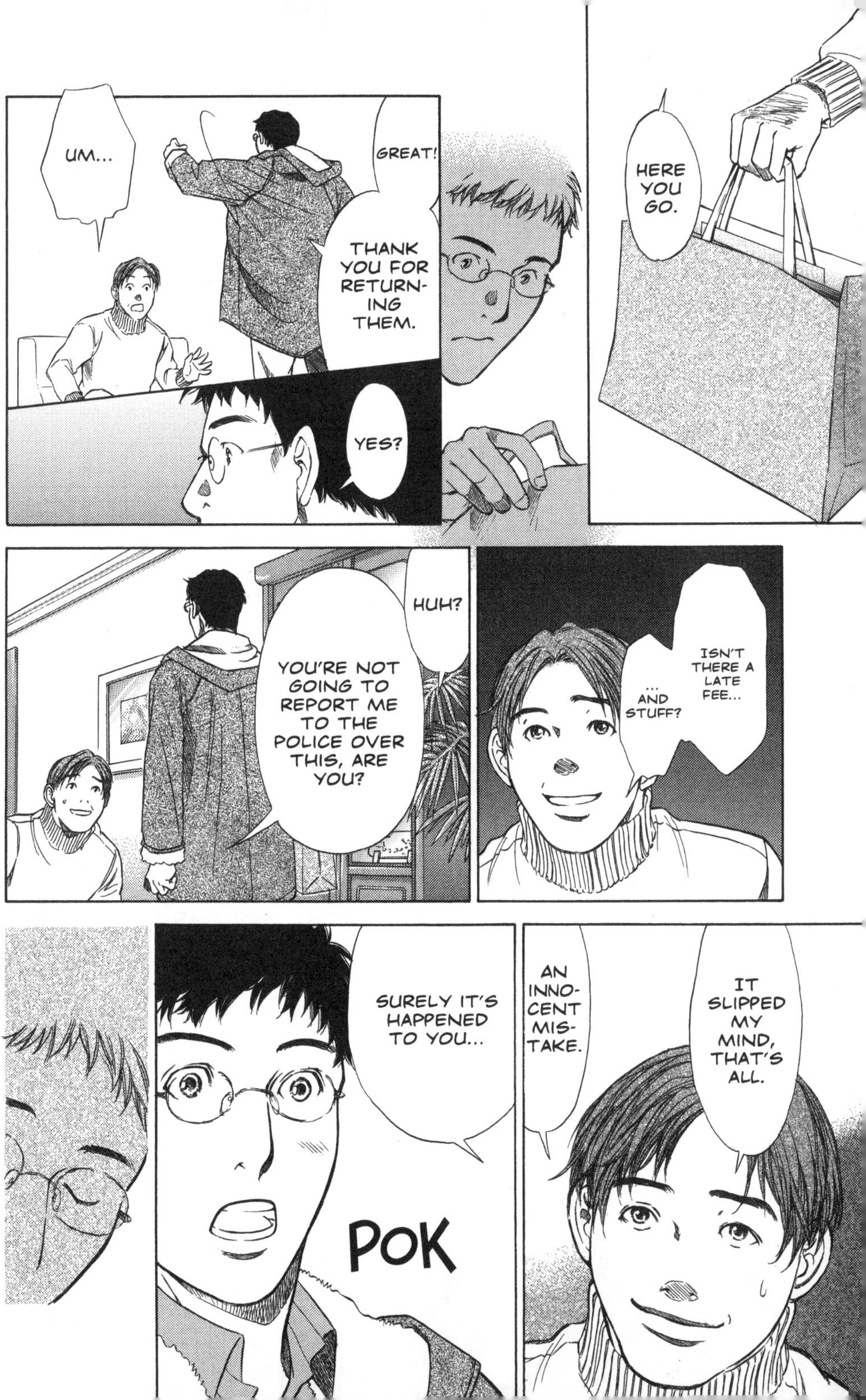
HERE YOU GO.
GREAT!
THANK YOU FOR RETURNING THEM.
UM...
YES?
ISN'T THERE A LATE FEE...
... AND STUFF?
HUH?
YOU'RE NOT GOING TO REPORT ME TO THE POLICE OVER THIS, ARE YOU?
IT SLIPPED MY MIND, THAT'S ALL.
AN INNOCENT MISTAKE.
SURELY IT'S HAPPENED TO YOU...
POK

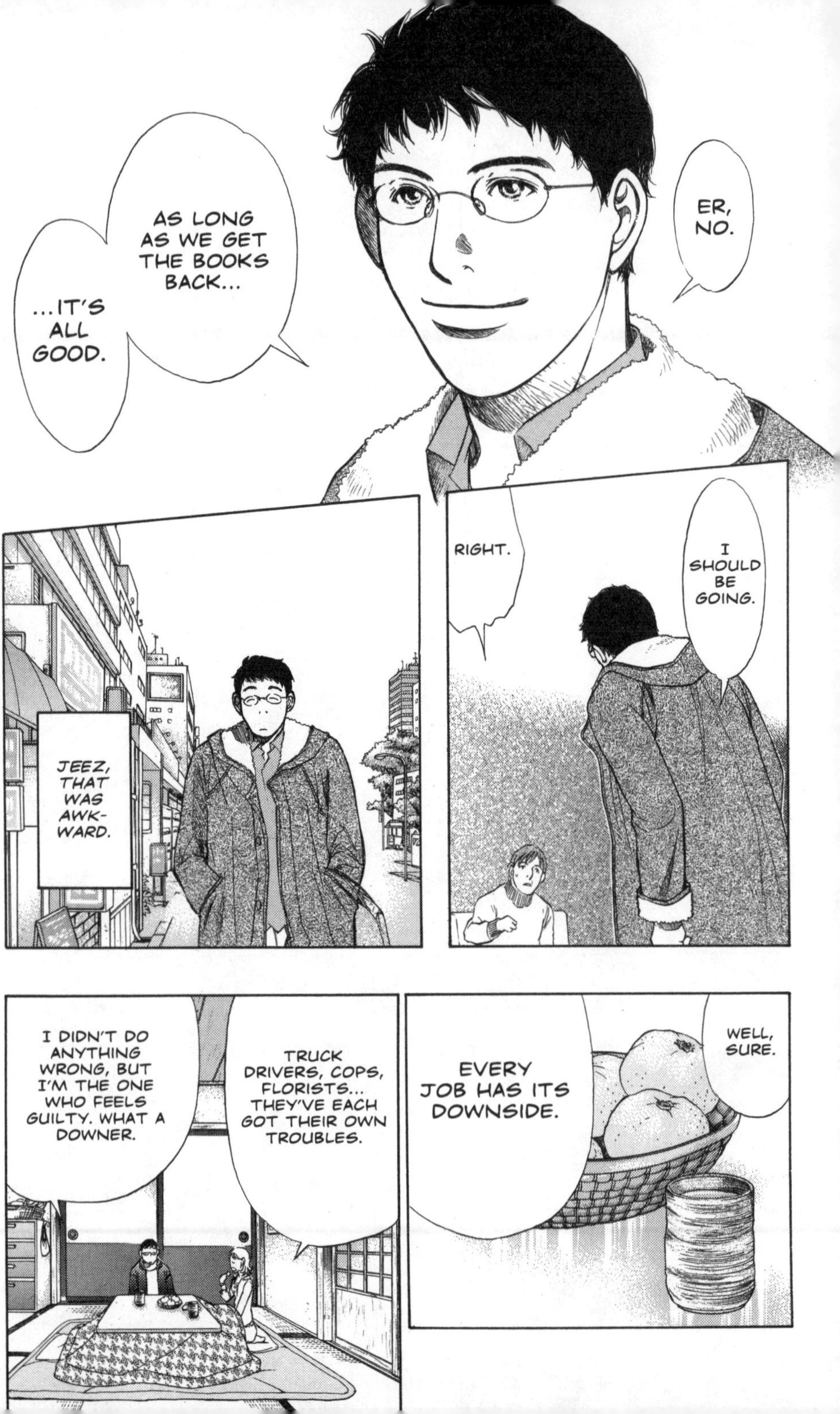
ER, NO.
AS LONG AS WE GET THE BOOKS BACK...
...IT'S ALL GOOD.
I SHOULD BE GOING.
RIGHT.
JEEZ, THAT WAS AWK-WARD.
WELL, SURE.
EVERY JOB HAS ITS DOWNSIDE.
TRUCK DRIVERS, COPS, FLORISTS... THEY'VE EACH GOT THEIR OWN TROUBLES.
I DIDN'T DO ANYTHING WRONG, BUT I'M THE ONE WHO FEELS GUILTY. WHAT A DOWNER.

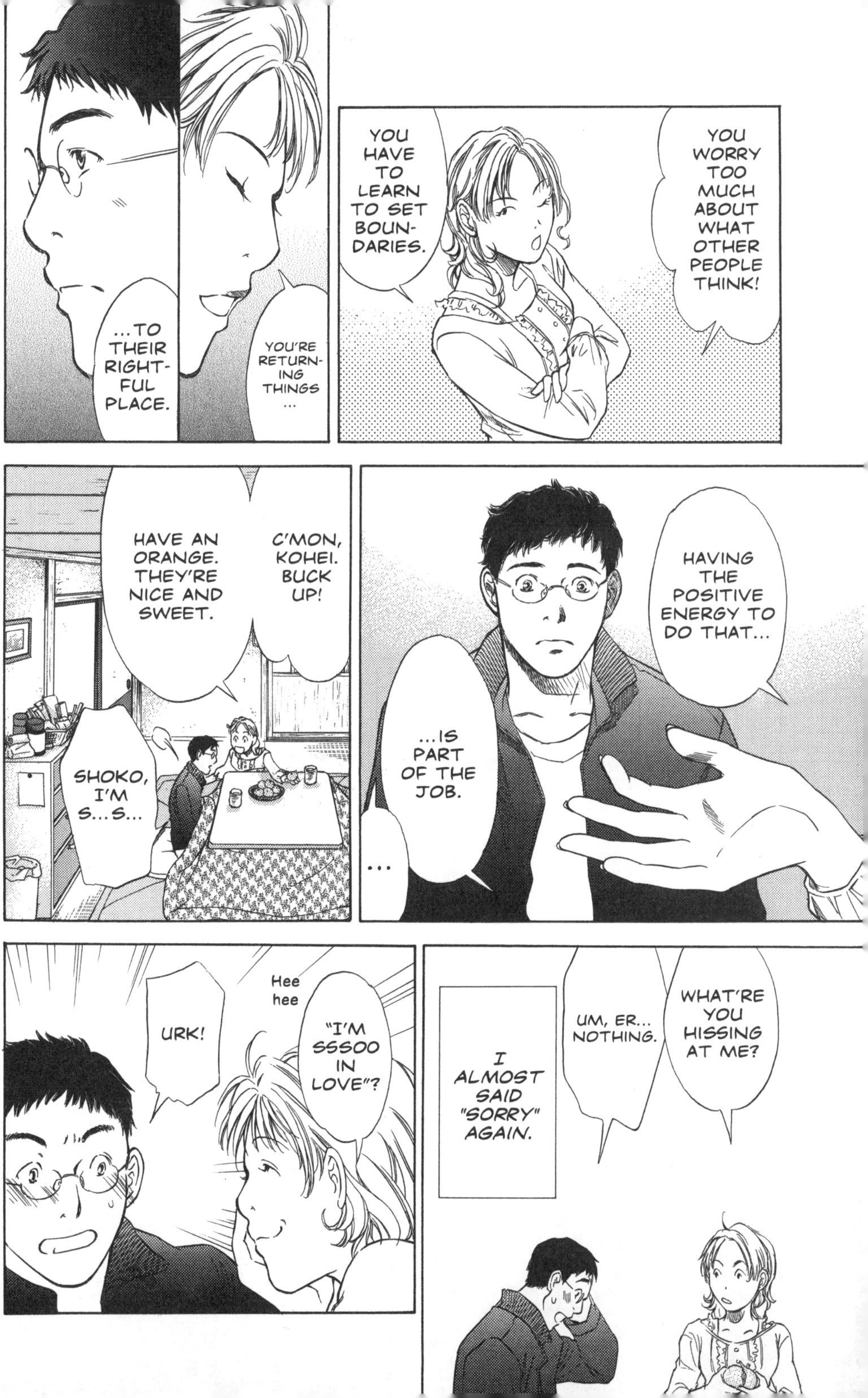
YOU WORRY TOO MUCH ABOUT WHAT OTHER PEOPLE THINK!
YOU HAVE TO LEARN TO SET BOUN-DARIES.
YOU'RE RETURN-ING THINGS ...
...TO THEIR RIGHT-FUL PLACE.
HAVING THE POSITIVE ENERGY TO DO THAT...
...IS PART OF THE JOB.
...
C'MON, KOHEI. BUCK UP!
HAVE AN ORANGE. THEY'RE NICE AND SWEET.
SHOKO, I'M S...S...
WHAT'RE YOU HISSING AT ME?
UM, ER... NOTHING.
I ALMOST SAID "SORRY" AGAIN.
Hee hee
"I'M SSSOO IN LOVE"?
URK!

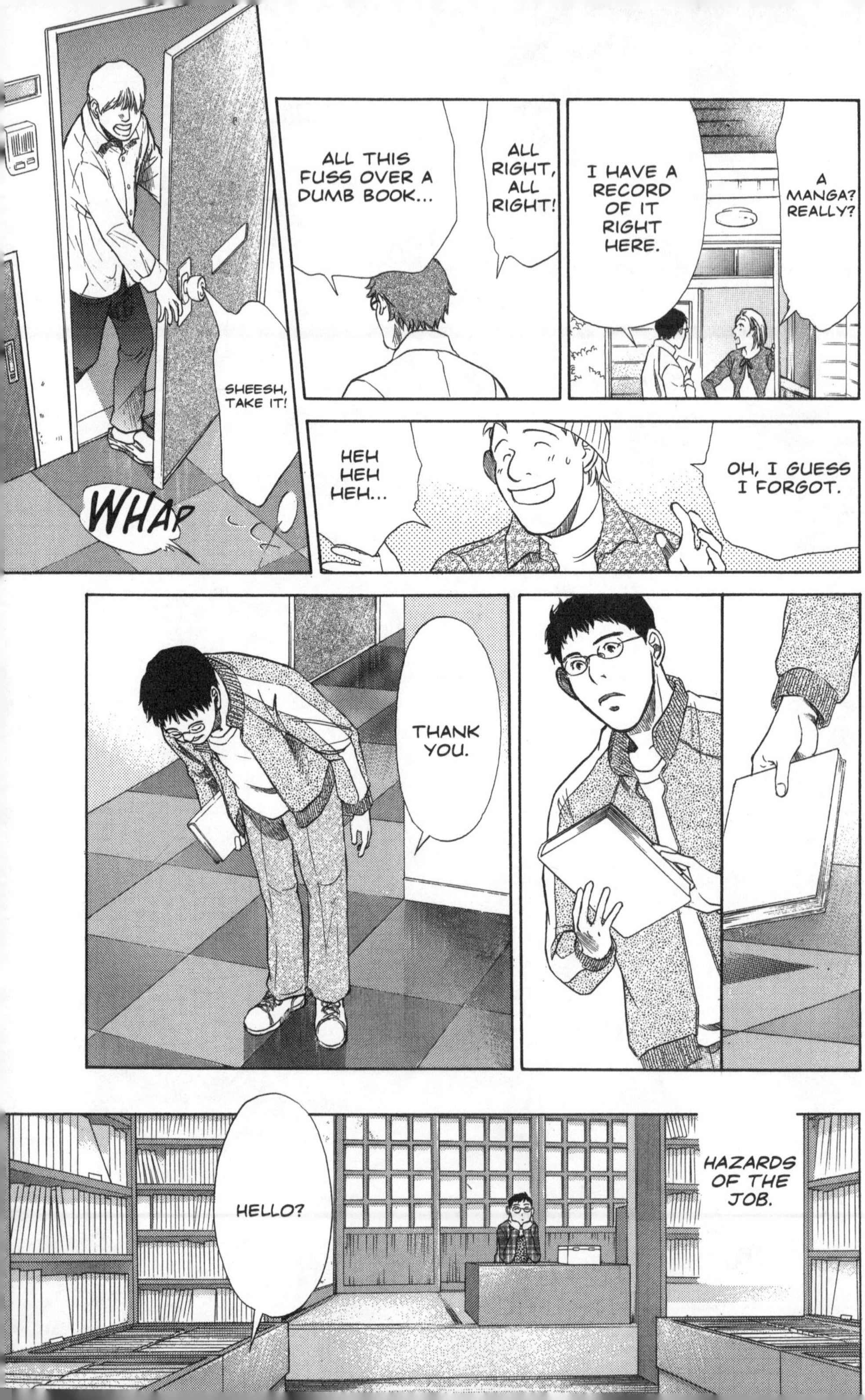
A MANGA? REALLY?
I HAVE A RECORD OF IT RIGHT HERE.
ALL RIGHT, ALL RIGHT!
ALL THIS FUSS OVER A DUMB BOOK...
OH, I GUESS I FORGOT.
HEH HEH HEH...
SHEESH, TAKE IT!
WHAP
THANK YOU.
HAZARDS OF THE JOB.
HELLO?

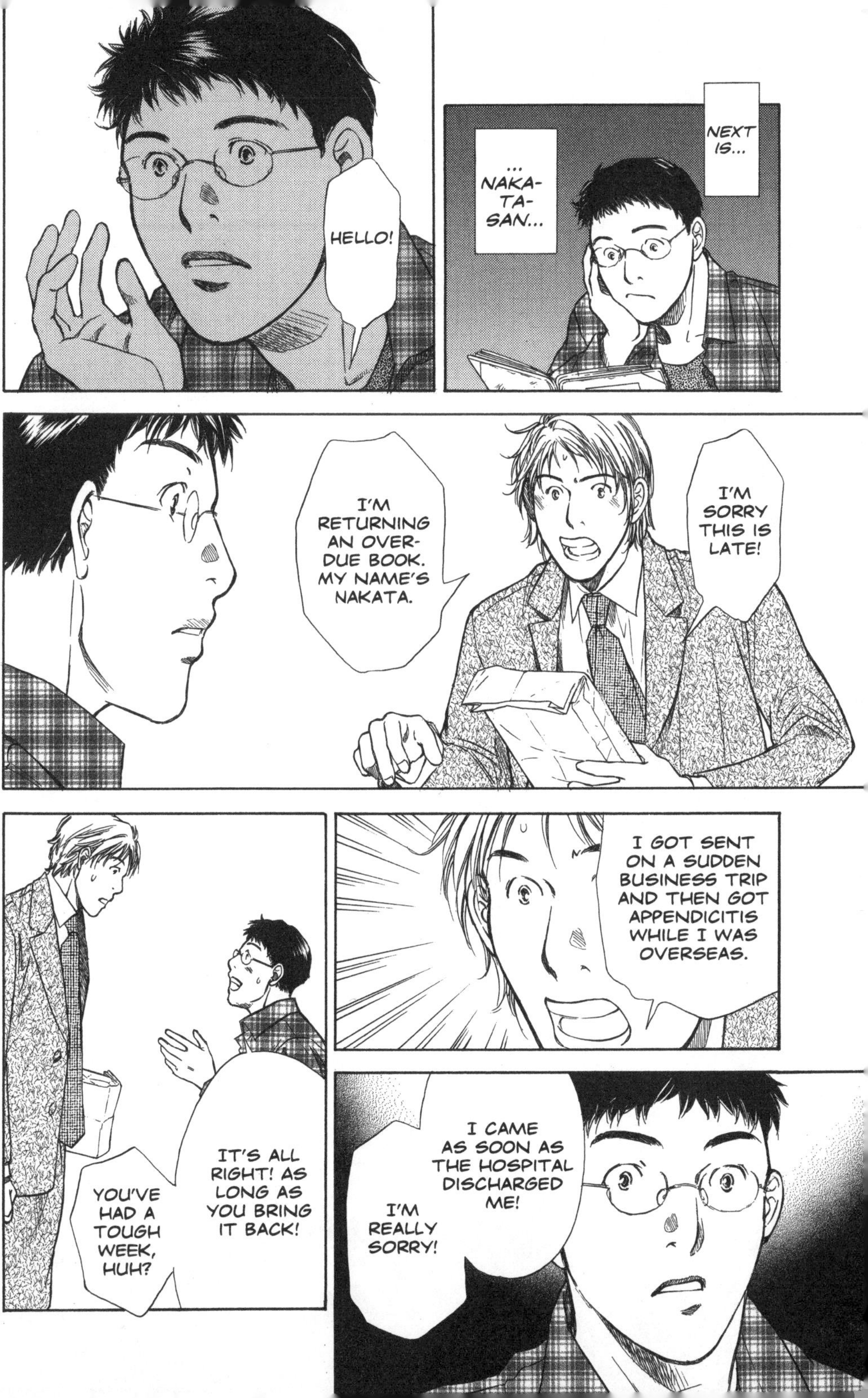
NEXT IS...
...NAKA-TA-SAN...
HELLO!
I'M SORRY THIS IS LATE!
I'M RETURNING AN OVER-DUE BOOK. MY NAME'S NAKATA.
I GOT SENT ON A SUDDEN BUSINESS TRIP AND THEN GOT APPENDICITIS WHILE I WAS OVERSEAS.
I CAME AS SOON AS THE HOSPITAL DISCHARGED ME!
I'M REALLY SORRY!
IT'S ALL RIGHT! AS LONG AS YOU BRING IT BACK!
YOU'VE HAD A TOUGH WEEK, HUH?

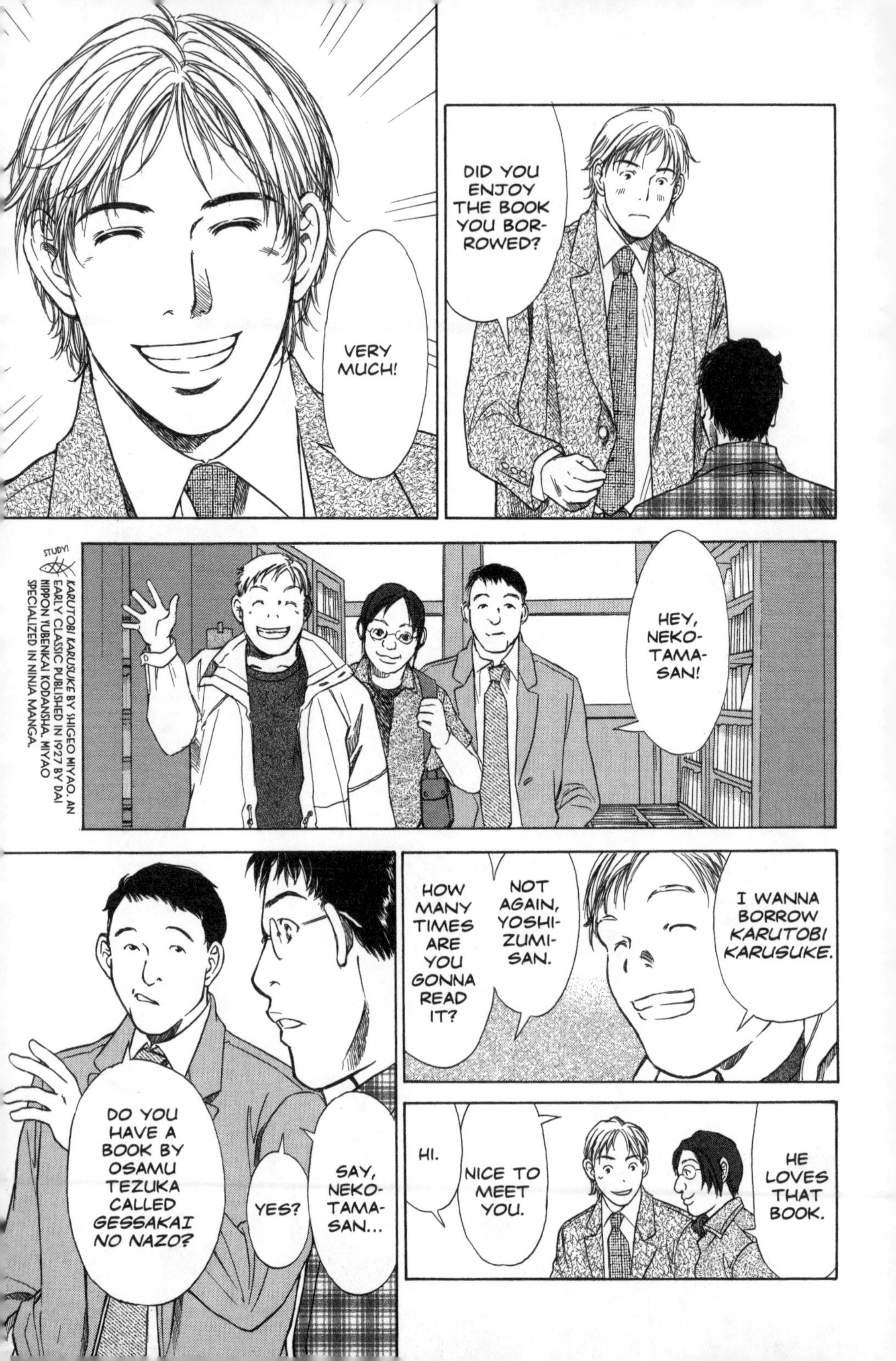
DID YOU ENJOY THE BOOK YOU BORROWED?
VERY MUCH!
STUDY!
KARUTOBI KARUSUKE BY SHIGEO MIYAO. AN EARLY CLASSIC PUBLISHED IN 1927 BY DAI NIPPON YUBENKAI KODANSHA. MIYAO SPECIALIZED IN NINJA MANGA.
HEY, NEKO-TAMA-SAN!
I WANNA BORROW KARUTOBI KARUSUKE.
NOT AGAIN, YOSHIZUMI-SAN.
HOW MANY TIMES ARE YOU GONNA READ IT?
HE LOVES THAT BOOK.
NICE TO MEET YOU.
HI.
SAY, NEKO-TAMA-SAN...
YES?
DO YOU HAVE A BOOK BY OSAMU TEZUKA CALLED GESSAKAI NO NAZO?

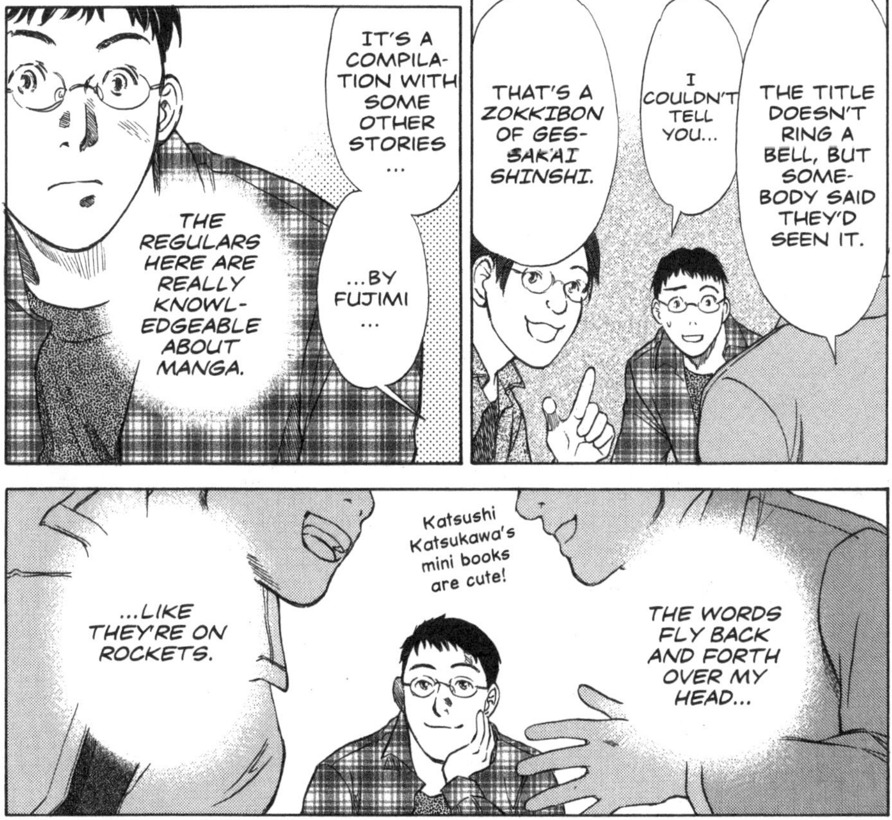
THE TITLE DOESN'T RING A BELL, BUT SOMEBODY SAID THEY'D SEEN IT.
I COULDN'T TELL YOU...
THAT'S A ZOKKIBON OF GES-SAKAI SHINSHI.
IT'S A COMPILATION WITH SOME OTHER STORIES...
...BY FUJIMI...
THE REGULARS HERE ARE REALLY KNOWLEDGEABLE ABOUT MANGA.
THE WORDS FLY BACK AND FORTH OVER MY HEAD...
Katsushi Katsukawa's mini books are cute!
...LIKE THEY'RE ON ROCKETS.

STUDY!

GESSEKAI SHINSHI (MOONY MAN): BY OSAMU TEZUKA. PUBLISHED IN 1948 BY FUJI SHOBO. A SCIENCE FICTION STORY BASED ON THE FOLKTALE *TAKETORI MONOGATARI* (THE TALE OF THE BAMBOO CUTTER). *ZOKKIBON* ARE BARGAIN BOOKS SOLD THROUGH ALTERNATIVE DISTRIBUTION METHODS. *GESSEKAI NO NAZO* (MOON SECRET) IS A *ZOKKIBON* COLLECTING *GESSEKAI SHINSHI* AND TWO OTHER STORIES, PUBLISHED IN 1956 BY FUJIMI SHUPPAN.

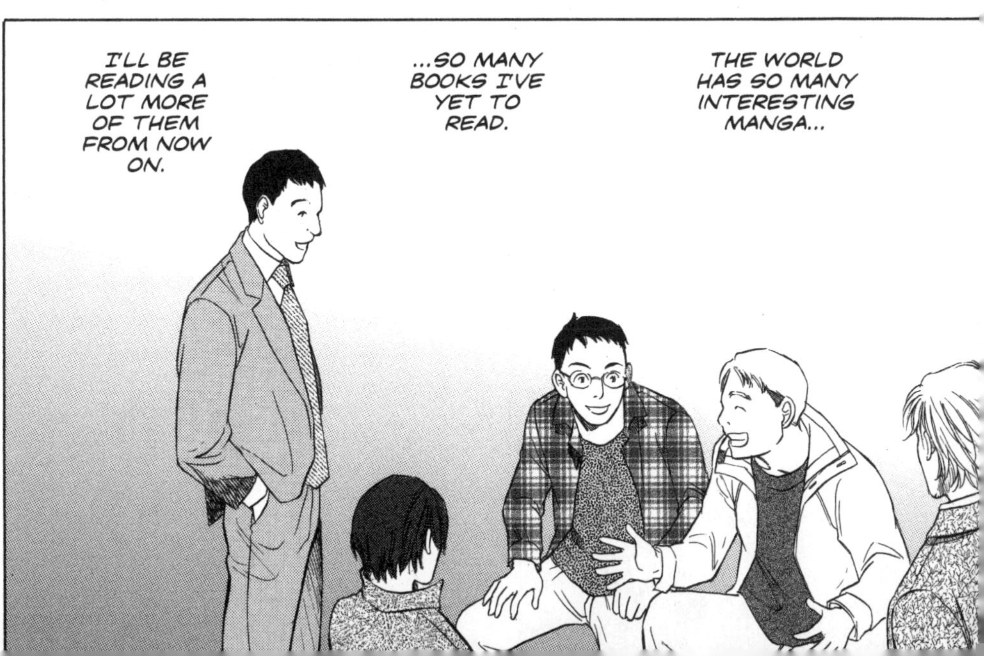
THE WORLD HAS SO MANY INTERESTING MANGA...
...SO MANY BOOKS I'VE YET TO READ.
I'LL BE READING A LOT MORE OF THEM FROM NOW ON.

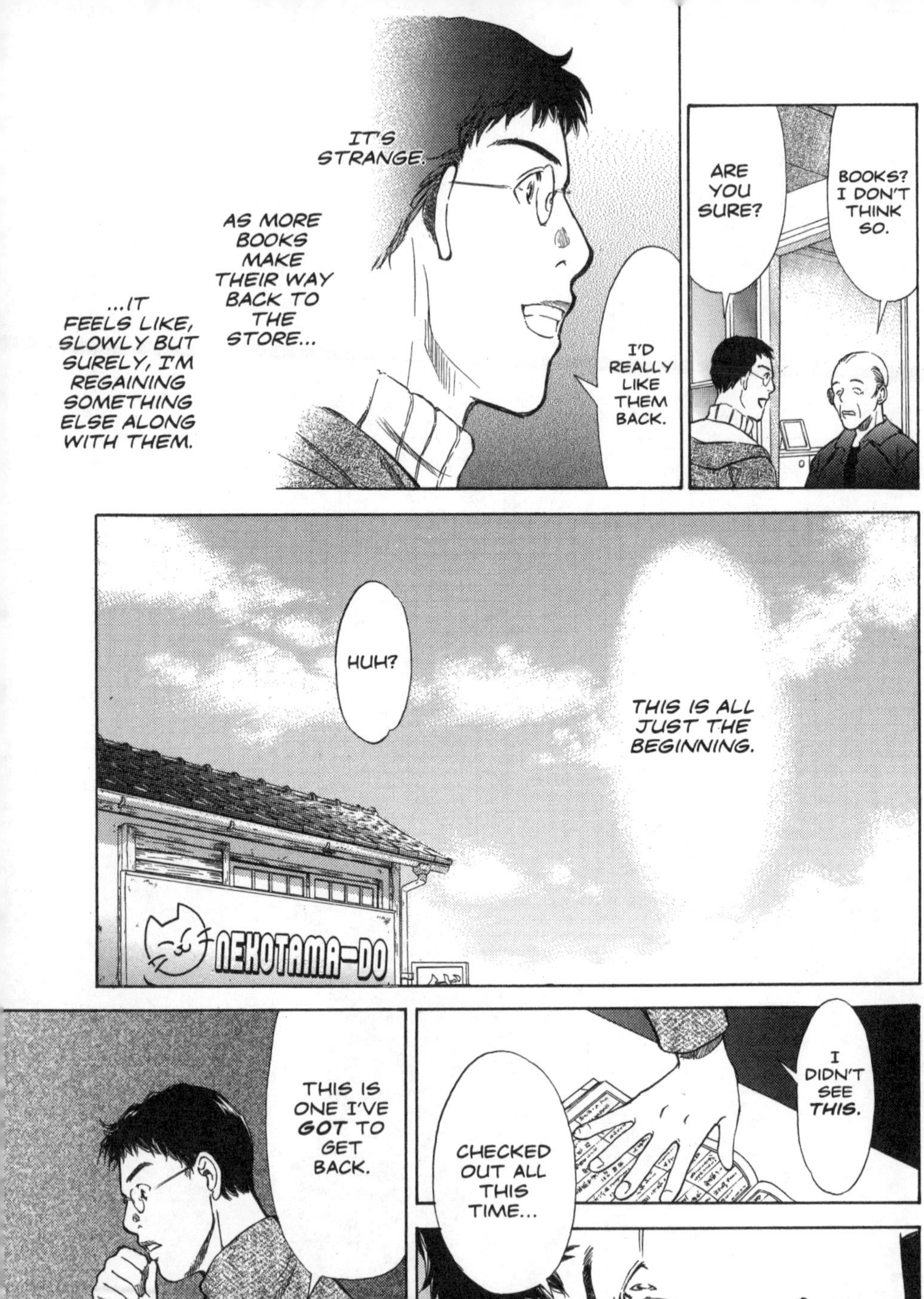
BOOKS? I DON'T THINK SO.
ARE YOU SURE?
I'D REALLY LIKE THEM BACK.
IT'S STRANGE.
AS MORE BOOKS MAKE THEIR WAY BACK TO THE STORE...
...IT FEELS LIKE, SLOWLY BUT SURELY, I'M REGAINING SOMETHING ELSE ALONG WITH THEM.
THIS IS ALL JUST THE BEGINNING.
HUH?
NEKOTAMA-DO
I DIDN'T SEE **THIS**.
CHECKED OUT ALL THIS TIME...
THIS IS ONE I'VE **GOT** TO GET BACK.

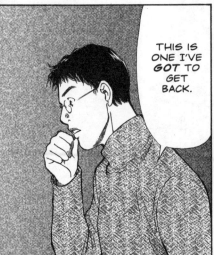

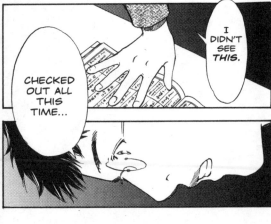

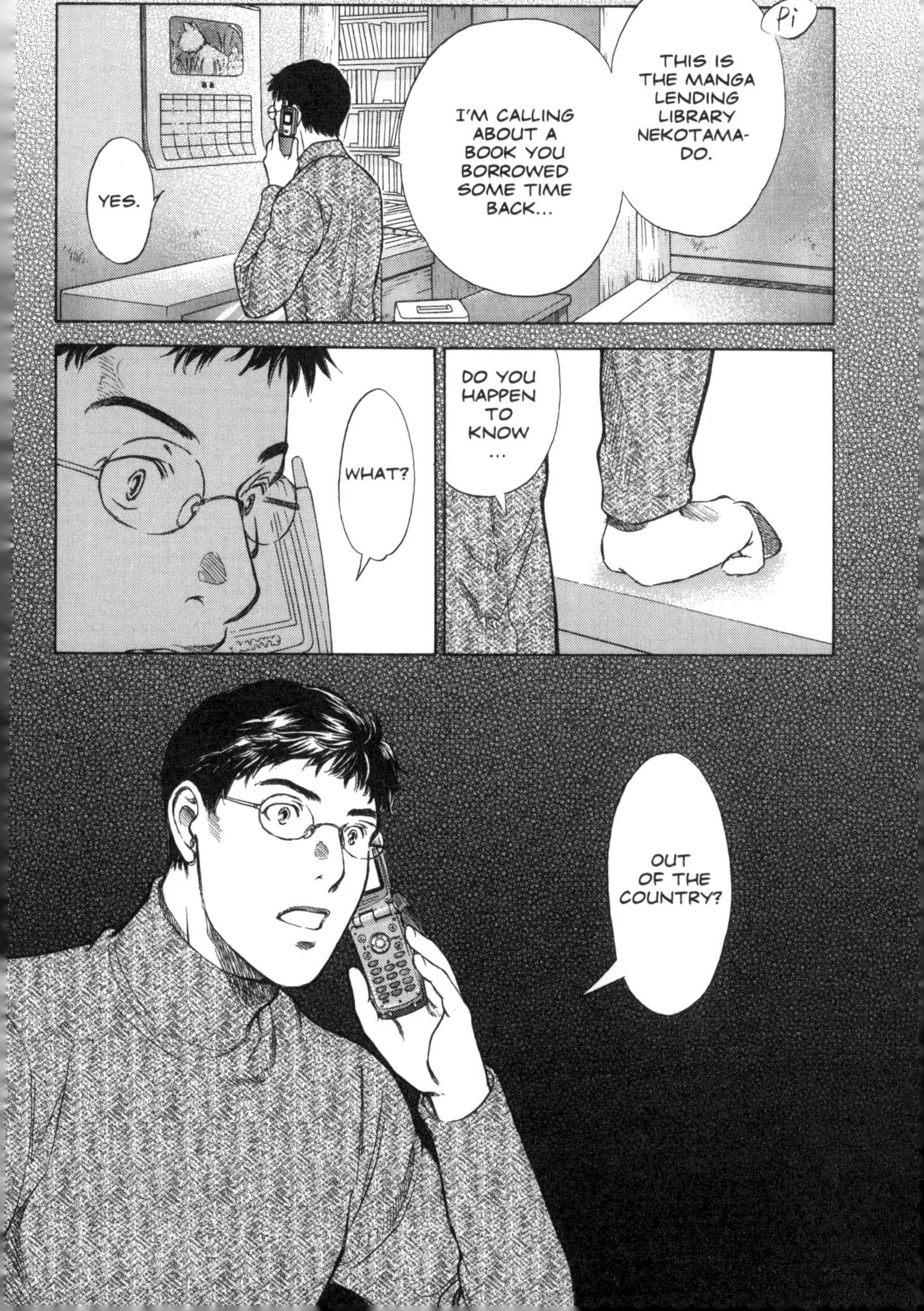
Pi
THIS IS THE MANGA LENDING LIBRARY NEKOTAMA-DO.
I'M CALLING ABOUT A BOOK YOU BORROWED SOME TIME BACK...
YES.
DO YOU HAPPEN TO KNOW ...
WHAT?
OUT OF THE COUNTRY?

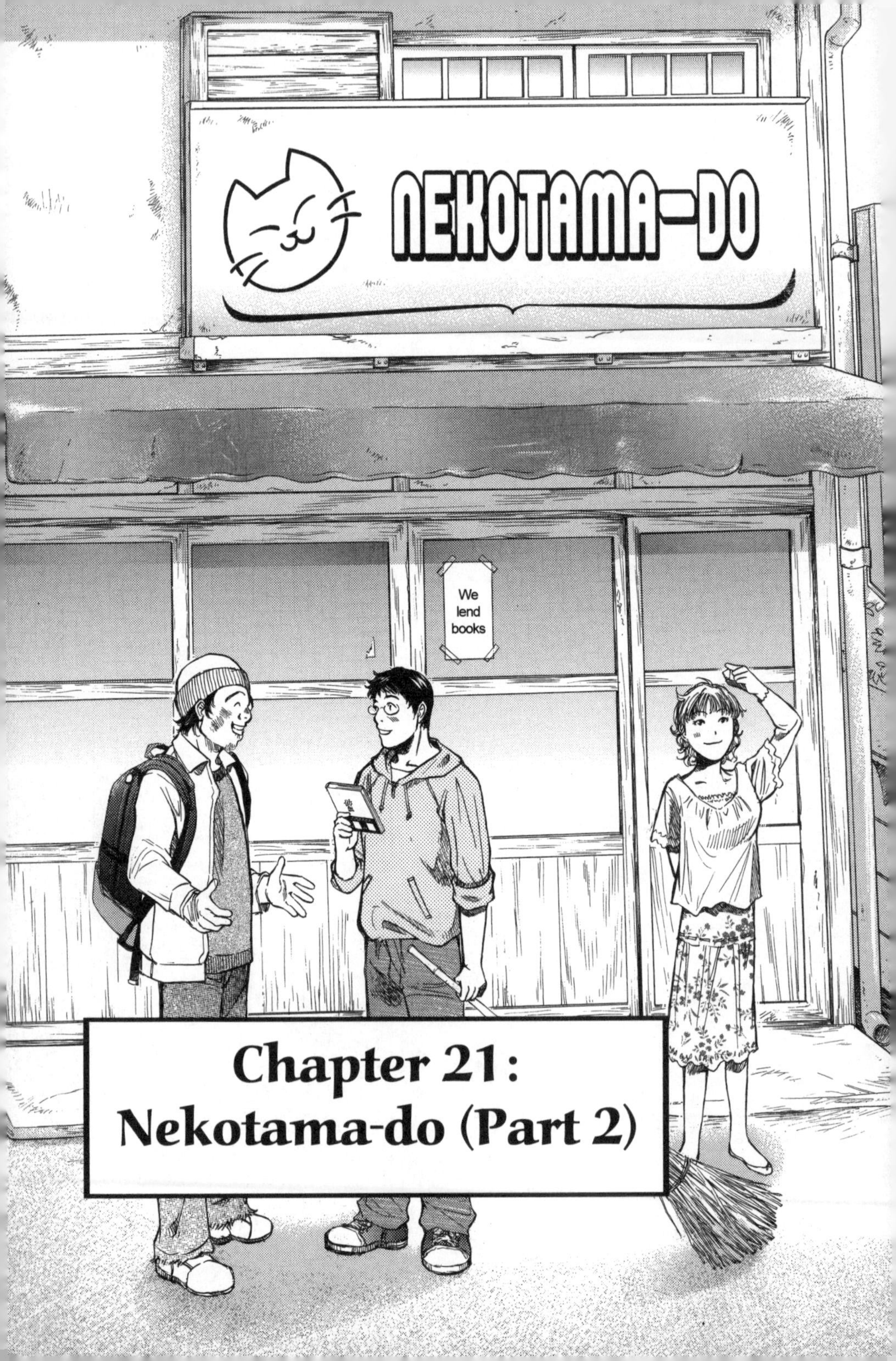
NEKOTAMA-DO
We lend books

Chapter 21: Nekotama-do (Part 2)

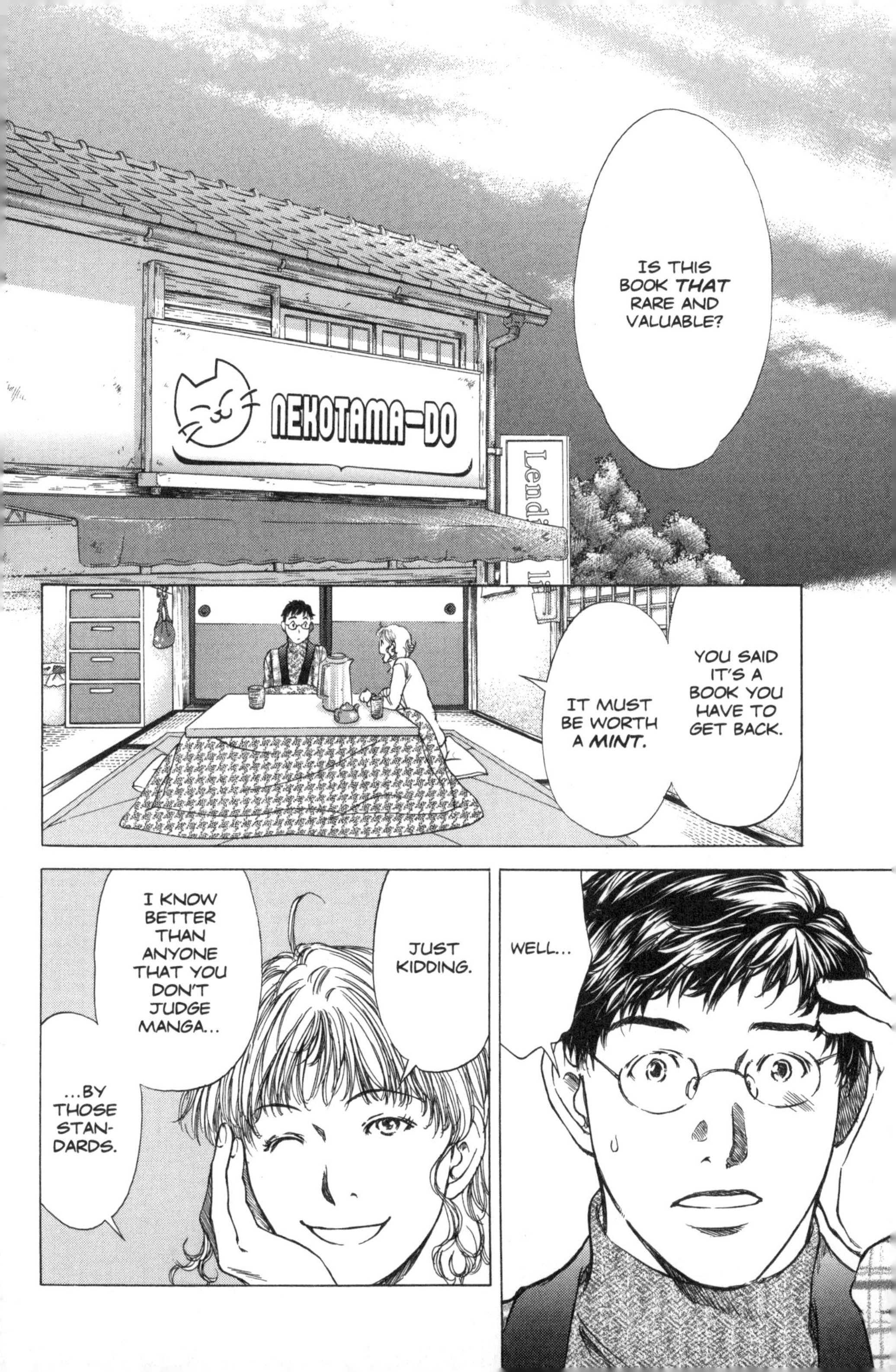
NEKOTAMA-DO
IS THIS BOOK THAT RARE AND VALUABLE?
YOU SAID IT'S A BOOK YOU HAVE TO GET BACK.
IT MUST BE WORTH A MINT.
WELL...
JUST KIDDING.
I KNOW BETTER THAN ANYONE THAT YOU DON'T JUDGE MANGA...
...BY THOSE STANDARDS.

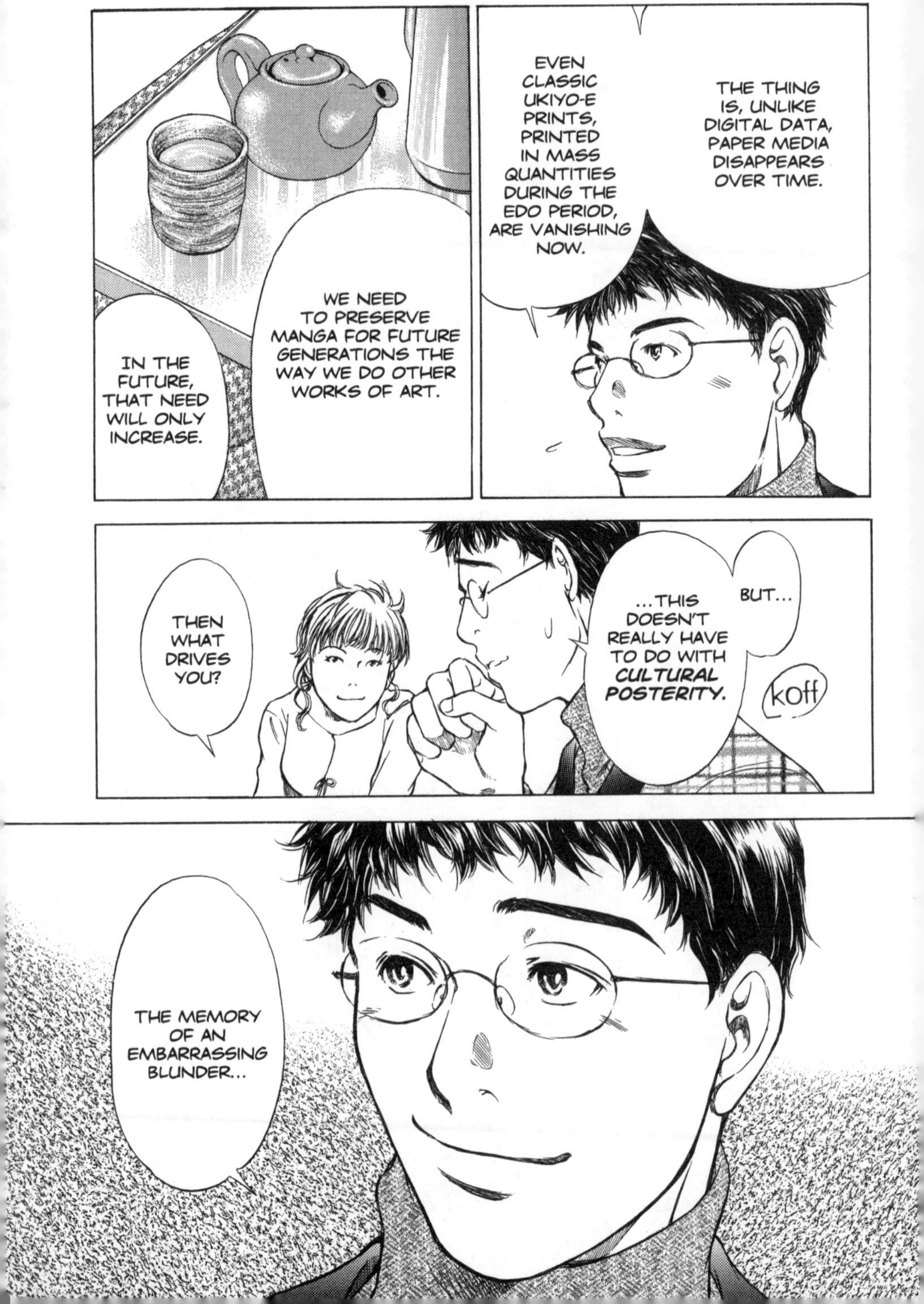
THE THING IS, UNLIKE DIGITAL DATA, PAPER MEDIA DISAPPEARS OVER TIME.
EVEN CLASSIC UKIYO-E PRINTS, PRINTED IN MASS QUANTITIES DURING THE EDO PERIOD, ARE VANISHING NOW.
WE NEED TO PRESERVE MANGA FOR FUTURE GENERATIONS THE WAY WE DO OTHER WORKS OF ART.
IN THE FUTURE, THAT NEED WILL ONLY INCREASE.
koff
BUT...
...THIS DOESN'T REALLY HAVE TO DO WITH *CULTURAL POSTERITY.*
THEN WHAT DRIVES YOU?
THE MEMORY OF AN EMBARRASSING BLUNDER...

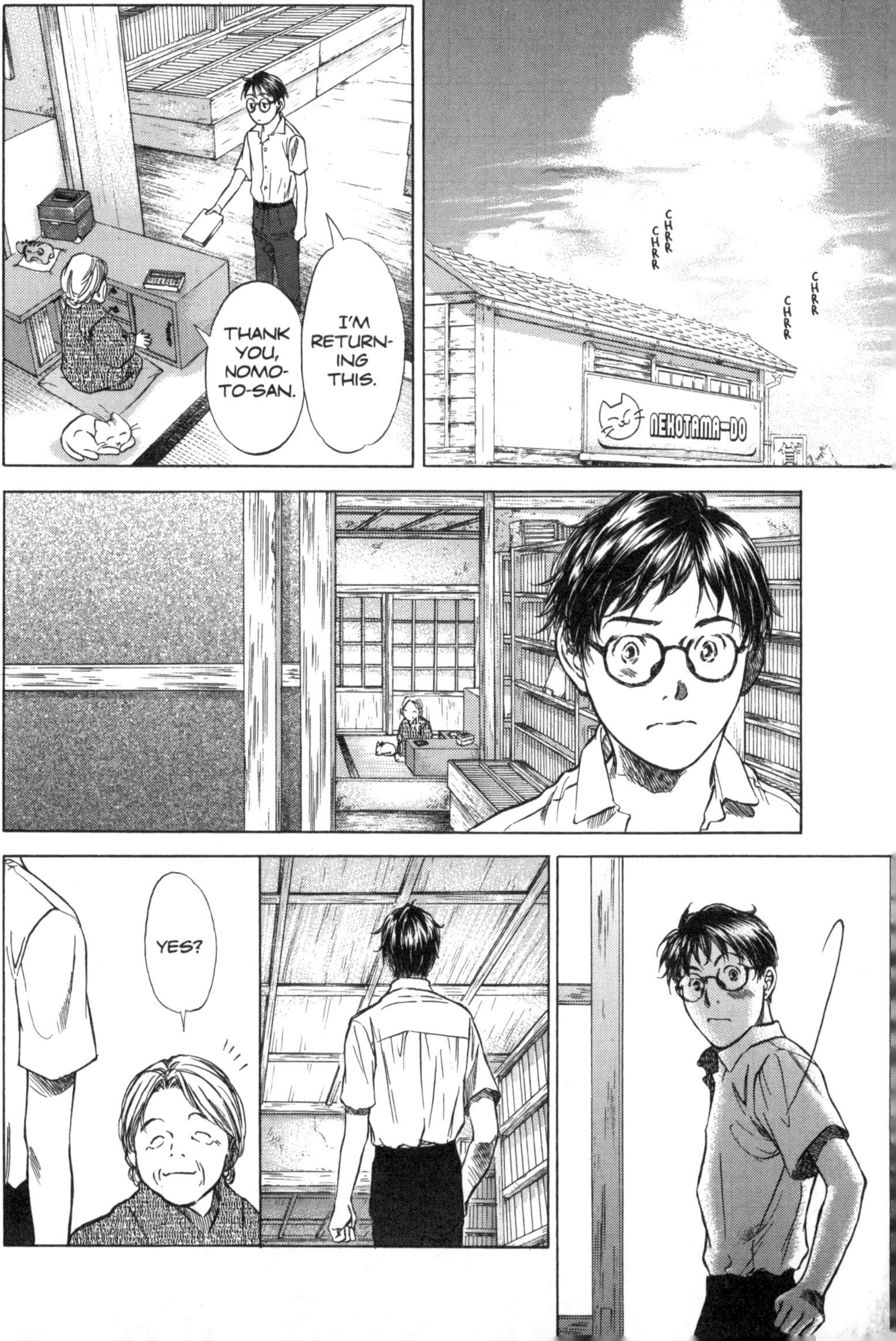
CHRR CHRR
CHRR CHRR
NEKOTAMA-DO
I'M RETURNING THIS.
THANK YOU, NOMOTO-SAN.
YES?

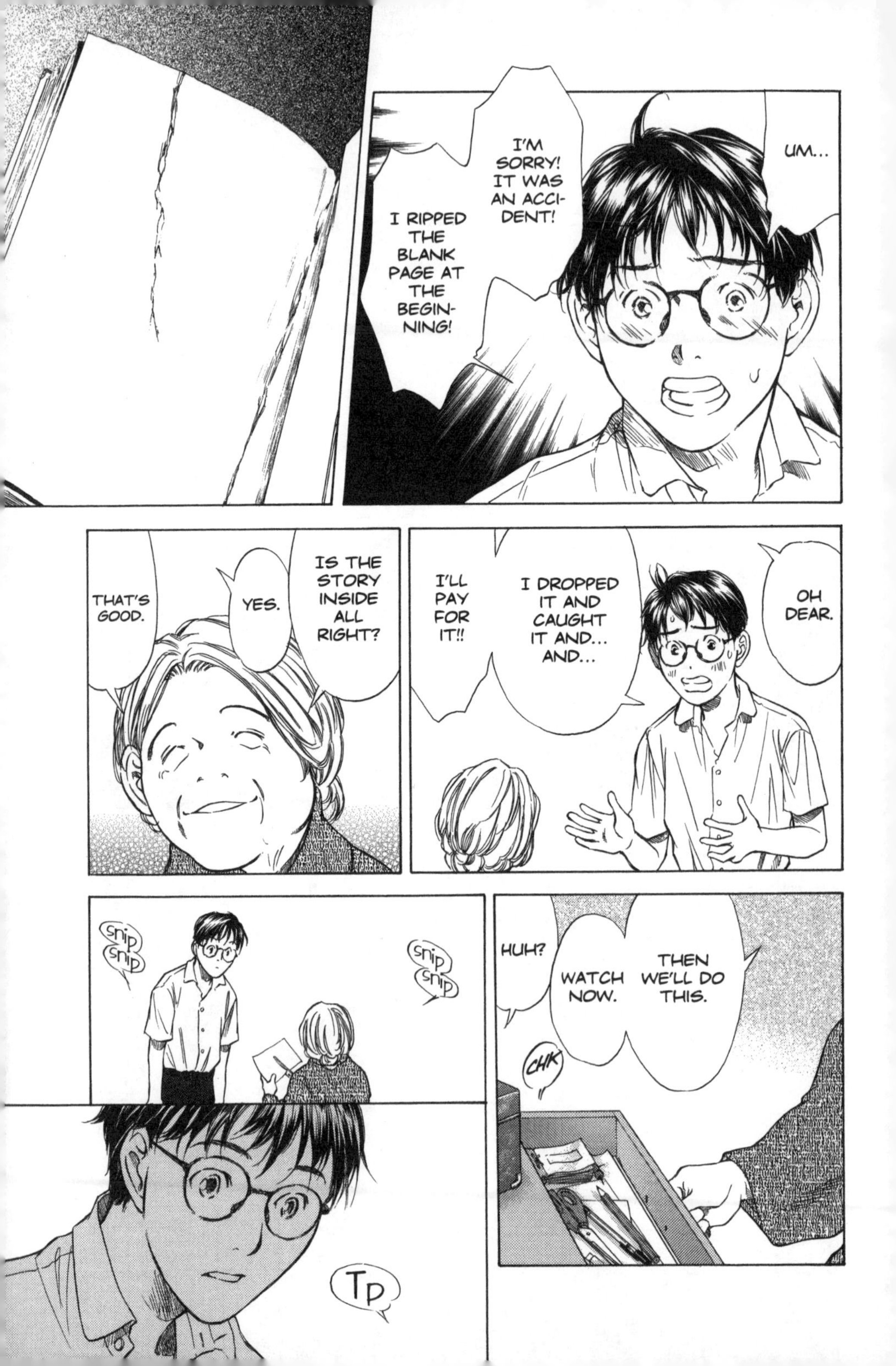
UM...
I'M SORRY! IT WAS AN ACCI-DENT!
I RIPPED THE BLANK PAGE AT THE BEGIN-NING!
OH DEAR.
I DROPPED IT AND CAUGHT IT AND... AND...
I'LL PAY FOR IT!!
IS THE STORY INSIDE ALL RIGHT?
YES.
THAT'S GOOD.
THEN WE'LL DO THIS.
WATCH NOW.
HUH?
CHK
snip snip
snip snip
Tp

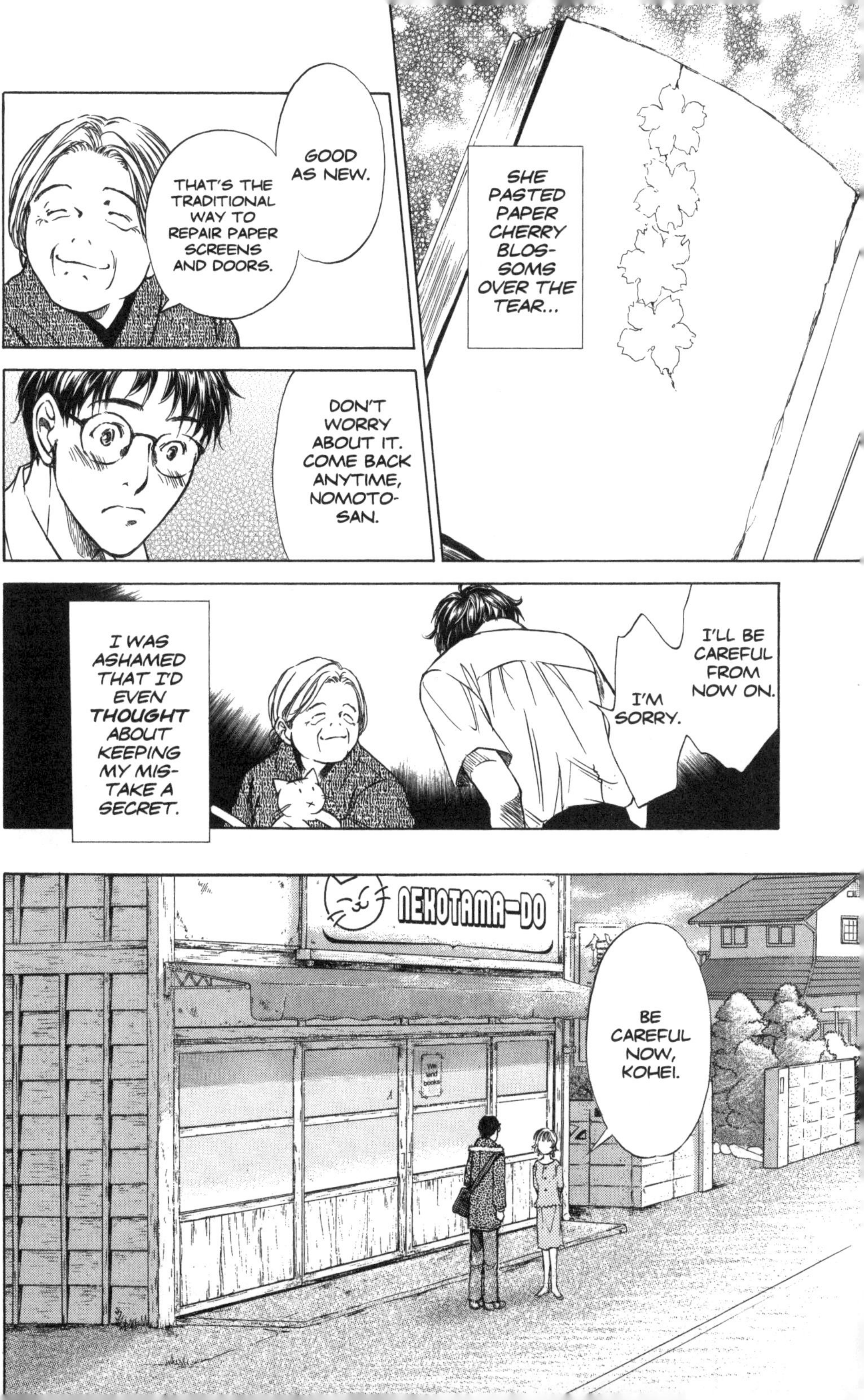
SHE PASTED PAPER CHERRY BLOSSOMS OVER THE TEAR...
GOOD AS NEW.
THAT'S THE TRADITIONAL WAY TO REPAIR PAPER SCREENS AND DOORS.
DON'T WORRY ABOUT IT. COME BACK ANYTIME, NOMOTO-SAN.
I'LL BE CAREFUL FROM NOW ON.
I'M SORRY.
I WAS ASHAMED THAT I'D EVEN **THOUGHT** ABOUT KEEPING MY MISTAKE A SECRET.
NEKOTAMA-DO
BE CAREFUL NOW, KOHEI.

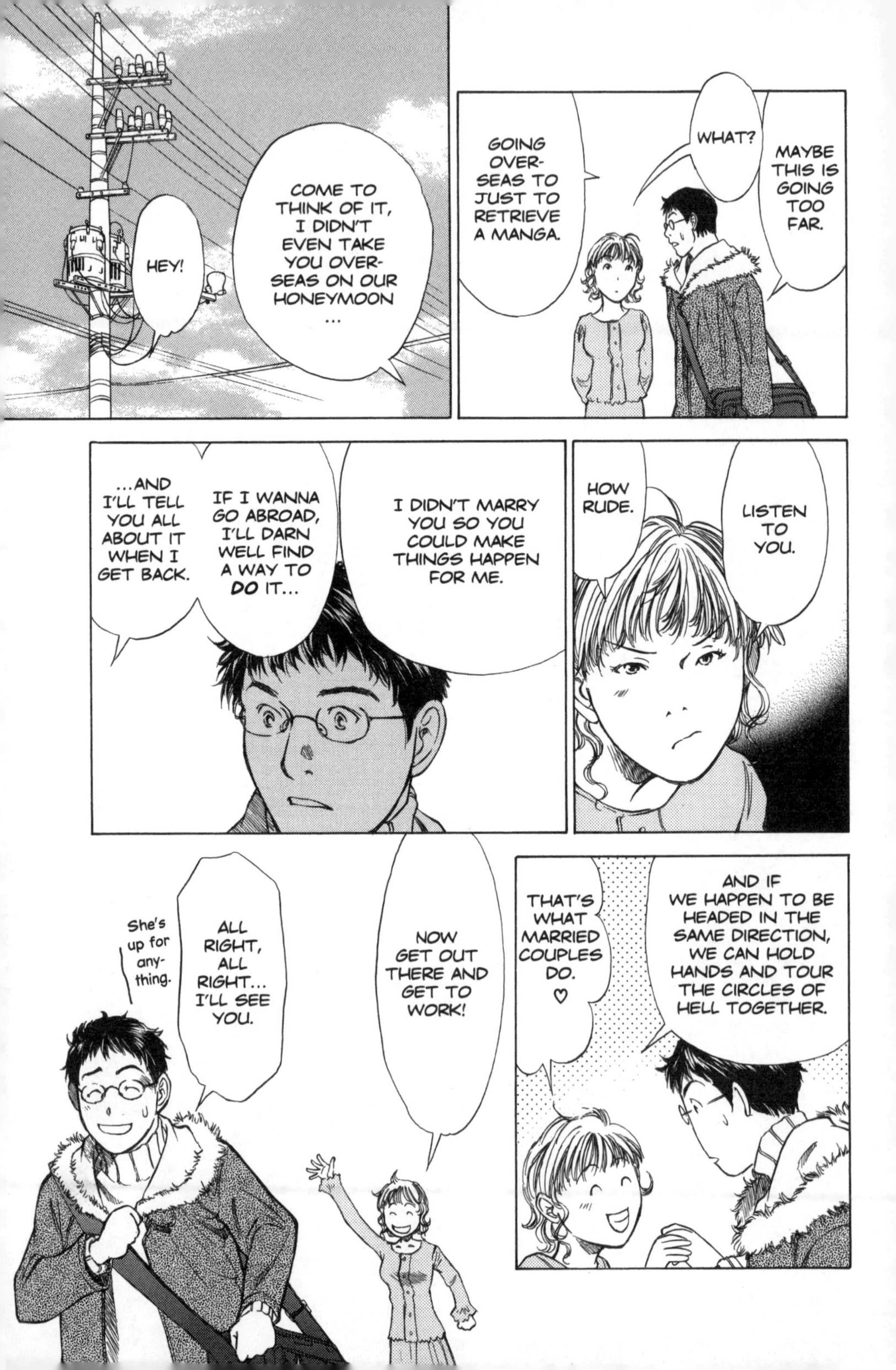
MAYBE THIS IS GOING TOO FAR.
WHAT?
GOING OVER-SEAS TO JUST TO RETRIEVE A MANGA.
COME TO THINK OF IT, I DIDN'T EVEN TAKE YOU OVER-SEAS ON OUR HONEYMOON ...
HEY!
LISTEN TO YOU.
HOW RUDE.
I DIDN'T MARRY YOU SO YOU COULD MAKE THINGS HAPPEN FOR ME.
IF I WANNA GO ABROAD, I'LL DARN WELL FIND A WAY TO **DO** IT...
...AND I'LL TELL YOU ALL ABOUT IT WHEN I GET BACK.
AND IF WE HAPPEN TO BE HEADED IN THE SAME DIRECTION, WE CAN HOLD HANDS AND TOUR THE CIRCLES OF HELL TOGETHER.
THAT'S WHAT MARRIED COUPLES DO. ♡
NOW GET OUT THERE AND GET TO WORK!
ALL RIGHT, ALL RIGHT... I'LL SEE YOU.
She's up for any-thing.

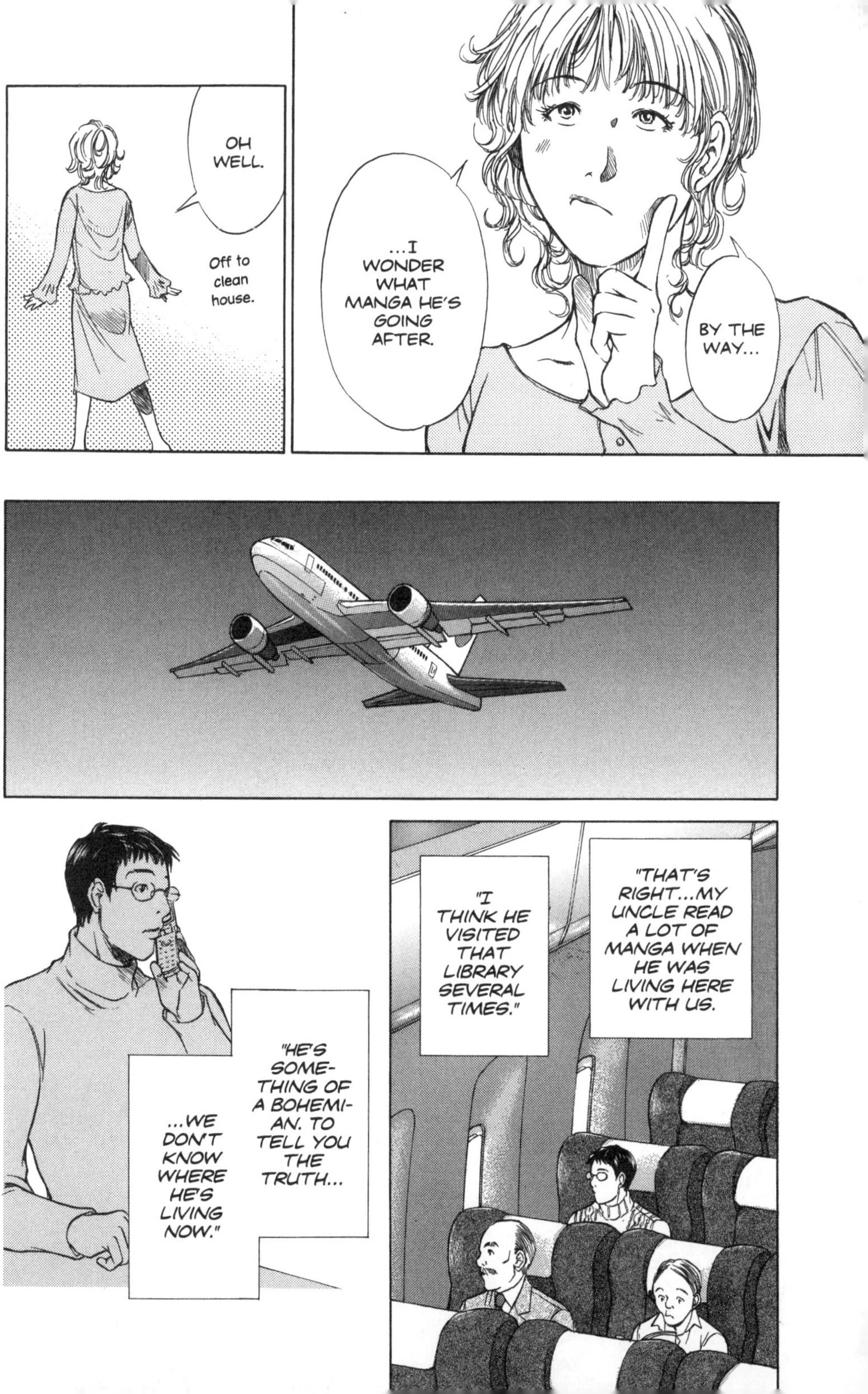
BY THE WAY...
...I WONDER WHAT MANGA HE'S GOING AFTER.
OH WELL.
Off to clean house.
"THAT'S RIGHT...MY UNCLE READ A LOT OF MANGA WHEN HE WAS LIVING HERE WITH US.
"I THINK HE VISITED THAT LIBRARY SEVERAL TIMES."
"HE'S SOME-THING OF A BOHEMI-AN. TO TELL YOU THE TRUTH...
...WE DON'T KNOW WHERE HE'S LIVING NOW."

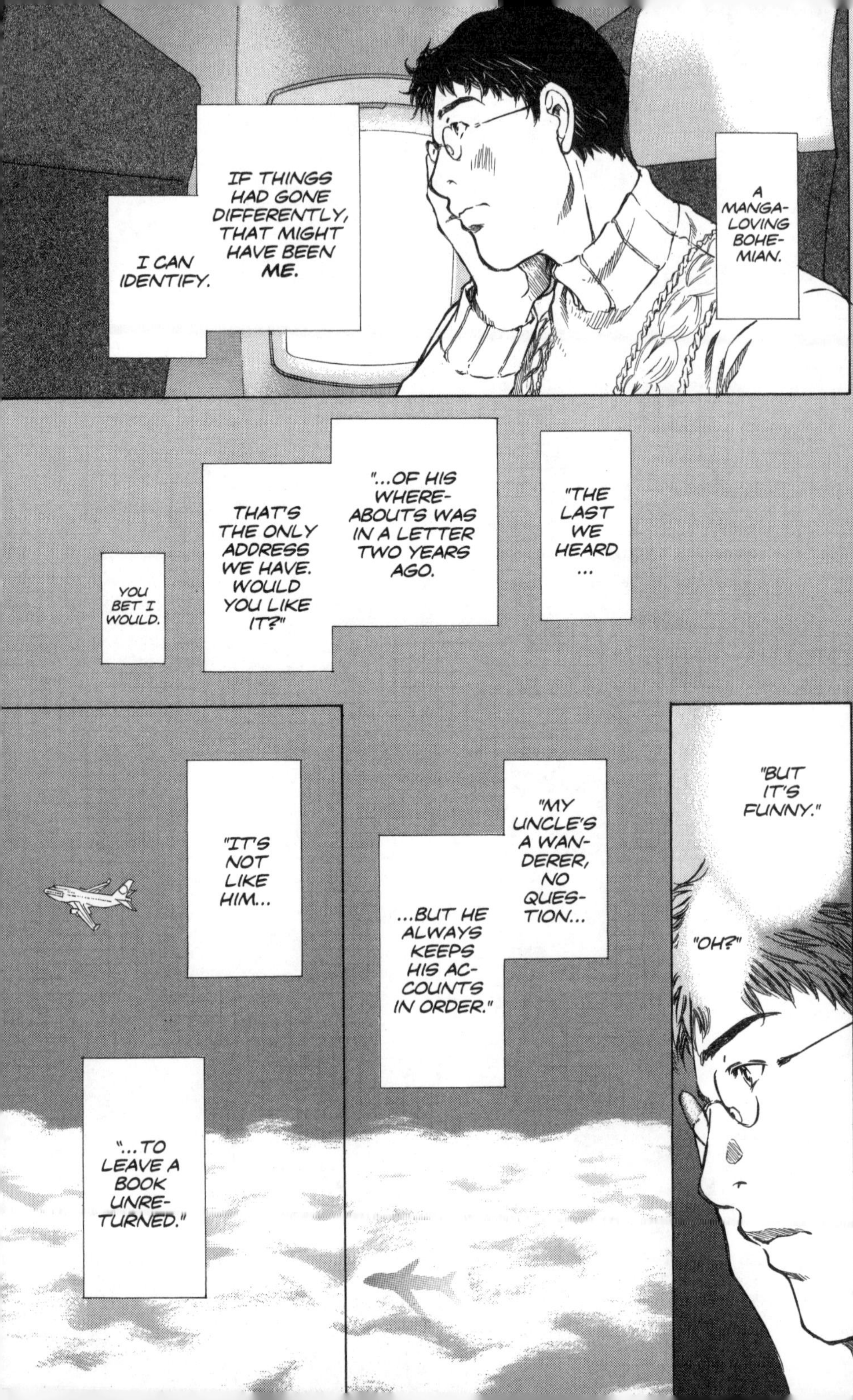
A MANGA-LOVING BOHEMIAN.
IF THINGS HAD GONE DIFFERENTLY, THAT MIGHT HAVE BEEN ME.
I CAN IDENTIFY.
"THE LAST WE HEARD...
"...OF HIS WHEREABOUTS WAS IN A LETTER TWO YEARS AGO.
THAT'S THE ONLY ADDRESS WE HAVE. WOULD YOU LIKE IT?"
YOU BET I WOULD.
"BUT IT'S FUNNY."
"OH?"
"MY UNCLE'S A WANDERER, NO QUESTION...
...BUT HE ALWAYS KEEPS HIS ACCOUNTS IN ORDER."
"IT'S NOT LIKE HIM...
"...TO LEAVE A BOOK UNRETURNED."

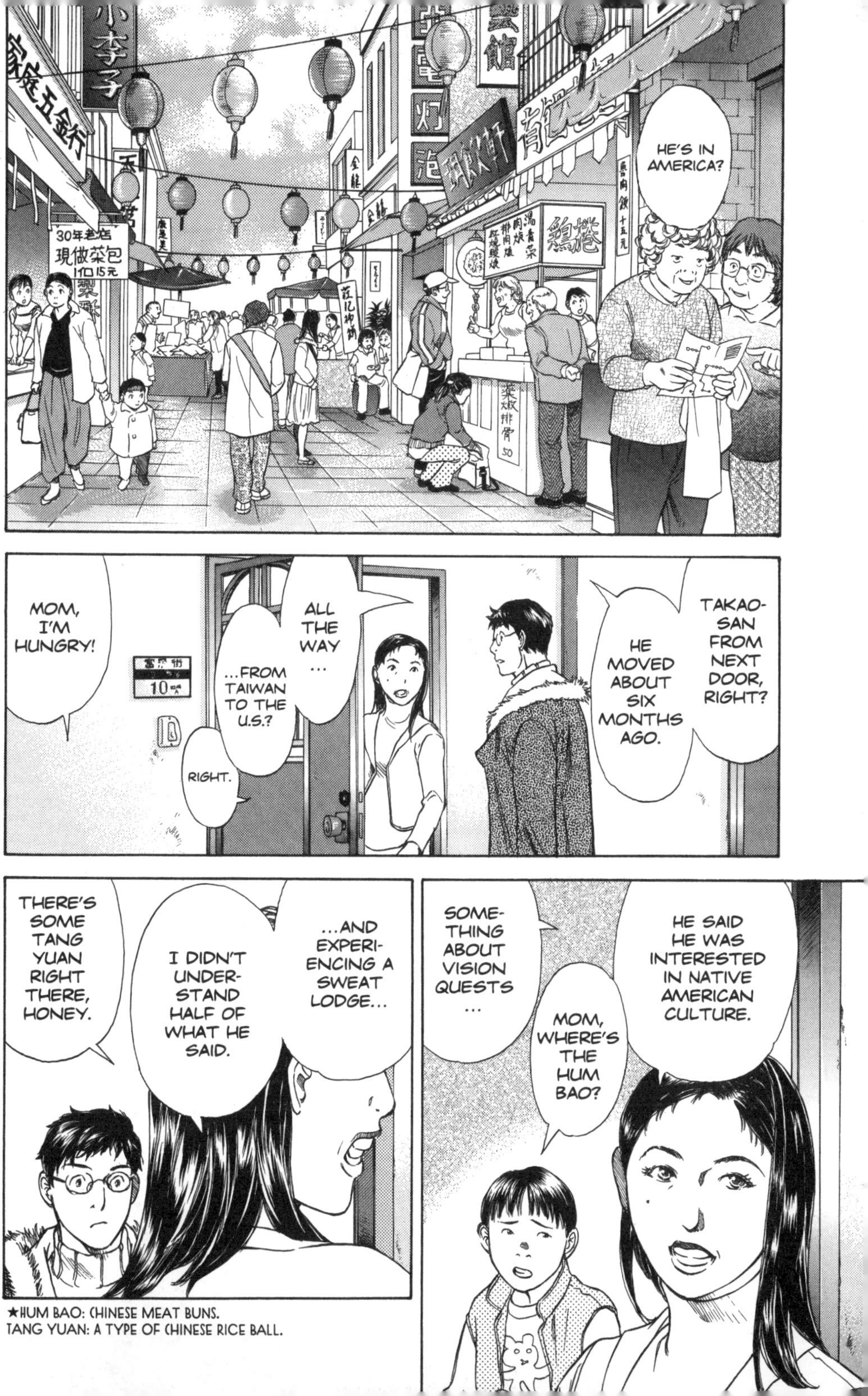
HE'S IN AMERICA?
TAKAO-SAN FROM NEXT DOOR, RIGHT?
HE MOVED ABOUT SIX MONTHS AGO.
ALL THE WAY...
...FROM TAIWAN TO THE U.S.?
RIGHT.
MOM, I'M HUNGRY!
HE SAID HE WAS INTERESTED IN NATIVE AMERICAN CULTURE.
SOMETHING ABOUT VISION QUESTS...
MOM, WHERE'S THE HUM BAO?
...AND EXPERIENCING A SWEAT LODGE...
I DIDN'T UNDERSTAND HALF OF WHAT HE SAID.
THERE'S SOME TANG YUAN RIGHT THERE, HONEY.

★HUM BAO: CHINESE MEAT BUNS.
TANG YUAN: A TYPE OF CHINESE RICE BALL.

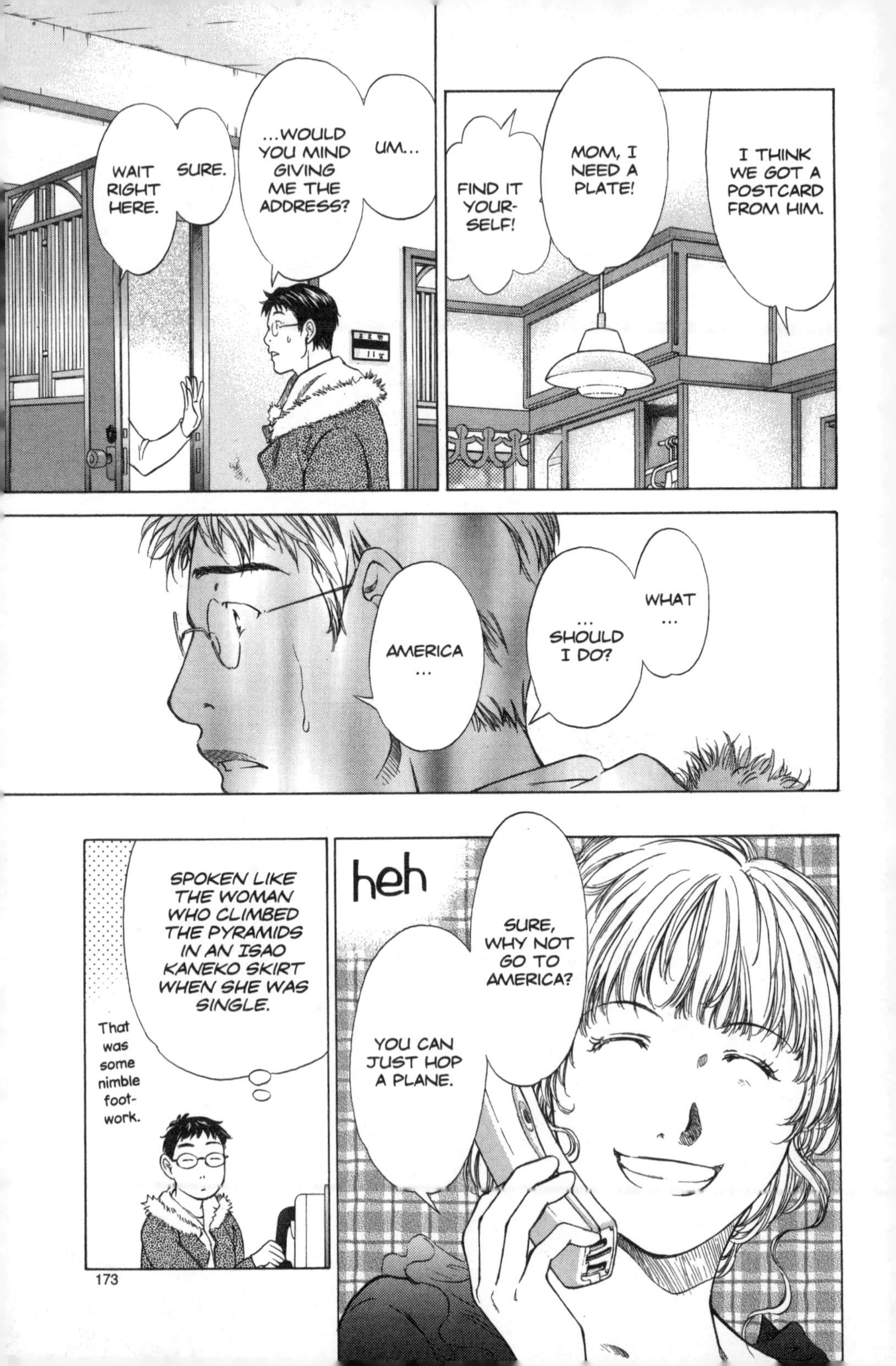
I THINK WE GOT A POSTCARD FROM HIM.
MOM, I NEED A PLATE!
FIND IT YOURSELF!
UM...
...WOULD YOU MIND GIVING ME THE ADDRESS?
SURE.
WAIT RIGHT HERE.
WHAT ... SHOULD I DO?
AMERICA ...
heh
SURE, WHY NOT GO TO AMERICA?
YOU CAN JUST HOP A PLANE.
SPOKEN LIKE THE WOMAN WHO CLIMBED THE PYRAMIDS IN AN ISAO KANEKO SKIRT WHEN SHE WAS SINGLE.
That was some nimble foot-work.

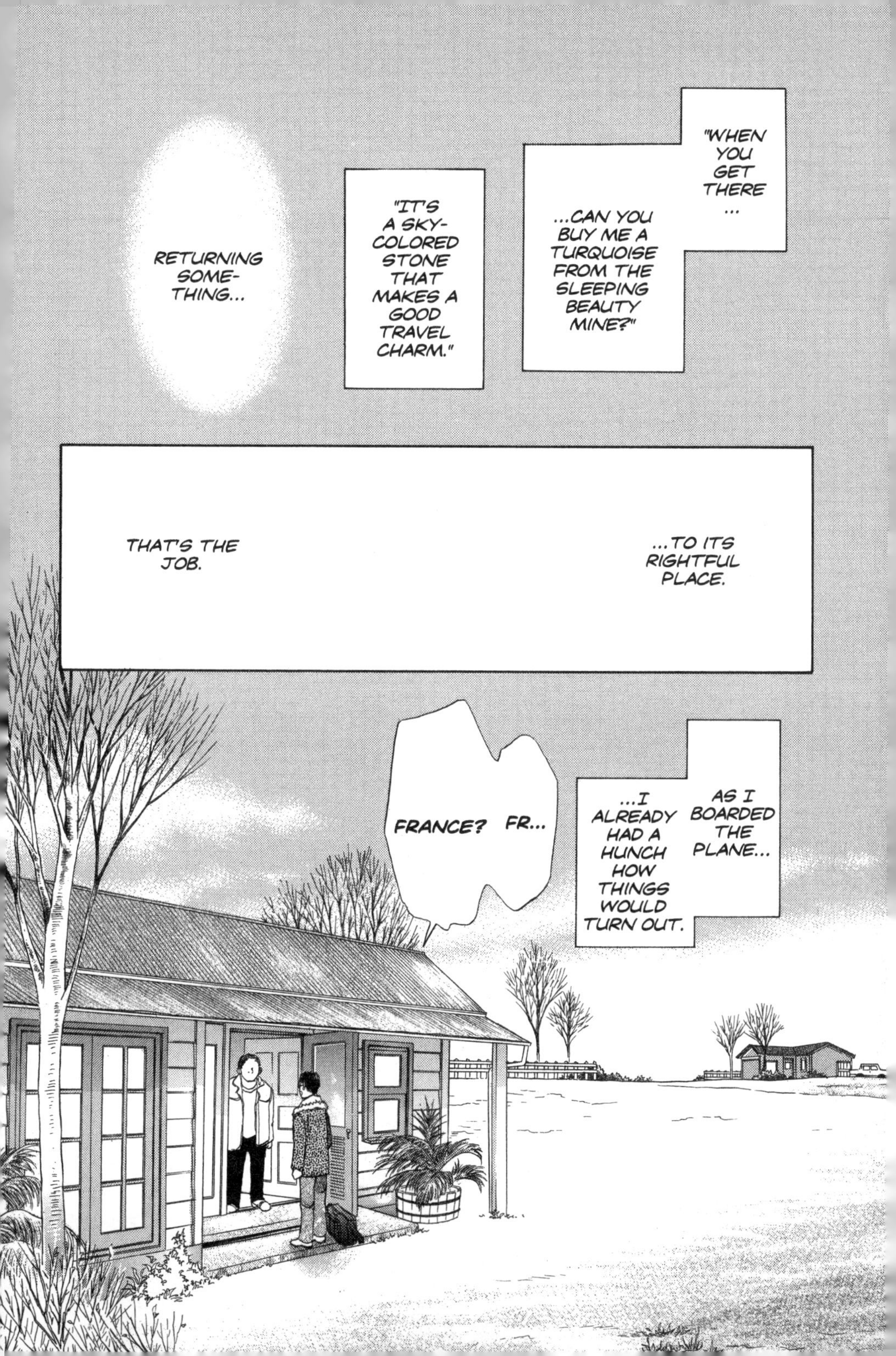
"WHEN YOU GET THERE ...
...CAN YOU BUY ME A TURQUOISE FROM THE SLEEPING BEAUTY MINE?"
"IT'S A SKY-COLORED STONE THAT MAKES A GOOD TRAVEL CHARM."
RETURNING SOME-THING...
...TO ITS RIGHTFUL PLACE.
THAT'S THE JOB.
AS I BOARDED THE PLANE...
...I ALREADY HAD A HUNCH HOW THINGS WOULD TURN OUT.
FR... FRANCE?

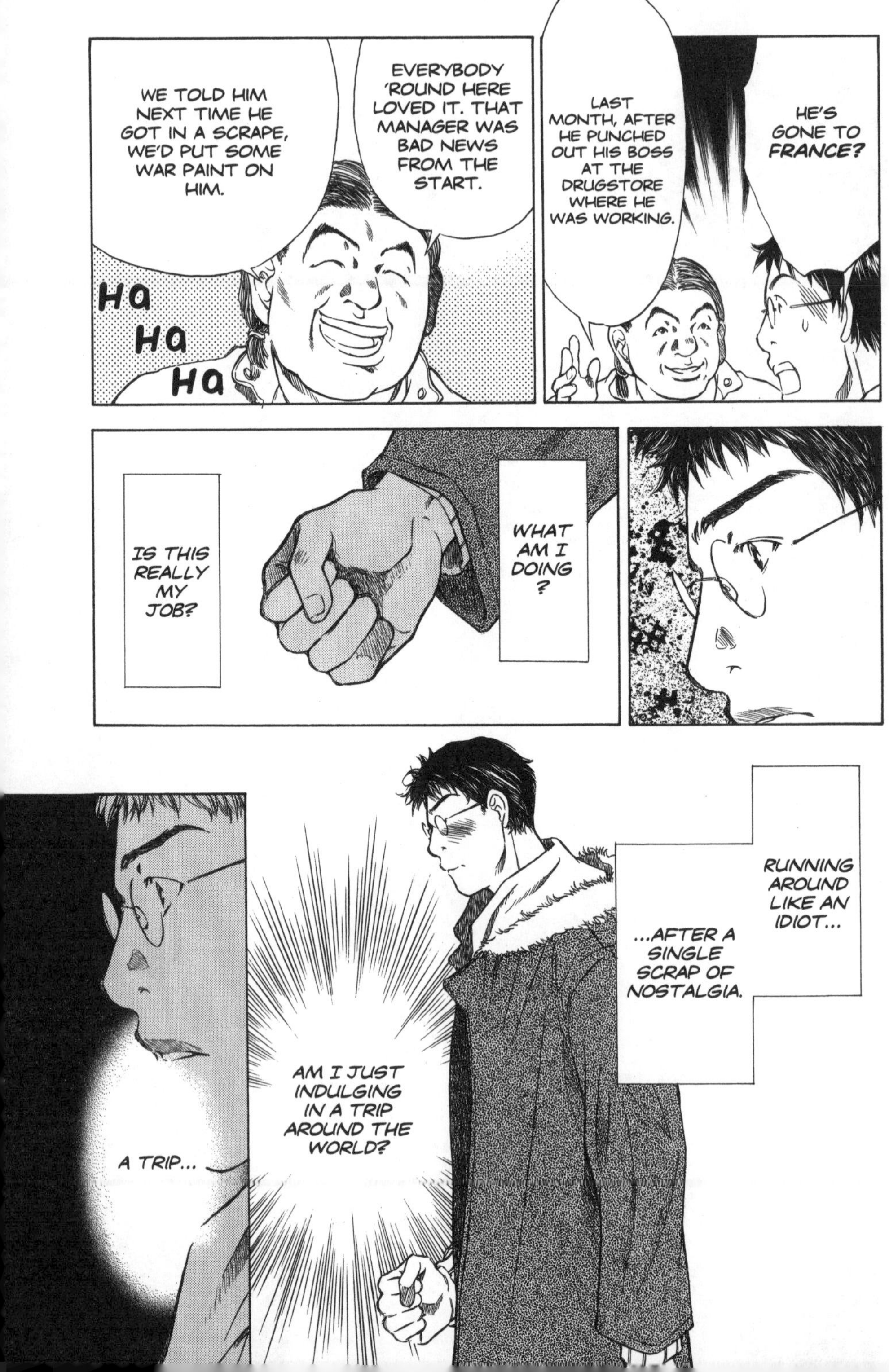
HE'S GONE TO FRANCE?
LAST MONTH, AFTER HE PUNCHED OUT HIS BOSS AT THE DRUGSTORE WHERE HE WAS WORKING.
EVERYBODY 'ROUND HERE LOVED IT. THAT MANAGER WAS BAD NEWS FROM THE START.
WE TOLD HIM NEXT TIME HE GOT IN A SCRAPE, WE'D PUT SOME WAR PAINT ON HIM.
Ha Ha Ha
WHAT AM I DOING?
IS THIS REALLY MY JOB?
RUNNING AROUND LIKE AN IDIOT...
...AFTER A SINGLE SCRAP OF NOSTALGIA.
AM I JUST INDULGING IN A TRIP AROUND THE WORLD?
A TRIP...

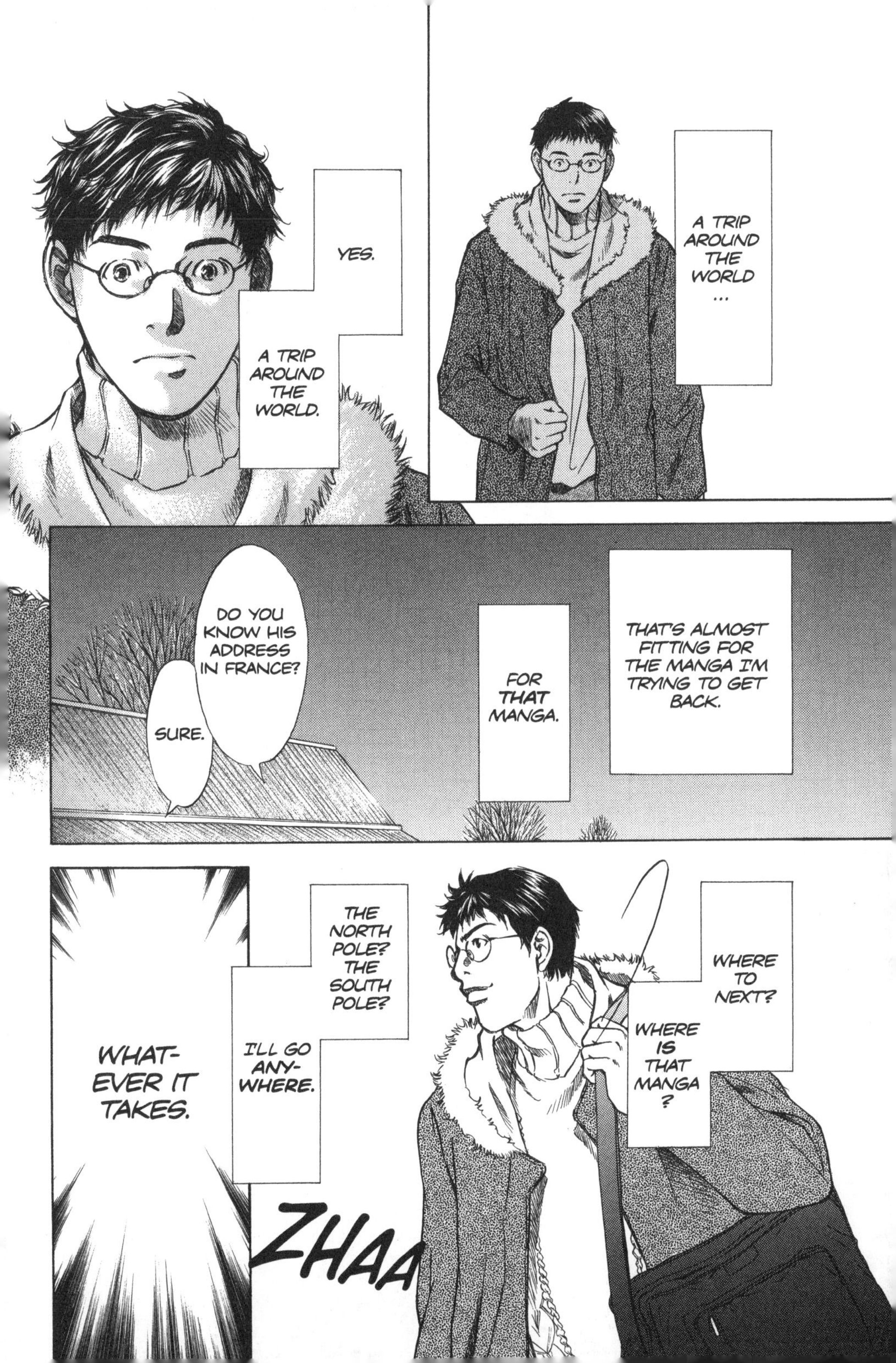
A TRIP AROUND THE WORLD ...
YES.
A TRIP AROUND THE WORLD.
THAT'S ALMOST FITTING FOR THE MANGA I'M TRYING TO GET BACK.
FOR THAT MANGA.
DO YOU KNOW HIS ADDRESS IN FRANCE?
SURE.
WHERE TO NEXT?
WHERE IS THAT MANGA?
THE NORTH POLE? THE SOUTH POLE?
I'LL GO ANY-WHERE.
ZHAA
WHAT-EVER IT TAKES.

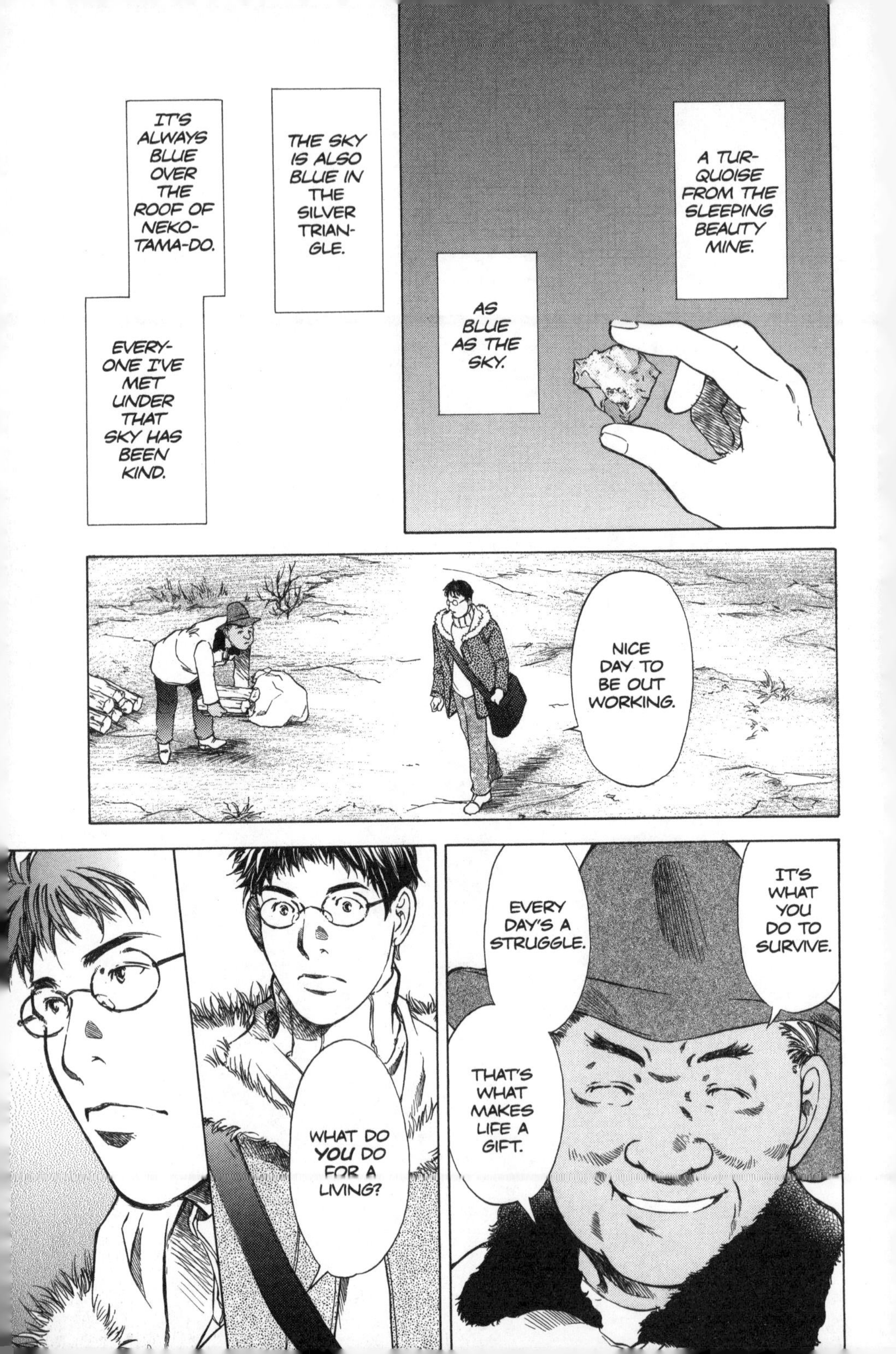
IT'S ALWAYS BLUE OVER THE ROOF OF NEKO-TAMA-DO.
EVERYONE I'VE MET UNDER THAT SKY HAS BEEN KIND.
THE SKY IS ALSO BLUE IN THE SILVER TRIANGLE.
A TURQUOISE FROM THE SLEEPING BEAUTY MINE.
AS BLUE AS THE SKY.
NICE DAY TO BE OUT WORKING.
WHAT DO *YOU* DO FOR A LIVING?
EVERY DAY'S A STRUGGLE.
IT'S WHAT YOU DO TO SURVIVE.
THAT'S WHAT MAKES LIFE A GIFT.

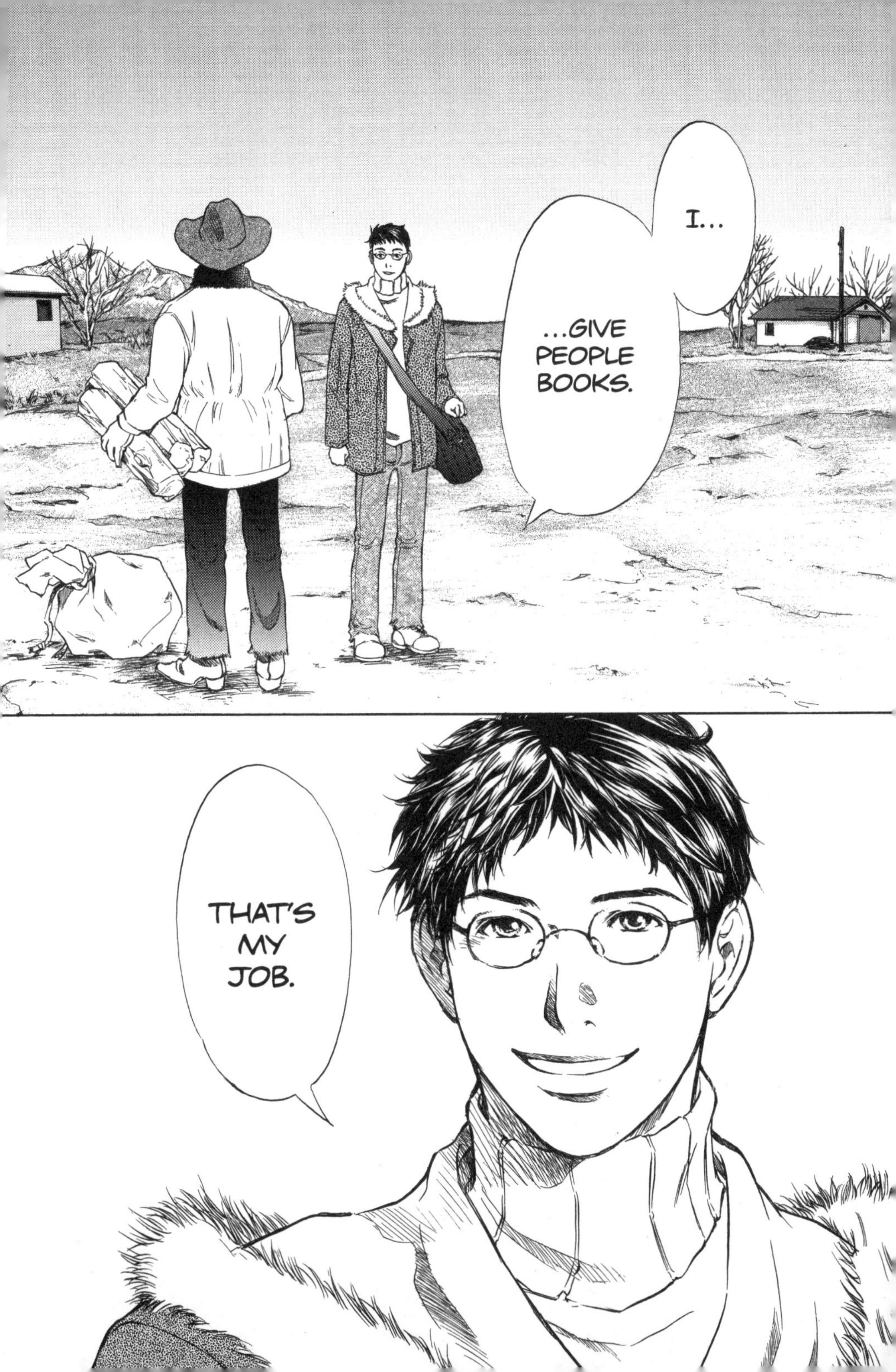
I...
...GIVE PEOPLE BOOKS.
THAT'S MY JOB.

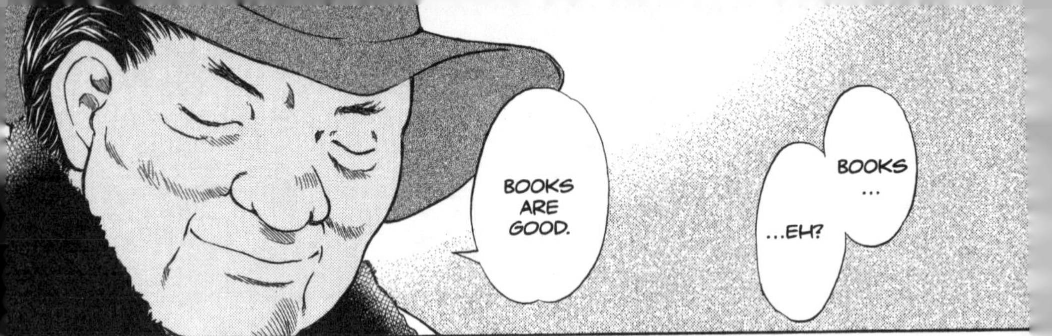
BOOKS ...
...EH?
BOOKS ARE GOOD.

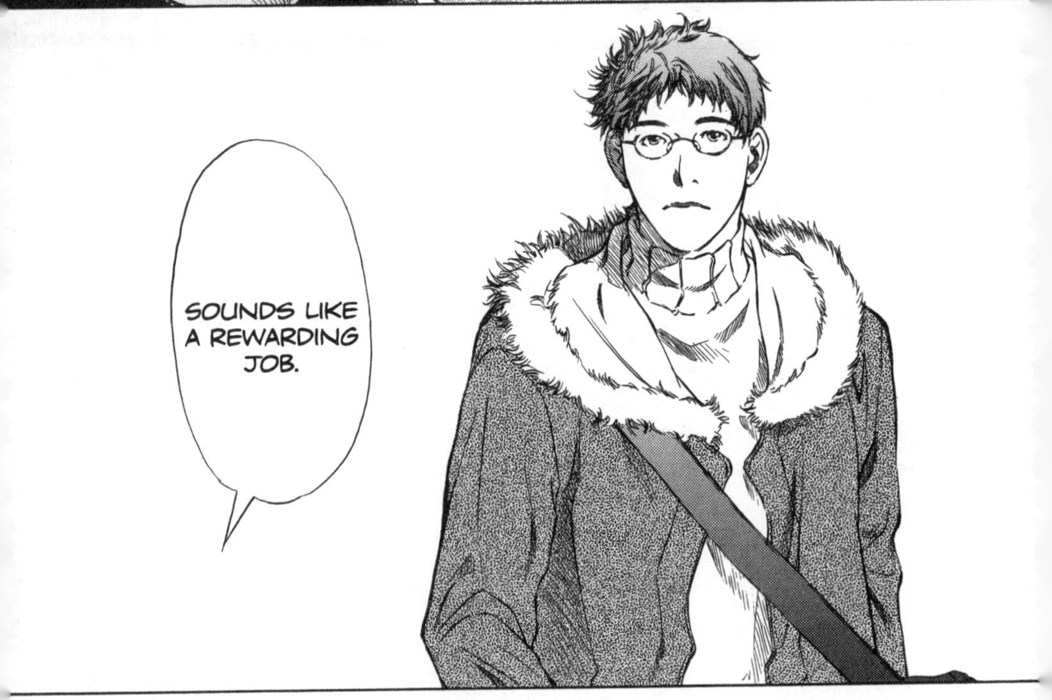
SOUNDS LIKE A REWARDING JOB.

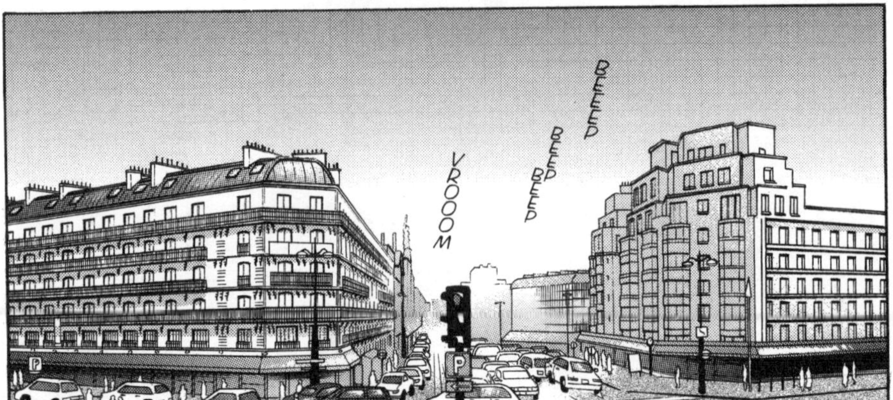
BEEED
BEEP BEED
VROOOM

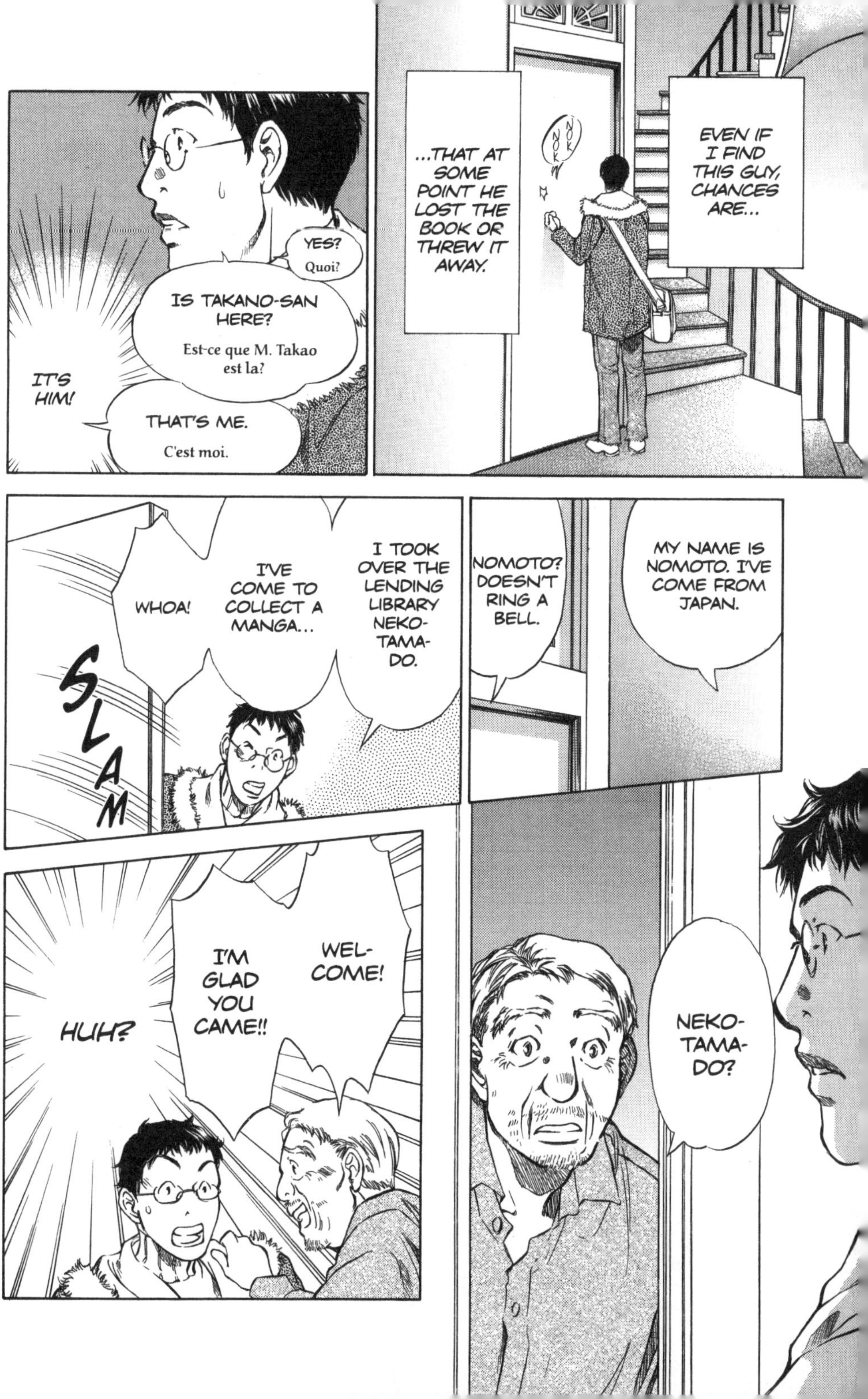
EVEN IF I FIND THIS GUY, CHANCES ARE...
...THAT AT SOME POINT HE LOST THE BOOK OR THREW IT AWAY.
YES? Quoi?
IS TAKANO-SAN HERE? Est-ce que M. Takao est la?
IT'S HIM!
THAT'S ME. C'est moi.
MY NAME IS NOMOTO. I'VE COME FROM JAPAN.
NOMOTO? DOESN'T RING A BELL.
I TOOK OVER THE LENDING LIBRARY NEKO-TAMA-DO.
I'VE COME TO COLLECT A MANGA...
WHOA!
SLAM
NEKO-TAMA-DO?
WEL-COME!
I'M GLAD YOU CAME!!
HUH?

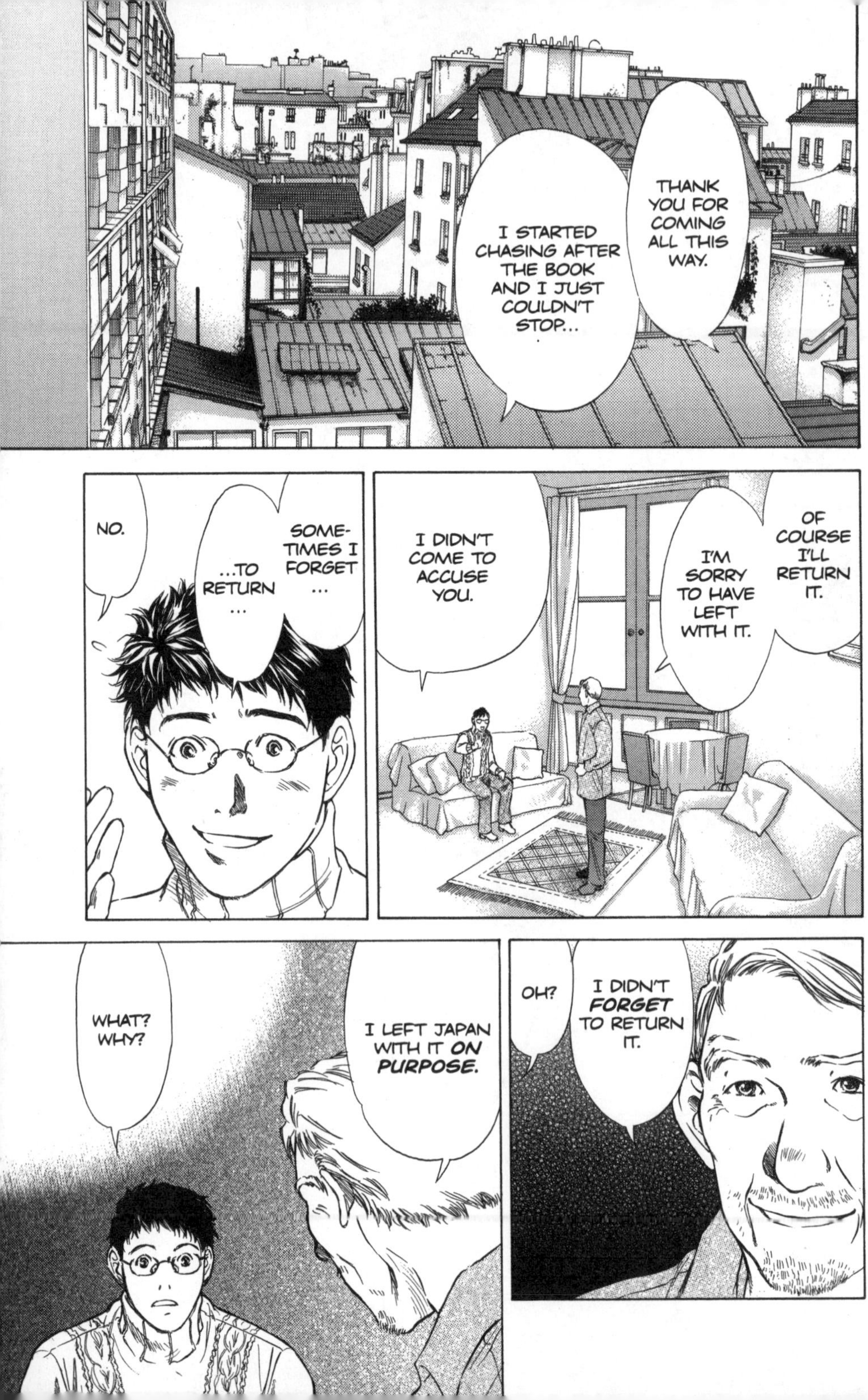
THANK YOU FOR COMING ALL THIS WAY.
I STARTED CHASING AFTER THE BOOK AND I JUST COULDN'T STOP...
OF COURSE I'LL RETURN IT.
I'M SORRY TO HAVE LEFT WITH IT.
I DIDN'T COME TO ACCUSE YOU.
SOME-TIMES I FORGET ...
...TO RETURN ...
NO.
I DIDN'T *FORGET* TO RETURN IT.
OH?
I LEFT JAPAN WITH IT ***ON PURPOSE.***
WHAT? WHY?

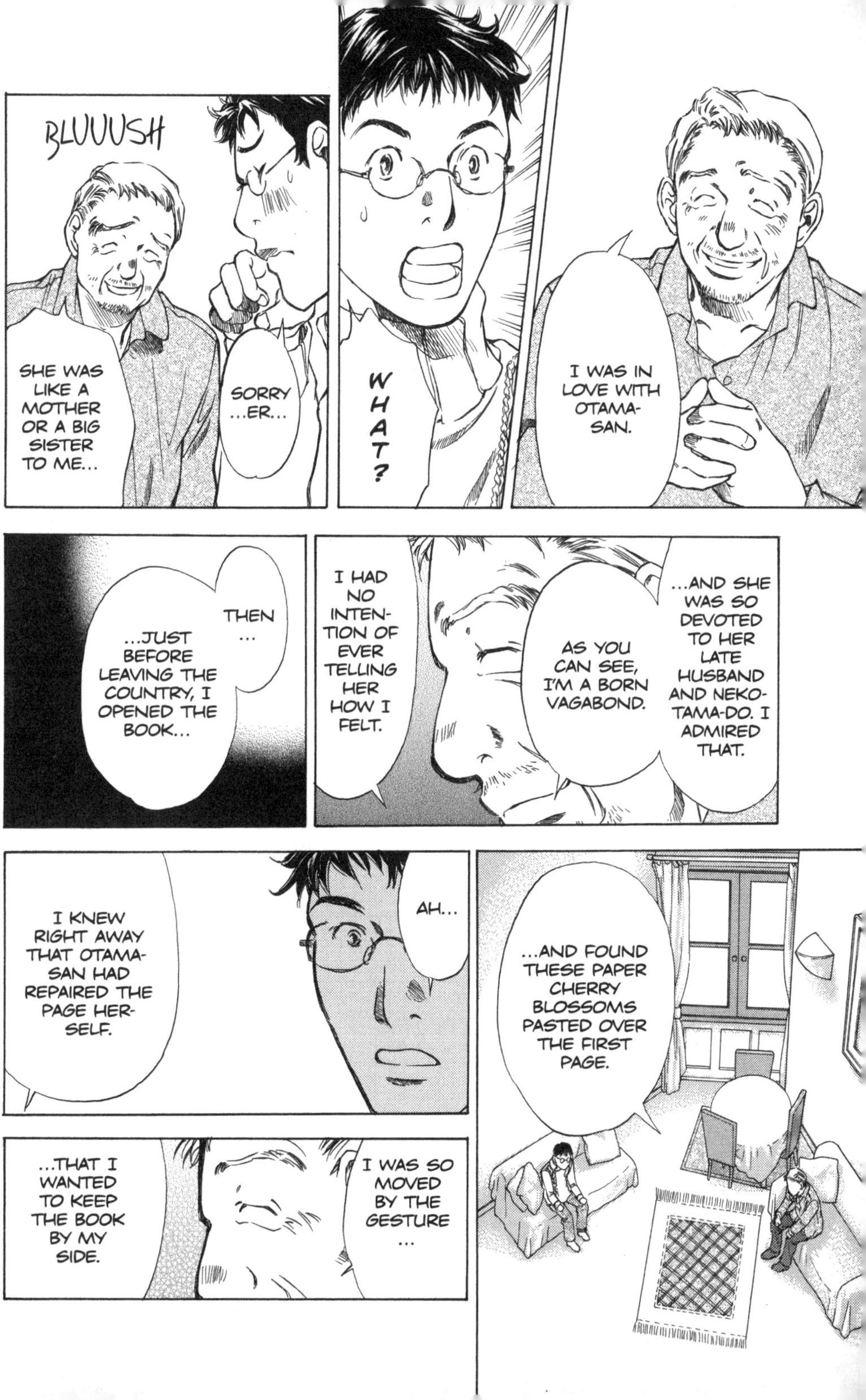
I WAS IN LOVE WITH OTAMA-SAN.
WHAT?
BLUUUSH
SORRY ...ER...
SHE WAS LIKE A MOTHER OR A BIG SISTER TO ME...
...AND SHE WAS SO DEVOTED TO HER LATE HUSBAND AND NEKO-TAMA-DO. I ADMIRED THAT.
AS YOU CAN SEE, I'M A BORN VAGABOND.
I HAD NO INTENTION OF EVER TELLING HER HOW I FELT.
THEN...
...JUST BEFORE LEAVING THE COUNTRY, I OPENED THE BOOK...
...AND FOUND THESE PAPER CHERRY BLOSSOMS PASTED OVER THE FIRST PAGE.
AH...
I KNEW RIGHT AWAY THAT OTAMA-SAN HAD REPAIRED THE PAGE HER-SELF.
I WAS SO MOVED BY THE GESTURE...
...THAT I WANTED TO KEEP THE BOOK BY MY SIDE.

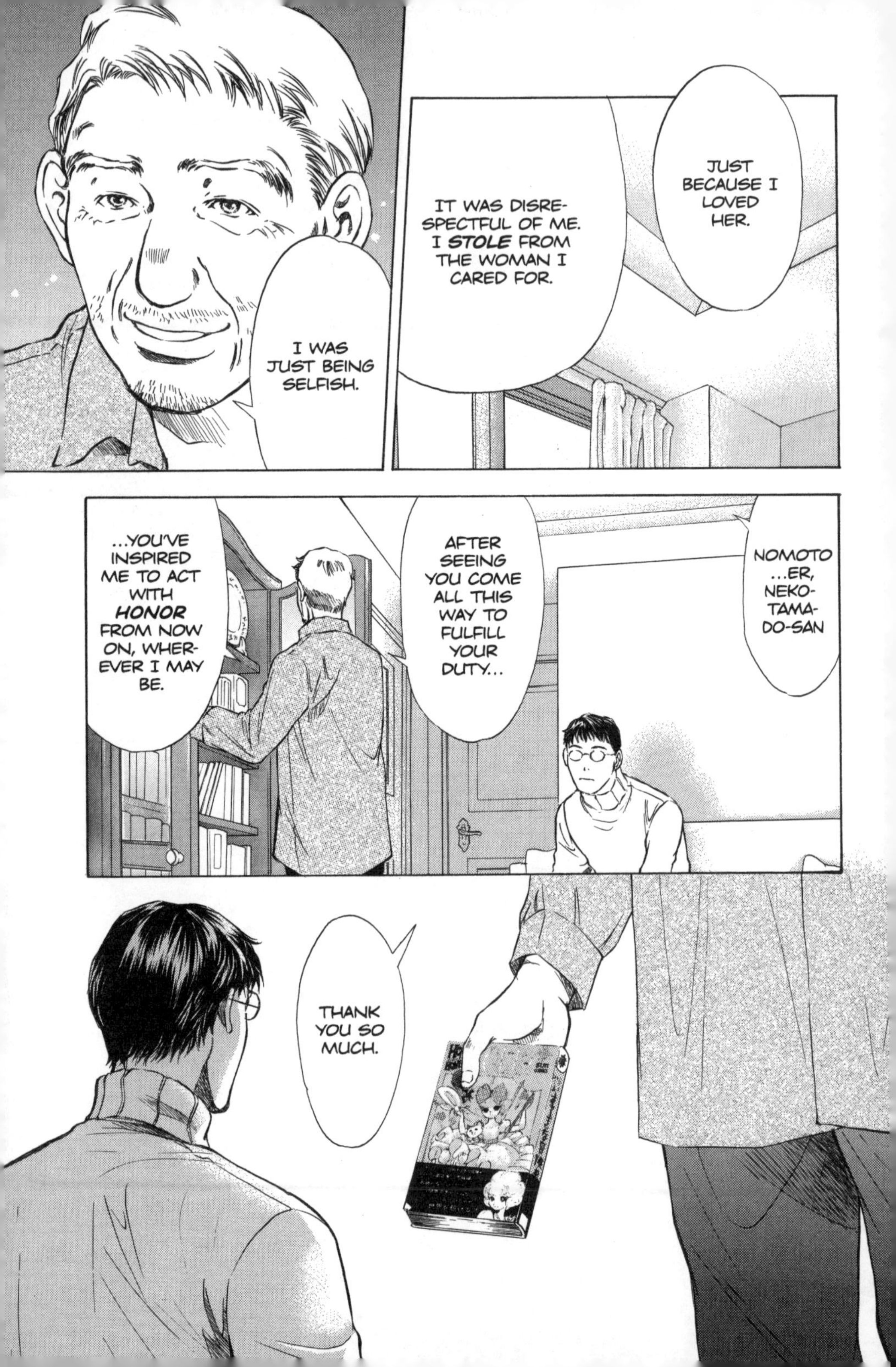
JUST BECAUSE I LOVED HER.
IT WAS DISRE-SPECTFUL OF ME. I **STOLE** FROM THE WOMAN I CARED FOR.
I WAS JUST BEING SELFISH.
NOMOTO ...ER, NEKO-TAMA-DO-SAN
AFTER SEEING YOU COME ALL THIS WAY TO FULFILL YOUR DUTY...
...YOU'VE INSPIRED ME TO ACT WITH **HONOR** FROM NOW ON, WHER-EVER I MAY BE.
THANK YOU SO MUCH.

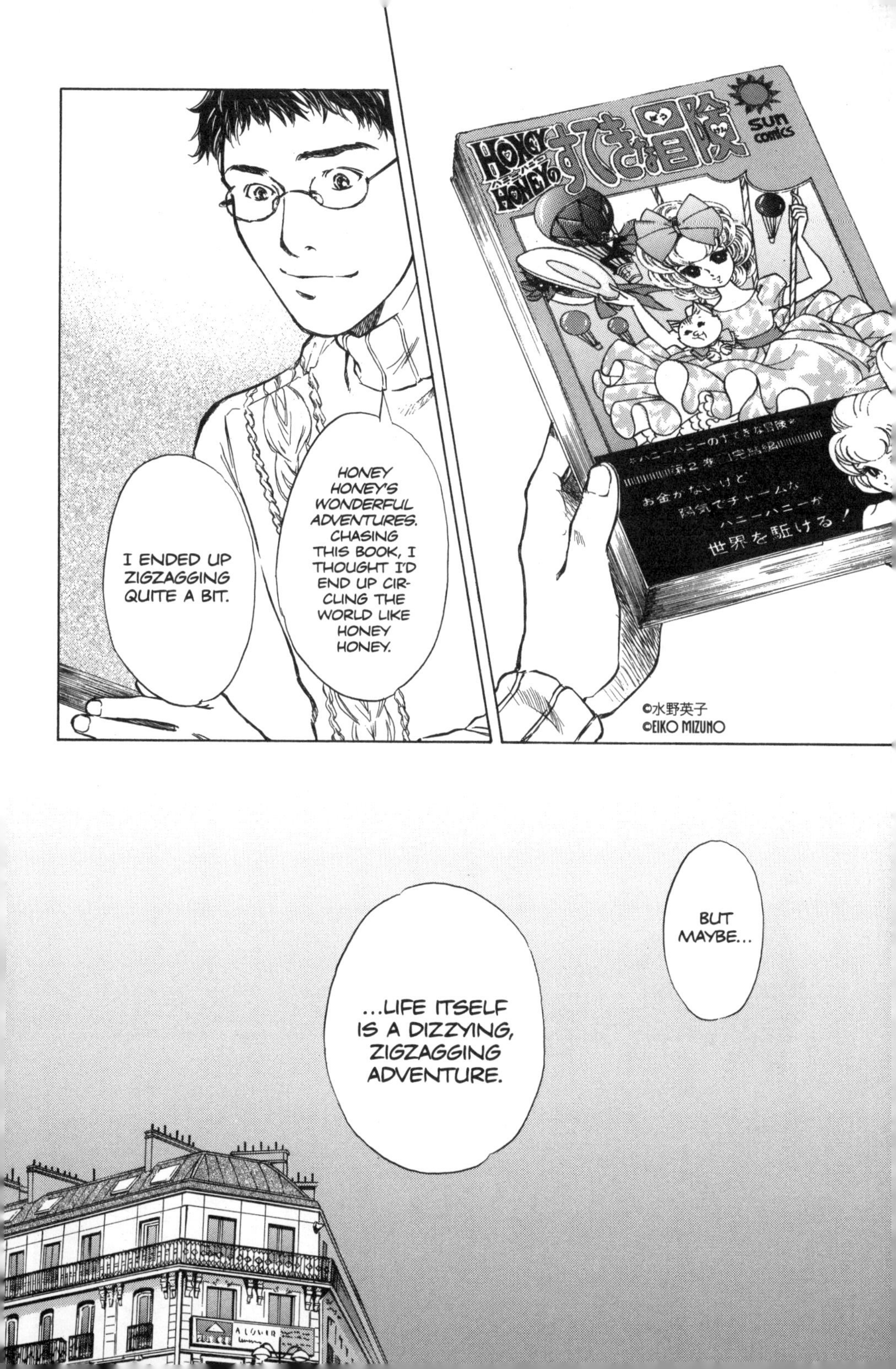
HONEY HONEY のすてきな冒険
SUN comics
ハニーハニーのすてきな冒険
第2巻 完結編
お金がないけど 陽気でチャームな ハニーハニーが 世界を駆ける！
©水野英子
©EIKO MIZUNO
HONEY HONEY'S WONDERFUL ADVENTURES. CHASING THIS BOOK, I THOUGHT I'D END UP CIR-CLING THE WORLD LIKE HONEY HONEY.
I ENDED UP ZIGZAGGING QUITE A BIT.
BUT MAYBE...
...LIFE ITSELF IS A DIZZYING, ZIGZAGGING ADVENTURE.

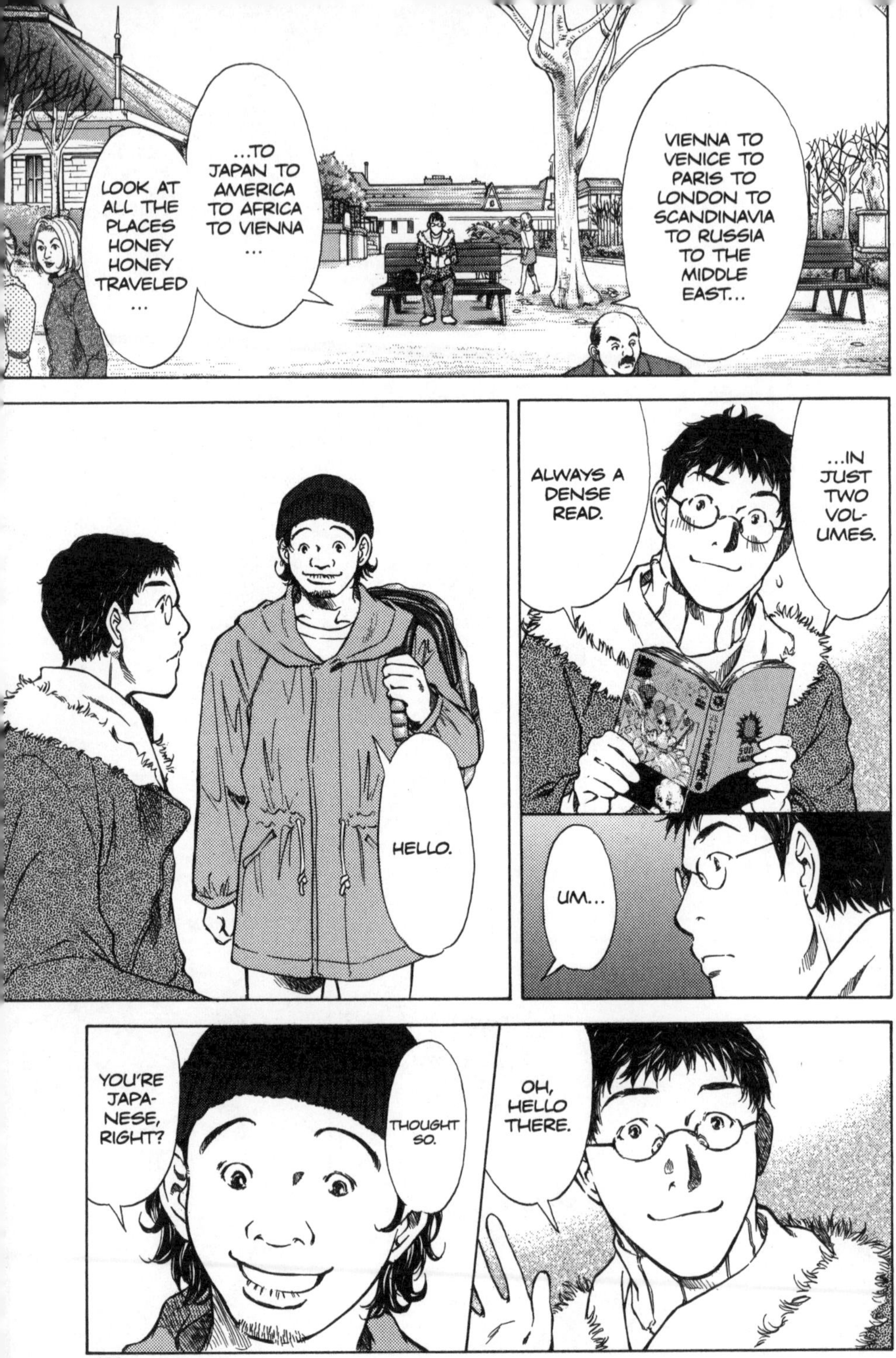
VIENNA TO VENICE TO PARIS TO LONDON TO SCANDINAVIA TO RUSSIA TO THE MIDDLE EAST...
...TO JAPAN TO AMERICA TO AFRICA TO VIENNA ...
LOOK AT ALL THE PLACES HONEY HONEY TRAVELED ...
...IN JUST TWO VOL-UMES.
ALWAYS A DENSE READ.
UM...
HELLO.
OH, HELLO THERE.
YOU'RE JAPA-NESE, RIGHT?
THOUGHT SO.

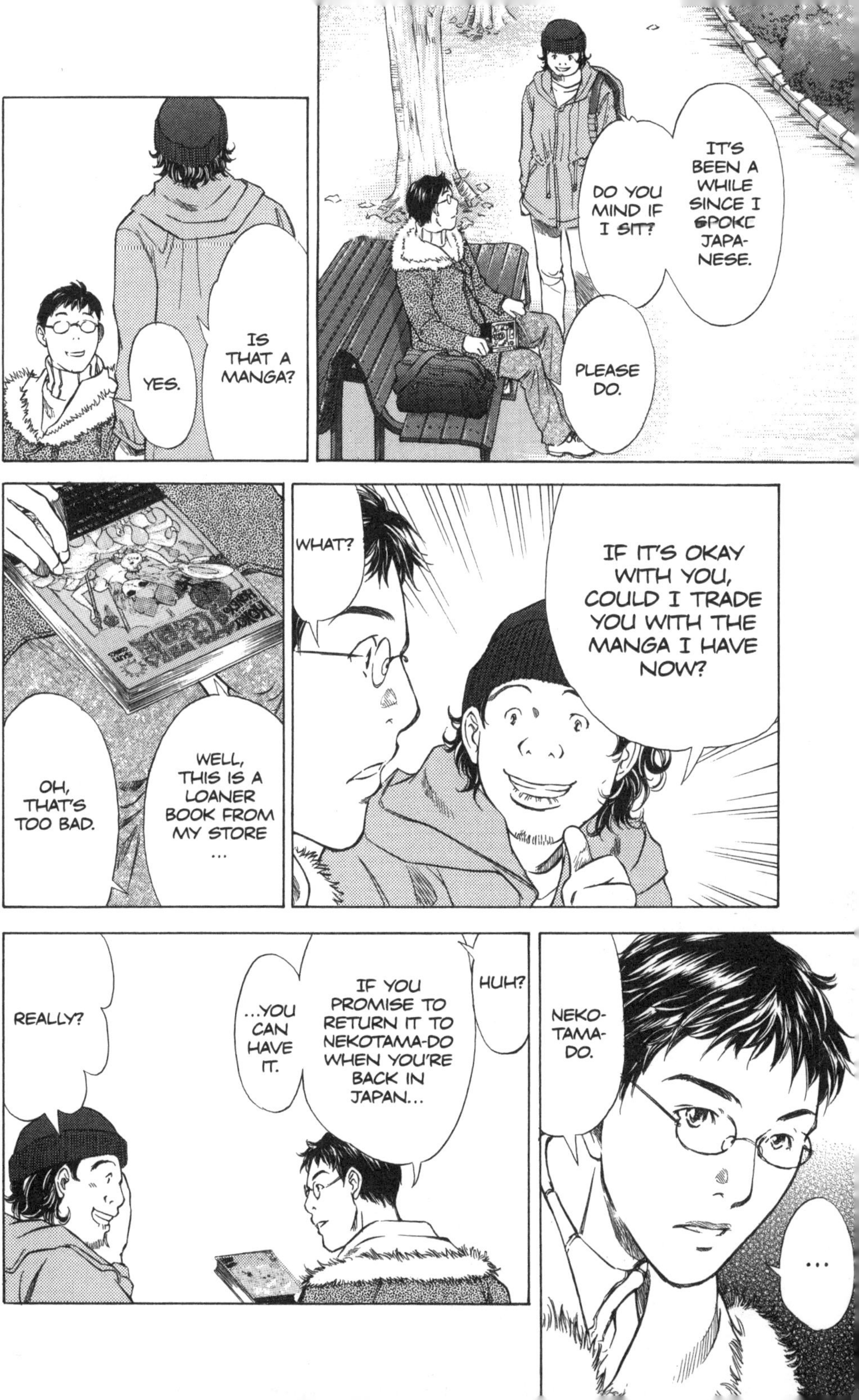
IT'S BEEN A WHILE SINCE I SPOKE JAPANESE.
DO YOU MIND IF I SIT?
PLEASE DO.
IS THAT A MANGA?
YES.
IF IT'S OKAY WITH YOU, COULD I TRADE YOU WITH THE MANGA I HAVE NOW?
WHAT?
WELL, THIS IS A LOANER BOOK FROM MY STORE...
OH, THAT'S TOO BAD.
NEKO-TAMA-DO.
...
HUH?
IF YOU PROMISE TO RETURN IT TO NEKOTAMA-DO WHEN YOU'RE BACK IN JAPAN...
...YOU CAN HAVE IT.
REALLY?

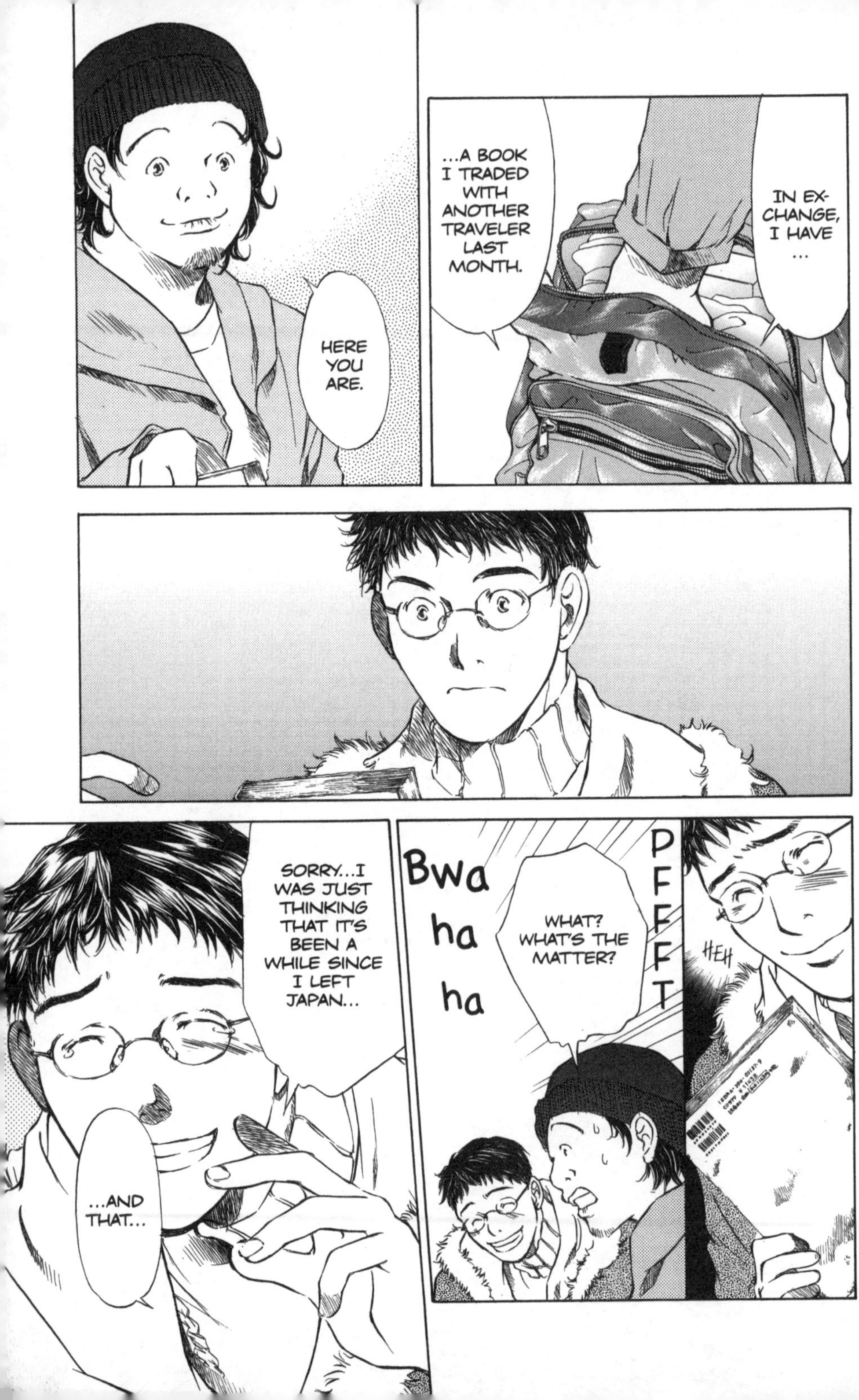
IN EX-CHANGE, I HAVE ...
...A BOOK I TRADED WITH ANOTHER TRAVELER LAST MONTH.
HERE YOU ARE.
PFFFT
HEH
WHAT? WHAT'S THE MATTER?
Bwa ha ha
SORRY...I WAS JUST THINKING THAT IT'S BEEN A WHILE SINCE I LEFT JAPAN...
...AND THAT...

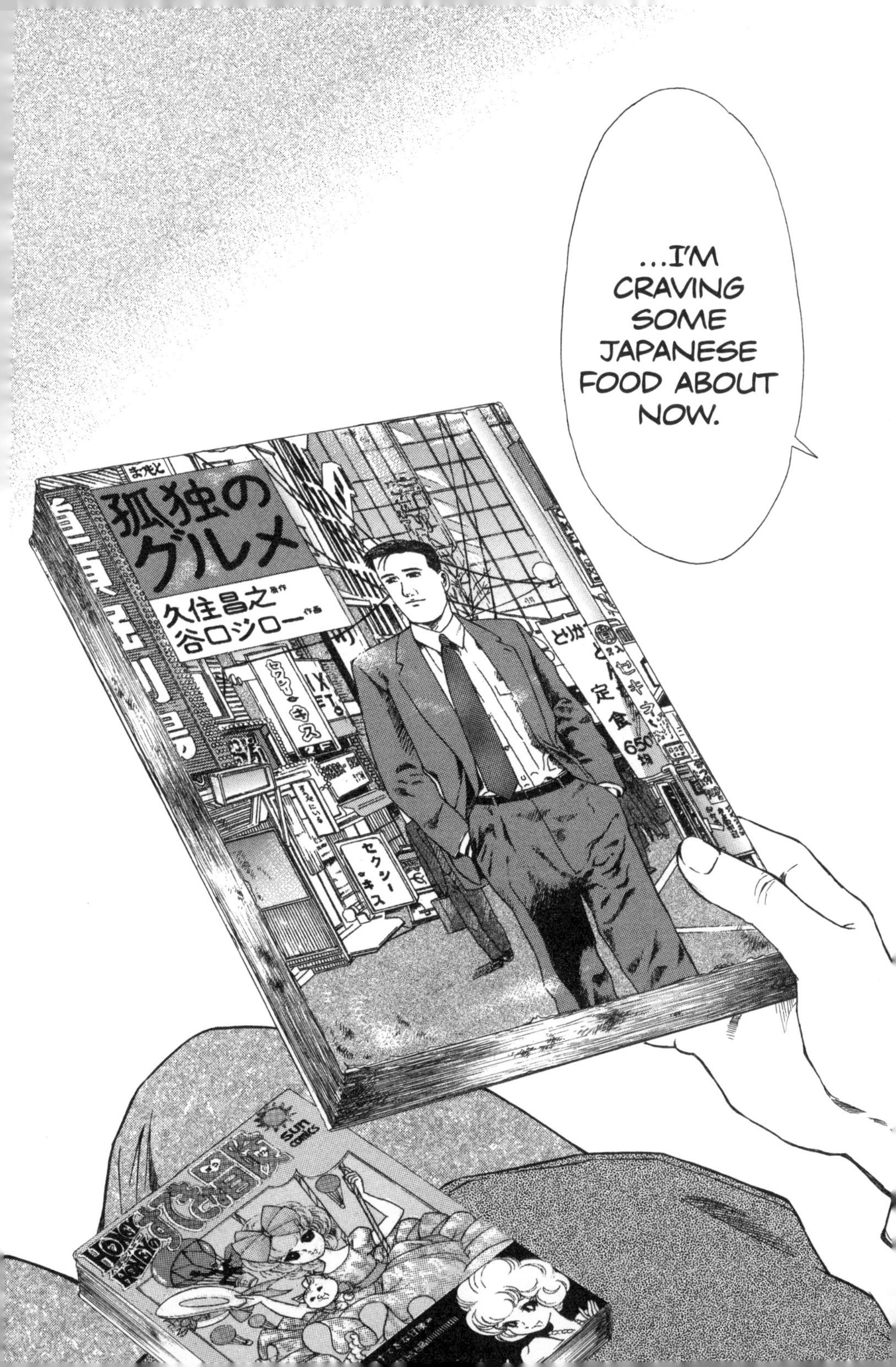
...I'M CRAVING SOME JAPANESE FOOD ABOUT NOW.
孤独のグルメ
久住昌之 原作
谷口ジロー 作画
セクシーキス
定食 650円

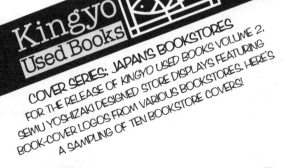

Kingyo Used Books

COVER SERIES: JAPAN'S BOOKSTORES

FOR THE RELEASE OF KINGYO USED BOOKS VOLUME 2, SEIMU YOSHIZAKI DESIGNED STORE DISPLAYS FEATURING BOOK-COVER LOGOS FROM VARIOUS BOOKSTORES. HERE'S A SAMPLING OF TEN BOOKSTORE COVERS!

三省堂書店
BOOKS SANSEIDO
JUNKUDO

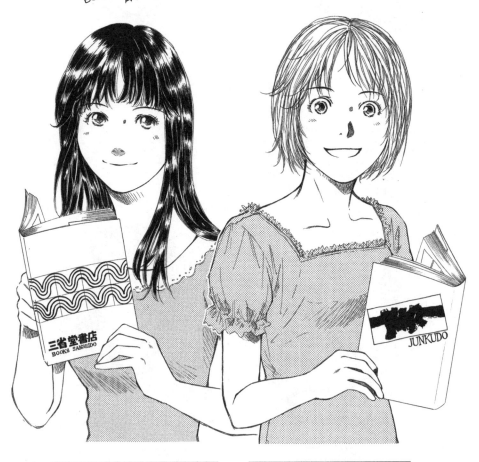

SANSEIDO SHOTEN

JUNKUDO SHOTEN

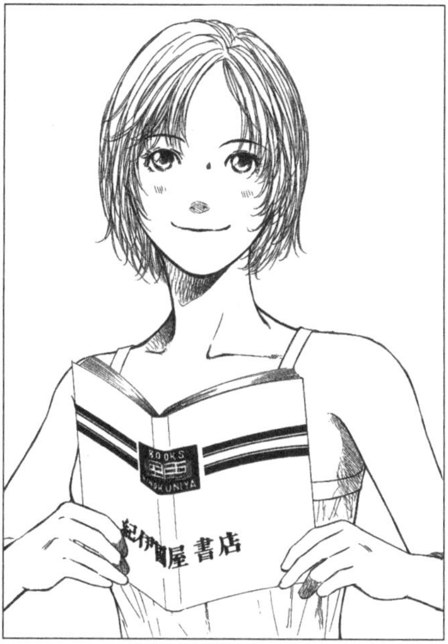
BOOKS
KINOKUNIYA
紀伊國屋 書店

KINOKUNIYA SHOTEN

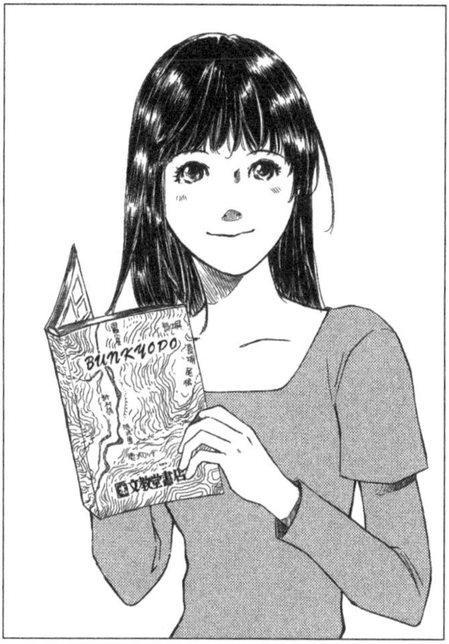
BUNKYODO
文教堂書店

BUNKYODO SHOTEN

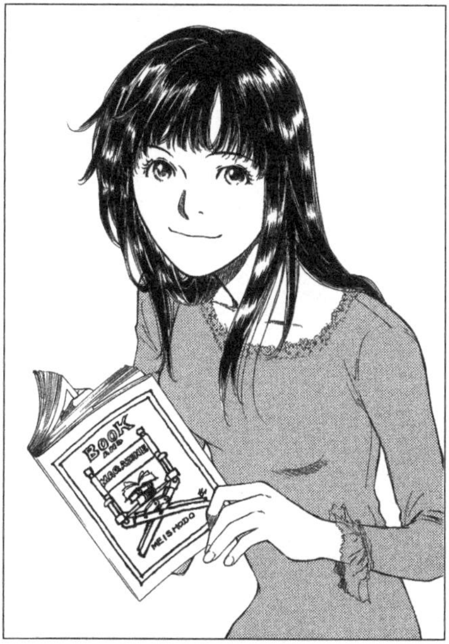
BOOK
AND
MAGAZINE
MEISHODO

MEISHODO SHOTEN

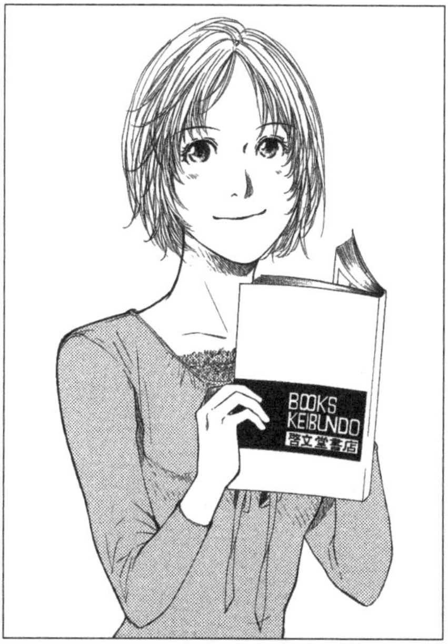
BOOKS
KEIBUNDO
啓文堂書店

KEIBUNDO SHOTEN

Kingyo Used Books

COVER SERIES: JAPAN'S BOOKSTORES

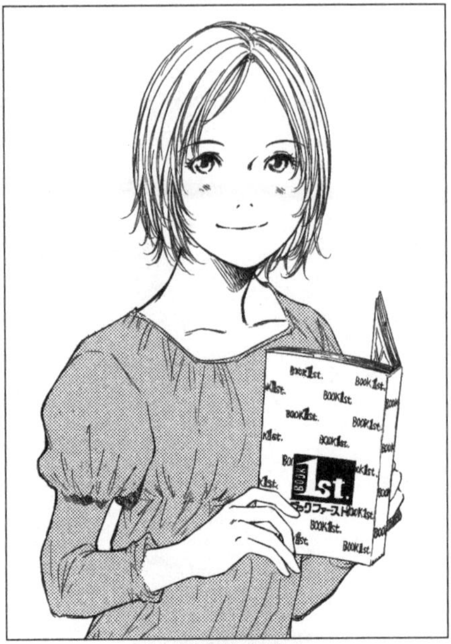
BOOK 1st.

BOOK FIRST

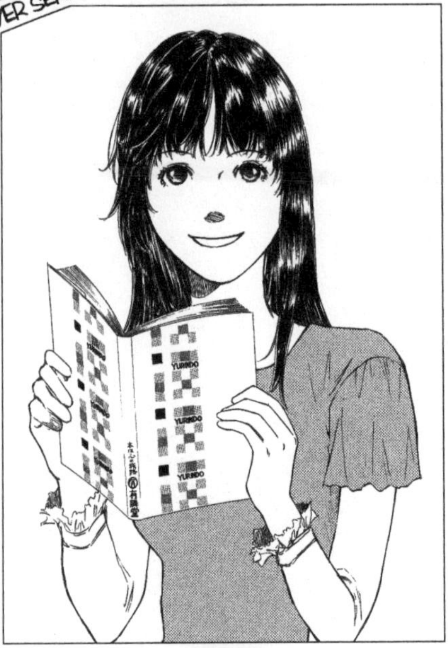
YURINDO

YURINDO

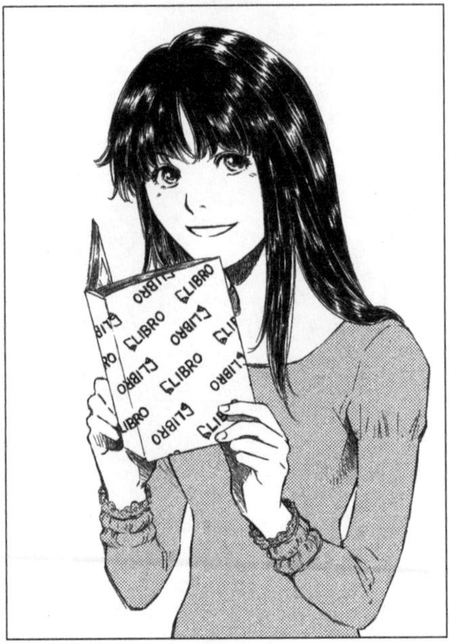
LIBRO

LIBRO

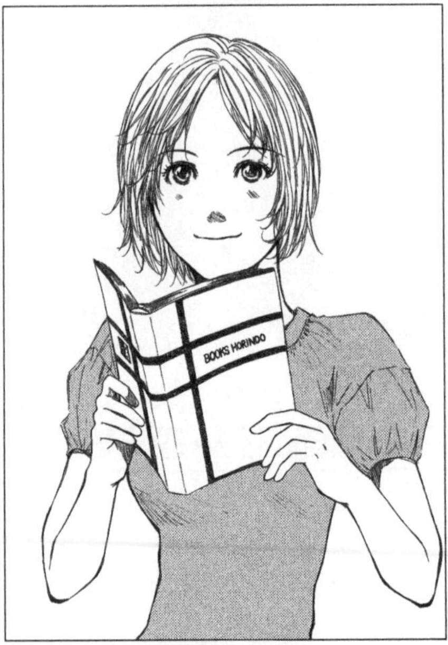
BOOKS HORINDO

HORINDO SHOTEN

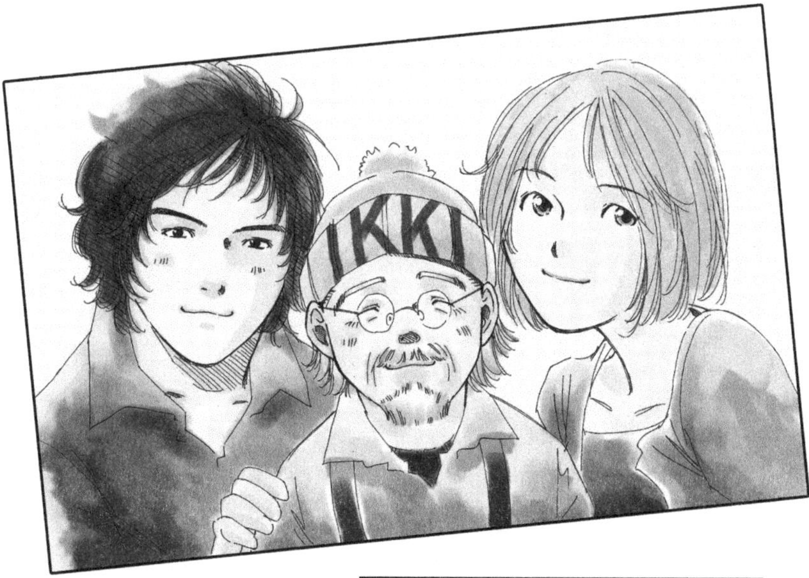
IKKI

BONUS IMAGE: IKKI PREMIUM CARD, 2005 VERSION

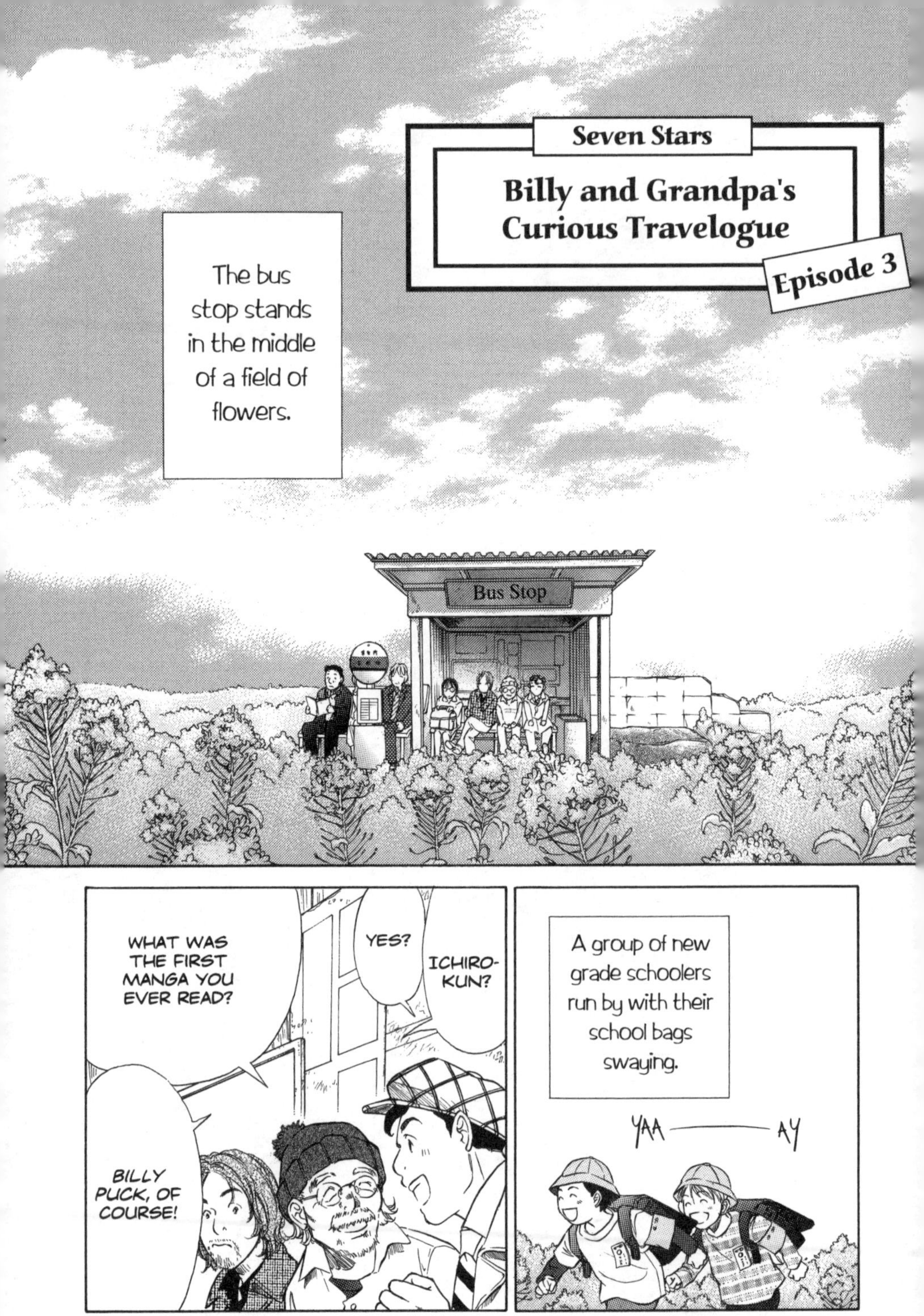
Seven Stars
Billy and Grandpa's Curious Travelogue
Episode 3
The bus stop stands in the middle of a field of flowers.
Bus Stop
A group of new grade schoolers run by with their school bags swaying.
YAA——AY
ICHIRO-KUN?
YES?
WHAT WAS THE FIRST MANGA YOU EVER READ?
BILLY PUCK, OF COURSE!

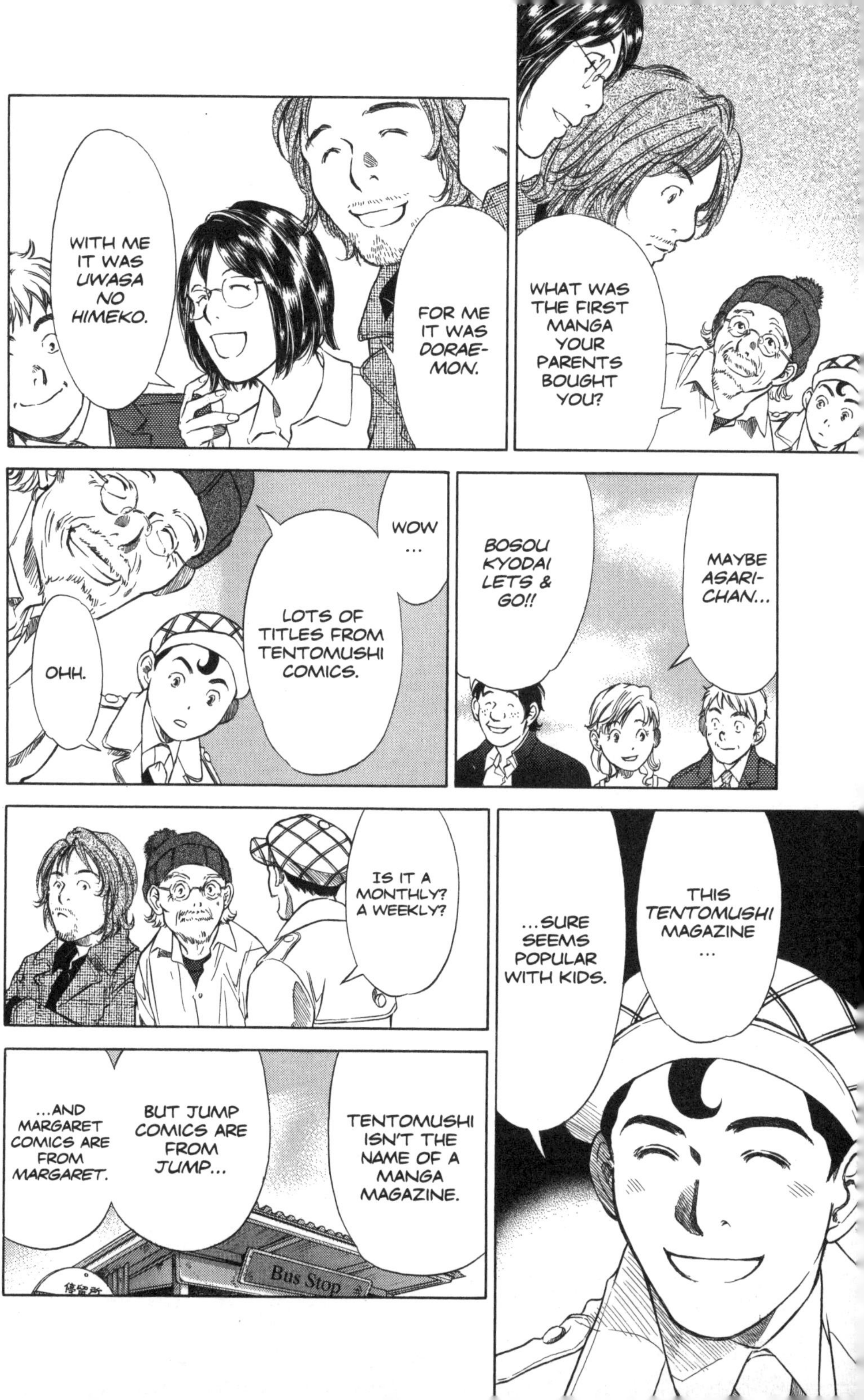
WHAT WAS THE FIRST MANGA YOUR PARENTS BOUGHT YOU?
FOR ME IT WAS DORAE-MON.
WITH ME IT WAS UWASA NO HIMEKO.
MAYBE ASARI-CHAN...
BOSOU KYODAI LETS & GO!!
WOW ...
LOTS OF TITLES FROM TENTOMUSHI COMICS.
OHH.
THIS TENTOMUSHI MAGAZINE ...
...SURE SEEMS POPULAR WITH KIDS.
IS IT A MONTHLY? A WEEKLY?
TENTOMUSHI ISN'T THE NAME OF A MANGA MAGAZINE.
BUT JUMP COMICS ARE FROM JUMP...
...AND MARGARET COMICS ARE FROM MARGARET.
Bus Stop

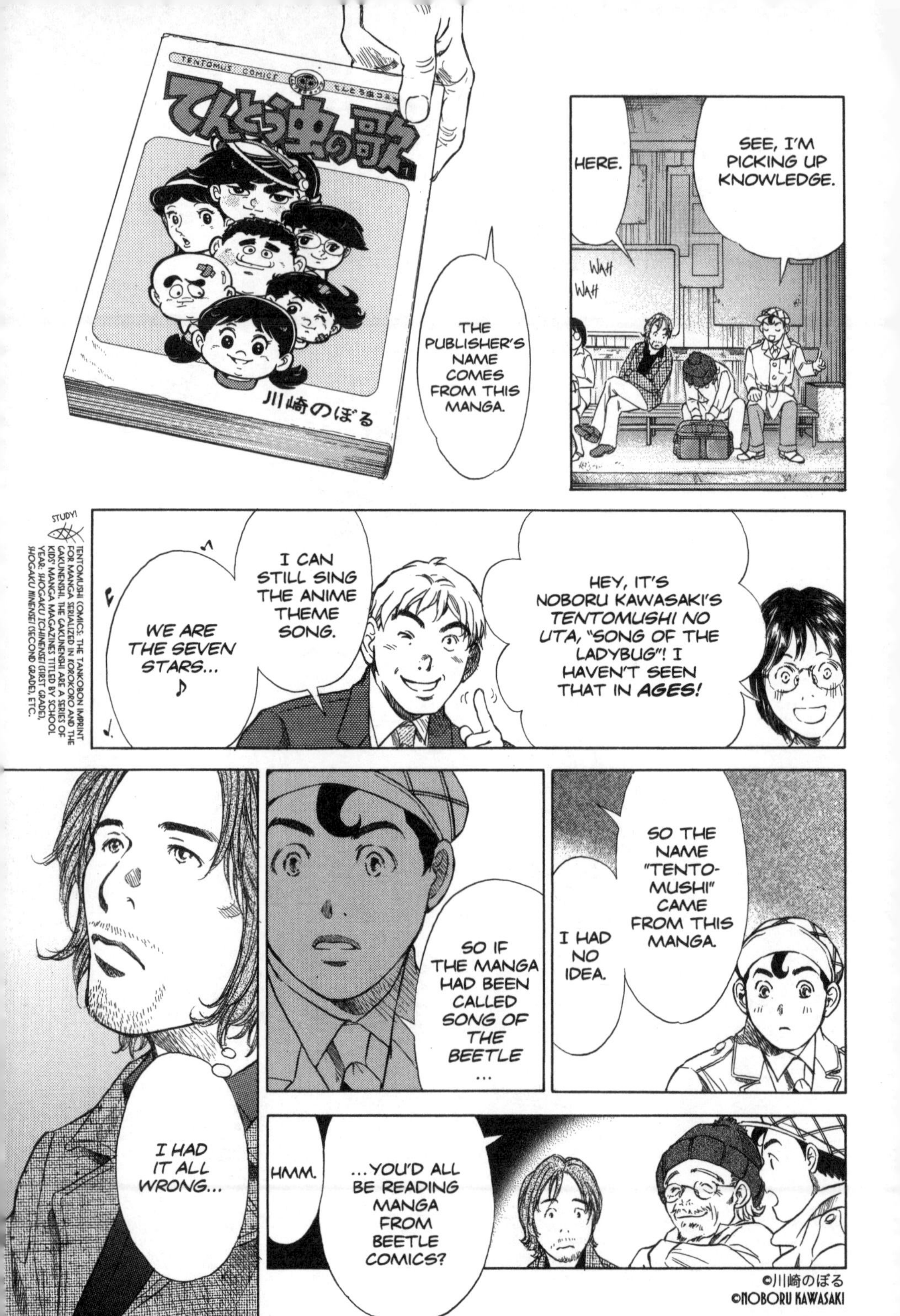
SEE, I'M PICKING UP KNOWLEDGE.
HERE.
WAH WAH
TENTOMUS COMICS
てんとう虫の歌 1
川崎のぼる
THE PUBLISHER'S NAME COMES FROM THIS MANGA.
HEY, IT'S NOBORU KAWASAKI'S *TENTOMUSHI NO UTA*, "SONG OF THE LADYBUG"! I HAVEN'T SEEN THAT IN **AGES!**
I CAN STILL SING THE ANIME THEME SONG.
WE ARE THE SEVEN STARS... ♪
STUDY!
TENTOMUSHI COMICS: THE TANKOBON IMPRINT FOR MANGA SERIALIZED IN KOROKORO AND THE GAKUNENSHI. THE GAKUNENSHI ARE A SERIES OF KIDS' MANGA MAGAZINES TITLED BY SCHOOL YEAR: SHOGAKU ICHINENSEI (FIRST GRADE), SHOGAKU NINENSEI (SECOND GRADE), ETC.
SO THE NAME "TENTOMUSHI" CAME FROM THIS MANGA.
I HAD NO IDEA.
SO IF THE MANGA HAD BEEN CALLED SONG OF THE BEETLE ...
...YOU'D ALL BE READING MANGA FROM BEETLE COMICS?
HMM.
I HAD IT ALL WRONG...

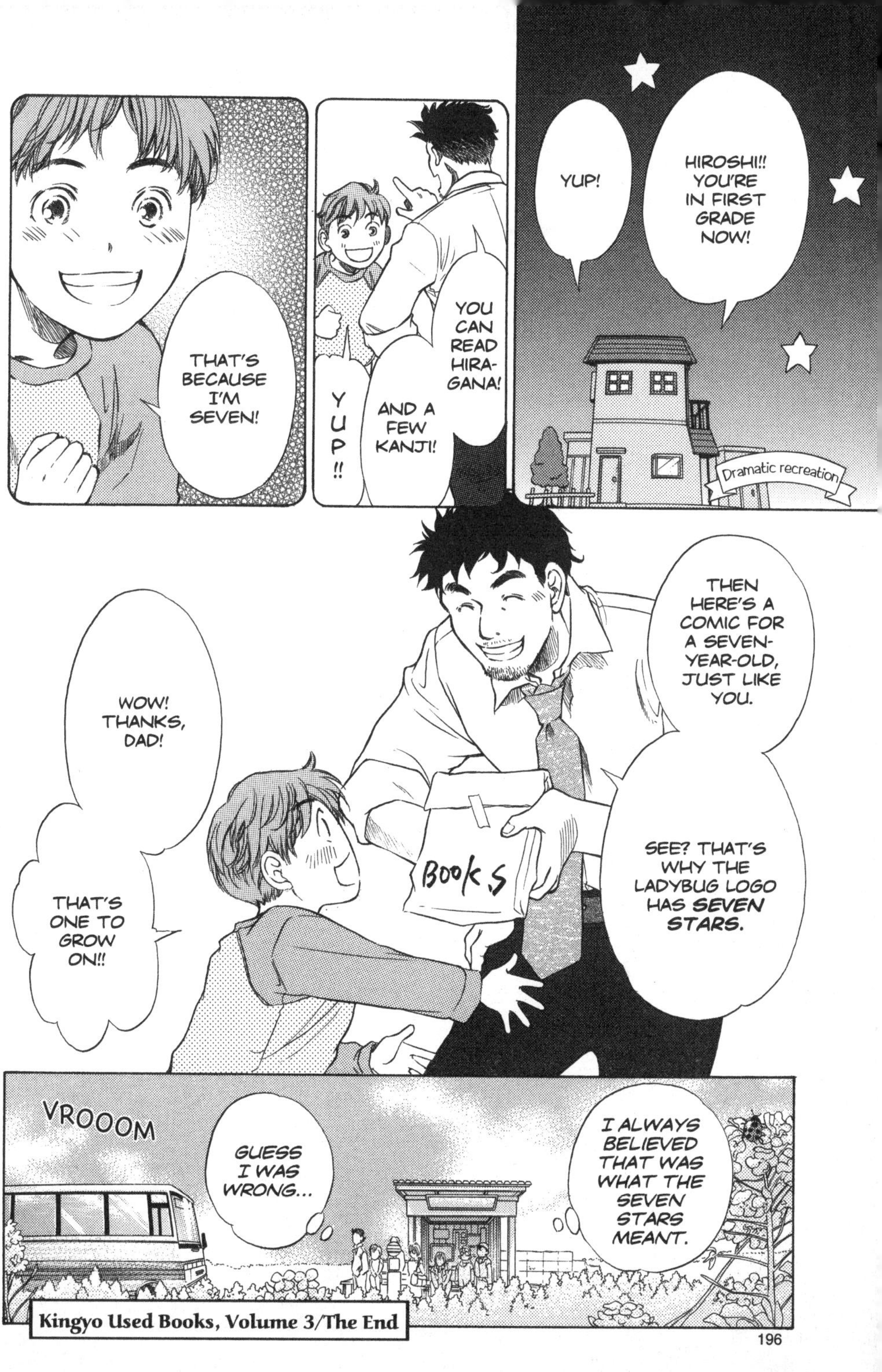
HIROSHI!! YOU'RE IN FIRST GRADE NOW!
YUP!
Dramatic recreation
YOU CAN READ HIRA-GANA!
AND A FEW KANJI!
YUP!!
THAT'S BECAUSE I'M SEVEN!
THEN HERE'S A COMIC FOR A SEVEN-YEAR-OLD, JUST LIKE YOU.
SEE? THAT'S WHY THE LADYBUG LOGO HAS **SEVEN STARS.**
BOOKS
WOW! THANKS, DAD!
THAT'S ONE TO GROW ON!!
I ALWAYS BELIEVED THAT WAS WHAT THE SEVEN STARS MEANT.
GUESS I WAS WRONG...
VROOOM
Kingyo Used Books, Volume 3/The End

KINGYO USED BOOKS NOTEBOOK

More useful information about the manga found on the shelves of **Kingyo Used Books**!

Text by Hiroshi Hashimoto.

Born in 1948 in Kumamoto, Japan. Owner of the used bookstore Kirara Bunko. Aside from running his bookstore, he also teaches at a preparatory school and is active in a nonprofit organization. Fellow alumni of his elementary school include manga commentators Hiroshi Yonezawa and Yukari Fujimoto. His dream is to build a manga library in Aso. Hashimoto was asked to write this column when being interviewed for information for this series.

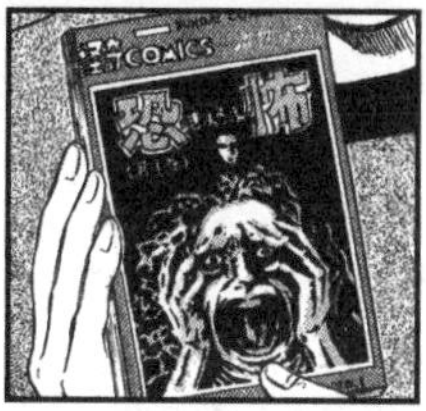

This title is featured in Chapter 15: Umezu Salon

The Manga of Kazuo Umezu

The manga at left is *Kyofu*

Published by Akita Shoten beginning in 1971

This chapter of *Kingyo Used Books* features the works of Kazuo Umezu, the dark prince of horror manga. Umezu made his debut with *Mori no Kyodai* (Brother and Sister's Forest), which he wrote when he was in eighth grade. His exceptional artistry garnered immediate attention and was said to have sparked the jealousy of Osamu Tezuka himself.

At the height of the popularity of manga lending libraries, Umezu exploded onto the scene with the *Hebi Onna* (Snake Women) series and *Mama ga Kowai* (Scared of Mama), which appeared in *Shojo Friend*. In these stories, beautiful women and reassuring mothers suddenly turn into snakes and slither menacingly. Each weekly installment relentlessly stirred the visceral fear of creatures like snakes, spiders, centipedes and cats. My younger sister was traumatized by horror manga for a long time after reading Umezu's stories.

As *Kyofu* (Terror) ran in *Heibon* magazine and *Hangyojin* (Half-Man Half-Fish) ran in *Shonen* magazine, Umezu's work evolved from external scares to a more internal, psychological brand of horror. *Iara*, which began serialization in the premier issue of *Big Comic*, is a classic that raises the question: "Is there only one reality?" When I read it as a kid, I didn't quite understand what the manga was trying to say. I only felt an uneasy fear in the pit of my stomach. Even when I read *Iara* now, my heart shrivels instantly. That's how powerfully Umezu's manga bored into the hearts of readers.

After Umezu began publishing exclusively with Shogakukan, he launched his masterpiece, *The Drifting Classroom*. Any Hollywood sci-fi thriller is reduced to a B movie in comparison. Umezu followed it with an unexpected gag manga, *Makoto-chan*. With regard to these two seemingly disparate genres, Umezu has said, "If you're doing the chasing, it's comedy. If you're being chased, it's horror." A spot-on appraisal indeed.

Hopefully this overview gives you a glimpse of just how vast Umezu's world is. That's why the Umezu Salon is necessary. It's not too late! Perhaps you'd like to visit the secret salon in Kingyo's basement.

※ *Kyofu* (Terror) is available in *Kyofu: Umezu Perfection* (two volumes) from Shogakukan.

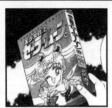

© Naoko Takeuchi

This title is featured in Chapter 16: Makeup

Sailor Moon (18 volumes)

By Naoko Takeuchi

Published by Kodansha beginning in 1992

The series featured in this chapter, Naoko Takeuchi's *Bishojo Senshi Sailor Moon* (Pretty Soldier Sailor Moon), can be read today in a new 12-volume edition from Kodansha. *Codename wa Sailor V* (Codename Sailor V) appeared in Kodansha's *Run-Run* in July 1991, laying the foundation for the monster hit series, which launched in *Nakayoshi* in December of the same year.

The franchise broke sales records for books, games and merchandise; it also set attendance records for its theatrical films and stage musicals and hit the top of the ratings for TV anime. *Sailor Moon* was also a hit overseas and became a fan phenomenon worldwide.

The overwhelming success of *Sailor Moon* is, in no small part, due to the fact that the main characters battle their foes in school uniforms. There's no doubt that the stylish uniforms color-coded for each character made a big impression on kids. The huge cast of characters was another factor in the manga's success. Up until then, it was customary to have no more than five main characters in an action manga, as seen in the Super Sentai series *Goranger*. By increasing that number to ten, Takeuchi gave every reader at least one character with whom to closely identify. As *Sailor Moon* expanded into a multimedia franchise, kids became hooked on the anime, games and character merchandise.

Nearly twenty years later, those kids are all grown up. But for the adults who experienced the *Sailor Moon* craze as children, it isn't so easy to escape the powerful hold it had over them. The same goes for Misaki, who makes a return appearance in this chapter of *Kingyo Used Books*. *Sailor Moon* has the power to transport her back to her childhood. For Misaki, who was beginning to question her career path, reading the beloved manga again takes her back to a time when she was able to just enjoy anything that came her way.

If you're feeling down and looking for a good manga, try picking up one you used to read as a kid. The manga you've dismissed as too childish or mainstream to merit a second read just may give you the shot in the arm you need to get out of your funk.

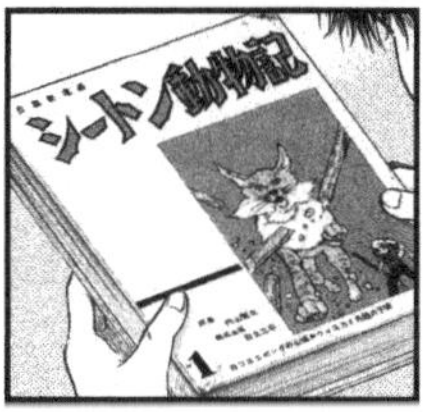
シートン動物記
1

This title is featured in Chapter 17:
Same Time Tomorrow

The Manga of Sanpei Shirato

The manga at left is *Seton Dobutsuki*

Published by Toho Tosho Publishing beginning in 1961

The manga featured in this chapter are all series by Sanpei Shirato. *Sasuke* and *Watari* feature young ninja as protagonists. *Ninpou Hiwa* (Secret Stories of Ninja), *Kamui Gaiden* (The Tale of Kamui) and *Sanada Kenryu* (Sanada Swordsmanship) depict the cruel destinies of ninja. *Seton Dobutsuki* (Seton Animal Chronicles) is the first manga told from an ecological perspective. All of these titles were published more than thirty years ago, but none of them have lost their luster.

For baby boomers like myself, Shirato's manga are indispensable to any conversation about the turbulent era of the late '60s. The young people of the time lashed out against society with massive student protests. At the time we truly believed we had the power to change the world.

That was when Shirato's *Ninja Bugeicho* (Band of Ninja) and *Kamui-den* (The Legend of Kamui), depicting characters who fight against the establishment, became like Holy Bibles for student activists. In Shirato's stories, peasants rise up against the powerful ruling class and the ninja group known as the *Kage Ichizoku* (Shadow Clan) with the help of Kamui, a fugitive ninja. College students identified with the heroes and became enthralled with Shirato's stories.

But the youth movement fizzled and those student warriors began to drift apart. Some joined extremist groups, while others dispersed to the countryside to join grassroots movements like anti-pollution organizations; many more became corporate warriors, contributing to Japan's economic revival. But the indelible message of Shirato's manga echoed in their minds. Shirato's works may be the first and last manga to make such a powerful and lasting social impact.

Beginning in 2005, *Kamui-den* was re-released in 38 volumes to commemorate Shirato's fifty years as an artist. The project was timed to coincide with the approaching retirement of the baby boom generation and remind them once again of Shirato's message. I hope Kamui's ninjutsu will provide a much-needed spark to Japan's languishing revolutionary spirit.

If you want to know how the long journeys of Shirato's lone swordsmen, ninja and wolves come to an end, pay a visit to Kingyo Books. You just may find a book that's destined for you!

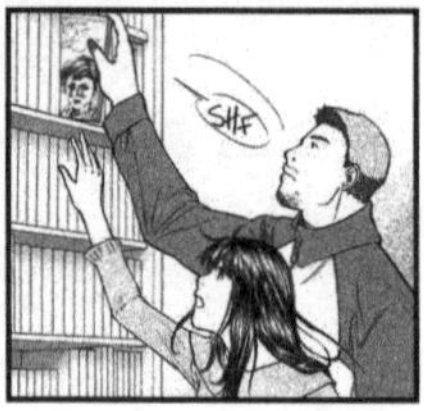
SHF

This title is featured in Chapter 18:
The Kingyo Diaries (The Yamabuki Episode)

Stuff About Sedori

Sedori means "taking from the spine"...

Ready to put your eyes and brain to the test?

Let's learn a bit about the sedori business. The word *sedori* (背取り), first used in used bookstore circles, refers to the practice of buying underpriced books from used bookstores and other sources and reselling them at a profit. It's called *sedori* because you grab the books as you scan their spines.

But the sedori business isn't as easy as it looks. For starters, you have to know which books are valuable at resale. In *Kingyo*, both Ayu and Okadome are incredibly knowledgeable about which out-of-print manga are rare, how much they typically sell for, which stores they can be found at, and which stores will offer a fair buyback price. That's why the two seem to bump into each other so frequently all over the city.

In the world of out-of-print manga, some books have much greater resale value than others. For example, shonen (boys') manga from publishers like Mushi Comics, Sun Comics and Fujiko Fujio Land no longer garner as high a price as they have in the past. With so many popular shonen manga being reprinted and sedori competing fiercely for books, the market has become saturated.

On the other hand, kiddie manga, shojo (girls') manga and video game-based manga are becoming increasingly valuable. Also keep an eye out for out-of-print *bunko* and *shinsho* collectors' editions, children's "mooks" (a cross between a magazine and a book) and illustrated reference books! It's fun to check bookstore and online catalogs and try to predict the next big thing. As for where to sell, try to find a bookstore that is as fair and conscientious as Kingyo.

Incidentally, there are several golden rules to keep in mind if you decide to try your hand at sedori. The first is to consider the feelings of the bookstore where you do your treasure hunting. While it's only natural to buy at places that tend to price their books low, never check the market price of the books on your cell phone or talk about how cheap the books are while you're in the store. Pulling too many books from the shelves at once is also a no-no. Not only will you put the store on alert, you should approach the sedori trade with the mindset of sharing the wealth.

In this respect, Ayu and Okadome are ideal sedori. What's great about them is they're not seduced by money; they're not just about reselling books to turn a profit. Sometimes their goal is to cheer someone up with a book; other times it's to find a book that expresses their feelings; other times it's to lend support to places like Kingyo Books. If you go into the business with a genuine love of books and a desire to spread good cheer to those around you, no doubt the books will be happy too.

Perhaps you'd like to take a cue from Ayu and Okadome and try your hand at becoming a true sedori.

※ *Sedori* can also be written with characters signifying "to outbid." [競取り]

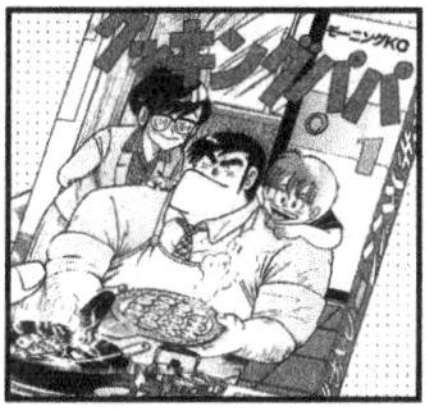
モーニングKC
1

This title is featured in Chapter 19: The Joy of Living

Cooking Papa (84+ volumes)

By Tochi Ueyama

Published by Kodansha beginning in 1986

The manga featured in this chapter is the long-running series *Cooking Papa.* It began its run in *Shuukan Morning* (Weekly Morning) back in 1985 and is still ongoing, with 110 tankobon volumes to date. The manga stars Ichimi Araiwa, a cheerful salaryman who manages to juggle a career and housework; his wife Nijiko, a first-rate newspaper reporter who's not very good at keeping house; their growing son Makoto; and their cute-as-a-button daughter Miyuki. The Araiwa family's dinner table is always overflowing with delicious dishes and delicious smiles.

While there are plenty of cooking manga out there, few focus on home cooking and are filled with recipes anyone can make. I get excited at the sight of dads and kids, who rarely spend much time in the kitchen, seriously but happily preparing a meal from the recipes they jotted down from *Cooking Papa*. This manga has the curious ability to make readers feel the joy of eating, the joy of living and the joy of reading.

Cooking Papa is especially popular on the island of Kyushu, where the manga is set. The huge cast of characters has spread from the Hakata ward to all of Kyushu, with cooking connoisseurs from each area enlivening the story with their culinary skills. With endless story lines about heartbreak, retirement, illness, school admissions, child rearing and travel among the cast, the series keeps going strong, having lost none of its power over the years.

It's common for a long-running series to grow stale, but this manga gets better and better, its characters becoming more clearly defined with each episode. Why is that? For one thing, it's chock-full of useful cooking ideas. *Cooking Papa* uses not only the author's ideas, but ideas sent in by readers from far and wide. Its painstaking research is another secret to its unwavering popularity. And perhaps readers feel an affinity for the manga because it's based on easily identifiable stories from everyday life.

In this chapter, Natsuki's ever-impulsive mother makes a return appearance, and we see her employed as a cooking instructor. She uses *Cooking Papa* as a textbook! I truly envy the people of Kingyo, who live in a world where such a charming instructor teaches them to cook delectable dishes with manga.

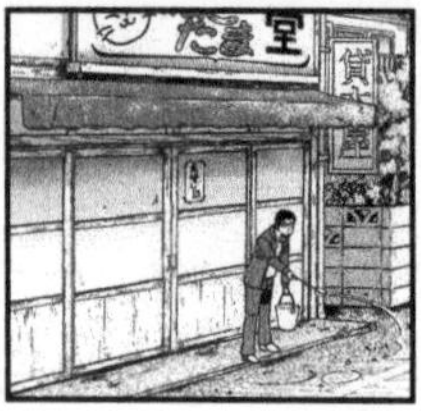

This title is featured in Chapter 20: Nekotama-do (Part 1)

Stuff About Lending Libraries

The vanishing lending library...

Have you ever been to this place with a different ambiance than a manga café?

Old manga are cultural artifacts that must be passed down to future generations. Used bookstores like Kingyo Used Books and lending libraries like Nekotama-do have acted as bridges between generations. Recently, however, as new bookstores, manga cafés and rental bookstores have become influential, traditional used bookstores and lending libraries have begun to disappear. They're time-consuming businesses with little profit or time off, and, without anyone to succeed the previous owners, they are on the brink of extinction.

This is the situation faced by Nomoto-kun, the former salaryman who takes over Nekotama-do in this chapter. His decision to run a lending library because he wants to follow his heart truly inspires hope. It's true there are plenty of easier ways to make money than to manage a lending library. But for someone who loves manga and children and values human relationships, running a used bookstore or lending library just may be the perfect job.

Twenty years have flown by since the owner of the used bookstore I used to frequent entrusted me with taking over his business. He and the couple managing the lending library I used to visit since I was a kid were wonderful advisers to me during crucial turning points in my life, such as choosing a college, seeking employment, getting married, studying overseas and changing jobs.

"When I close the store, I'll pass on all of these books to you," were words that soon became reality, and here I am now writing about classic manga. There's not much money in it, but no other job suits me quite so well.

Incidentally, did you know that older lending libraries like Nekotama-do are completely different from the current rental bookstores? In the 1950s, over 20,000 lending libraries across the country loaned out books that weren't offered at general bookstores and were only available through rental distribution. Many of the publishers were small businesses whose primary focus was not publishing, like candy stores, toy stores and open-air vendors, all of which hired manga creators to write one-shots. These B6- and A5-sized books were called *kashihon manga* (loaner manga) and *kashihon shosetsu* (loaner novels). Masterpieces by some of the top mangaka featured in *Kingyo*, including Kazuo Umezu, Sanpei Shirato, Osamu Tezuka and Fujio Akatsuka, were published as *kashi manga* during this period.

After the 1960s, it became more common for the manga serialized in magazines to be reprinted in book format, and lending libraries began to stock the same material as general bookstores. During this period, kashihon manga disappeared from the shelves of lending libraries, only to be replaced by the portably slim shinsho format. As more and more manga were published in greater volume, the shelves of lending libraries became glutted with a constant stream of new titles and older manga that had lost their currency were thrown away.

Thanks to places like Nekotama-do and Kingyo, which continued to preserve old manga through these turbulent times, we are able to enjoy classic manga today. Now it's our turn to support them! Let's run down there to enjoy the classic manga of the '50s and '60s!

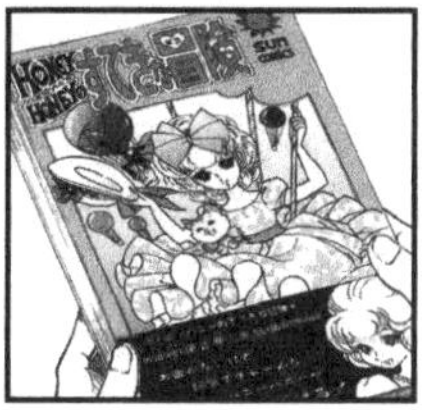

This title is featured in Chapter 21: Nekotama-do (Part 2)

Honey Honey no Suteki na Bouken **(2 volumes)**

By Eiko Mizuno

Published by Asahi Sonorama beginning in 1968

Nekotama-do's new owner, Nomoto, embarks on a trip around the world (more or less) to track down a checked-out manga that was never returned. The book in question is Eiko Mizuno's *Honey Honey no Suteki na Bouken* (Honey Honey's Wonderful Adventures), released in 1968 from Asahi Sonorama. It's the story of a girl named Honey Honey and her kitten, Mimi, who find themselves traveling around the world, entangled in one incident after another. The cast of this slapstick comedy includes a cute romantic heroine, a hysterical queen, a handsome and mysterious thief, a Viking and a suspicious inventor.

Creator Eiko Mizuno started drawing in third grade and was identified as an artistic prodigy from an early age. With the encouragement of Osamu Tezuka she began contributing to *Shojo Club* magazine, and in 1956 her series *Gin no Hanabira* (The Silver Flower Petals) was a big hit. The only female resident of Tokiwa-so, the apartment in Tokyo where Tezuka, Fujio Akatsuka and other classic manga creators lived as fledgling artists, Mizuno displayed a design aesthetic that hadn't been seen in shojo manga before.

Honey Honey no Suteki na Bouken began serialization in 1968 in *Ribon*. Although Asahi Sonorama has since published both a shinsho edition and an oversize edition, both have been out of print for quite some time. By popular demand, Futabasha released bunko editions in 2002, but these too are out of print and are now hard to find. The manga was also adapted into an anime series in 1981, which is indicative of how popular Mizuno was at the time.

In this chapter, the globetrotting Takano is so moved by the careful repairs done to the ripped pages by Otama-san's own hand that he feels compelled to take the book with him when he leaves the country. As depicted in this episode, traditional lending libraries put a lot of care and affection into each book that they make available for their customers.

In order to offer books in the best possible condition and to as many people as possible, lending libraries have developed methods of preserving them. First they remove the cover, drill holes and reinforce the binding with nails so the pages don't fall out. Then they cut a plastic sheet down to size to make a cover so the original cover doesn't get damaged. If the edge of a book comes back dirty, they clean it with sandpaper or an eraser. And, of course, if a page is ripped, it's repaired with thin, translucent paper. Library owners also make a point of remembering their customers and offer recommendations if there are any new arrivals.

Up until the '60s, when manga were still rare and people shared copies with one another because there were few other sources of entertainment, both the lender and borrower treated books very seriously. Perhaps Nekotama-do and Kingyo are reminders that this bygone era existed just a few decades ago.

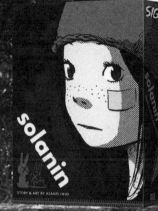

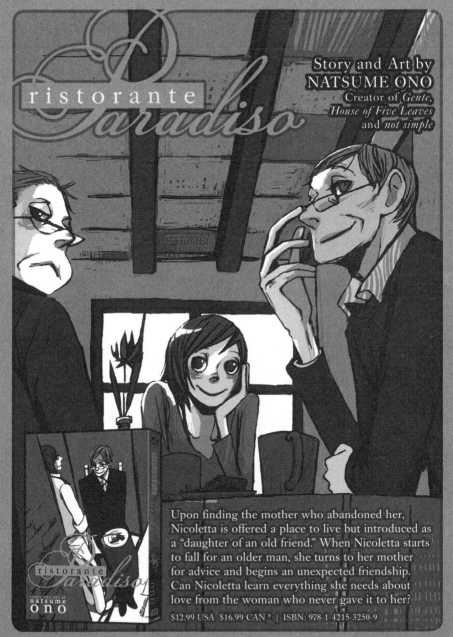

The information in this volume is current up to March 2006.

Thanks to every creator, publisher and property owner of manga titles mentioned in this volume for your understanding and cooperation.

Information provided by Gendai Manga Toshokan/Kirara Bunko.

KINGYO USED BOOKS
Volume 3
VIZ Signature Edition

Story and Art by **SEIMU YOSHIZAKI**

© 2005 Seimu YOSHIZAKI/Shogakukan
All rights reserved.
Original Japanese edition "KINGYOYA KOSHOTEN"
published by SHOGAKUKAN Inc.

Original Japanese cover design by Kei Kasai

Translation: Takami Nieda
Touch-up Art & Lettering: Erika Terriquez
Design: Fawn Lau
Editor: Shaenon K. Garrity

Printed in Canada

Published by VIZ Media, LLC
P.O. Box 77010
San Francisco, CA 94107

10 9 8 7 6 5 4 3 2 1
First printing, April 2011

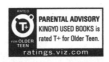

PARENTAL ADVISORY
KINGYO USED BOOKS is rated T+ for Older Teen.
ratings.viz.com

www.viz.com

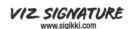

VIZ SIGNATURE
www.sigikki.com

>✕✕· Kingyo = Goldfish ·✕✕‹